D1621496

DATE			

SOFTWARE DEVELOPMENT USING EIFFEL:

THERE CAN BE LIFE OTHER THAN C++

D. COLEMAN, P. ARNOLD, S. BODOFF,
C. DOLLIN, H. GILCHRIST, F. HAYES
AND P. JEREMAES
Object-Oriented Development:
The Fusion Method

S. COOK AND J. DANIELS
Designing Object Systems

B. HENDERSON-SELLERS
A Book of Object-Oriented Knowledge

B. HENDERSON-SELLERS
Book Two of Object-Oriented Knowledge

H. KILOV AND J. ROSS
Information Modelling

P. KRIEF
Prototyping with Objects

K. LANO AND H. HAUGHTON
Object-Oriented Specification Case Studies

J. LINDSKOV KNUDSEN, M. LÖFGREN,
O. LEHRMANN MADSEN AND B. MAGNUSSON
Object-Oriented Environments:
The Mjølner Approach

M. LORENZ
Object-Oriented Software Development:
A Practical Guide

M. LORENZ
Object-Oriented Software Metrics

D. MANDRIOLI AND B. MEYER (eds)
Advances in Object-Oriented
Software Engineering

B. MEYER
An Object-Oriented Environment

B. MEYER
Eiffel: The Language

B. MEYER
Reusable Software

B. MEYER AND J. M. NERSON
Object-Oriented Applications

POMBERGER AND BALSCHEK
An Object-Oriented Approach in
Software Engineering

P. J. ROBINSON
Hierarchical Object-Oriented Design

R. SWITZER
Eiffel: An Introduction

K. WALDEN AND J. M. NERSON
Seamless Object-Oriented Software Architecture

R. WIENER
Software Development Using Eiffel

SOFTWARE DEVELOPMENT USING EIFFEL:
THERE CAN BE LIFE OTHER THAN C++

RICHARD WIENER

 Prentice Hall PTR, Englewood Cliffs, New Jersey 07632

Library of Congress Cataloging-in-Publication Data

Wiener, Richard, 1941–
     Software development using Eiffel : there can be life other than
C++ / Richard Wiener.
        p.   cm. — (Prentice Hall object-oriented series)
     Includes index.
     ISBN 0-13-100686-X (hardcover)
     1. Computer software—Development. 2. Eiffel (Computer program
language) I. Title. II. Series.
QA76.76.D47W52 1995   94-37783
005.13'3—dc20   CIP

Editorial/Production Management: *Digital Communications Services*
Cover Design: *Miguel Ortiz*
Manufacturing: *Alexis R. Heydt*
Acquisitions Editor: *Paul W. Becker*

© 1995 Prentice Hall PTR
Prentice-Hall, Inc.
A Simon & Schuster Company
Englewood Cliffs, New Jersey 07632

The publisher offers discounts on this book when ordered in bulk
quantities. For more information, contact Corporate Sales Department,
Prentice Hall PTR, 113 Sylvan Avenue, Englewood Cliffs, NJ 07632.
Phone: 800-382-3419; Fax: 201-592-2249; e-mail: dan_rush@prenhall.com

Printed in the United States of America

10 9 8 7 6 5 4 3 2 1

ISBN 0-13-100686-X

Prentice-Hall International (UK) Limited, *London*
Prentice-Hall of Australia Pty. Limited, *Sydney*
Prentice-Hall Canada Inc., *Toronto*
Prentice-Hall Hispanoamericana, S.A., *Mexico*
Prentice-Hall of India Private Limited, *New Delhi*
Prentice-Hall of Japan, Inc., *Tokyo*
Simon & Schuster Asia Pte. Ltd., *Singapore*
Editora Prentice-Hall do Brasil, Ltda., *Rio de Janeiro*

*This book is dedicated
to my best friend, my wife
and my love, Hanne.*

Contents

Part 1 The Language

Chapter 7: C++ && Eiffel or is it C++ & Eiffel or is it C++ and Eiffel? A Clash of Cultures 191

Part 2 Case Studies

Chapter 8: Object-Oriented Analysis and Design   239

Chapter 9: An Ecological Simulation   277

Preface

THE BOOK

This book is aimed at computer scientists, software development professionals, educators and students, programmers, and in particular C++ programmers, who wish to examine a compelling alternative to the C++ programming language for implementing object-oriented software systems. This alternative is Eiffel. This book is also about object-oriented analysis and design using the Booch '94 method with Eiffel implementation. The reader is assumed to have prior experience with object-oriented programming, most likely using C++ or Smalltalk, and at least basic familiarity with the concepts of object-oriented programming.

Part 1 of the book, Chapters 1 through 7, presents the major features of the Eiffel language from a programmer's perspective. These chapters contain many small but complete examples of Eiffel coding. These are used to illustrate the typical use of various language features. Part 2 of the book, Chapters 8 through 11, shows Eiffel in action. These chapters present case studies that, in addition to Eiffel implementation, show the use of the Booch '94 method of object analysis and design.

The standard reference book for the Eiffel programming language is *Eiffel: The Language,* written by Bertrand Meyer (Prentice Hall, 1992), the creator of Eiffel. This present book is meant to complement this reference, not compete with it. It is recommended that the reader also acquire this standard reference about Eiffel since there is no attempt in this book to duplicate the rigorous and fine-grained details concerning some of the "legal" issues related to the Eiffel language. Such issues are typically of greater concern to compiler writers but not programmers.

ITS CONTENT

Chapter 1, "The Flavor of Eiffel," presents a broad overview of the language, showing its major features. No attempt is made to provide detailed explanations of the many language features that are previewed in this chapter. A small class hierarchy associated with writing instruments is used to sample the flavor of Eiffel.

Chapter 2, "Classes and Objects," introduces and illustrates the various components of an Eiffel class. An Eiffel class serves as an implementation of an abstract data type, as well as a software module. The main issues discussed in this chapter include the creation of objects, features and their visibility, object assignment and equality, copying and cloning objects, polymorphism and dynamic-binding, generic classes and expanded types.

Chapter 3, "Correct Programs," introduces the powerful assertion-handling facilities of Eiffel. Pre and postconditions and class invariants are explained and illustrated. The notions of programming by contract and subcontracting are explored. Finally, Eiffel's exception-handling mechanism is presented.

Chapter 4, "Generic Container Classes," introduces the concept of constrained and unconstrained "genericity" and the construction of reusable software components. Several container classes, including a list, ordered list, stack, queue, search tree and sortable array, are presented to illustrate the basic ideas.

Chapter 5, "Inheritance in Eiffel," discusses the role of inheritance in object-oriented programming. The overall structure of an Eiffel inheritance clause and its many possible subclauses are presented and illustrated. These include redefinition, renaming, export scope and "undefining." Repeated inheritance structures are examined. The construction and role of abstract classes using deferred routines are explored. The issue of "mix-ins" or code inheritance is discussed.

Chapter 6, "Polymorphism and Conformance," focuses on the rules associated with late-binding in Eiffel. An application of polymorphism involving the concept of the "generality of numbers" is presented as a non-trivial application of polymorphism.

Chapter 7, "C++ && Eiffel or is it C++ & Eiffel or is it C++ and Eiffel? : A Clash of Cultures," provides a direct technical comparison of C++ an Eiffel.

Chapter 8, "Object-Oriented Analysis and Design," introduces the Booch '94 method and its notation. A supermarket checkout line simulation is used to illustrate the basic ideas.

Chapter 9, "An Ecological Simulation," presents a case study involving the construction of several dozen classes that illustrates the Booch analysis and design process and the use of the Eiffel language. After completing the initial design, some simple maintenance is performed to illustrate the importance of building a robust software structure.

Chapter 10, "A Game of Strategies and Investment," presents another case study that again involves the construction of several dozen classes. This example focuses on the extensive use of late-binding as a central design principle. After the initial design is completed, it is critically examined and replaced with an improved design.

Chapter 11, "Simulated Annealing," shows the application of object-oriented analysis, design and programing in a less traditional area — heuristic algorithm design. An abstract class that encapsulates the basic mechanism of simulated annealing is constructed. A concrete class that solves the classic "Travelling Salesperson Problem" is constructed as a subclass of the abstract simulated annealing class to demonstrate the use and power of inheritance in this non-traditional setting.

STYLE AND FORMAT

An area of potential controversy in this book is the deviation from the "standard" Eiffel style recommended in Bertrand Meyer's reference *Eiffel: The Language* (ETL).

The arguments in favor of using a "standard" style are understood and appreciated by this author. It is this author's deep conviction that programming is as much an art as a science. It is an aesthetic and expressive activity that involves the personality as well as the intellect of the programmer. This author believes that every programmer, Eiffel or otherwise, should develop a style that is personal, comfortable and most importantly consistent. Of course, consistent is different from uniform. The programs in this book hopefully illustrate this principle.

The "standard" Eiffel style recommends that multiple word identifiers use an underscore to separate individual words. For example, *average_force* to represent the idea of average force. This book sometimes adheres to this recommendation, but not always. A more Smalltalk influenced style is often evident. This Smalltalk style would use the identifier *averageForce* to represent the idea of average force.

The "standard" Eiffel style involves a myriad of details related to the layout of various language artifacts, formation of identifier names, as well as the use of boldface fonts for all keywords. This recommended style is presented in Appendix A of the ETL. Since there are about 15 pages of details presented there, no attempt will be made here to summarize the "standard" style recommendations. The reader is urged to read this Appendix in the ETL and then decide for himself or herself.

A sample of "standard" Eiffel style is presented in the Appendix of this book so that the reader can either see what they are missing or be further encouraged to develop their own personal style.

ACKNOWLEDGMENTS

Several people contributed to this book through discussions of many of the later examples. In particular, thanks go to two computer scientists very close to me: Erik, my son, and Hanne, my wife.

Jim McKim, of the Hartford Graduate Center, did more than review the first draft manuscript. He poured over every line of code in every example, making constructive suggestions, and contributed significantly to improvements in the book. Thank you so much Jim for your extremely constructive and useful effort.

The case studies in Chapters 8, 9 and 10 were class tested in a graduate course at the University of Colorado at Colorado Springs. I wish to thank Wes Munsil, a student in the class, for his constructive feedback throughout the course.

Other useful reviews that led to the improvement of the final manuscript were provided by Dr. Stuart Greenfield of Marist College and Paul Blanco of Object Center in Boston. I wish to thank Paul for his enthusiastic encouragement and help at every stage of this project.

A special thanks goes to Bertrand Meyer, not only for creating the fine language Eiffel, but for his encouragement, friendship and support throughout this project. His classic work, *Object-Oriented Software Construction*, published by Prentice Hall in 1988 has served as an inspiration to me and many other workers in this field. His work associated with Eiffel and his writings in general have made significant contributions to our field.

I wish to thank Interactive Software Engineering (ISE) in Goleta, California, for providing me with the latest versions of their compiler and tools as Eiffel has evolved over the years. In particular, I wish to thank Annie Meyer and Frederik Deramat for their help.

I thank Tower Technology in Austin, Texas, for also providing me with the latest versions of their compiler and tools. Their president, Robert Howard, and marketing director, Madison Cloutier, have provided tremendous help and encouragement throughout this project. Many of the programs and examples in this book were developed and tested using the TowerEiffel system.

I am most grateful to Paul Becker, Publisher at Prentice Hall, for his continuing support.

Finally, on a personal note, I am so grateful for the patience, encouragement, love and support of my wife Hanne. It is to you that this book is dedicated.

The Language

The Flavor of Eiffel

1.1 INTRODUCTION

Eiffel is a pure object-oriented language developed in the 1980s by Dr. Bertrand Meyer, President, Interactive Software Engineering (ISE), Goleta, California. His book *Object-Oriented Software Construction*, considered by many to be a classic and inspirational work, was published by Prentice Hall in 1988. The Eiffel language is introduced in this book and used primarily as a vehicle for supporting Meyer's ideas related to the construction of safe and robust object-oriented software systems. Up until Prentice Hall's publication of Meyer's *Eiffel: The Language* in 1992, there was no "official" book describing the Eiffel language. This huge reference work of almost 600 pages is written for programmers as well as potential compiler writers. It is and shall remain the definitive reference on the Eiffel language. Most importantly, *Eiffel: The Language* describes the latest version of Eiffel, Eiffel 3. The only other book published on Eiffel, as of the time of this writing, is *Eiffel: An Introduction*, by Robert Switzer. This short book of 161 pages describes a particular implementation of Eiffel, namely, Eiffel/S, being manufactured in Gottingen, Germany. Although Eiffel/S conforms, in large measure, to the standard developed at ISE, its class libraries are different and much more limited than those developed at ISE. TowerEiffel, a product of Tower Technology, is another major Eiffel 3 product recently released. The code presented in this book was developed using both ISE Eiffel and TowerEiffel.

Programming languages embody not only syntax and associated semantics, but cultural attributes, as well. The programming "culture" and use pattern associated with a language may be correlated with its level of success in solving a problem from a particular application area. Some programming languages have in fact been associated with specialized application areas. As an example, the now highly popular C programming language was originally created as a system programming language, allowing a programmer relatively easy access to low-level abstractions associated with the underlying machine. In recent years, the C language has been used in many non-system programming applications. But what has been the price? The price has been an occasional loss of reliability resulting from undetected memory leakage problems or perhaps an increase in maintenance costs because of the relative lack of "readability" of C. I certainly do not wish to offend either C programmers or users of any particular programming language. It has certainly been known for a long time that a good programmer in a weak language is more effective than a mediocre programmer using a strong language. Many programmers hold their particular favorite language more sacred than their religion.

We can often get a clue and perhaps some insight about the culture and purpose associated with programming languages by seeing what their authors say about them.

Brian W. Kerrighan and Dennis M. Ritchie in their book, "Programming In C,"[1] state: "C is a relatively 'low-level' language... . C retains the basic philosophy that programmers know what they are doing; it only requires that they state their intentions explicitly." In the interest of performance, C provides programmers with a relatively poor support system and safety net. This is completely consistent with the philosophy stated above. Do programmers always know what they are doing? Speaking for myself, I can answer in the negative. I believe that most programmers would confess the same. Yet, the sometimes blinding speed of C, compared with some other languages, makes it quite attractive even though it may be dangerous.

Adele Goldberg and David Robson in their book, "Smalltalk-80 — The Language and its Implementation,"[2] state: "As suggested by the personal computing vision, Smalltalk is designed so that every component in the system that is accessible to the user can be presented in a meaningful way for observation and manipulation... . The Smalltalk-80 system provides a rich environment for prototyping new applications and refining old ones... . In the early 1970s, the Xerox Palo Alto Research Center Learning Research Group began work on a vision of the ways different people might effectively and joyfully use computing power." It is clear from the above statements that Smalltalk was designed to support personal computing (as opposed to large-scale multi-programmer projects), experimentation and prototyping. Furthermore, the emotional reference to "joyfully use computing power" suggests a commitment to a strong programming framework. Smalltalk has certainly lived up to these expectations.

In Bjarne Stroustrup's book *The C++ Programming Language — Second Edition*,[3] he states: "C++ is a general-purpose programming language; its core application domain is systems programming in the broadest sense. In addition, C++ is successfully used in many application areas that are not covered by this label." So C++, like its substrate language C, is a system programming language. It is, at the time of this writing, the most widely used "object-oriented" language. Like the language C, C++ provides a thin safety net and support system. But it provides the programmer with constructs and capabilities for writing safer code (compared to C) through the disciplined construction of classes. Because C++ is a hybrid language, it does not tend to encourage (or discourage) any particular paradigm of programming. For this reason, many programmers, particularly beginners, do not use C++ as an object-oriented language. For many programmers, the culture of C++ programming has become an extension of the C culture. For some C++ programmers, this culture implies writing clever but cryptic code that is maximally efficient but perhaps difficult to maintain. A growing consensus is that the most common deficiency of many C++ systems is memory leakage — exacerbated by the presence of pointers, references, and constructors and destructors. The general level of thinking in C++ is still fairly close to the machine.

In Bertrand Meyer's book *Object-Oriented Software Construction,*[4] he states: "We study the object-oriented approach as a set of principles, methods and tools which can be instrumental in building 'production' software of higher quality than is the norm today." In the Preface to *Eiffel: The Language,* by Bertrand Meyer,[5] and referenced above, it is stated, "Eiffel embodies a 'certain idea' of software construction: the belief that it is possible to treat this task as a serious engineering enterprise, whose goal is to yield quality software through the careful production and continuous enhancement of parameterizable, scientifically specified reusable components, communicating on the basis of clearly defined contracts and organized in systematic multi-criteria classifications."

It is clear that Eiffel's stated purpose is to provide support for the engineering of high quality, reliable software systems and components. The important concept of "programming by contract" is inherent in the Eiffel philosophy and supported in the Eiffel language. This is in fact the inspirational force behind my own interest in the Eiffel language. I have always believed that as language technology moves forward, we the programmers should be liberated from the programming micro-management and hazards fostered by the use of pointers and references and also liberated from the micro-management of system module organization. The Eiffel language does both; it does not allow the explicit use of pointers, and it provides automatic tools for the physical management of large software systems. Most importantly, the language provides advanced facilities that support the construction of safe, robust and reusable generic software components based on a pure object-oriented approach to programming. In my view, Eiffel provides an excellent match between the concerns of the software designer and the programmer. I have effectively used Eiffel purely as a program design language and have later been required to translate the design to a lower-level language such as C++. This process produced a better-designed C++ program than would have been possible doing the coding completely in C++ from the beginning.

In this book, I hope to inspire the joy of software engineering using Eiffel.

1.2 THE FLAVOR OF EIFFEL — SOME WRITING INSTRUMENTS

Before delving into the technical aspects of Eiffel and object-oriented software development, let us preview a taste of things to come by examining a complete Eiffel system — a relatively simple one, but one that is sufficiently rich to provide a flavor of the power and elegance of this pure object-oriented language. Let us model and implement a collection of writing instruments — a pencil-pen case that contains an array of pens and pencils. Only a general high-level explanation of the code will be provided in this warm-up example. The reader may wish to revisit this example after completing Chapters 2 through 7 of this book.

1.2.1 A Quick Specification

Our case of writing instruments contains various pens and pencils. The case is a container class, a class that holds zero or more objects from other classes. The case is a container because its existence is independent of the objects that it holds. Each object in the case is an instance of a subclass of WRITING_INSTRUMENT. Included among the writing instruments are the following "instances" (an instance of a class is an actual object whose properties are described in its class definition): an old black fountain pen with a medium/heavy metal point, a much newer and more expensive red fountain pen with a gold medium point, an equally expensive yellow ball-point pen with a roller type point, several inexpensive ball-point pens with non-roller type points, a "mechanical" pencil with 7mm lead, small eraser, and a capacity of 20 pieces of lead, and three number 2 ordinary pencils, each with a medium sized eraser.

1.2.2 Some Analysis

The first step in our construction is to perform object classification. This process is explained and illustrated in great detail in Chapters 8 through 10. The reader may wish to revisit the analysis done below after reading Chapter 8.

Two types of pens have been identified: fountain and ball-point. Two types of pencils have been identified: ordinary and mechanical. An important goal of classification is to factor common attributes and behavior into ancestor classes. Although there is no absolute standard by which to judge a classification, the following consistency principles are highly recommended:

- All subclasses should satisfy the "is kind of" or "is a" relationship with respect to their parents;
- All of the attributes inherited from ancestor classes should logically fit a subclass;
- All of the methods inherited from ancestor classes should logically fit a subclass, and
- Any subclasses of a given parent should have a clear and logical basis for discrimination. This discrimination can be manifested by a subclass having one or more additional attributes than its parent, having one or more addi-

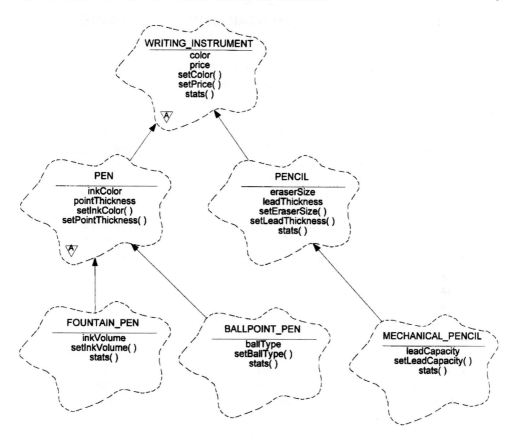

Fig. 1.1 Class Diagram For Writing Instruments

tional methods than its parent, or having one or more inherited methods redefined.

A simple class hierarchy of writing instruments is shown in Figure 1.1 using Booch notation. This notation is explained in detail in Chapters 8, 9 and 10. Each cloud represents a class. Each class name is shown above the solid line within the cloud. Under the line are the attributes and the methods of the class. The attributes represent the data model of the class. The methods represent the actions that can be taken on the data. Together, the attributes and methods implement an abstract data type.

The triangular adornment in two of the classes indicates that these are "abstract" classes. No instances of these classes can be created. Their purpose is to factor attributes and methods that are needed in the "effective" classes (a class is "effective" if instances can be created).

The abstract class WRITING_INSTRUMENT contains the attributes *color* and *price*. This suggests that all writing instruments can be characterized by a color and a price. The methods also inherited by all subclasses of WRITING_INSTRUMENT include *setColor, setPrice* and *stats*. This latter method, *stats*, is deferred. This is a display method. Its implementation must be done in each effective subclass of WRITING_INSTRUMENT.

The abstract class PEN, contains the two additional attributes *inkColor* and *pointThickness* as well as two methods for setting the values of these attributes. There are two effective subclasses of PEN—FOUNTAIN_PEN and BALLPOINT_PEN. Class FOUNTAIN_PEN contains the additional attribute *inkVolume* and a method for setting its value as well as an implementation of *stats*. Class BALLPOINT_PEN contains the additional attribute *ballType* and a method for setting its value as well as an implementation of stats.

The effective class PENCIL introduces the attributes *eraserSize, leadThickness* and two methods for setting their values. It also implements *stats*. Its subclass, MECHANICAL_PENCIL, introduces the additional attribute *leadCapacity* and a method for setting its value as well as an implementation of *stats*.

The reader may be wondering why there are no methods for getting the value of any attributes. This will be discussed in connection with the Eiffel implementation below.

1.2.3   Naming Conventions

In this book, object names, routine names and formal parameters of routines always start with a lowercase character. Class names are always in upper-case characters. Names that involve more than one word either use a mixed-case style (inspired by Smalltalk) or underscores to separate words (more of a C style and one that is recommended in Meyer's book *Eiffel: The Language*). For example, an identifier that refers to the terminal velocity of a falling object might be declared as *terminalVelocity* or as *terminal_velocity*. Both styles are used throughout the book, often in the same application.

Some additional conventions that will be attempted (there may occasionally be an exception due to carelessness) are: (1) using a verb name for all procedures (e.g. *push, pop, setValue*), (2) using noun names for non-Boolean functions, (e.g. *top, the_temperature, theSpeed*) and (3) using yes/no type names for Boolean functions, (e.g. isEmpty or *is_full*).

The reader may wish to review the section of the Preface that makes further comments about Eiffel style conventions.

1.2.4   The Eiffel Implementation

Class WRITING_INSTRUMENT is presented in Listing 1.1.

Listing 1.1   Class WRITING_INSTRUMENT

```
deferred class WRITING_INSTRUMENT
-- Abstract class for pens and pencils
```

```
feature
    color  : STRING;
    price  : INTEGER;

    setPrice( aPrice : INTEGER ) is
    do
        price := aPrice;
    end; -- setPrice

    setColor( aColor : STRING ) is
    do
        color := clone( aColor);
    end; -- setColor

    stats is
    -- Displays a writing instrument
    deferred
    end; -- stats

end -- WRITING_INSTRUMENT
```

1.2.4.1 Discussion of Class WRITING_INSTRUMENT All text from the right of a double dash (--) to the end of a line is a comment in Eiffel.

The attributes *color* and *price* are declared in a feature section that by default is public. As discussed in Chapter 2, each feature clause of an Eiffel class can specify its own export scope; the name of the class(es) and the descendants that can access the features contained in the feature clause directly. For example, *class LIST feature { NODE }* implies that within class NODE all of the LIST features contained within this feature clause have a read-only status. A feature clause without an explicit export scope, such as the one given in Listing 1.1, exports its features to all clients. In Eiffel, features are read-only even when they are public features. It is illegal to attempt to set the value of a feature directly through an object. This must be done using a "set" routine given in the class. Class WRITING_INSTRUMENT contains two such "set" routines, *setColor* and *setPrice*.

If class A has a public feature *b,* it would be illegal to set the value of *b* through *objectA* as follows: *objectA.b := some_expression;.* The proper way to do this would be *objectA.setB(someValue);* where *setB* is a routine in class A.

Languages such as C++ and Smalltalk encourage the use of "get" functions that allow the value of attributes to be returned. Such "get" functions are never needed in the public section of an Eiffel class because the attributes have read-only semantics.

The routine *stats* is deferred. This causes class WRITING_INSTRUMENT to be a deferred class, or abstract class. No instances of this class can be created. An Eiffel class is deferred if one or more of its routines are deferred.

STRING and INTEGER are class types available in the standard Eiffel library. Function *clone* is defined in the Eiffel root class and is available to all Eiffel classes. This function allocates storage for a new instance of STRING and copies the data from the old instance to the new instance.

In Listing 1.2, the details of class PEN are presented.

Listing 1.2   Class PEN

```
deferred class PEN

  inherit
     WRITING_INSTRUMENT

  feature
     inkColor        : STRING;
     pointThickness : INTEGER;

     setInkColor( aColor : STRING ) is
     do
         inkColor := clone( aColor );
     end; -- setInkColor

     setPointThickness( thickness : INTEGER ) is
     do
         pointThickness := thickness;
     end; -- setPointThickness

end -- PEN
```

1.2.4.2 Discussion of Class PEN   The inherit clause is used to indicate that class PEN is a descendant of class WRITING_INSTRUMENT. Chapter 5 discusses the inheritance mechanism in great detail. As a consequence of the inheritance relationship, instances of class PEN have attributes *color* and *price* (inherited from WRITING_INSTRUMENT) in addition to the attributes *inkColor* and *pointThickness*. Instances of class PEN can also respond to the messages *setColor* and *setPrice*.

Class PEN is a deferred class because routine *stats*, inherited from class WRITING_INSTRUMENT, has not yet been defined.

Class FOUNTAIN_PEN is presented in Listing 1.3.

Listing 1.3   Class FOUNTAIN_PEN

```
class FOUNTAIN_PEN

  inherit
    PEN

  creation
    make

  feature
     inkVolume : INTEGER;

     make( aColor : STRING; aPrice : INTEGER; anInkColor : STRING;
     aPointThickness : INTEGER; anInkVolume : INTEGER ) is
     do
```

```
        setColor( aColor );
        setPrice( aPrice );
        setInkColor( anInkColor );
        setPointThickness( aPointThickness );
        setInkVolume( anInkVolume );
    end; -- make

    setInkVolume( volume : INTEGER ) is
    do
        inkVolume := volume;
    end; -- setInkVolume

    stats is
    do
        io.putstring( "Displaying Fountain Pen%N" );
        io.putstring( "-------------------------%N" );
        io.putstring( "Color: " );
        io.putstring( color ); io.new_line;
        io.putstring( "Price: $" );
        io.putint( price ); io.new_line;
        io.putstring( "Point thickness: " );
        io.putint( pointThickness ); io.new_line;
        io.putstring( "Ink color: " );
        io.putstring( inkColor ); io.new_line;
        io.putstring( "Ink volume: " );
        io.putint( inkVolume ); io.new_line;
    end; -- stats

end -- FOUNTAIN_PEN
```

1.2.4.3 Discussion of Class FOUNTAIN_PEN Class FOUNTAIN_PEN is an effective class. It has a creation clause. The routine *make* with five parameters *aColor, aPrice, anInkColor, aPointThickness* and *anInkVolume* is used to create an instance of class FOUNTAIN_PEN with an initial state given by the parameters. An instance of FOUNTAIN_PEN has a data model characterized by five attributes: *color, price, inkColor, pointThickness* and *inkVolume*. The *stats* routine is implemented in this class. The object, *io*, is initialized by the system. The routines *putstring* and *putint* are implemented in the library class STANDARD_FILES. The symbol %N is used as a new-line character.

Class BALLPOINT_PEN is implemented in Listing 1.4.

Listing 1.4 Class BALLPOINT_PEN

```
class BALLPOINT_PEN

  inherit
    PEN

  creation
    make

  feature
    ballType : STRING;
```

```
make( aColor : STRING; aPrice : INTEGER; anInkColor : STRING;
aPointThickness : INTEGER; aBallType: STRING ) is
do
    setColor( aColor );
    setPrice( aPrice );
    setInkColor( anInkColor );
    setPointThickness( aPointThickness );
    setBallType( aBallType );
end; -- make

setBallType( type : STRING ) is
do
    ballType := clone( type );
end; -- setBalltype

stats is
do
    io.putstring( "Displaying Ballpoint Pen%N" );
    io.putstring( "--------------------------%N" );
    io.putstring( "Color: " );
    io.putstring( color ); io.new_line;
    io.putstring( "Price: $" );
    io.putint( price ); io.new_line;
    io.putstring( "Point thickness: " );
    io.putint( pointThickness ); io.new_line;
    io.putstring( "Ink color: " );
    io.putstring( inkColor ); io.new_line;
    io.putstring( "Ball type: " );
    io.putstring( ballType ); io.new_line;
end; -- stats

end -- BALLPOINT_PEN
```

1.2.4.4 Discussion of Class BALLPOINT_PEN   All of the details of class
BALLPOINT_PEN should be familiar from the previous listing.

Listing 1.5 shows the details of class PENCIL.

Listing 1.5   Class PENCIL

```
class PENCIL

inherit
  WRITING_INSTRUMENT

creation
  make

feature
  eraserSize    : INTEGER;
  leadThickness : INTEGER;
```

```
      make( aColor : STRING; aPrice : INTEGER; anEraserSize :
         INTEGER; aLeadThickness : INTEGER )is
       do
          setColor( aColor );
          setPrice( aPrice );
          setEraserSize( anEraserSize );
          setLeadThickness( aLeadThickness );
       end; -- make

      setEraserSize( size : INTEGER ) is
       do
          eraserSize := size;
       end; -- setEraserSize

      setLeadThickness( thickness : INTEGER ) is
       do
          leadThickness := thickness;
       end; -- setLeadThickness

      stats is
       do
          io.putstring( "Displaying Pencil%N" );
          io.putstring( "----------------------%N" );
          io.putstring( "Color: " );
          io.putstring( color ); io.new_line;
          io.putstring( "Price: $" );
          io.putint( price ); io.new_line;
          io.putstring( "Eraser size: " );
          io.putint( eraserSize ); io.new_line;
          io.putstring( "Lead thickness: " );
          io.putint( leadThickness ); io.new_line;
       end; -- stats

end -- PENCIL
```

Class MECHANICAL_PENCIL is shown in Listing 1.6.

Listing 1.6   Class MECHANICAL_PENCIL

```
class MECHANICAL_PENCIL

 inherit
    PENCIL
        redefine
            stats
        end

 creation
    makeLeadPencil

 feature
    leadCapacity : INTEGER;
```

```
    makeLeadPencil( aColor : STRING; aPrice : INTEGER;
                anEraserSize : INTEGER; aLeadThickness :
                INTEGER; theLeadCapacity : INTEGER ) is
    do
        setColor( aColor );
        setPrice( aPrice );
        setEraserSize( anEraserSize );
        setLeadThickness( aLeadThickness );
        setLeadCapacity( theLeadCapacity );
    end; -- make

    setLeadCapacity( capacity : INTEGER ) is
    do
        leadCapacity := capacity;
    end; -- setLeadCapacity

    stats is
    do
        io.putstring( "Displaying Mechanical Pencil%N" );
        io.putstring( "-----------------------------%N" );
        io.putstring( "Color: " );
        io.putstring( color ); io.new_line;
        io.putstring( "Price: $" );
        io.putint( price ); io.new_line;
        io.putstring( "Eraser size: " );
        io.putint( eraserSize ); io.new_line;
        io.putstring( "Lead thickness: " );
        io.putint( leadThickness ); io.new_line;
    end; -- stats
end -- MECHANICAL_PENCIL
```

1.2.4.5 Discussion of Class MECHANICAL_PENCIL   The inherit clause of MECHANICAL_PENCIL specifies a *redefine* subclause. In this subclass, the routine *stats* is declared. It was not necessary to include a *redefine* subclause in classes FOUNTAIN_PEN and BALLPOINT_PEN because the parent of these subclasses is not an effective class. Therefore, the definitions of *stats* provided in these subclasses are not redefinitions but merely original definitions.

Having built a small hierarchy of WRITING_INSTRUMENT classes, how do we construct a case of writing instruments? How do we initiate "flow of control?" How do we build a "main application" program?

Since the class in Eiffel is the basic logical and modular unit, we must build a class whose purpose is to trigger the application. Such an application class is presented in Listing 1.7 and is called class APPLICATION (any class name will suffice). An Eiffel Ace file specifies the name of the main application class and the routine for triggering the application. A typical Ace file is shown in Listing 1.8.

Listing 1.7   Main APPLICATION class

```
class APPLICATION

creation
    start
```

```
feature

    start is
    local
        pen1        : FOUNTAIN_PEN;
        pen2        : BALLPOINT_PEN;
        pen3        : BALLPOINT_PEN;
        pencil1     : PENCIL;
        pencil2     : MECHANICAL_PENCIL;
        pencil_case : ARRAY[ WRITING_INSTRUMENT ];
        index       : INTEGER;
    do
        -- Create various writing instruments
        !!pen1.make( "Red", 239, "Blue", 1, 5 );
        !!pen2.make( "Green", 6, "Black", 2, "Ordinary" );
        !!pen3.make( "Red", 175, "Blue-black", 2, "Roller" );
        !!pencil1.make( "Yellow", 1, 6, 2 );
        !!pencil2.makeLeadPencil( "Grey", 8, 4, 7, 20 );
        -- Initialize the pencil_case array
        !!pencil_case.make( 1, 10 );
        -- Load up the pencil case with writing instruments
        pencil_case.put( pen1, 1 );
        pencil_case.put( pen2, 2 );
        pencil_case.put( pen3, 3 );
        pencil_case.put( pencil1, 4 );
        pencil_case.put( pencil2, 5 );
        -- Allow user to change the sequence of writing
        -- instruments
        io.putstring(
          "%NInterchange pencil 1 and pencil 2 (y/n)? " );
        io.readchar;
        if io.lastchar = 'y' or io.lastchar = 'Y' then
            pencil_case.put( pencil2, 4 );
            pencil_case.put( pencil1, 5 );
        end;
        -- Display each writing instrument
        from index := 0
        until index = 5
        loop
            index := index + 1;
            pencil_case.item( index ).stats; io.new_line;
        end;
        -- Modify point thickness of mechanical pencil
        pencil2.setLeadThickness( 5 );
        -- Output the new point thickness of mechanical pencil
        io.putstring( "New point thickness of pencil2 = " );
        io.putint( pencil2.leadThickness ); io.new_line;
    end; -- start

end -- APPLICATION
```

The output of the program is given below:

```
Interchange pencil 1 and pencil 2 (y/n)? y
Displaying Fountain Pen
```

```
----------------------
Color: Red
Price: $239
Point thickness: 1
Ink color: Blue
Ink volume: 5

Displaying Ballpoint Pen

----------------------
Color: Green
Price: $6
Point thickness: 2
Ink color: Black
Ball type: Ordinary

Displaying Ballpoint Pen

----------------------
Color: Red
Price: $175
Point thickness: 2
Ink color: Blue-black
Ball type: Roller

Displaying Mechanical Pencil

----------------------------
Color: Grey
Price: $8
Eraser size: 4
Lead thickness: 7

Displaying Pencil

-----------------
Color: Yellow
Price: $1
Eraser size: 6
Lead thickness: 2

New point thickness of pencil2 = 5
```

1.2.4.6 Discussion of Class APPLICATION   Five objects — *pen1*, *pen2*, *pen3*, *pencil1* and *pencil2* — are declared in the *local* section of routine *start*. The collection object, *pencil_case*, is also declared in this *local* section. It is declared as type ARRAY containing WRITING_INSTRUMENT as its parameter. The class ARRAY is one of many standard library Eiffel classes that is a parameterized class. Such a parameterized class allows the user to specify the base type contained within the class when an instance of the class is created. The conformance rules of Eiffel discussed in detail in Chapter 6 allow an instance of any descendant of WRITING_INSTRUMENT to be put into the array. Therefore, the *pencil_case* array can contain several types of writing instruments, each an instance of one of the subclasses of WRITING_INSTRUMENT.

After creating and initializing five writing instrument objects (two ball point pens, one fountain pen, one ordinary pencil and one mechanical pencil), the pencil case array is created and initialized using the *make* routine of class ARRAY. The parameters 1 and 10 specify the lower and upper index range of the array object being created. The objects are inserted into the array in the order *pen1*, *pen2*, *pen3*, *pencil1* and *pencil2*. The user is then given the choice of interchanging the order of *pencil1* and *pencil2*.

Next, an iteration is performed on the pencil case collection (ARRAY). Each object in the array is accessed and sent the message *stats*. Because of Eiffel's late-binding polymorphism, the subject of Chapter 6, the correct *stats* method is bound to the *stats* message call at run-time (the one associated with the class to which the particular object belongs). This iteration is accomplished as follows:

```
from index := 0
until index = 5
loop
    index := index + 1;
    pencil_case.item( index ).stats; io.new_line;
end;
```

The expression *pencil_case.item(index)* gets the writing instrument object in the specified index location of the array.

Listing 1.8   Ace File for Application

```
system test
root application : start

cluster

 local: "."

 kernel: "$EIFFEL/clusters/kernel"

 support: "$EIFFEL/clusters/support"

 serial: "$EIFFEL/clusters/serial"

 booch_subset: "$EIFFEL/clusters/booch/subset"

end
```

The reader is urged to review the construction of an Ace file in the documentation associated with Eiffel compiler being used.

1.2.5   Implementation in C++ — A Big Problem With No Easy Solution

A C++ implementation of the pencil case requires that base class `Writing_Instrument` contain downward references to member functions defined in several subclasses. This is a major design compromise because superior classes in a hierarchy should stand independent of lesser classes in the hierarchy and make no references to them. This is not possible in C++ because of the need for the system to build a virtual table in the base class. This virtual table must contain placeholders for all member functions that are to enjoy late-binding (the default binding mode in C++ is early-binding).

The C++ `Writing_Instrument` class definition would look as shown in Listing 1.9.

Listing 1.9   Class Writing_Instrument in C++ with required design compromise

```
class Writing_Instrument
{
    private:
        char *color;
        int price;
    public:
        Writing_Instrument() { }

        void setColor( char *aColor ) { /* Details not
            shown */ }

        void setPrice( int aPrice ) { /* Details not shown
            */ }

        char* getColor() { return color; }

        int getPrice() { return price; }

        virtual void stats() = 0; /* Equivalent to a deferred
            routine in Eiffel */

        virtual int getLeadThickness() = 0;
};
```

1.2.5.1   Discussion of of C++ Class Writing_Instrument The two "pure" virtual member functions, *stats( )* and *getLeadThickness( )*, allow late-binding to prevail when these member functions are invoked on a pointer or reference to any publically derived instance of class Writing_Instrument. It is not unreasonable to specify an output function *stats( )* in class Writing_Instrument. It is totally unreasonable to have to specify a stub for member function *getLeadThickness( )* at the base-class level. This access function refers to an attribute that is introduced in a subclass.

C++ classes need "get" type access functions (e.g. *getColor( )* and *getPrice( )*) because public data members are not read-only as in Eiffel. It is generally a bad practice in C++ to define data members in the public section of a class because such data members could be written to directly. Thus data members are generally defined in either a private section or protected section. Access to the data is provided through "get" type member functions.

In strongly typed languages such as C++ and Eiffel, there is a tension between providing type safety and the flexibility associated with dynamic languages such as Smalltalk. Eiffel's various mechanisms for performing run-time type identification help to resolve this conflict. There is currently some discussion in the C++ standards committee for providing run-time type identification in C++, as well. Perhaps by the time this book is published, this proposed new feature of C++ will have become a reality.

1.3 A FINAL WARM-UP EXAMPLE

One more small Eiffel application will be examined as part of the "warm-up" process. This application allows us to preview some of Eiffel's libraries and powerful assertion-handling facilities. Again, no attempt will be made to describe all of the details. The reader may wish to revisit this example after completing Chapters 2 through 7.

The specifications for this problem are taken directly from the "Blue Book," more commonly known by the title *Smalltalk-80 — The Language and Its Implementation*, by Goldberg and Robson. This example is found early in the book (page 10) and is used to introduce many basic concepts of object-oriented programming in Smalltalk. The following is an informal statement of the problem:

Develop a financial history application that:

1. Creates a new financial history object with a certain initial amount of money available.

2. Maintains and provides archival capability for a database that contains the following information: amounts spent in various categories, amounts received from various sources.

3. Allows one to output the balance currently available.

For the purposes of this "warm-up" example, the user interface is quite primitive and simple. Instead of taking input from the user, the input will be "hardwired" into the program.

There are two classes that must be constructed for this application. The first class, FINANCIAL, encapsulates the protocol given in the problem specifications. The three key attributes of this class are: (1) balance, (2) expenditures, and (3) revenues.

Class FINANCIAL is shown in Listing 1.10. A detailed discussion of this class is presented after the listing.

Listing 1.10   Class FINANCIAL

```
class FINANCIAL
-- Used to maintain financial history

 inherit
    STORABLE -- for archiving

 creation
    make

 feature { NONE } -- Accessible to classes that conform to
    -- FINANCIAL
    expenditure : HASH_TABLE[ REAL, STRING ];
    revenues    : HASH_TABLE[ REAL, STRING ];

    make( initialAmount : REAL ) is
    require
    initial_amount_positive: initialAmount > 0.0;
    do
        !!expenditures.make( 1 );
        !!revenues.make( 1 );
        balance := initialAmount;
    end; -- create

    display( table : HASH_TABLE[ REAL, STRING ] ) is
    local
        index        :INTEGER;
        categories   :ARRAY[ STRING ];
        category     :STRING;
    do
      categories := table.current_keys;
        from index := 0
        until index = categories.count
        loop
            index := index + 1;
            category := categories.item( index );
            put( category, table @ category );
        end;
    end; -- display

    put( category : STRING; amount : REAL ) is
    do
        io.putstring( category );
        io.putstring( ": $" );
        io.putreal( amount );
        io.new_line;
    end; -- put

 feature { ANY } -- Public
    balance : REAL;

    valid_expenditure_category( category : STRING ) :
       BOOLEAN is
```

```
do
    Result := expenditures.has( category );
end; -- valid_expenditure_category

valid_revenue_category( category : STRING ) : BOOLEAN is
do
    Result := revenues.has( category );
end; -- valid_revenue_category

spend( amount : REAL; category : STRING ) is
require
    amount_positive: amount > 0.0;
    valid_amount: amount <= balance;
    category_not_void: category /= Void
local
    currentValue : REAL;
do
    if expenditures.has( category ) then
       currentValue := expenditures @ category;
       expenditures.replace( amount + currentValue,
          category );
    else
        expenditures.put( amount, category );
    end;
    balance := balance - amount
ensure
    balance = old balance - amount;
    valid_expenditure_category( category );
end; -- spend

earn( amount : REAL; category : STRING ) is
require
    category_not_void: category /= Void;
    amount_positive: amount > 0.0;
local
    currentValue : REAL;
do
    if revenues.has( category ) then
        currentValue := revenues @ category;
        revenues.replace( amount + currentValue,
           category );
    else
        revenues.put( amount, category );
    end;
    balance := balance + amount;
ensure
    balance = old balance + amount;
    valid_revenue_category( category );
end; -- spend

expenditure( category : STRING ) : REAL is
require

    category_not_void: category /= Void;
```

```
            valid_category: valid_expenditure_category
               ( category );

    do

        Result := expenditures @ category;

    end; -- expenditure

    revenue( category : STRING ) : REAL is
    require
        category_not_void: category /= Void;
        valid_category: valid_revenue_category( category );
    do
        Result := revenues @ category;
    end; -- revenue

    displayRevenues is
    do
        display( revenues );
    end; -- displayRevenues

    displayExpenditures is
    do
        display( expenditures );
    end; -- displayExpenditures

    displayTable is
     do
        display( revenues );
        display( expenditures );
     end; -- displayTable

invariant -- Imposed on entire class
    balance >= 0.0;

end -- FINANCIAL
```

1.3.1 Discussion of Class FINANCIAL

Class FINANCIAL inherits from STORABLE, a standard Eiffel 3 class, because it needs two methods from this class for storing and retrieving objects. It can be argued that class FINANCIAL is a "kind of" STORABLE. In any case, the protocol for storing and retrieving objects is provided in class STORABLE. It is, therefore, essential that class FINANCIAL be a subclass of STORABLE.

Some may disagree that class FINANCIAL is a "kind of" STORABLE and object to the "code inheritance" (sometimes called a "mix-in") from class STORABLE. There is no other way to accomplish the "archiving" without this type of inheritance. Eiffel 3 does not support a "use" clause that allows one class to use resources from another class without either an aggregation or inheritance relationship.

The three attributes of FINANCIAL are *expenditures*, *revenues* and *balance*. The first two of these attributes are declared to be instances of class HASH_TABLE[REAL, STRING]. These attributes are declared in a feature section that exports to NONE (i.e. *feature { NONE }*). This implies that no client (a class that uses FINANCIAL) can access these attributes directly. They are for internal use and the use of any descendant of class FINANCIAL. The semantics are identical with a *protected* section in C++ with *public* derivation. The attribute *balance* is in the public section of class FINANCIAL (i.e. *feature { ANY }* or just *feature*). It is important that clients can access the current account balance directly. As indicated before, such a public attribute has read-only semantics.

A hash-table is a container that stores entities at particular keys. In this case, the entities that will be stored are real numbers (instances of class REAL), and the key values are instances of class STRING.

In the first hash-table, *expenditures*, the total quantity of money spent in various categories is stored. When a certain amount is spent on an item of a given category, the total expenditure associated with this category must get incremented by the amount spent. Thus, the totals in each category can only increase with time. These categories would normally be input by the user.

In the second hash-table, *revenues*, we store revenue from various sources. As funds are earned, we increment the totals associated with each revenue source.

Both the revenue sources as well as the expenditure categories are character strings. By "reusing" code in the Eiffel base class library HASH_TABLE, much of the coding work required to solve this problem is taken care of.

In the *make* routine, the two hash-tables are initialized to have a capacity of 1. The protocol of HASH_TABLE indicates that the size can change dynamically and on demand when greater capacity is needed. The *balance* is set to the value passed through the parameter *initialAmount*.

The *make* routine is placed in the "for internal use only," NONE, export section of class FINANCIAL because clients should be denied the opportunity to invoke the routine through an existing instance of class FINANCIAL. The only use of the *make* routine is for object creation and initialization.

In routine *spend*, a precondition type of assertion is used. In order for the routine to fulfill its obligations or contract, the client (the routine using feature *spend*) must satisfy two conditions: the parameter *amount* must be positive, and the string *category* must not be *void*. If either of these conditions is not met, an exception will be triggered in the calling routine. This is where the offense has taken place. The caller must respect the preconditions of the routine being called or be able to handle an exception if one occurs.

In the body of routine *spend*, the *if* clause tests to see whether category already exists in the hash-table. If not, the value *amount* is *put* into the hash-table. The *put* method is defined in class HASH_TABLE. If *category* already exists in the hash-table, the current total in the hash-table for the given key (*category*) is computed. This value is added to the *amount* and the sum is put back into the table using the message *replace*. The infix operator "@" allows access to the total in the given *category* for the hash-table *expenditure*. This operator notation is a deviation from the normal noun-verb metaphor in which an instance of a class (an object) receives a message according to the style **object.message**. Lastly, the value of *balance* is decremented by *amount*.

The *ensure* clause, or postcondition type of assertion, indicates what the routine guarantees to the caller if the precondition has been met. In this case, the new *balance* will always be smaller by *amount* than the old *balance*. Also, the category will be guaranteed to be a valid category in the future.

The *earn* routine is similar to the *spend* routine.

The routines *expenditure* and *revenue* each return a real value in response to a valid category. If the caller sends in an invalid category, a precondition of the called routine is violated and an exception is triggered in the calling routine.

The routine *displayTable* invokes the protected routine *display*. This protected routine and the routine *put* are in the "protected" section because they are for internal use only.

The class that triggers the application, class APPLICATION, is presented in Listing 1.11.

Listing 1.11   Class APPLICATION

```
class APPLICATION
-- Financial history application

  creation
    start

  feature { NONE } -- For internal use
    database: FINANCIAL;
    myFile   : UNIX_FILE;

    incomeSource1 : STRING is "Main Job";
    incomeSource2 : STRING is "Editing";
    incomeSource3 : STRING is "Consulting";
    incomeSource4 : STRING is "Royalties";

    spendingCat1 : STRING is "Food";
    spendingCat2 : STRING is "Mortgage";
    spendingCat3 : STRING is "Utilities";
    spendingCat4 : STRING is "Entertainment";
    spendingCat5 : STRING is "Insurance";
    spendingCat6 : STRING is "Fuel";
    spendingCat7 : STRING is "Computer equipment";
    spendingCat8 : STRING is "Clothes";
    spendingCat9 : STRING is "Miscellaneous";

  feature -- Public

    start is
    do
        -- Create database with initial amount of $2500
        !!database.make( 2500.0 );
        io.putstring( "The current balance in account: $" );
        io.putreal( database.balance );
        io.new_line;
        -- Enter data into database
```

```
database.earn( 4000.0, incomeSource1 );
database.earn( 1800.0, incomeSource2 );
database.earn( 2000.0, incomeSource3 );
database.earn( 250.0, incomeSource4 );
if database.balance >= 800.0 then
    database.spend( 800.0, spendingCat1 );
else
    io.putstring(
        "Cannot spend 800.00 because of insufficient
         balance%N" );
end;

if database.balance >= 900.0 then
    database.spend( 900.0, spendingCat2 );
else
    io.putstring(
        "Cannot spend 900.00 because of insufficient
         balance%N" );
end;
if database.balance >= 120.0 then
    database.spend( 120.0, spendingCat3 );
 else
    io.putstring(
        "Cannot spend 120.00 because of insufficient
         balance%N" );
end;

if database.balance >= 400.0 then
    database.spend( 400.0, spendingCat4 );
else
    io.putstring(
        "Cannot spend 400.00 because of insufficient
         balance%N" );
end;
if database.balance >= 160.0 then
    database.spend( 160.0, spendingCat5 );
else
    io.putstring(
        "Cannot spend 160.00 because of insufficient
         balance%N" );
end;
if database.balance >= 60.0 then
    database.spend( 60.0, spendingCat6 );
else
    io.putstring( "Cannot spend 60.00 because of
        insufficient balance%N" );
 end;
 if database.balance >= 400.0 then
    database.spend( 400.0, spendingCat7 );
else
    io.putstring(
        "Cannot spend 400.00 because of insufficient
         balance%N" );
 end;
 if database.balance >= 150.00 then
```

```
      database.spend( 150.0, spendingCat8 );
else
   io.putstring(
      "Cannot spend 150.00 because of insufficient
         balance%N" );
end;
if database.balance >= 200.0 then
   database.spend( 200.0, spendingCat9 );
else
   io.putstring(
      "Cannot spend 200.00 because of insufficient
         balance%N" );
end;
io.putstring( "End of month balance in account: $" );
io.putreal( database.balance );
io.new_line;
database.displayTable; io.new_line;
io.putstring( "The amount spent on mortgage is: $" );
io.putreal( database.expenditure( spendingCat2 ) );
   io.new_line;
io.new_line;
-- Save database
!!myFile.make_open_binary_write( "finances" );
database.basic_store( myFile );
myFile.close;

-- Open database and make two changes
!!myFile.make_open_binary_read( "finances" );
database ?= database.retrieved( myFile );
myFile.close;
if database /= Void then
   io.putstring( "Current account balance after
      retrieving data is: $" );
   io.putreal( database.balance );
   io.new_line;
else
   io.putstring( "Cannot retrieve database file from
      disk" );
   io.new_line;
end;
database.earn( 1700.0, incomeSource3 );
 if database.balance >= 6000.0 then
    database.spend( 6000.0, spendingCat7 );
else
      io.putstring(
         "Cannot spend 6000.00 because of insufficient
            balance%N" );
end;
io.new_line;
database.displayTable;
io.new_line;
io.putstring( "Final account balance: $" );
io.putreal( database.balance );
io.new_line;
```

```
         -- Make one final change that is illegal
      if database.balance >= 3061.00 then
         database.spend( 3061, spendingCat9 );
      else
         io.putstring(
            "Cannot spend 3061.00 because of insufficient
             balance%N" );
      end;
      -- One final display of database
      io.new_line;
      database.displayTable;
      io.new_line;

    io.putstring( "The final account balance is: $" );
    io.putreal( database.balance );
    io.new_line;
   end; -- start

end -- APPLICATION
```

1.3.2 Discussion of Class APPLICATION

The attributes of the APPLICATION class include *database*, an instance of FINANCIAL, and *myFile*, an instance of UNIX_FILE. This last attribute is used to provide archiving capability for the *database*. The additional attributes provide the "hard-wired" user input. Four income sources and nine spending categories are defined using manifest strings (i.e. string attributes that are initialized at their point of declaration).

In the creation method, *start*, the *database* is initialized with $2500. Next, the *database* is loaded with values for both *revenue* and *expenditures*. The *database* is displayed. The amount spent in a particular category, mortgage, is next output.

Saving an object (archiving) is more complicated than simply saving scalar data such as an integer or character. An object may have many dependent objects. These are the objects associated with the attributes of the given class and, recursively, their dependents. When an object is stored, all of its dependents, both direct and indirect, must also be stored. In languages that do not provide standard class libraries, such as C++, a great deal of effort is usually expended to implement object storage and retrieval. In fact, several database vendors have dedicated their business to providing class libraries that provide for object persistence in C++.

Class STORABLE provides the Eiffel programmer with important facilities for object persistence. As indicated earlier, in order for an object to be stored, its class must inherit from class STORABLE. The mechanism for storing an object is first to open an instance of UNIX_FILE for write-only. This is accomplished in the *start* routine by sending the message *make_open_binary_write* to the object *myFile* with a file name string as a parameter. If you recall, class FINANCIAL inherits from class STORABLE. This allows the message *basic_store*, with parameter *myFile*, to be sent to *database*. The file *myFile* is closed after *database* is stored.

To retrieve the *database* object and perform additional operations on it, *myFile* is opened for read-only. This is accomplished by sending the message *make_open_binary_read* with the file name string as a parameter to the object *myFile*. Next, the *database* is assigned using the reverse assignment operator, to the result of sending the message *retrieved* with parameter *myFile* to *database*. If the assignment yields a non-void result, then *database* has been restored. It is always necessary to test for a non-void value whenever a reverse assignment is performed. In this case, the current account *balance* is output.

The remainder of the *start* routine adds $1700 to the Consulting income source and $6000 to the Computer equipment spending category.

Finally, an expenditure of $3061 in the Miscellaneous category is sent to the *database*. The precondition of the *spend* routine is not violated because of the test condition used in routine *start*. Without this test, an exception would be raised in routine *start* resulting from the pre-condition violation in class FINANCIAL. Chapter 3 discusses assertion handling in detail.

1.4   SOME GENERAL OBSERVATIONS ABOUT EIFFEL

In the previous two sections, two small Eiffel systems were presented and discussed briefly. Many important technical details and issues were omitted because they will be discussed in later chapters. From these two examples, some general observations and some opinions are offered.

Eiffel is a relatively easy language to read. Every object that is used belongs to a specified class with well-defined protocol. The style of message call, **object.message,** prevails except when a call is made to the current object. Then the object *Current* may be used explicitly or may be omitted as is normally the case. There are a minimum of cryptic operators and symbols. There are no pointers and their associated hazards. The reserved words in the language are descriptive and convey meaning.

Eiffel is a relatively easy language to write. It is a **pure** object-oriented language. This implies that all routines must be sent through an object and all types that are used must be associated with a class. There is no temptation to mix a procedural approach with an object approach to programming, as is the case with C++ and Object Pascal. Although Eiffel functions exist as the routines of a class, they cannot exist by themselves. Routines provide the vehicle in Eiffel for abstracting class behavior. An Eiffel routine must be applied to an object.

Since the semantics of late-binding prevail in Eiffel, the actual function definition (routine implementation) is bound to the message call at run-time. This promotes a flexible style of programming. Along with this flexibility, Eiffel employs static type checking to promote safety. This is a powerful combination not found in many other languages. For example, in C++, static checking is accompanied by early-binding. Late-binding must be enabled explicitly using a complex mechanism that involves virtual functions, a base class and its polymorphic cluster of derived classes, and pointers or references to objects. Furthermore, in C++, functions can exist independently of a class. This promotes a mixed paradigm of procedural and object-oriented programming. This may account for the relative difficulty that most beginning object-oriented programmers experience when using C++ to support their learning of object-oriented programming.

Eiffel has a clean and simple syntax for constructing and using generic classes. Class HASH_TABLE in the previous section is an example of such a class. Class ARRAY in the two previous sections is another example. In both of these classes, the underlying base type is specified by the client. The behaviors defined in a generic class are defined independent of any base type.

Eiffel's predefined class library provides a programmer with significant leverage in reusing code that would otherwise take a major effort to develop. With these class libraries and Eiffel's program development tools, Eiffel is more than a language; it is a framework for thinking about, designing and implementing object-oriented software.

In the next six chapters of Part 1, the Eiffel language is described in some detail. I hope you are excited about learning this elegant and powerful language for object-oriented problem solving.

Let's get on with it ...

REFERENCES

1. Kerrighan, Brian W. and Dennis M. Ritchie, *Programming In C — Second Edition*, Prentice-Hall, Inc., 1988.
2. Goldberg, Adele and David Robson, *Smalltalk-80: The Language and its Implementation*, Addison-Wesley, 1983.
3. Stroustrup, Bjarne, *The C++ Programming Language — Second Edition,* Addison-Wesley, 1986.
4. Meyer, Bertrand, *Object-Oriented Software Construction*, Prentice-Hall, Inc., 1988.
5. Meyer, Bertrand, *Eiffel: The Language*, Prentice-Hall, Inc., 1992.

Classes and Objects

2.1 CLASSES AND OBJECTS

The noun *class*, in English, is related to the word *classification*. In many branches of science, entities are classified according to their basic properties or behaviors. Classification is used to help us understand complex systems. Groups of entities are classified based on their common properties as well as the differences in their properties. The periodic table in Chemistry is a classic example that illustrates the power of classification. Many basic properties of an element are known simply by knowing its position or group in the table. All metals, for example, are bound by certain common and basic properties. The inert elements possess common characteristics quite distinct from metals. Biological systems serve as a model to demonstrate the power and effectiveness of classification. Biological classification exploits the power of inheritance in which a subclass inherits properties from its parent class. The subclass also introduces more specialized characteristics distinct from the parent class. Much can be known about the characteristics of an organism by simply knowing what subclass it belongs to. Biological classification has served as an inspiration and role model for object-oriented analysis.

An object-oriented analysis begins with the classification of the physical or abstract entities that comprise a problem space. All the entities that share common behavior and a common data model can be considered instances of the same class. Entities that share a common data model with an existing class but exhibit more specialized behavior can be considered instances of a subclass of the existing class. Much of the literature describing object-oriented analysis discusses techniques for class identification and the construction of a class hierarchy.

The word *object* implies a physical boundary or shape. In the abstract world of object-oriented software modeling, the word *object* is used to represent any entity that is an instance of a class. An object's properties are specified by its class description. What about an object's physical boundary or shape?

The concept of boundary is more elusive in describing software objects, but a meaningful concept exists. This is the concept of encapsulation. The "boundary" that abstractly surrounds a software object is represented by the external interface of the object. More precisely, the set of *messages* that can be sent to an object to either modify its internal state or produce some output defines this abstract "boundary," The internal state of an object is given by the data model of its class. The actions that can be taken with the object, or equivalently, the *messages* that can be sent to the object, are defined by the *methods* of its class. For each *message* that an object can accept, there must be a corresponding *method* in its class. This method provides the details for implementing the message.

The unification of methods with a data model provided by a class is one of the fundamental pillars of object-oriented software technology. It provides the basis for specifying *abstract data types*. Abstract data types are given by a data model and a set of operations that may be performed on the data model — the very essence of a class. Such abstract data types can form the basis for developing a software component technology in which a software system is designed by interconnecting individual software components, each with a precisely specified external interface. Such a component technology has proven very effective in designing electronic systems.

2.2   EIFFEL CLASSES

An Eiffel class is the basic logical and physical unit of an Eiffel software system.

As a logical unit, an Eiffel class specifies a data model that is unified with a set of methods. The data model is comprised of the **attributes** of the class. The methods are called **routines** and are analogous to functions or procedures in a structured language. The combination of attributes and routines is called the feature of the class. An Eiffel class can contain many feature sections, each containing a set of attributes and routines. Each feature section can specify its own export scope, the set of classes and their descendants that can access the given features directly. In this export scope, the attributes can be accessed on a read-only basis.

In Eiffel, all routines must be invoked either explicitly or implicitly through an instance of the class. This is in sharp contrast to ordinary functions or procedures of a structured language that are invoked independent of any object.

A routine can be invoked directly within the body of a class or its descendants. Such a direct invocation, although it may appear to occur independent of any object, is actually invoked implicitly through the self reference object *Current*. Otherwise, a routine must be invoked explicitly through an instance of the class.

As a physical unit, an Eiffel class is a module. Both the external interface and internal specification of an Eiffel class are contained in a single file. There is, therefore, less chance for the interface and implementation to get out of synchronization. To promote a consistent organization of Eiffel software, it is recommended that the file be given the same name as the class (in lower case letters) with a ".e" extension. For example, if the class name is POINT, the file name should be *point.e*.

The disadvantage of combining the external interface of a class with its implementation is that it makes it more difficult for a user of a class to see only the relevant external interface details. These are the details that are typically of interest to a user of a class. To offset this disadvantage, Eiffel systems provide a tool called *short*. This tool extracts the relevant interface details for a given class. These details include the assertions and signature (parameters and return type) for each routine, the class invariant, if one is present, and the attributes of the class. As an illustration, *short* is applied to Listing 1.10, class FINANCIAL. The result is shown in Listing 2.1. Compare Listing 2.1 to Listing 1.10.

Listing 2.1   The tool short applied to class FINANCIAL from Listing 1.10

```
class interface FINANCIAL

creation
    make

feature specification {ANY}
    balance : REAL

    valid_expenditure_category (category : STRING) : BOOLEAN

    valid_revenue_category (category : STRING) : BOOLEAN

    spend (amount : REAL; category : STRING)
    require
        amount_positive : amount > 0.0;
        valid_amount : amount <= balance;
        category_not_void : category /= void;
    ensure
        balance = ((old balance) - amount);
        valid_expenditure_category (category);

    earn (amount : REAL; category : STRING)
    require
        category_not_void : category /= void;
        amount_positive : amount > 0.0;
    ensure
        balance = ((old balance) + amount);
        valid_revenue_category (category);

    expenditure (category : STRING) : REAL
    require
        category_not_void : category /= void;
        valid_category : valid_expenditure_category
```

```
            (category);

        revenue (category : STRING) : REAL
        require
            category_not_void : category /= void;
            valid_category : valid_revenue_category (category);

        displayrevenues

        displayexpenditures

        displaytable

    invariant
        balance >= 0.0;

    end interface -- class FINANCIAL
```

Only the "public" section of class FINANCIAL is shown after processing with *short*. All of the pre and postconditions are shown, and the class invariant is shown.

In C++, the physical organization of a software system is left to the programmer. He or she has the option of specifying the external interface in a ".h" file and putting all of the implementation details (member function definitions) in a single ".c" file that can be compiled independently. This desirable style of organization for a C++ system is neither enforced or even encouraged. A C++ programmer may also elect to provide a separate implementation file (.c file) for each member function or combine subsets of member functions into separate implementation files.

2.3 FEATURES

As indicated earlier, an Eiffel class has two kinds of features: **attributes** (the data model) and **routines**. We examine each in this subsection.

A client of a class need not know whether a feature is defined as an attribute or as a routine. The client should be able to access any service of the class regardless of whether the service is provided through storage (an attribute) or through computation (a routine). Features that have no parameters can often be defined either as attributes or as routines. This is illustrated in Listing 2.2.

Listing 2.2   Access through storage versus computation

```
class APPLICATION
creation
    start

feature
    start is
    local
```

```
                object1 : NEWTON1;
                object2 : NEWTON2;
        do
                !!object1;
                object1.setMass( 2.0 );
                object1.setAcceleration( 3.0 );
                io.putstring( "object1.force = " );
                io.putreal( object1.force ); io.new_line;
                !!object2;
                object2.setMass( 2.0 );
                object2.setAcceleration( 3.0 );
                io.putstring( "object2.force = " );
                io.putreal( object2.force ); io.new_line;
            end; -- start

end -- APPLICATION

class NEWTON1

  feature
        mass         : REAL;
        acceleration : REAL;
        force        : REAL;

      setMass( value : REAL ) is
        do
            mass := value;
            updateForce;
        end; -- setMass

      setAcceleration( value : REAL ) is
        do
            acceleration := value;
            updateForce;
        end; -- setAcceleration

  feature { NONE }

      updateForce is
        do
            force := mass * acceleration;
        end; -- updateForce

end -- NEWTON1

class NEWTON2

feature
        mass         : REAL;
        acceleration : REAL;

      setMass( value : REAL ) is
        do
            mass := value;
        end; -- setMass
```

```
setAcceleration( value : REAL ) is
do
    acceleration := value;
end; -- setAcceleration

force : REAL is
do
    Result := mass * acceleration;
end; -- force

end -- NEWTON2
```

In Listing 2.2, *object1* is an instance of class NEWTON1, and *object2* is an instance of class NEWTON2. Both objects are created with no initialization using *!!object1* and *!!object2*. The *mass* of each of the objects is set to 2.0 and the *acceleration* to 3.0. Then, the *force* of each object is determined using identical syntax. If you do not inspect the source code of the two NEWTON classes, it is impossible to determine whether the *force* is being determined by storage (the case for *object1*) or by computation (the case for *object2*).

In class NEWTON1, each time either the *mass* or *acceleration* is updated using one of the "set" routines, the *force* attribute is automatically updated using the "protected" routine *updateForce*. This is not required in class NEWTON2 since *force* is always determined by computation.

2.3.1   Visibility

The key word *feature* with a class name in braces to its right controls the visibility of the attributes and routines contained within a given feature section. The export scope of the feature section is given by the class name in braces next to the word *feature*. For example, the class NONE, which has no descendants, may be used to obtain a "protected" section for a class. In such a section, all of the attributes and routines that are defined are visible only from within the routines of the class and the routines of any descendant class.

```
feature { NONE }
    ...
    -- All attributes and routines are for internal use only
```

A public section may be obtained by using a feature clause:

```
feature { ANY }
    ...
    -- All attributes and routines are exported to any client
```

The class ANY is at the top of the Eiffel hierarchy. All classes are descendants of ANY. If the brace and the class ANY are omitted (i.e. just the keyword *feature* is used), the effect is the same (e.g. *feature* by itself is the same as *feature { ANY }*).

In general, the clause:

```
feature { CLASS_NAME }
    ...
```

defines a scope that consists of the CLASS_NAME and all of its descendant classes. This is useful when the class producer wishes to limit the visibility of some features to only a subtree of classes. Practical examples of this will be shown in later programs.

2.3.2 Routines

Routines represent the actions that may be taken on instances of a class. An Eiffel routine is a function or procedure. As a procedure, a routine may change the state of an object. As a function, a routine returns a value of a given type based on the state of the object. An Eiffel function can also alter the internal state of an object — thus it can produce a side-effect. But this side-effect is localized to the object through which the function is sent. It is not the global kind of side-effect that has proven to be so potentially damaging in structured languages. It is undesirable for a function to change the state of an object in a way that is visible from outside the object.

Routines contain the algorithms that represent the low-level design of a system. A routine often performs a computation. In contrast with hybrid languages such as C++, and as indicated earlier, **an Eiffel routine is always applied through an object** (either an explicit object or the implicit object *Current*).

A routine may be **effective** or **deferred**. An effective routine provides all implementation details in its body, whereas a deferred routine provides no implementation details. Such details must be provided by some descendant class.

The value of a *function* routine is associated with the object *Result*. Storage for *Result* may be allocated within the routine, or *Result* may be assigned to an existing object. Its type is specified by the return type of the routine.

Several names may be specified for a routine. For example:

```
function1, funct2, function3 ( x : REAL ) : REAL is
    . . .
```

One or more formal arguments may be associated with a routine. Callers of the routine must adhere to the type specification given in the routine declaration when passing actual arguments to the routine.

A routine contains a body and some optional components. These optional components include *require, local, rescue* and *ensure,* as well as others discussed in Chapter 5.

The *require* clause of a routine, if present, introduces an assertion or precondition that must be satisfied in order for the routine to do its work correctly. If the precondition is not satisfied, an exception is raised in the caller that may result in program execution stopping with an error trace that indicates which precondition has failed.

The *local* clause of a routine, if present, declares objects that must be re-initialized every time the routine is invoked unless the default values are acceptable. These "local" variables are useful in supporting the computation given in the main body of the routine.

The body of a routine begins with the reserved word *do*. Within the body of a routine, assignments can be performed only on attributes and local entities. It is illegal to assign to a parameter of a routine. That is, **a parameter cannot be the target of an assignment**.

The *rescue* clause of a routine, if present, describes the action that is taken if an exception occurs during the execution of the routine body. The absence of a *rescue* clause invokes a call to the procedure *default_rescue* contained within the universal class ANY. The *default_rescue* routine does nothing but any class may redefine it to perform exception handling relevant to the class.

The *ensure* clause of a routine, if present, introduces a postcondition that must be satisfied upon exit from the routine.

Chapter 3 discusses pre and postconditions and *rescue* clauses for routines in detail.

External routines permit access to important libraries that reside outside of the Eiffel environment, such as C libraries. Listing 2.3 presents a random number class constructed using several external routines. This class is used in several important applications in later chapters.

Listing 2.3   Class RANDOM and External Routines

```
class RANDOM
-- generates pseudo-random numbers
creation
   initialize
feature { NONE } -- For internal use

   c_init is
   -- C function seeds random number generator using
         current clock time
   external "C"
   alias
      "initial"
   end; -- c_init

   c_valueBetween( low : INTEGER; high : INTEGER ) :
      INTEGER is
   -- C function returns a uniform number between low
         and high
   external "C"
   alias
      "nextBetween"
   end; -- c_valueBetween

   c_uniform : DOUBLE is
   external "C"
   alias
      "rrandom"
   end; -- c_uniform

feature -- public

   initialize is
```

```
once
    c_init;
end; -- initialize

valueBetween( low: INTEGER; high : INTEGER ) : INTEGER
    is
do
    Result := c_valueBetween( low, high );
end; -- valueBetween


uniform : DOUBLE is
-- Returns a uniform random real number between 0.0 and
    1.0
do
    Result := c_uniform;
end; -- uniform

end -- class RANDOM
```

In class RANDOM, the protected routines *c_init*, *c_valueBetween* and *c_uniform* are all implemented in terms of calls to external C language functions. The syntax is:

```
function_name is
external "C"
alias
    "C_function_name"

end;
```

In the public section of the class, function *initialize* uses the key word *once* instead of *do* as a delimiter for the function body. This causes the routine to be executed exactly one time. If the routine were a function (*initialize* is a procedure), subsequent calls to the routine would cause the original value to be returned. When the routine is a procedure, as in this case, subsequent calls to the procedure have no effect.

Once function routines act as computed constants since they return the same value with every invocation. See section 2.9 for more details.

In Listing 2.4, the file containing the C functions is presented.

Listing 2.4   C file containing random number functions

```
#include <time.h>
#include <stdlib.h>
#include <math.h>
double drand48();
void initial()
{
    long seed;
    time_t t;
    time( &t );
```

```
        seed = ( long ) t;
        seed *= seed;
        seed = abs( seed );
        srand48( seed );
}

double rrandom()
{
        return drand48(); /* Unix random number function */
}

int nextBetween( int low, int high )
{
        double r, t;
        r = ( double ) high - ( double ) low + 1.0;
        t = r * drand48();
        return low + ( int ) t;
}
double power( double exponent )
{
        return exp( exponent );

}
```

2.3.3 Attributes

Attributes come in two flavors: variable and constant. Variable attributes can be the target of an assignment in any routine of the class. Constant attributes maintain the same value for all instances of the class.

Attributes play a central role in object-oriented analysis. They represent the data model of a class. Attributes are generally used to represent the descriptive features of an object (e.g. height, weight, cost, depth, etc.). Attributes are also used to represent aggregations, (e.g. a VEHICLE class is composed of an ENGINE object), targets (push a button object [the target] to activate some action), and delegates (an object that is used to perform some action on behalf of another object). Chapter 8 discusses the role of attributes in detail.

Every instance of a class has the same collection of attributes to characterize its current state. This state may be modified only by the routines of the class.

The storage for a constant attribute does not need to be physically attached to every instance of the class. The following is a list of possible constant attributes:

- BOOLEAN: True and False
  Example: IS_TRUE : BOOLEAN is True;
- CHARACTER: 'A', 'B', ... ,'Z', ...
  Example: LETTER_F : CHARACTER is 'f';
- INTEGER: decimal digits possibly preceded by a sign
  Example: FIVE : INTEGER is 5;
- REAL: normal formation of a floating point number
  Example: SIXTY_SIX : REAL is 66.0;

- DOUBLE: precision based on particular compiler
- Bit_Type: Sequence of 0's and 1's terminated with B
  Example: FOUR : Bit_Type is 100B;
- STRING: string literals in double quotes
  Example: MY_NAME : STRING is "Richard";

For types other than the ones given above, the use of *once* functions can achieve the same effect. For example, a unit matrix of size 10 by 10 can be declared and used like a constant, as shown in Listing 2.5.

Listing 2.5   Once routine for a UNIT_VECTOR

```
UNIT_VECTOR : ARRAY2[ REAL ] is
local
    vector    : ARRAY2[ REAL ];
    row, col  : INTEGER;
once
    !!vector.make( 10, 10 ); -- Initializes storage for a 10
    -- x 10 matrix
    from row := 0
    until row = 10
    loop
        row := row + 1;
        from col := 0
        until col = 10
        loop
            col := col + 1;
            vector.put( row, col, 0 );
        end;
    end;
    from row := 0
    until row = 10
    loop
        row := row + 1;
        vector.put( row, row, 1 );
    end;
    Result := vector;
end; -- UNIT_VECTOR
```

Every time the function UNIT_VECTOR is used in an expression, the value of a two-dimensional array with 1's along the main diagonal and 0's everywhere else is returned. This structured constant is computed only once.

Attributes can be declared as *unique*. Such attributes are assigned a distinct integer value by the compiler. An example is given next.

```
-- Traffic light colors
red, amber, green : INTEGER is unique;
...
inspect -- Eiffel's "switch-like" statement
    color
when red then
    stop_cars;
```

```
when amber then
    proceed_with_caution;
when green then
    go;
else
    default_action;
end;
```

2.4 THE CREATION OF OBJECTS

One or more routines of an Eiffel class may be used to create an instance of a class with specified initial values for its attributes. Such a "creation" routine must be included in the creation clause of a class.

A creation routine may be used either to create a new instance of a class or, if placed in the "public" section of the class, as a normal routine used typically to assign value(s) to the attributes of the class. In order for a creation routine to produce a new class instance, the operator "!!" must be used in front of the expression involving the creation routine.

For example, if *make_my_day* is a creation routine of class CLINT_EASTWOOD, the expression *!!cowboy.make_my_day(10)* would create a new CLINT_EASTWOOD object and assign it the initial value 10. On the other hand, the expression *cowboy.make_my_day(4)* would merely assign the value 4 to the existing CLINT_EASTWOOD object.

All variables in a class (i.e. local variables and attributes) must be initialized (storage allocated) before they can be used. Storage for all instances is allocated dynamically after a creation routine is invoked. The initial value of all class instances is *Void* before initialization. If a message is sent to a class instance that has not been initialized, a run-time exception will be raised with a trace indicating the offending message call.

In addition to the form shown above, the syntax for invoking a creation routine can take several other forms. Suppose C is a class without any creation clause (i.e. no creation routine). The expression *!!c* causes c to become a new instance of class C with all its attributes initialized to their default values. The variable name *c* is attached to the object just created. The above syntax is not valid if one or more creation routines exist in class C. Then only one of these can be used to create a new instance.

The following list of default values exists for various types of entities:

- An instance of a class (reference type): Void
- BOOLEAN: False
- CHARACTER: null character
- INTEGER, REAL, DOUBLE: 0(.0)
- Bit_Type: a sequence of zeros

When an object that contains attributes from the above list is created, the default initial values are assigned to the appropriate attributes of the newly created class.

Another option in invoking a creation routine is to use an explicit type that is a descendant of the declared class of the object. As an example, suppose CAR is a subclass of VEHICLE. Consider the following code:

```
myCar : VEHICLE;
!CAR!myCar
or
!CAR!myCar( ... )
```

A creation clause, like a feature clause, can specify an export scope such that only the classes in the export scope and their descendants can use the routines that are designated to create instances. An example is the following:

```
Creation { VEHICLE }
    ...
```

Here, only from within the VEHICLE class or any of its descendants can instances of the given class be created.

2.5 SOME SIMPLE CLASSES

Some simple Eiffel classes are presented in this section to illustrate the syntax and introduce some basic concepts associated with class construction. In later sections of this chapter, the various parts of an Eiffel class are examined much more closely.

2.5.1 A Simple Class POINT

Let us illustrate the construction of a simple class, class POINT. Such a class is useful as a building block in geometric applications.

The data model for a POINT class involves two fields of data, each a real number, say x and y. The operations that need to be specified include creating a point with default values of 0.0 for both x and y, creating a point with specified initial values of x_0 and y_0, setting the value of x to *xvalue* and setting the value of y to *yvalue*. Because the attributes x and y are put in the "public" section of the class, all clients have read-only accessibility to these attributes.

The definition of such a POINT class is given in Listing 2.6.

Listing 2.6   Class POINT

```
class POINT
    creation
        make

  feature -- public section
     x, y : DOUBLE;

    make( x0 : DOUBLE; y0: DOUBLE ) is
    do
```

```
        x := x0;
        y := y0;
    end; -- make

    setX( xvalue: DOUBLE ) is
    do
        x := xvalue;
    end; -- setX

    setY( yvalue: DOUBLE ) is
    do
        y := yvalue;
    end; -- yvalue

end -- class POINT
```

Listing 2.7   Class APPLICATION

```
class APPLICATION

    creation
        make

  feature
    make is
    local
        pt1, pt2 : POINT
    do
        !!pt1;
        !!pt2.make( 3, 4 );
        io.putstring( "The coordinates of pt1 are: " );
        io.putdouble( pt1.x ); io.putstring( ", " );
        io.putdouble( pt1.y ); io.new_line;
        io.putstring( "The coordinates of pt2 are: " )
        io.putdouble( pt2.x ); io.putstring( ", " );
        io.putdouble( pt2.y ); io.new_line;
    end; -- make
end -- APPLICATION
```

The program output is:

```
The coordinates of pt1 are: 0, 0
The coordinates of pt2 are: 3, 4
```

In the *make* routine of class APPLICATION, the POINT variables *pt1* and *pt2* must be brought to life explicitly, otherwise they assume the default value *Void*.

The result of applying the tool *short* to class POINT is given in Listing 2.8. It contains the information that a user of this class needs.

Listing 2.8   The tool *short* applied to class POINT

```
class interface POINT

creation specification
    make
```

```
feature specification
    x, y : DOUBLE

    make (x0 : DOUBLE; y0 : DOUBLE)

    setx (xvalue : DOUBLE)

    sety (yvalue : DOUBLE)

end interface -- class POINT
```

2.5.2 A Simple Class LINE_SEGMENT

A line may be defined by two points. Therefore, the data model for class
LINE_SEGMENT will consist of two points. A simple LINE_SEGMENT class is pre-
sented in Listing 2.9. It uses a design principle called composition. A
LINE_SEGMENT object is composed of two POINT objects. In order to initialize a
LINE_SEGMENT object, it is necessary to specify the two POINT objects.

Listing 2.9   Class LINE_SEGMENT

```
class LINE_SEGMENT

  creation
     make

  feature { NONE }-- Protected section
     a, b      : POINT;
     deltaX    : DOUBLE;
     deltaY    : DOUBLE;

  feature - Public section
     make( pt1 : POINT; pt2 : POINT ) is
     do
         a := pt1;
         b := pt2;
         deltaY := ( b.y - a.y );
         deltaX := ( b.x - a.x );
     end; -- make

     length : DOUBLE is
     do
         Result := ( deltaX ^ 2 + deltaY ^ 2 ) ^ 0.5;
     end; -- length

     slope : DOUBLE is
     do
         Result := deltaY / deltaX;
     end; -- slope

end -- LINE_SEGMENT
```

The data model of class LINE_SEGMENT, in addition to containing two points
a and *b*, also has attributes *deltaX* and *deltaY*. These protected features (they are

exported to NONE) are useful in computing the length of the line and its slope. In a later section of this chapter that examines the semantics of object assignment, we closely examine the consequence of assigning *a* to *p1* and *b* to *pt2* in the *make* routine. We note that both *length* and *slope* could be defined as part of the data model (i.e. as attributes) instead of routines. No changes would have to be made in class APPLICATION. The expressions *line1.length* and *line1.slope* remain unchanged and are independent of whether *length* and *slope* are attributes or routines.

In Listing 2.10, a new APPLICATION class is defined to exercise the features of class LINE_SEGMENT.

Listing 2.10   Class APPLICATION

```
class APPLICATION
 creation
    make

 feature
    make is
    local
        pt1, pt2 : POINT;
        line1    : LINE_SEGMENT;
    do
        !!pt1.create;
        !!pt2.make( 3, 4 );
        !!line1.make( pt1, pt2 );
        io.putstring( "The length of line1 = " );
        io.putdouble( line1.length ); io.new_line;
        io.putstring( "The slope of line1 = " );
        io.putdouble( line1.slope ); io.new_line;
    end; -- make

    end -- APPLICATION
```

The program output is:

```
The length of line1 = 5
The slope of line1 = 0.927295
```

2.5.3   Some Additions to Classes POINT and LINE_SEGMENT

What additional features might we wish to add to classes POINT and LINE_SEGMENT?

Regarding class POINT, it might be desirable to be able to compute the distance between two points. We will add a routine *distance*, and infix operator "@" to class POINT. We might also wish to be able to add and subtract two points. We will add the routines *add* and *subtract*, and infix operators "+" and "-" to class POINT.

Regarding class LINE_SEGMENT, we might wish to be able to find the point of intersection between two line segments. We will add a routine *intersection* and infix operator @ to class LINE_SEGMENT. A supporting routine *intersects* will also be needed.

The infix operators provide an alternative way of invoking the routine. For example, two alternative ways of computing the distance between pt1 and pt2 would be:

distance := pt1.distance(pt2);

distance := pt1 @ pt2;

Before presenting the code for the more complete classes POINT and LINE_SEGMENT, let us discuss briefly the algebra underlying the computation of the intersection of two line segments.

2.5.3.1 The Intersection of Two Line Segments

The reader who is not interested in the mathematical details relating to the development of the *intersection* routine of class LINE_SEGMENT may wish to skip this sub-section.

A necessary but not sufficient condition for the two line segments to intersect is that their slopes must not be the same. If they were, this would imply that the segments were parallel.

The approach that is used to determine the point of intersection, if one exists, is to extend each line segment and compute the x-coordinate of their intersection, *xLoc*. Such a value must exist if the line segments have unequal slopes. After computing *xLoc*, a test is performed to determine whether this x-coordinate lies within the range of x values for both line segments. If it does, a bona-fide intersection of the two segments exists, otherwise the two line segments do not intersect. Figure 2.1 shows several possibilities regarding the intersection of line segments 1 and 2

Consider the two line segments given in Figure 2.1(a). The equations of the two lines, expressed in terms of their slopes s_1 and s_2 and their left-most end point, are:

Line 1: $y = s1(x - a_{1x}) + a_{1y}$

Line 2: $y = s2(x - a_{2x}) + a_{2y}$

where a_{1x} and a_{1y} are the x and y coordinate of the left end point of line 1 and a_{2x} and a_{2y} are the x and y coordinates of the left end point of line 2.

After equating the y values for line 1 and line 2, the following equation may be solved for *xLoc*: $s_1(x - a_{1x}) + a_{1y} = s_2(x - a_{2x}) + a_{2y}$

(a) Segments intersect   (b) Segments do not intersect   (c) Segments parallel

Fig. 2.1 Intersecting and Non-intersecting Line Segments

The solution for *xLoc* is:

$$xLoc = (a_{2y} - a_{1y} + s_1a_{1x} - s_2a_{2x}) / (s_1 - s_2)$$

The complete classes for `POINT` and `LINE_SEGMENT` are given in the next sub-section.

2.5.3.2 Classes POINT and LINE_SEGMENT

Class `POINT` is presented in Listing 2.11. As indicated earlier, self references to an instance of a class are given by the reserved word *Current*. This reserved word is used in class `POINT`.

Listing 2.11   Class POINT

```
class POINT

 creation
   make

 feature -- Public section
   x, y : DOUBLE;

   make( xvalue : DOUBLE; yvalue: DOUBLE ) is
   do
      x := xvalue;
      y := yvalue;
   end; -- make

   -- Access methods
   setX( xvalue: DOUBLE ) is
   do
      x := xvalue;
   end; -- setX

   setY( yvalue: DOUBLE ) is
   do
      y := yvalue;
   end; -- yvalue

   -- Output
   display is
   do
      io.putstring( "< "); io.putdouble( x );
      io.putstring( ", "); io.putdouble( y );
      io.putstring( " > "); io.new_line;
   end; -- display

   -- Operations involving another point
   distance, infix "@" ( anotherPoint : POINT ) : DOUBLE is
   local
      aLine : LINE_SEGMENT;
   do
```

```
        !!aLine.make( Current, anotherPoint );
        Result := aLine.length;
    end; -- distance

    add, infix "+" ( anotherPoint : POINT ) : POINT is
    do
        !!Result.make( x + anotherPoint.x, y + anotherPoint.y
            );
    end; -- add

    subtract, infix "-" ( anotherPoint : POINT ) : POINT is
    do
        !!Result.make( x - anotherPoint.x, y - anotherPoint.y
            );
    end; -- subtract

end -- class POINT
```

The routine *distance*, used for computing the distance from the receiver to another point, also defines a prefix operator "@." This may be used as an alternative to *distance*. To compute the distance, a line segment composed of the receiver *Current* and *anotherPoint* is defined locally. The length of this line is computed and returned by the function *distance*.

The details of class LINE_SEGMENT are given in Listing 2.12.

Listing 2.12   Class LINE_SEGMENT

```
class LINE_SEGMENT

inherit
    C_MATH  -- a "mix-in" for sqrt from the TowerEiffel
            -- library

creation
    make

feature { NONE }
    deltaX : DOUBLE;
    deltaY : DOUBLE;

feature -- Public section
    a, b : POINT; -- End points of line segment

    -- Creation methods
    make( pt1 : POINT; pt2 : POINT ) is
    do
        a := pt1;
        b := pt2;
        deltaY := ( b.y - a.y );
        deltaX := ( b.x - a.x );
    end; -- make
```

```
-- Access methods
length : DOUBLE is
do
   Result := sqrt( deltaX * deltaX + deltaY * deltaY );
end; -- length

slope : DOUBLE is
do
   Result := deltaY / deltaX;
end; -- slope

intersects( anotherLine : LINE_SEGMENT ) : BOOLEAN is
-- Determines whether receiver intersects anotherLine
local
   xLoc : DOUBLE;
do
   if slope = anotherLine.slope then
      Result := False
   else
      xLoc := ( anotherLine.a.y - a.y + slope * a.x -
            anotherLine.slope * anotherLine.a.x
            ) / ( slope - anotherLine.slope );
      Result := not ( xLoc < a.x or xLoc > b.x or xLoc <
         anotherLine.a.x or xLoc > anotherLine.b.x );
   end;
end; -- intersects

-- Operations involving another line
intersection, infix "@" ( anotherLine : LINE_SEGMENT ) :
   POINT is
require
   lines_intersect: intersects( anotherLine );
local
   xLoc : DOUBLE;
do
   xLoc := ( anotherLine.a.y - a.y + slope * a.x -
         anotherLine.slope * anotherLine.a.x ) /
            ( slope - anotherLine.slope );
   !!Result.make( xLoc, slope * ( xLoc - a.x ) + a.y );
end; -- intersection

end -- LINE_SEGMENT
```

Class LINE_SEGMENT inherits from class C_MATH (using the TowerEiffel library for this example) so that the routine *sqrt* is accessible directly. This type of "mix-in" is fairly common in Eiffel. As discussed earlier, it represents a violation of the "is a" relationship associated with inheritance. It does not make sense to argue that LINE_SEGMENT "is a" kind of C_MATH. If Eiffel had an import or "uses" capability, inheritance would not have to be compromised in this way. This is discussed further in Chapter 5.

Routine *intersection* has an infix operator "@" that may be used as an alternative. The routine has a precondition that assures that a valid intersection actually exists between the two line segments. A client can test for this before invoking the *intersection* routine since the *intersects* routine is in the public section of class LINE_SEGMENT.

Class APPLICATION, given in Listing 2.13, exercises some of the features of the new LINE_SEGMENT class. Valid intersections are tested for before invoking *intersection*.

Listing 2.13   Class APPLICATION — Testing class LINE_SEGMENT

```
class APPLICATION

creation
    start

feature

    start is
    local
        pt1, pt2, pt3 : POINT;
        pt4, pt5      : POINT;
        line1, line2  : LINE_SEGMENT;
    do
        !!pt1.make( 4, 5 );
        !!pt2.make( 3, 4 );

        io.putstring( "The distance from pt1 to pt2 = " );
        io.putdouble( pt1 @ pt2 ); io.new_line;
        io.putstring( "The distance from pt2 to pt1 = " );
        io.putdouble( pt2.distance( pt1 ) ); io.new_line;

        io.putstring( "The sum of pt1 and pt2 = " );
        pt3 := pt1 + pt2;
        pt3.display;
        io.putstring( "The difference of pt1 and pt2 = " );
        pt3 := pt1 - pt2;
        pt3.display;

        pt1.make( 0, 1 );
        pt2.make( 2, -1 );
        !!line1.make( pt1, pt2 );
        !!pt4.make( 0, -1 );
        !!pt5.make( 2, 1 );
        !!line2.make( pt4, pt5 );
        if line1.intersects( line2 ) then -- Test for validity of
        -- intersection
            pt3 := line1 @ line2;
            pt3.display;
        else
            io.putstring( "line1 does not intersect line2" );
            io.new_line;
        end;
```

```
            pt4.make( 0, -1 );
            pt5.make( 5, -1 );
            line2.make( pt4, pt5 );
            if line1.intersects( line2 ) then -- Test for validity
            -- of intersection
                pt3 := line1 @ line2;
                pt3.display;
            else
                io.putstring( "line1 does not intersect line2" );
                io.new_line;
            end;

            pt4.make( 3, -1 );
            pt5.make( 5, 1 );
            line2.make( pt4, pt5 );
            if line1.intersects( line2 ) then -- Test for validity
            -- of intersection
                pt3 := line1 @ line2;
                pt3.display;
            else
                io.putstring( "line1 does not intersect line2" );
                io.new_line;
            end;

        end; -- start

    end -- APPLICATION
```

The program output is:

```
The distance from pt1 to pt2 = 1.41421
The distance from pt2 to pt1 = 1.41421
The sum of pt1 and pt2 = < 7, 9 >
The difference of pt1 and pt2 = < 1, 1 >
< 1, 0 >
< 2, -1 >
line1 does not intersect line2
```

It is noted that the routine *make* is used both as a creation routine and as a normal routine.

2.6   SEMANTICS OF OBJECT ASSIGNMENT AND EQUALITY

Three basic, important and common operations in object-oriented programming are: copying, cloning and comparing two objects.

Copying involves transferring information from one object to an existing object. Cloning involves the creation of a new object, as well as the transfer of information from the cloned object.

Copying, cloning and comparing have shallow as well as deep semantics. We examine each in the next few subsections.

2.6.1 Deep and Shallow Copies

All Eiffel objects inherit the *copy* routine from class ANY. If a and b are instances of class C and properly initialized (a creation routine is used to initialize each), b is copied to a as follows: *a.copy(b)*.

Note: If object b contains one or more references as its attributes (normal objects), these reference values are copied to the corresponding fields of object a. This creates a potentially dangerous situation in which fields of the target point to the same data as fields of the source. If any of the source field values should change, these changes would affect the target. In Listings 2.14 and 2.15, the potential hazards of such aliasing are demonstrated.

Listing 2.14   The hazards of shallow copy — Class SHALLOW_COPY

```
class SHALLOW_COPY
-- To illustrate shallow copying

 creation
    make

 feature

    make is
    local
       w1, w2 : POINT_WRAPPER;
    do
       !!w1.make( 1, 1 );
       !!w2.make( 2, 2 );
       w1.copy( w2 );
       io.putstring( "w1 after copy is: " );
       w1.display;
       w2.setX( 3 ); w2.setY( 3 );
       io.putstring(
       "w1 after w2 is changed from < 2, 2 > to < 3, 3 > is: "
       );
       w1.display;
    end; -- make

end -- class SHALLOW_COPY
```

The program output is:

```
w1 after copy is: < 2, 2 >
w1 after w2 is changed from < 2, 2 > to < 3, 3 > is: < 3, 3 >
```

Listing 2.15   Class POINT_WRAPPER

```
class POINT_WRAPPER
-- Used to illustrate shallow versus deep semantics for copy,
-- clone, and equality test
```

```
creation
    make

  feature -- Public section
     pt : POINT;

    make( x0 : INTEGER; y0 : INTEGER ) is
       do
          !!pt.make( x0, y0 );
       end; -- make

     setX( xvalue : INTEGER ) is
     do
        pt.setX( xvalue );
     end; -- setX

     setY( yvalue : INTEGER ) is
     do
        pt.setY( yvalue );
     end; -- setY

     display is
     do
        pt.display;
     end; -- display

  end -- class POINT_WRAPPER
```

The creation routine, *make*, in class SHALLOW_COPY defines two local variables of type POINT_WRAPPER. This class is defined in Listing 2.15 and contains a point reference (point object) as an attribute.

Two point_wrapper objects, *w1* and *w2*, are created in class SHALLOW_COPY. Object *w2* is copied to *w1*. The value < 2, 2 > of object *w2* is successfully copied to *w1*. Now *w2* sets the value of its point attribute to < 3, 3 >. Unfortunately, this has the effect of changing the value of object *w1* since its point field is aliased with the point field of *w2* because of the shallow copy. Unless done intentionally, and this would be most unusual, the error exhibited in this shallow copy application is quite serious. The program compiles, runs and produces output. It is only upon very close examination of the output that the error is detected.

Figure 2.2 shows the result of the shallow copy of *w2* to *w1*.

As a result of shallow copying, the *pt* attribute of *w1* points to the storage of the *pt* attribute of *w2*.

Figure 2.3 shows the result of the deep copy of *w2* to *w1*.

As a result of deep copying, the *pt* attribute of *w1* has autonomous storage for its *pt* attribute. The value of the *pt* attribute of *w2* is copied to the *pt* attribute of *w1*.

Listing 2.16 shows the revised code for making a deep copy.

Listing 2.16   Deep Copy — Class DEEP_COPY

```
class DEEP_COPY
-- To illustrate deep copy
```

Fig. 2.2 Shallow Copying

Fig. 2.3 Deep Copying

```
.creation
   make

feature

    make is
    local
       w1, w2 : POINT_WRAPPER;
    do
       !!w1.make( 1, 1 );
       !!w2.make( 2, 2 );
       w1.deep_copy( w2 );
       io.putstring( "w1 after copy is: " );
       w1.display;
       w2.setX( 3 ); w2.setY( 3 );
       io.putstring(
          "w1 after w2 is changed from < 2, 2 > to < 3, 3 > is: "
          );
       w1.display;
    end; -- make

end -- class DEEP_COPY
```

The output of Listing 2.16 is:

```
w1 after copy is: < 2, 2 >
w1 after w2 is changed from < 2, 2 > to < 3, 3 > is: < 2, 2 >
```

In making a deep copy of *w2*, the data in the fields of *w2* are recursively copied to *w1*. The aliasing problem that was evident in the code of Listing 2.14 is now corrected.

2.6.2 Deep and Shallow Clones

Cloning can be accomplished when an existing object is used to create a new object with the same field values as the existing object. If *a* and *b* are instances of class C, *b* is initialized and *a* is *Void*, then the expression *a* := *clone(b)* will create a new object *a* with the fields of *b*.

The same difficulties of aliasing discussed in connection with copying in section 2.6.1 prevail with cloning. In a shallow clone (plain clone), the fields of object *a* that are object references will point to the same data as in the cloned object *b*. This is potentially dangerous, as outlined in 2.6.1.

The alternative to using *clone* is using *deep_clone*. For example, *a* := *deep_clone(b)*. The data in the fields of *b* are recursively copied to *a* after *a* is created.

2.6.3   Deep and Shallow Equality Testing

When two objects of the same class, say *a* and *b*, are compared, either a shallow comparison that compares the object references or a deep comparison that recursively compares the data fields is performed. The class SHALLOW_COPY of Listing 2.14 is modified in Listing 2.17 to demonstrate each type of equality testing.

Listing 2.17   Class SHALLOW_COPY modified to illustrate equality testing

```
class SHALLOW_COPY
-- To illustrate shallow copy and equality testing

  creation
     make

  feature

     make is
     local
        w1, w2 : POINT_WRAPPER;
     do
        -- See Listing 2.14 for missing code
        if equal( w1, w2 ) then
           io.putstring( "w1 and w2 are equal in a shallow sense"
           ); io.new_line;
        end;
        if deep_equal( w1, w2 ) then
           io.putstring( "w1 and w2 are equal in a deep sense"
           ); io.new_line;
     end;
  end; -- make

end -- class SHALLOW_COPY
```

The program output is:

```
w1 after copy is: < 2, 2 >
w1 after w2 is changed from < 2, 2 > to < 3, 3 > is: < 3, 3 >
```

```
w1 and w2 are equal in a shallow sense
w1 and w2 are equal in a deep sense
```

The reader may be wondering why the output of the program of Listing 2.17 indicates that *w1* and *w2* are equal in a deep sense. Only a shallow copy was performed.

A deep equality test verifies that the data fields of the two objects are recursively equal. They are in this example because when the field of *w2* is changed, the field of *w1* becomes the same.

2.6.4 Assignment Operation

At any moment in the execution of an Eiffel software system, every variable is either attached to a particular object or has the value *Void*. A variable may be attached or reattached using one of the following four operations: assignment, reverse assignment, use of creation instruction or the association of an actual argument of a routine to the formal argument at the time of a call.

Reverse assignment is discussed in later sections. Creation operations are discussed in section 2.4. We focus on the assignment operator here.

Object *b* is assigned to object *a* using the expression, *a* := *b*. If objects *a* and *b* are normal reference type objects (expanded types are introduced later), then the same storage is pointed to by *a* and *b*.

An assignment is valid if and only if the source type (right side) conforms to its target type (left side). This implies that the source type is the same as the target type or a descendant of the target type. This is discussed in more detail in the next section, polymorphism and dynamic-binding.

2.7 POLYMORPHISM AND DYNAMIC-BINDING — LEARNING TO SKI, WALK AND RUN

In addition to encapsulation and inheritance, dynamic-binding and polymorphism are fundamental pillars of object-oriented programming. They promote a flexible style of programming in which messages are associated with particular methods at run-time. This is in sharp contrast to languages such as Pascal, C and C++, in which the predominant binding is performed at compile/link time

The word polymorphism means to assume various forms. In the context of object-oriented programming, polymorphism implies that a given message produces various responses based on the particular subclass of the receiving object. In the writing instrument application presented in Chapter 1, the message *stats* is sent to a collection (pencil case) of pens and pencils. When a WRITING_ INSTRU-MENT object receives the message *stats*, this message is attached to the appropriate *stats* routine.

At a technical conference on Object-Oriented Programming a few years ago, Brad Cox, the author of the seminal book *Object-Oriented Programming: An Evolutionary Approach*[1], presented a cute slide showing a boy born with skis bound to his feet. Brad pointed out that this "early-binding" promotes a high degree of efficiency in skiing but not much flexibility in walking or running. In contrast, ordinary feet, which may be bound to ski-boots, running shoes or plain walking shoes, are much more flexible but slightly less efficient for skiing. The analogy is quite good. Early-binding imposes an intellectual straight-jacket on the software designer in exchange for a potentially greater degree of code optimization and resulting run-time performance. Dynamic-binding promotes greater design flexibility in exchange for a small performance penalty.

Programmers accustomed to languages such as Pascal, C and Ada may find early-binding more natural simply because it is more familiar. C++, bound in many ways closely to C, favors early-binding as its default mode. A limited form of dynamic-binding may be enabled in C++. To do so requires the use of either pointers or references. A C++ class may in fact promote a mixed-mode of design in which some member functions are bound at compile/link time (early-binding) and other member functions are bound at run-time (late-binding). This mixed-mode of design can lead to confusion, inconsistency and greater difficulty in software maintenance. More details are provided in Chapter 7.

Eiffel, like Smalltalk, promotes a totally consistent mode of programming in which all message calls are interpreted semantically as dynamic-binding calls at run-time. During the optimization phase of compilation, those message calls that obviously can be bound at compile/link time are converted to early-binding calls to achieve improved run-time performance. This optimization is done by the compiler and does not require any programmer intervention. The programmer can focus on high-level design issues and does not have to be burdened with the micro-management details associated with specifying the kind of binding to be employed. This, in my view, is the right way to do business.

Dynamic-binding derives its strength from the principle that what matters when a message is sent to a target object is the type of object that receives the message, not the static specification of the object type (the declaration given in the program text). The writing instrument example presented in Chapter 1 provides a simple model of this principle. When the pencil case is declared, its base type is specified as WRITING_INSTRUMENT. When the message *stats* is sent to each object in the case, the response is based on whether the receiver is a PENCIL, MECHANCAL_PENCIL, FOUNTAIN_PEN or BALLPOINT_PEN. These subclasses conform to (are descendants of) WRITING_INSTRUMENT. It should be clear from this discussion that dynamic-binding and polymorphism are intimately associated with inheritance. Without a hierarchy of classes, conforming subclasses has no meaning and neither does polymorphism and dynamic-binding.

As an example, consider a small portion of an Eiffel class hierarchy consisting of the classes A, B, C, D and E each defining a routine *dynamic*. The hierarchy of the subtree is shown in Figure 2.4.

If a declaration of the following form is given:

```
target : B;
```

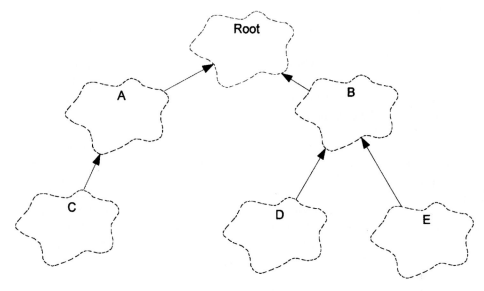

Fig. 2.4 A Class Hierarchy

and if messages of the form:

```
!D!target.create;
target.dynamic;
```

are applied to *target*, then late-binding will assure that the correct version of method *dynamic* is executed if the actual type of *target* is D (or E). The message *dynamic* cannot be dynamically-bound to *target* if the actual type of *target* is A or C since these class types are not heirs of the formal type of *target*, namely B. Such an attempt would cause a compilation error. The classes B, D and E form a polymorphic cluster with respect to the root class B.

2.8 GENERIC CLASSES

A generic class is defined in terms of one or more parameters that are unspecified by the class producer but specified when an instance of the class is created by the class consumer (the user). The operations defined in the class are implemented in terms of the generic parameters.

A generic class provides a high potential for reuse since the consumer is able to set values for the generic parameters that are relevant to the application. Several instances of a generic type may be created, each having a different basetype. For example, if a STACK class is defined in terms of a generic base type, a user could declare a stack of integers, stack of personnel records, and a stack of cafeteria trays all within the same application. The syntax for these various stacks might look as follows:

```
intStack               : STACK[ INTEGER ];
personnelRecords       : STACK[ PERSONNEL_RECORD ];
trays                  : STACK[ TRAYS ];
```

It is assumed that PERSONNEL_RECORD and TRAYS classes have been defined. If the STACK class were not generic, the user would have to create three separate stack classes such as INTEGER_STACK, RECORD_STACK and TRAY_STACK. Only a single generic class need be defined instead.

From the viewpoint of the producer, the operations associated with a stack such as *push* and *pop* may be implemented in terms of the generic base type parameter. In more complex classes, the generic parameters may have to be constrained to assure that they can respond to certain operations. As an example, in a generic ARRAY class, the operation of sorting the array can be assured only if the generic base type is a member of a class that responds to the comparison operators. Such a parameter would have to conform to class COMPARABLE. Eiffel allows the class producer to specify constraints on each generic parameter to assure that the parameter is capable of responding to appropriate messages.

In the next chapter, several important generic container classes, including LIST, STACK, QUEUE and TREE, are presented.

In Listing 2.18, we consider a simple generic class, SORTABLE_ARRAY. This class has a generic parameter T -> COMPARABLE and has an attribute, *data,* that is of type ARRAY[T]. The actual parameter that is substituted by the user in creating an instance of SORTABLE_ARRAY must be an heir of class COMPARABLE. This assures that the operations of "<" and ">" may be used on instances of T in the routines of class SORTABLE_ARRAY.

The basic operations provided are *sort, maximum* and *minimum,* which return an ordered array and the largest and smallest values in the array. In addition, the operation of *display* is provided that outputs the elements of the sorted array.

Listing 2.18   Class SORTABLE_ARRAY

```
class SORTABLE_ARRAY[ T -> COMPARABLE ]
  creation
    make

  feature -- Public
    data : ARRAY[ T ];
    size : INTEGER;

    make( anArray : ARRAY[ T ]; sz : INTEGER ) is
    do
        data := deep_clone( anArray );
        size := sz;
    end; -- make

    sort is
    local
        i, j       : INTEGER;
        maxindex   : INTEGER;
```

```
        temp      : T;
        max       : T;
do
    from i := 0
    until i = size - 1
    loop
        i := i + 1;
        max := data.item( 1 );
        maxindex := 1;
        from j := 0
        until j = size + 1 - i
        loop
            j := j + 1;
            if data.item( j ) > max then
                max := data.item( j );
                maxindex := j;
            end;
        end;
        temp := data.item( size + 1 - i );
        data.put( data.item( maxindex ), size + 1 - i );
        data.put( temp, maxindex );
    end;
end; -- sort

display is
local
    i : INTEGER;
do
    from i := 0
    until i = size
    loop
        i := i + 1;
        print( data.item( i ) ); -- print defined in class
        -- GENERAL
        io.new_line;
    end;
end; -- display

maximum : T is
local
    i      : INTEGER;
do
  Result := data.item( 1 );
    from i := 1
    until i = size
    loop
        i := i + 1;
        if data.item( i ) > Result then
          Result := data.item( i );
        end;
    end;
end; -- maximum

minimum : T is
```

```
        local
            i       : INTEGER;
        do
          Result := data.item( 1 );
            from i := 1
            until i = size
            loop
               i := i + 1;
               if data.item( i ) < Result then
                  Result := data.item( i );
               end;
            end;
        end; -- minimum

    end -- SORTABLE_ARRAY
```

Routine *sort* declares two local variables, *temp* and *max*, of type T. The ">"
operation is performed on *max*. Because T is an heir of class COMPARABLE, this
operation is defined.

Listing 2.19 presents a main driver class, SORTING, that exercises the functions of class SORTABLE_ARRAY.

Listing 2.19   Class SORTABLE_ARRAY

```
    class SORTING

      creation
        define

      feature

          sortable1 : SORTABLE_ARRAY[ INTEGER ];
          sortable2 : SORTABLE_ARRAY[ STRING ];
          -- The following line would produce an error:
          -- actual type is not an heir of formal type
          -- sortable3 : SORTABLE_ARRAY[ POINT ];

          define is
          do
             !!sortable1.make( << 1, 2, 3 >>, 3 );
             sortable1.sort;
             sortable1.display;
             io.putstring( "The maximum value in array = " );
             io.putint( sortable1.maximum ); io.new_line;
             io.putstring( "The minimum value in array = " );
             io.putint( sortable1.minimum ); io.new_line;
             io.new_line;

             !!sortable2.make( << "Henrik", "Hanne", "Erik",
                "Richard", "Marc" >>, 5 );
             sortable2.sort;
             sortable2.display;
```

```
            io.putstring( "The maximum value in array = " );
            io.putstring( sortable2.maximum ); io.new_line;
            io.putstring( "The minimum value in array = " );
            io.putstring( sortable2.minimum ); io.new_line;

            io.new_line;
         end; -- define

      end -- SORTING
```

The program output is:

```
1
2
3
The maximum value in array = 3
The minimum value in array = 1

Erik
Hanne
Henrik
Marc
Richard
The maximum value in array = Richard
The minimum value in array = Erik
```

The first line of code in function *define* is:

```
   !!sortable1.make( << 1, 2, 3 >>, 3 );
```

Here, the manifest array << *1, 2, 3* >> is passed as a parameter to *make*, the creation routine for the SORTABLE_ARRAY *sortable1*. Later, the line of code:

```
   !!sortable2.make( << "Henrik", "Hanne", "Erik", "Richard",
      "Marc" >>, 5 );
```

passes the manifest array << *"Henrik", "Hanne", "Erik", "Richard", "Marc"* >> to the creation routine for *sortable2*.

As seen by the output, both arrays are sorted, and their minimum and maximum values are output.

2.9 CONSTANT OBJECTS

The data fields of an object normally can be changed by sending messages to the object. There are times, however, when it is useful to define constant objects. Such objects cannot have their data fields modified once they are set.

When the reserved word *once* is used instead of *do* as the delimiter of a routine body, the routine computes a return value one time. All subsequent calls of the function cause the same return value to be returned, but not re-computed.

In Listing 2.20, a class COMPLEX is presented. This class defines two constant objects through the use of "once" routines. Included are the "constants" *one* and *j*. The constant *one* represents the complex number with real part 1.0 and imaginary part 0.0. The constant *j* represents the complex number with real part 0.0 and imaginary part 1.0.

Listing 2.20   Class COMPLEX

```
class COMPLEX
  inherit
    C_MATH -- TowerEiffel library that includes required
    -- mathematical functions

  creation
    make, make1, make2

  feature -- Public section
    real_part    : DOUBLE;
    imag_part    : DOUBLE;
    modulus      : DOUBLE;
    angle        : DOUBLE;

    convert is
    do
      modulus := sqrt( real_part * real_part + imag_part *
        imag_part );
      if real_part /= 0.0 then
        angle := atan( imag_part / real_part );
      elseif imag_part > 0.0 then
        angle := 2.0 * atan( 1.0 ); -- pi / 2 radians
      elseif imag_part < 0.0 then
        angle := -2.0 * atan( 1.0 ); -- -pi / 2 radians
      end;
    end; -- convert

    make is
    do
      real_part := 0.0;
      imag_part := 0.0;
      convert;
    end; -- make

    make1( rePart : DOUBLE ) is
    do
      real_part := rePart;
      imag_part := 0.0;
      convert;
    end; -- make1

    make2( rePart : DOUBLE; imPart : DOUBLE ) is
    do
      real_part := rePart;
      imag_part := imPart;
      convert;
    end; -- make2
```

```
    -- other make routines not shown
        display is
        do
            io.putstring( "< " ); io.putdouble( real_part );
            io.putstring( ", " );
            io.putdouble( imag_part );
            io.putstring( " > " ); io.new_line;
        end; -- display

        one : COMPLEX is
        once
            !!Result.make1( 1.0 );
        end; -- one

        j : COMPLEX is
        once
            !!Result.make2( 0.0, 1.0 );
        end; -- j

        setReal( rePart : DOUBLE ) is
        do
            real_part := rePart;
            convert;
        end; -- setReal

        setImag( imPart : DOUBLE ) is
        do
            imag_part := imPart;
            convert;
        end; -- setImag

        infix "+" ( other : COMPLEX ) : COMPLEX is
        do
            !!Result.make2( real_part + other.real_part, imag_part +
            other.imag_part );
        end; -- "+"

        -- Other arithmetic operators not shown

end -- COMPLEX
```

Missing from Listing 2.20 are operators for multiplication, division and subtraction. The reader may wish to write these as an exercise.

Each time the routines *one* and *j* are sent to an instance of COMPLEX, the "constant" values < 1.0, 0.0 > and < 0.0, 1.0 > are returned. This is as close as Eiffel gets to constant objects.

Listing 2.21 presents a test class that exercises some of the functions of class COMPLEX.

Listing 2.21   Class to test COMPLEX

```
class TEST
creation
```

```
            make

    feature
        value : COMPLEX;

        make is
        local
            c1, c2, c3 : COMPLEX;
        do
            !!value.make;
            c1 := value.one;
            c2 := value.j;
            c3 := c1 + c2;
            c3.display;
            c3 := c3 + c3;
            c3.display;
            c3.setImag( 10 );
            c3.display;
            io.putstring( "The modulus of c3 = " );
            io.putdouble( c3.modulus );
            io.new_line;
        end; -- make

    end -- TEST
```

The program output is:

```
< 1, 1 >
< 2, 2 >
< 2, 10 >
The modulus of c3 = 10.198
```

2.10 TYPES

In this section, we discuss anchored types and expanded types.

2.10.1 Anchored Types

The reserved word "like" may be used to establish an anchored type. List-ings 2.22, 2.23 and 2.24 illustrate the typical use of an anchored type.

Listing 2.22   Class ANCHORED

```
class ANCHORED

creation
    create

feature { NONE }
    field1 : INTEGER;
```

```
feature

    create( anInt : INTEGER ) is
    do
        field1 := anInt;
    end; -- create

    duplicate : like Current is
    do
        Result := deep_clone( Current );
    end; -- duplicate

    display is
    do
        io.putstring( "Instance of anchored" ); io.new_line;
        io.putint( field1 );
        io.new_line;
    end; -- display

end -- ANCHORED
```

Listing 2.23   Class ANCHORED_CHILD

```
class ANCHORED_CHILD

inherit ANCHORED
    redefine
        display
    end;

 creation
    make

 feature { NONE }
    field2 : INTEGER;

 feature

    make( value1 : INTEGER; value2 : INTEGER ) is
    do
        field1 := value1;
        field2 := value2;
    end; -- make

    display is
    do
        io.putstring( "Instance of anchored_child" );
        io.new_line;
        io.putint( field1 ); io.new_line;
        io.putint( field2 ); io.new_line;
    end; -- display

end -- ANCHORED_CHILD
```

Listing 2.24   Class APPLICATION

```
class APPLICATION

 creation
     start

 feature

     start is
     local
         a1 : ANCHORED;
         a2 : ANCHORED_CHILD;
         b1 : ANCHORED;
         b2 : ANCHORED_CHILD;
     do
         !!a1.create( 15 );
         !!a2.make( 20, 25 );
         b1 := a1.duplicate;
         b1.display;
         b2 := a2.duplicate;
         b2.display;
     end; -- start

 end -- MAIN
```

The program output is:

```
Instance of anchored
15
Instance of anchored_child
20
25
```

Routine *duplicate* in class ANCHORED returns *like Current*. This implies that all descendant classes return copies of the appropriate descendant class and not an ANCHORED type.

As another example, we look at parts of the deferred class COMPARABLE given in the standard Eiffel library in Listing 2.25.

Listing 2.25   Class COMPARABLE

```
deferred class COMPARABLE
    inherit PART_COMPARABLE
        redefine
            infix "<", infix "<=",
            infix ">", infix ">="
        end

feature -- Comparison

    infix "<" (other: like Current): BOOLEAN is
    -- Is 'Current' less than 'other'?
```

```
    deferred
    end;

    infix "<=" (other: like Current): BOOLEAN is
    -- Is 'Current' less than or equal to 'other'?
    do
        Result := not (other < Current)
    end;

    ...

end -- class COMPARABLE
```

The parameter *other: like Current* in routines *infix "<"* and *infix "<="* assure that descendants of class COMPARABLE have a parameter *other* that is of the same type as the receiver. Otherwise, the type of the two objects being compared would not be the same.

Another common use for anchored types occurs when there are several attributes of a particular type and a reasonable likelihood that a subclass will need to redefine all of the attributes. This situation is illustrated in Listing 2.26. Portions of several classes are shown in the same listing.

Listing 2.26   Redefinition of attributes using anchored types

```
class GAME_PLAYER
  feature
    piece        : GAME_PIECE; -- Defined elsewhere
    p1, p2, p3   : like piece;
  -- other features not shown
end -- GAME_PLAYER

class PLAYER
  inherit
      GAME_PLAYER
          redefine
              piece
          end
  feature
      piece : SPECIAL_PIECE; -- inherited from GAME_PIECE
      -- other features not shown
end -- PLAYER
```

Class PLAYER acquires the attributes *p1*, *p2* and *p3* through inheritance from GAME_PLAYER. The type associated with *p1*, *p2* and *p3* in class GAME_PLAYER is SPECIAL_PIECE because of the use of the anchored type declaration *like piece* in class GAME_PLAYER.

2.10.2 Expanded Types

Normal objects in Eiffel are reference objects (instances of reference types).

When an object is declared, it assumes a default value of *Void*. This value remains until the object is initialized using a creation routine. Normal assignment and equality testing have reference semantics — when one object is assigned to another, the target object gets the same address as the source. Of course, deep copies or deep equalities may be performed using methods from class ANY (*deep_copy* and *deep_equal*). As we have seen, reference objects provide a high level of flexibility in dynamically allocating storage and supporting polymorphism.

An Eiffel class may be declared as "expanded." When an expanded type object is declared, its fields assume their default values. One never uses *!!x* if x's type is expanded. A small improvement in efficiency may be obtainable using expanded types because pointers and indirection are avoided. An assignment statement $x := y$, where x and y are instances of an expanded class, copies the fields of object y to the corresponding fields of object x. These fields reside in separate storage. Similarly, the comparison $x = y$ must compare the objects field by field.

The basic numeric classes, such as INTEGER and REAL, are expanded classes.

The rules for defining expanded classes are the following:

- The class cannot be deferred (deferred classes are discussed in Chapter 5); and
- The class can have at most one creation routine that has no parameters.

We compare the semantics of object assignment in expanded classes and ordinary reference classes in Listings 2.27 through 2.32.

Listings 2.27 through 2.29 present two expanded classes, *A* and *B,* and a test class, APPLICATION, that exercises the assignment operation on two expanded classes. Listings 2.30 through 2.32 present the same application using ordinary reference type classes.

Listing 2.27   An expanded class A

```
expanded class A
  creation
    make

  feature
    field1 : INTEGER;
    field2 : B; -- Class B defined in Listing 2.28

    make is
    do
        field1 := 5;
        field2.setValue( 6 );
    end; -- make

    setField1( value : INTEGER ) is
    do
        field1 := value;
```

```
      end; -- setField1

      setField2( value : INTEGER ) is
      do
         field2.setValue( value );
      end; -- setField2

      display is
      do
         io.putstring( "field1 = " ); io.putint( field1 );
         io.new_line;
         field2.display;
      end; -- display

   end -- A
```

Listing 2.28   Expanded class B

```
expanded class B

  feature
    field : INTEGER;

    setValue( value : INTEGER ) is
    do
       field := value;
    end; -- setValue

    display is
    do
          io.putstring( "field = " ); io.putint( field );
          io.new_line;
    end; -- display

  end -- B
```

Listing 2.29   Class APPLICATION for testing expanded classes A and B

```
class APPLICATION

  creation
    make

  feature

    make is
    local
       a : A;
       b : A;
    do
       io.putstring( "Object a: " );
       a.display;
       b := a;
```

```
            io.putstring( "Object b after assignment to a: " );
            b.display;
            a.setField1( 20 );
            a.setField2( 25 );
            io.putstring( "Object a after setting its fields: "
               );
            a.display;
            io.putstring( "Object b again: " );
            b.display;
         end; -- make

   end -- APPLICATION
```

The program output is:

```
Object a: field1 = 5
field = 6
Object b after assignment to a: field1 = 5
field = 6
Object a after setting its fields: field1 = 20
field = 25
Object b again: field1 = 5
field = 6
```

The assignment of a to b copies the two fields of b to a. The storage for a and b is separate.

Let us examine the reference versions of classes A and B and a new test program in Listings 2.30 and 2.31.

Listing 2.30   Reference class A

```
   class A
    creation
      make

    feature
      field1 : INTEGER;
      field2 : B;

      make is
      do
         field1 := 5;
         !!field2.make( 6 );
         field2.display;
      end; -- make

      setField1( value : INTEGER ) is
      do
         field1 := value;
      end; -- setField1

      setField2( value : INTEGER ) is
      do
         field2.setValue( value );
```

```
          end; -- setField2

          display is
          do
              io.putstring( "field1 = " ); io.putint( field1 );
              io.new_line;
              field2.display;
          end; -- display

    end -- A
```

Listing 2.31   Reference class B

```
class B
 creation
     make

  feature { NONE }
     field : INTEGER;

     make( value : INTEGER ) is
     do
         field := value;
     end; -- make

     setValue( value : INTEGER ) is
     do
         field := value;
     end; -- setValue

    display is
    do
            io.putstring( "field = " ); io.putint( field );
            io.new_line;
    end; -- display
end -- B
```

Listing 2.32   Class APPLICATION for testing reference classes A and B

```
class APPLICATION

  creation
    make

  feature

    make is
    local
        a : A;
        b : A;
    do
        !!a.make;
        io.putstring( "Object a: " );
```

```
      a.display;
      b := a;
      io.putstring( "Object b after assignment to a: " );
      b.display;
      a.setField1( 20 );
      a.setField2( 25 );
      io.putstring( "Object a after setting its fields: "
         );
      a.display;
      io.putstring( "Object b again: " );
      b.display;
   end; -- make

end -- APPLICATION
```

The program output is:

```
field = 6
Object a: field1 = 5
field = 6
Object b after assignment to a: field1 = 5
field = 6
Object a after setting its fields: field1 = 20
field = 25
Object b again: field1 = 20
field = 25
```

From the output of Listing 2.32, it is evident that the semantics associated with the assignment of an instance of reference class a to b cause a serious problem. After resetting the fields of object a to 20 and 25, the fields of object b become 20 and 25. This is because the object assignment causes the address of object b to be the same as that of object a. Storage for only one object has been created.

The reader is urged to note carefully the differences in the three listings for the expanded classes and the three listings for the reference classes.

2.11 SUMMARY

The unification of methods with a data model provided by a class is a fundamental pillar of object-oriented software technology. It provides the basis for specifying *abstract data types*. Such abstract data types form the basis for developing a software component technology in which a software system is designed by interconnecting individual software components, each with a precisely specified external interface.

This chapter has explored the construction of Eiffel classes and the creation of class instances, namely, objects. Objects are the "players" that populate the stage of an object-oriented application. Each object maintains its own internal state. This state may be affected by receiving messages (routines invoked through the object). Upon receiving a message, an object may emit output as well as send messages to other objects.

Some of the important facts relating to classes and objects that are presented in this chapter include:

- The declaration of an ordinary (reference type) object does not bring the object to life. All objects have a default value of *Void* until a creation routine is sent to the object.
- The declaration of an expanded type object sets all the attributes of the object to their default values. Storage for instances of such a class is statically allocated. An assignment x := y, where x and y are instances of an expanded class, causes the fields of y to be copied recursively to the fields of x.
- A creation routine can be used to initialize the fields (attributes) of the object when it is brought to life. The same routine can be used as an ordinary routine after an object is created in order to modify its fields.
- The syntax for invoking a routine without parameters is the same as accessing an attribute (i.e. *object.routine* or *object.attribute*).
- The keyword *Current* refers to the receiver of a message (it is the object through which the routine is invoked).
- "Mix-ins" are sometimes useful in Eiffel for allowing a class to have direct access to the routines of another class. The "is a" relationship is violated in such cases.
- Eiffel classes have two types of features: attributes and routines.
- Some features are commands that change the internal state of the object to which the command is applied.
- Some features are queries that return information about the object to which the query is applied without changing the internal state of the object.
- Class ANY is at the top of the Eiffel class hierarchy. All Eiffel classes are descendants of ANY. Class NONE is at the bottom of the Eiffel class hierarchy. No classes are descendants of class NONE.
- The export scope of Eiffel features are specified in the braces to the right of a feature clause. If no explicit export scope is specified, the default scope is ANY (i.e. features accessible in all client classes). A class may contain many feature clauses, each specifying a different export scope.
- A creation clause, like a feature clause, can specify an export scope. Only the class and its descendants given in the export scope of the creation clause can create instances of the given class.
- The export scope NONE implies that the features are for internal use only. Such internal features are also directly accessible in descendant classes.
- A routine may be effective or deferred. An effective routine specifies all of its implementation details whereas a deferred routine provides no implementation details. These must be provided in a descendant class.
- A routine may contain the following optional components: *require, local, rescue and ensure*.
- The *require* clause, if present, provides a precondition that must be satisfied

by the caller. If it is not satisfied, an exception is sent to the caller.

- The *local* clause of a routine, if present, declares objects that must be re-initialized every time the routine is invoked unless the default values are acceptable.
- Within the body of a routine, assignments can only be performed on attributes and local entities. It is illegal to assign to a parameter of a routine.
- The *rescue* clause of a routine, if present, describes the action that is taken if an exception is raised during the execution of the routine body.
- The *ensure* clause of a routine, if present, introduces a postcondition that must be satisfied upon exit from the routine.
- If a routine begins with the reserved word *once*, it can execute exactly once if it is a procedure, and it returns the original value if it is a function.
- The attributes of a routine can be declared as *unique*. Each such attribute is assigned an integer value by the compiler.
- A generic class is defined in terms of one or more parameters that are unspecified by the class producer but specified when an instance of the class is created.
- A generic class may constrain one or more of its generic parameters to conform to a particular class. This may be done to assure that the operations defined in the routines of the class are implemented by the actual type that is defined when an instance of the class is created.
- "Genericity" provides a compromise between strong typing that requires every attribute of a class to have a specified type versus the need to provide a high level of reuse to the consumer by allowing one or more attribute types to be defined by the user of the class.

REFERENCES

1. Cox, Brad J., *Object-Oriented Programming: An Evolutionary Approach*, Addison-Wesley, 1986.

Correct Programs

3.1 QUALITY SOFTWARE

In many crafts, extremes in quality, whether they be very high or very low, are usually easy to detect. One usually knows when something has been designed "right" or designed "wrong." This "feel" comes from experience. It is always wonderful to marvel at a piece of work that is a "masterpiece"—albeit a relatively rare event! Such a great work usually displays an unusual degree of balance in its shape, design, efficiency and strength.

Software development is a craft and also displays extremes in quality. A software "masterpiece" also exhibits balance. Such software is very useful but not overly complex—an increasingly common phenomenon resulting from an attempt to do everything for everybody. A software "masterpiece" must have an attractive and simple interface. The software must work predictably, consistently and with a level of efficiency commensurate with the application area. Most importantly, the software must work correctly. It must never falter or fail. Software that falters may occasionally produce erroneous output for some input data. Software that fails causes a system "crash" for certain input data. Neither failure nor falter is acceptable. Unfortunately, as the complexity of software systems grows, the likelihood of defects producing such problems increases.

Change is a natural part of the software development process. In the past, it has typically accounted for over 50 percent of the time and money spent on a given project over its lifetime. Much of the impetus for the development of more modern programming languages and associated development tools has been to lower the cost of maintenance and increase the robustness of commercial software.

In recent years there has been an increasing amount of interest on the part of the software development community in seeking tools, languages, environments and methodologies that promote the construction of robust (i.e. highly maintainable) and correct software systems. The familiar benchmark that software is only as good as it is fast is being replaced by the notion that software is only as good as it is correct and robust. Robust software is stable and remains stable under reasonable change. The fact that a program "runs" does not imply that it is stable. The fact that a program is stable does not imply that it is robust. Its level of "robustness" can be determined only when change is attempted. Its "robustness" is a function of its design. Object-oriented design is the subject of Chapter 8. This chapter focuses on the issue of "correctness" and the supplier-client relationship achievable with Eiffel's assertion technology and "programming by contract."

Some of the fundamental issues related to software correctness that will be the focus of this chapter are:

- What is a software component?
- How does one specify the desired behavior of a software component?
- How does inheritance affect the specification of the desired behavior of a software component?
- How does a software system detect and report faults if they are present?
- What type of faults can be "handled," and whose responsibility is it to "handle" the faults?
- How does one provide for exception handling to permit a graceful escape from an error condition?
- What is "programming by contract," and how does it provide the potential to improve software "correctness"?

3.2   SOFTWARE COMPONENTS AND THE NOTION OF A SOFTWARE CONTRACT

The notion of a *supplier* and *client* or *producer* and *consumer* is fundamental in understanding the responsibilities and benefits that occur when a consumer (client) contracts with a producer (supplier) to perform some services. Contracts always exist whether they be formal or informal. The supplier must understand precisely the conditions that are guaranteed by the client before undertaking the project (this usually implies the payment schedule and/or penalties, the materials that are available or to be supplied by the client and other conditions relevant to performing the mission — these are the preconditions), whereas the client must understand precisely the conditions that the supplier promises if the preconditions are met (this usually takes the form of performance specifications). These are the postconditions.

To illustrate the high-level concepts before discussing software components, let us consider the business relationship between a homeowner and a painting company (this example is partly inspired by the fact that at the time of writing this section, the author's house is surrounded by ladders and half-empty buckets of exterior paint). The homeowner wishes to enter into a contract with the "Roll-On" Painting Company. Bob, the homeowner, is the client, and Jill, the owner of "Roll-On," is the supplier.

The preconditions expected by the supplier are $2500 payable before the job begins. In addition, the supplier expects Bob to clear the deck of all outside furniture and plants. Jill also expects access to the windows at prearranged times.

If Bob meets all of these preconditions, Jill, the supplier, agrees to the following postconditions: the rear deck of Bob's house will be sanded and stained, the body of Bob's house will be painted with two coats of paint applied by brush or roller, the window trim will be painted in a different color with two coats of paint and the wood surrounding the window will be stained.

Each party in this agreement has clear expectations and responsibilities.

Jill, the owner and general contractor, plans to hire subcontractors to perform the required work. Jill, in her relation to the subcontractors, Lewis and Fred, becomes the client, and Lewis and Fred are the suppliers.

Bob does not need to know the details of the contract that binds Jill with her two subcontractors. Bob is concerned only about the preconditions that he must meet and the postconditions that his supplier, Jill, guarantees.

The contract that binds Bob and Jill affects the contract between Jill and her two subcontractors. Jill is at liberty to relax the precondition (i.e. pay Lewis and Fred less than the $2500) but not at liberty to relax the postcondition (i.e. the requirements that the deck be sanded and stained, the body and trim painted and the windows stained). Jill, if she chooses, can strengthen the postconditions by requiring Lewis and Fred to do even more than Jill has bargained with Bob to accomplish. She might do this to establish her reputation and create good will. But, Jill cannot allow Lewis and Fred to do less than the work promised to Bob.

Now let us go back to the world of software development in Eiffel. If Jill's "Roll-On" painting company is modelled as a class, then Lewis and Fred's sub-contracting company may be modelled as a subclass. After all, Lewis and Fred are a "kind of" painting company. The actions they can take (sand, paint, stain) are inherited from those of the parent class.

A fundamental principle of Eiffel software development is evident from this example. That principle is: *In any descendant class, the preconditions of the parent class may be left alone or weakened, and the postconditions of the parent class may be left alone or strengthened.*

3.3 PROGRAMMING BY CONTRACT

Bertrand Meyer, the developer of Eiffel, is the inspirational force behind a methodology for software development called, "Programming by Contract." We explore this style of programming in this section.

Every Eiffel class may be considered a software component. Each routine of a class can optionally declare one or more *preconditions* (Boolean expressions typically involving constraints on the routine's parameters that must be satisfied) and one or more *postconditions* (expressions that typically relate attribute values before and after the routine is invoked). In addition, the entire class can declare some *class invariants* (expressions involving attribute value constraints that must hold at all times for all routines of the class) that provide a client with some guarantees regarding the state of every class instance at any time. The software component guarantees that if the preconditions are met for a routine, then the postconditions will be met. Furthermore, the state of every instance of the class is constrained by the class invariant. Examples of preconditions, postconditions and class invariants are presented later in this chapter.

Every Eiffel class has the potential to offer "contracts" to its clients—one potential contract for each of its routines. As indicated above, if the client meets the preconditions of the routine, the routine guarantees to meet its end of the contract by satisfying its postconditions. Thus, a supplier (the routine offering the contract) is bound to a client through a precondition/postcondition contract.

Programming by contract through Eiffel's assertion technology provides only a semi-formal mechanism for controlling the "correctness" of a routine. Only a limited number of conditions can be specified. Assertion handling provides no guarantee or proof of "correctness." Instead, it provides the Eiffel developer with a systematic mechanism for detecting and correcting faults and documenting the responsibilities of the client and the supplier. This documentation can be of tremendous value to users of the routine who wish to understand better their responsibility to builders of descendants of the routine and to maintenance engineers who may be called upon to modify the routine in the future.

3.3.1 Contract Enforcement

If a contract between supplier and client is broken, it is because:

- The client has not met all of the preconditions of the supplier routine; and/or
- The code of a supplier routine is defective because the supplier has not met all of its postconditions; and/or
- The code in some supplier routine is defective and the class invariant is violated.

In all of the above cases, if exception handling has not been enabled by the client or supplier, a run-time error will occur and a trace will be emitted indicating the offending routine and the pre or postcondition that has been violated. If the supplier is at fault, the routine that has violated its postcondition must be repaired. If the client is at fault, the routine that has invoked the supplier routine must be repaired to satisfy the precondition of the supplier routine.

3.3.2 Location of Exception

Important and fundamental principles associated with Eiffel's assertion handling are:

- If a routine's precondition is not satisfied, the exception occurs in the client routine; if a handler has been written, it will be invoked in this client routine.
- If a routine's postcondition is not satisfied, the exception occurs in the supplier routine; if a handler has been written, it will be invoked in this supplier routine.
- If a class invariant is not satisfied, the exception occurs in the supplier routine that has caused the class invariant to fail; if a handler has been written, it will be invoked in this supplier routine.

3.3.3 Exception Handler

Exception handling in Eiffel is implemented within a routine by including a *rescue* clause. Such an optional clause must be defined at the end of the routine. Whenever an exception occurs within the routine (the routine may be either a client routine that has violated the preconditions of a supplier routine, or a supplier routine that is defective), an immediate jump to the *rescue* clause occurs.

The actions that might be taken in such a *rescue* clause include:

- Reporting the error through error messages;
- Changing the internal state of the object to restore it to a safe state, then re-invoking the routine; and
- Changing the internal state of the object to restore it to a safe state, but not re-invoking the routine.

The *retry* command causes the *rescue* clause to re-invoke the routine, typically after its internal state has been modified.

In the next several sections, the details of writing preconditions, postconditions and class invariants are presented.

3.4 PRECONDITIONS

An optional *require* clause located above the section *local*, if present, contains the totality of preconditions for the routine.

Within a *require* clause, a series of tags, each containing a specific precondition may be declared. The order of the assertions is important. Logically, each assertion is connected to its predecessor with an "and then" infix operator.

We illustrate a routine containing a precondition in Listing 3.1.

Listing 3.1   Illustration of routine containing a precondition

```
class PRECOND
-- Used to illustrate preconditions

 feature

    reciprocal( value : REAL ) : REAL is
    require
       value_non_zero: value /= 0.0;
       value_small_enough: value < 1000000.0;
       value_large_enough: value > -1000000.0
    do
       Result := 1.0 / value;
    end; -- reciprocal

end -- PRECOND

class APPLICATION

 creation
   make

 feature

    make is
    local
       myObject : PRECOND;
    do
       !!myObject;
       from
       until io.lastreal = -10000.0
       loop
          io.new_line;
          io.putstring( "Enter a real number (-10000.0 to
            quit): " );
          io.readreal;
          if io.lastreal /= 0.0 then -- Client verifies pre-
          -- condition as part of contract
             io.putstring( "The reciprocal of " );
             io.putreal( io.lastreal );
             io.putstring( " = " );
             io.putreal( myObject.reciprocal( io.lastreal )
                );
          end;
       end;
    end; -- make

end -- APPLICATION
```

In routine *reciprocal* of Listing 3.1, there are three preconditions that must be satisfied by the client. The first, *value_non_zero*, requires the parameter *value* to not equal zero. The second, *value_small_enough*, requires the parameter *value* to be less than one million. The third, *value_large_enough*, requires the parameter *value* to be larger than negative one million.

The *make* routine of class APPLICATION can be modified to include an exception handler. The revised class APPLICATION is shown with such an exception handler in Listing 3.2. Since the client class, APPLICATION, fails to satisfy the precondition of the supplier routine, *reciprocal*, the exception is raised in class APPLICATION.

Listing 3.2   Class APPLICATION with exception handling

```
class APPLICATION

  creation
     make

  feature

     make is
     local
        myObject  : PRECOND;
        numberErrors : INTEGER;
     do
        !!myObject;
        from
        until io.lastreal = -10000.0
        loop
           io.new_line;
           io.putstring( "Enter a real number (-10000.0 to
              quit): " );
           io.readreal;
           io.putstring( "The reciprocal of " );
           io.putreal( io.lastreal );
           io.putstring( " = " );
           io.putreal( myObject.reciprocal( io.lastreal ) );
        end;
     rescue
        numberErrors := numberErrors + 1;
        if numberErrors <= 3 then
           io.new_line; io.new_line;
           if io.lastreal = 0.0 then
              io.putstring( "Divide by zero error: " );
              io.putstring( "Please enter a non-zero real
                 number: " );
           else
              io.putstring( "Value too large or value too
                 small: " );
              io.putstring( "Enter a value less than one
                 million in magnitude: " );
           end;
           retry;
        end;
     end; -- make

  end -- APPLICATION
```

A counter, *numberErrors*, gets incremented each time the rescue clause is entered. The user is given three "strikes." If a fourth error occurs, the routine terminates with a run-time exception.

A clear error message is emitted within the *rescue* clause. Then the user is given another chance to enter a number and perform a calculation.

One final important technical requirement for preconditions: *A precondition of a routine, r, of class C is valid if and only if every feature whose name appears in any assertion clause is available to every class to which r is available.*

3.5 POSTCONDITIONS

The postconditions of a routine, if present, are embedded in an *ensure* clause just above the end of the routine.

The keyword *old* may be used in the postconditions of a routine. It allows one to express the new value of one or more attributes in terms of the "old" values that existed upon entering the routine.

Several additional examples of pre and postconditions are shown in the routines taken from class STRING and presented in Listing 3.3. The pre and postconditions are shown in boldface for extra emphasis.

Listing 3.3   Several routines from class STRING illustrating pre and postconditions

```
make (n: INTEGER) is
     -- Allocate space for at least 'n' characters.
  require
     non_negative_size: n >= 0
  do
     -- one extra character for a null terminator
     !!area.make (n+1);
     clear;
  ensure
     capacity >= n
  end;

count: INTEGER is
     -- Actual number of characters making up the string.
  do
     Result := strlen (area.to_external);
  ensure
     Result >= 0
  end;

put (c: CHARACTER; i: INTEGER) is
  -- Replace 'i'-th character by 'c'.
  require
     index_large_enough: i >= 1;
     index_small_enough: i <= count
  do
```

```
         area.put (c, i-1);
    ensure
        item (i) = c
    end;

    append (s: STRING) is
        -- Append a copy of 's' at end of 'Current'.
    require
        argument_not_void: s /= void
    local
        new_count : INTEGER;
    do
        new_count := count + s.count;
        if new_count > capacity then
        resize (new_count);
        end;
        strcat (area.to_external, s.area.to_external);
    ensure
        count = old count + s.count
    end;

    substring (n1: INTEGER; n2: INTEGER): STRING is
        -- Copy of substring starting at position 'n1' and
        -- ending at 'n2'
    require
        meaningful_origin: 1 <= n1;
        meaningful_interval: n1 <= n2;
        meaningful_end: n2 <= count
    do
        !!result.make(0) ;
        result.copy( Current ) ;
        result.shrink (n1, n2);
    ensure
        Result.count = n2 - n1 + 1
        -- for all 'i: 1..n2-n1', 'Result.item (i) = item (n1+i
        -- -1)'
    end;
```

In routine *make*, the client must ensure that the parameter n is non-negative. The *make* routine (supplier) must ensure that the *capacity* of the string is at least as large as the size n. If the client meets the requirements of the contract, then the supplier will meet its requirements. Programming by contract will assure a safe utilization of this creation routine.

In routine *count*, the supplier requires no preconditions but guarantees to the client that the result returned will be non-negative.

In routine *put*, the client must send in an integer index, i, that is at least as great as 1 and at least as small as *count*. The supplier then guarantees that *item* (i) contains the character c.

In routine *append*, the client must send a non-void string, and the supplier guarantees that the new value of the attribute *count* will equal the old value plus the size of the appended string, s.

In routine *substring*, several preconditions, each having a descriptive tag, require the client to send in integer parameters $n1$ and $n2$ that satisfy the following conditions: $1 <= n1 <= n2 <= count$. The supplier guarantees that the size of the resulting string equals $n2 - n1 + 1$.

3.6 CLASS INVARIANTS AND CONSISTENCY

The class invariants, if present, are included in an *invariant* clause that must appear at the end of the class definition. The invariants specify the properties that any instance of the class must satisfy at all times.

The invariants of a particular class are the invariants of all its ancestors concatenated.

A class is consistent if and only if the following condition is satisfied:

If a routine starts in a state such that its preconditions and class invariants are true, then the routine will end in a state such that its postconditions and class invariants are true.

Class consistency is an important requirement for constructing correct software.

In Listing 3.4, class ASSERTION contains a class invariant.

Listing 3.4   Class ASSERTION with a class invariant

```
class ASSERTION
-- Used to illustrate assertions

  creation
    make

  feature
    value     : REAL;
    inverse   : REAL;

    make is
    do
       value := 1.0;
       inverse := 1.0;
    ensure
      value = 1;
      inverse = 1;
    end; -- make

    change_value( val : REAL ) is
    require
       not_zero : val /= 0.0
    do
       value := val;
       inverse := 1.0 / value;
    ensure
      value = val;
      inverse = 1.0 / val;
```

```
        end; -- change_value

    invariant
        reciprocal : inverse = 1.0 / value

  end -- ASSERTION
```

If a supplier routine causes a class invariant to be violated, an exception is raised within the offending routine. If it has a *rescue* clause, it is executed. Otherwise a run-time exception is raised with an error message indicating the offending routine.

3.7 SUBCONTRACTING — PROPAGATION OF ASSERTIONS IN SUBCLASSES

Inheritance is the subject of Chapter 5. Here, we jump ahead and consider the effect of inheritance on assertions. The reader may wish to skip over this section until completing Chapter 5. Another option would be to read the section quickly now, and then more thoroughly reread the section after completing Chapter 5.

When one class is defined as a subclass of another (e.g. class B inherits from A), one or more of the parent's routines may be redefined in the subclass. A subclass routine that redefines a parent class routine is said to be a subcontractor of the parent. Through dynamic-binding, always present in Eiffel, the subcontractor will perform a service if a request (through a message) is sent to an instance of the subclass.

In section 3.2, the notion of subcontract is explored in the context of painting a house. There, it is observed that a subcontractor is bound by the contract of the parent. The subcontractor may not place more stringent demands on the client and may not deliver less than was promised by the parent.

This leads to a fundamental rule of assertion technology, the redefinition rule:

In the redefinition of a routine in a descendant class, the precondition must be equal or weaker than that of the parent and the postcondition must be equal or stronger than that of the parent.

Eiffel directly enforces the above principles through language rules. Specifically, in the redefined versions of a routine, it is not permitted to have a *require* clause or an *ensure* clause. A redefined version must instead use a *require else* clause for preconditions and an *ensure then* clause for postconditions.

The semantics of pre and postconditions for a redefined routine are:

For precondition: *new precondition or else original precondition*

For postcondition: *new postcondition and then original postcondition*

For the case of preconditions, if the new preconditions are satisfied, the original preconditions will not be tested. In the case of postconditions, if the new postcondition is satisfied, then the compiler verifies that the original postcondition is also satisfied.

An example that illustrates the above principle is presented in Listing 3.5.

Listing 3.5   Assertions through inheritance

```
class PARENT
-- Used to illustrate assertions

  feature

     operation( x : INTEGER ) : INTEGER is
      require
         x >= 10;
      do
         Result := x + 20;
      ensure
         Result >= 30;
      end; -- operation

end -- PARENT

 class CHILD

 inherit
    PARENT
        redefine
            operation
        end

 feature

     operation( x : INTEGER ) : INTEGER is
      require else
         non_negative: x >= 0;
      do
         Result := x + 50;
      ensure then
         result_size: Result >= 50;
      end; -- operation

    end -- CHILD
```

In Listing 3.5, the PARENT class requires the client to satisfy the condition $x >= 10$. In the CHILD class, this precondition is weakened so that $x >= 0$.

Class PARENT ensures that the *Result* will be greater than or equal to 30. Class CHILD ensures that the *Result* will be greater than or equal to 50. Here, we see that the CHILD class has weakened the precondition and strengthened the postcondition.

3.8 LOOP INVARIANTS

Loops are a potential source of errors. An "infinite loop"—one that never terminates—can produce major problems for an application.

Using loop variants and loop invariants, one can protect loops from the scourge of the "infinite loop" and help assure the correctness of the loop.

The general structure of an Eiffel loop, containing an invariant as well as variant is:

```
from
    -- initialization

invariant
    -- The loop invariant

variant
    -- An integer expression that decreases on each iteration
    -- but never becomes negative. Its value at the termination of
    -- the loop is zero.
until
    -- termination test

loop
    -- the executable code in the body

end
    -- termination of loop
```

A loop invariant is a Boolean expression that must initially have a value *True* and evaluate to *True* after every iteration of the loop. The combination of the loop invariant with the termination test should produce the statement that must be true upon the completion of the loop.

A loop variant is an integer expression that never becomes negative and is decremented by at least one after each iteration, becoming zero at the end.

Listing 3.6 shows a typical use of loop variants and invariants. Routine *go* from class LIST in the kernel library demonstrates the use of variants and invariants.

Listing 3.6   Loop variants and invariants

```
go( i : INTEGER ) is
    -- Move cursor to position i
require
    0 <= i; i <= nb_elements + 1
do
    if empty or i = 0 then
        go_offleft
    else
        from
            if position > i then start end
        invariant
            1 <= position;
            position <= i;
        variant
            i - position
        until position = i
```

```
        loop
            check not offright end;
            forth;
        end
    end
ensure
    ( i = 0 and offleft ) or
    ( i = nb_elements + 1 and offright ) or
    ( 1 <=i and i <= nb_elements and position = i )
end; -- go
```

3.9 THE CHECK ASSERTION

A check instruction allows you to express a property that should be satisfied when a statement (or group of statements) is executed. A test to assure that an object is not Void or more one or tests to assure that any preconditions of a routine about to be invoked are satisfied is a typical candidate for a *check* instruction.

The *check* assertion given in Listing 3.6 makes debugging easier. If the Boolean expression following the *check* is False, a run-time crash is induced in which an error message informs the user of the exact line of code that caused the crash.

3.10 ENABLING ASSERTIONS

An Eiffel software system can activate several levels of assertion handling. Typical Eiffel systems support the following choices:

- No assertion checking — *assertion(no)* in the system description file;
- Check preconditions — *assertion(require)* in the system description file;
- Check postconditions — *assertion(ensure)* in the system description file;
- Check class invariants — *assertion(invariant)* in the system description file; and
- Check all assertions — *assertion(all)* in the system description file.

Small improvements in performance may be obtainable by turning all assertion handling off. Except in rare cases when shaving CPU time is critical, the enforcement of "programming by contract" is highly recommended.

3.11 SUMMARY

In this chapter, Eiffel's assertion technology is explored—the notion of "programming by contract" in which a routine requires specific conditions to be satisfied by the client (preconditions) and then guarantees conditions about the state of the system upon exit from the routine (postconditions). These pre and postconditions form the basis for protecting a software component from misuse and provide the user with precise requirements for each routine of a class. Class invariants provide a specification to a user concerning the state of all instances of a class at any time.

When a subclass is created, it inherits all of the preconditions of the parent. These may be weakened by the descendant class. The subclass also inherits the postconditions of the parent. These can only be strengthened by the subclass. The class invariant that applies to a subclass is a concatenation of all the invariants of its ancestors. This provides a basis for "programming by subcontract" as well as "programming by contract."

Assertions provide the software designer with a precise documentation language that helps clarify the intended purpose and requirements for each routine.

Assertions offer the Eiffel developer improved safety, better documentation, significantly improved fault detection, exception handling and improved program correctness. It is highly recommended that you use Eiffel's assertion handling whenever possible.

Generic Container Classes

4.1 AN INTRODUCTION TO "GENERICITY"

A class may specify one or more generic parameters. When a client declares an instance of a generic class, it must specify actual types for each of the generic parameters of the class.

Some generic classes allow their parameter(s) to be of any type. Other classes impose a constraint on the generic parameter(s). Both types of generic classes (with unconstrained as well as constrained generic parameters) will be considered in this chapter.

Generic parameters allow general purpose reusable software to be constructed without compromising type safety. Eiffel is a statically typed language. The Eiffel static type system is able to verify that all of the operations on the formal generic parameters are defined. This type checking is performed without regard to the actual type or types that replace the generic parameter. If an operation is not defined for the generic parameter, this is flagged at compile time. Listing 4.1 illustrates this principle. It uses a "+" operator that is not defined for generic types.

Listing 4.1 A simple but defective generic class with undefined "+" operator

```
class SIMPLE[ T ]
 creation
    make

 feature -- Public
    value : T;
```

```
    make( aValue : T ) is
    do
        value := aValue;
    end; -- make

    infix "+" ( anotherValue : SIMPLE[ T ] ) : T is
    do
        Result := anotherValue.value + value;
    end; -- add

end -- class SIMPLE
```

The error message emitted when the code for this class is compiled is:

```
Operator, "+", not defined for class ANY.
Offending expression: 'anothervalue.value' {type: T}
Offending expression: 'value' {type: T}
```

In the infix "+" routine of class SIMPLE, the result returned is given by the sum of *anotherValue.value* and *value*. Unfortunately, there is no "+" operator defined in class ANY that can be applied to an arbitrary generic parameter. Therefore, the strict static type system of Eiffel emits an error message such as the one shown at the bottom of the class definition.

The C++ language, which supports generic classes through templates, takes a more relaxed approach to type checking. The C++ compiler checks that the actual parameter type that replaces the generic parameter has a meaningful definition for the "+" operation. Class *Simple* and a short main driver program written in C++ are presented in Listing 4.2.

Listing 4.2   A C++ implementation of generic class Simple

```
#include <iostream.h>
template < class T >
class Simple
{
    private:
        T value;
    public:
        Simple( T aValue ) : value( aValue ) { }
        T operator + ( const Simple< T >& anotherValue )
        {
            return ( anotherValue.value + value );
        }
};
void main()
{
    Simple< int > object1( 20 );
    Simple< int > object2( 5 );

    cout << "object1 + object2 = " << object1 + object2 <<
        endl;
}
```

The program output is:

```
object1 + object2 = 25
```

The C++ compiler verifies that for the actual parameter *int*, the "+" operation is defined. It, therefore, does not emit an error message. In Listing 4.3, the user attempts to create an instance of class *Simple* using a user-defined class *Counter* as the actual base type. A typical error message is shown.

Listing 4.3   An illegal instance of class Simple in C++

```
class Counter
{
 private:
     int count;
 public:
     Counter( int value = 0 )
     {
         count = value;
     }
     // Other details not shown
};

// Details of class Simple given in Listing 4.2

void main()
{
    Counter c1( 20 );
    Simple< Counter > object3( c1 );
}
```

The error message emitted from the C++ compiler is:

```
"simple.c", line 15: error: bad operands for +: const class
    Counter + class Counter
"simple.c", line 15: error detected during the instantiation
    of Simple <Counter>
"simple.c", line 28: is the site of the instantiation
"simple.c", line 15: error: cannot make a Counter from a any
"simple.c", line 15: error detected during the instantiation
    of Simple <Counter>
 "simple.c", line 28: is the site of the instantiation
2 errors
```

When the C++ compiler encounters the declaration *Simple< Counter > object3(c1)*, it statically determines that the "+" operation is not defined in class *Counter*.

In summary, the C++ compiler allows some instances of generic class *Simple* to be created but not others. The decision is based on whether the actual parameter type supports the "+" operation. The Eiffel compiler does not allow any instances of class SIMPLE to be created because the formal generic parameter, T, does not have a meaningful definition for the "+" operation.

In this author's view, the stricter type enforcement of the Eiffel system provides for a more consistent and safe process of software development compared with C++. Since the generic parameter, T, of the Eiffel class SIMPLE of Listing 4.1 cannot respond to the "+" operator, we must constrain class SIMPLE to take only parameters that conform to ADDABLE (a class that contains a deferred implementation of the "+" operator). This is done as follows:

```
class SIMPLE[ T -> ADDABLE ]
// Other details not shown
```

If a client attempts to create an instance of class SIMPLE using an actual parameter that does not conform to ADDABLE, an error will be emitted by the compiler. Such a client can see from SIMPLE's formal specification that the actual type used for T must conform to class ADDABLE.

We might wish the actual parameter to support a display operation as well as the "+" operation. This would enable us to display the result of adding two objects that are instances of class SIMPLE. So, instead of creating an abstract class ADDABLE, we create an abstract class ADDABLE_DISPLAYABLE.

The details of such an abstract class are shown in Listing 4.4.

Listing 4.4   Abstract class ADDABLE_DISPLAYABLE

```
deferred class ADDABLE_DISPLAYABLE

  feature
    infix "+" ( anotherValue : ADDABLE_DISPLAYABLE ) :
            ADDABLE_DISPLAYABLE is
    deferred
    end; -- infix "+"

    display is
    deferred
    end; -- display


  end -- ADDABLE_DISPLAYABLE
```

All effective classes (no deferred features) that conform to ADDABLE_DISPLAYABLE must define a "+" operation and display function.

An effective subclass of ADDABLE_DISPLAYABLE, CAN_ADD, is defined in Listing 4.5.

Listing 4.5   Class CAN_ADD

```
class CAN_ADD

  inherit
    ADDABLE_DISPLAYABLE

  creation
    make
```

```
feature
    value : INTEGER;

    make( aValue : INTEGER ) is
    do
        value := aValue;
    end; -- make

    infix "+" ( anotherValue : CAN_ADD ) : CAN_ADD is
    do
        !!Result.make( anotherValue.value + value );
    end; -- infix "+"

    display is
    do
        io.putint( value );
        io.new_line;
    end; -- display

end -- CAN_ADD
```

Class CAN_ADD defines an infix "+" function that returns a CAN_ADD object and also defines a display function.

Class NOT_SO_SIMPLE is presented in Listing 4.6. This class specifies that its generic parameter T must conform to ADDABLE_DISPLAYABLE.

Listing 4.6   Class NOT_SO_SIMPLE

```
class NOT_SO_SIMPLE[ T -> ADDABLE_DISPLAYABLE ]

  creation
    make

  feature
    value : ADDABLE_DISPLAYABLE;

    make( aValue : ADDABLE_DISPLAYABLE ) is
    do
        value := aValue;
    end; -- make

    infix "+" ( anotherValue : NOT_SO_SIMPLE[ T ] ) :
      NOT_SO_SIMPLE[ T ] is
    do
        !!Result.make( anotherValue.getValue + value );
    end; -- infix "+"

    display is
    do
        value.display;
    end; -- display

end -- class NOT_SO_SIMPLE
```

The infix "+" routine of class NOT_SO_SIMPLE returns an object of type NOT_SO_SIMPLE by applying the "+" operator to two instances of class ADDABLE_DISPLAYABLE. The Eiffel compiler allows this addition because objects that conform to this class must respond to the "+" operator.

The display routine sends the message *display* to *value*. Again, the Eiffel compiler allows this because objects of ADDABLE_DISPLAYABLE must respond to the *display* message.

By requiring the programmer to identify a constraint on the type of generic parameter that can be used in creating instances of class NOT_SO_SIMPLE, an easier to understand and easier to maintain software system is assured. The Eiffel system has required the programmer to specify the formal requirements that objects of class NOT_SO_SIMPLE must satisfy. In the case of the C++ system, it is not at all obvious that only actual parameters that support the "+" operation can legally be used in creating instances of class Simple.

In Listing 4.7, a "main driver" class, APPLICATION, is presented. Routine *start* of this class builds a small application that constructs two instances of class NOT_SO_SIMPLE using instances of class CAN_ADD. Routines "+" and *display* are exercised.

Listing 4.7   Class APPLICATION that exercises NOT_SO_SIMPLE

```
class APPLICATION

creation
    start

feature

    start is
    local
        object1  : NOT_SO_SIMPLE[ CAN_ADD ];
        object2  : NOT_SO_SIMPLE[ CAN_ADD ];
        object3  : NOT_SO_SIMPLE[ CAN_ADD ];
        s1, s2   : CAN_ADD;
    do
        !!s1.make( 20 );
        !!s2.make( 5 );
        !!object1.make( s1 );
        !!object2.make( s2 );
        object3 := object1 + object2;
        object3.display;
    end; -- start

end -- APPLICATION
```

The program output is : 25

If the *start* routine of class APPLICATION were to have the declaration:

```
object4 : NOT_SO_SIMPLE[ INTEGER ];
```

a typical error message might be:

```
Error: "./application.e": 13:
 Actual type is not an heir of formal type.
 Formal arg type: : ADDABLE_DISPLAYABLE
 Actual arg type: : INTEGER
emake: Error: "./application.e": 13:
 Element #1 in actual generic does not correspond-
    ing formal
 element in class NOT_SO_SIMPLE.
 Formal element type: T {ADDABLE_DISPLAYABLE}
 Offending element type: INTEGER
 Validity code: VTGC.
```

The Eiffel system in the code of Listings 4.4 through 4.7 has provided the user with a high degree of protection from potential misuse.

In the next two sections, more fully developed examples of practical reusable container classes are presented.

4.2 UNCONSTRAINED AND CONSTRAINED GENERIC CONTAINER CLASSES

This section presents several practical and important reusable software components. Although various versions of the classes presented are available in Eiffel libraries, the goal in this section is to illustrate some of the concepts that have been discussed earlier.

4.2.1 List

A list is an abstract data type (ADT) that is used to sequentially store and access data of arbitrary base type. It is impossible to access the nth element of a list without accessing all the elements up to and including the n-1st element first. The ADT is partially characterized by the following basic operations (other operations, such as *addAfter*, *addBefore*, *removeAfter*, *removeBefore*, etc., are not included in this implementation):

- **elements** – contains the number of elements currently in the list
- **front** – returns the element to the front of the list
- **back** – returns the element to the back of the list
- **insertFront** – adds a new item in front of all existing items in the list
- **insertBack** – adds a new item behind all existing items in the list
- **removeFront** – removes the first element, if present, from the list
- **removeBack** – removes the last element, if present, from the list

The LIST class, presented in Listing 4.8, uses an unconstrained type T.

Listing 4.8   Class LIST

```
class LIST[ T ]
  -- Unconstrained generic list

feature { NONE } -- Private data
```

```
      first : NODE[ T ];
      last : NODE[ T ];

feature -- Public section
      elements : INTEGER; -- The number of elements in the list

    front : T is
    require
        not_empty: elements > 0
    do
        Result := first.value;
    end; -- front

    back : T is
    require
        not_empty: elements > 0
    do
        Result := last.value;
    end; -- back

    insertFront( anItem : T ) is
    -- Add anItem to the front of the list
    local
        newItem : NODE[ T ];
    do
        if first = Void then
            !!first.make( anItem );
            last := first;
        else
            !!newItem.make( anItem );
            newItem.link( first );
            first := newItem;
        end;
        elements := elements + 1;
    ensure
        elements = old elements + 1;
        front = anItem;
        elements = 1 implies front = anItem
    end; -- insertFront

    insertBack( anItem : T ) is
    -- Add anItem to the end of the list
    local
        newItem : NODE[ T ];
    do
        if first = Void then
            !!first.make( anItem );
            last := first;
        else
            !!newItem.make( anItem );
            last.link( newItem );
            last := newItem;
        end;
        elements := elements + 1;
    ensure
```

```
                    elements = old elements + 1;
                    back = anItem;
                    elements = 1 implies front = anItem and back =
                        anItem;
           end; -- insertBack

        removeFront is
         -- Delete first item on list
         require
             not_empty: elements > 0;
         do
             first := first.next;
             if first = Void then
                 last := Void;
             end;
             elements := elements - 1;
         ensure
             elements = old elements - 1;
             -- front: If there is any value still on the List that was
             -- added by insertFront then "front" is the oldest such
             -- value. Otherwise "front" is the oldest value in the List
             -- added by insertBack.
         end; -- removeFront

        removeBack is
        -- Delete the last item on list
        require
            not_empty: elements > 0;
        local
            curr : NODE[ T ];
        do
            if elements = 1 then
                first := Void;
                last := Void;
        else
            from curr := first
            until curr.next = last
            loop
                curr := curr.next;
            end;
            last := curr;
            elements := elements - 1;
        end;
        ensure
            elements = old elements - 1;
            elements = 1 implies front = back;
            -- back: If there is any value still on the List that was
            -- added by insertFront then "back" is the oldest such
            -- value. Otherwise "back" is the oldest value in the List
            -- added by insertBack.
        end;
invariant
    elements >= 0;

end -- LIST
```

The attributes of class LIST are *first* and *last*, both of type NODE and in a protected section (*feature { NONE }*). This is done to assure that these attributes are for internal use only.

The reader is urged to study the pre and postconditions for the routines that contain them and the class invariant. These provide more precise specifications that make the LIST more usable and reusable.

The details of class NODE are given in Listing 4.9.

Listing 4.9   Class NODE

```
class NODE[ T ]
-- Unconstrained generic NODE

  creation
     make

  feature { LIST } -- Public section
     value : T;
     next  : NODE[ T ];

     make( initial : T ) is
     do
        value := initial;
     end; -- make

     setValue( aValue : T ) is
     do
        value := aValue;
     end; -- setValue

     link( target : NODE[ T ] ) is
     do
        next := target;
     end; -- link

  end -- NODE
```

The usual recursive definition of tree node is given in Listing 4.9. Class NODE has two attributes, *value* of generic type T and *next* of type NODE[T].

The export scope for all of the features of class NODE is defined as class LIST. This is designated by the statement *feature { LIST }*. These attributes and routines are visible to any class that conforms to LIST but not available to other clients.

A simple test program that exercises the routines of class LIST is given in Listing 4.10. The program protects itself from violating preconditions of routines *front, back, removeFront* and *removeBack.*

Listing 4.10   Test program for class LIST - class LIST_TEST

```
class LIST_TEST
  creation
     start
```

```
feature
    name1 : STRING is "AAA";
    name2 : STRING is "BBB";
    name3 : STRING is "CCC";

    start is
    local
        intList : LIST[ INTEGER ];
        strList : LIST[ STRING ];
        index   : INTEGER;
    do
        !!intList;
        from index := 7
        until index = 1
        loop
            index := index - 1;
            intList.insertFront( index );
        end;
        if intList.elements > 0 then -- to protect against
        -- precondition violation
            io.putstring( "The last item on the list is: " );
            io.putint( intList.back ); io.new_line;
        end;
        from index := 0
        until index = 3
        loop
            index := index + 1;
            if intList.elements > 0 then -- to protect against
            --  precondition violation
                io.putstring( "Removing from the back: " );
                io.putint( intList.back ); io.new_line;
                intList.removeBack;
            end;
        end;
        from index := 0
        until index = 2
        loop
            index := index + 1;
            if intList.elements > 0 then -- to protect against
        -- precondition violation
                io.putstring( "Removing from the front: " );
                io.putint( intList.front ); io.new_line;
                intList.removeFront;
            end;
        end;
        if intList.elements > 0 then -- to protect against
        -- precondition violation
            io.putstring("The first item on the list is: ");
            io.putint( intList.front ); io.new_line;
        end;
        !!strList;
        strList.insertBack( name1 );
        strList.insertBack( name2 );
        strList.insertBack( name3 );
        from index := 0
```

```
            until index = 3
            loop
                index := index + 1;
                if strList.elements > 0 then -- to protect against
                    -- precondition violation
                    io.putstring( "Removing from the front: " );
                    io.putstring( strList.front ); io.new_line;
                    strList.removeFront;
                end;
            end;
            io.putstring( "The number of items in intList = " );
            io.putint( intList.elements ); io.new_line;
            io.putstring( "The number of items in strList = " );
            io.putint( strList.elements ); io.new_line;
        end; -- start

    end -- LIST_TEST
```

The program output is:

```
The last item on the list is: 6
Removing from the back: 6
Removing from the back: 5
Removing from the back: 4
Removing from the front: 1
Removing from the front: 2
The first item on the list is: 3
Removing from the front: AAA
Removing from the front: BBB
Removing from the front: CCC
The number of items in intList = 1
The number of items in strList = 0
```

4.2.2   Ordered List

It is often useful to build a list in which the elements are strictly ordered. In such a list the operations of *insertFront* and *insertBack* are illegal. Only *insert* is defined; this operation places the item directly behind the item just "smaller" than it and just in front of the item just "larger" than it.

How should such a list be constructed? Should we start from scratch?

The protocol and even attributes of an ordered list are so different from an unordered list that we answer *yes* to the above question. We start from scratch.

The code for an ordered list is given in Listing 4.11.

Listing 4.11   Class ORDERED_LIST

```
class ORDERED_LIST[ T -> COMPARABLE ]
    -- Constrained generic ordered list

    feature { NONE } -- Private data
        first : NODE[ T ];
```

```
feature -- Public section
    elements : INTEGER; -- The number of elements in the list

    insert( anItem : T ) is
    local
        previous, curr : NODE[ T ];
        new_node : NODE[ T ];
    do
        !!new_node.make( anItem );
        if first = Void or else anItem < first.value then
            new_node.link( first );
            first := new_node;
        else
            from curr := first
            until curr = Void or else anItem < curr.value
            loop
                previous := curr;
                curr     := curr.next;
            end;
            previous.link( new_node );
            new_node.link( curr );
        end;
        elements := elements + 1;
    ensure
        elements = old elements + 1;
        -- anItem is inserted in the list so that all preceding
        -- items are less than or equal to anItem and all
        -- succeeding items are larger than anItem
    end; -- insert

    remove( anItem : T ) is
    require
        non_empty: elements > 0;
    local
        previous, curr : NODE[ T ];
    do
        if first.value.is_equal( anItem ) then
            first     := first.next;
            elements := elements - 1;
        elseif first.value < anItem then
            from previous := first
                curr := first.next
            until curr = Void or else curr.value >= anItem
            loop
                previous := curr;
                curr     := curr.next;
            end;
            if curr /= Void and then curr.value.is_equal(
                anItem ) then
                previous.link( curr.next );
                elements := elements - 1;
            end;
        end;
        -- automatic garbage collection removes curr's object
    ensure
```

```
         -- If the old version of the list contained anItem
         -- then the first such entry has been removed and
         -- elements has been decremented by one. Otherwise
         -- the list is unchanged.
      end; -- remove

      display is
      require
         non_empty: elements > 0;
      local
         count : INTEGER;
         curr  : NODE[ T ];
      do
         from curr := first
         until count = elements
         loop
            count := count + 1;
            print( curr.value );
            io.new_line;
            curr := curr.next;
         end;
      end; -- display

   invariant
      elements >= 0;
      -- The list is sorted from smallest to largest

   end -- LIST
```

The generic parameter in class ORDERED_LIST is constrained using T->
COMPARABLE. Therefore, the actual parameter assigned by the client must conform to class COMPARABLE; this guarantees that comparison operators are defined
for the actual parameter T.

The reader should verify that all of the special cases in routines *insert* and
remove have been taken care of. In the case of routine *insert*, the special cases
are inserting the first element or the smallest element. In the case of routine
remove, the special case involves removing the first element and the case where
the item is not in the list.

Both routines *insert* and *remove* utilize a precondition that requires that
the list is non-empty. Class NODE must be modified so that the feature section
containing the routines exports to ORDERED_LIST.

A test program for class ORDERED_LIST is given in Listing 4.12.

Listing 4.12   Test program for class ORDERED_LIST

```
class ORDERED_LIST_TEST
   creation
      start

   feature
      name1 : STRING is "AAA";
      name2 : STRING is "BBB";
      name3 : STRING is "CCC";
```

```
      start is
      local
          ordered_list : ORDERED_LIST[ STRING ];
      do
          !!ordered_list;
          ordered_list.insert( name2 );
          ordered_list.insert( name3 );
          ordered_list.insert( name1 );
          ordered_list.display;
          io.new_line;
          ordered_list.remove( name2 );
          ordered_list.display;
          io.new_line;
          ordered_list.remove( name1 );
          ordered_list.display;
          io.new_line;
      end; -- start

end -- ORDERED_LIST_TEST
```

The program output is:

```
"AAA"
"BBB"
"CCC"

"AAA"
"CCC"

"CCC"
```

The test routine, *start*, of class ORDERED_LIST_TEST uses class STRING, which conforms to COMPARABLE and is, therefore, legal.

4.2.3   Stack

A stack is a "kind of" list. This might suggest an inheritance relationship in which class STACK is defined as a subclass of class LIST. But this poses several basic problems.

The protocol of STACK is much simpler than the protocol of LIST. Only the operations of *push*, *pop*, *depth* and *top* are defined in addition to a creation routine *make*. Several list operations have no meaning for a stack and should not be available for stack objects. This problem can be solved by having class STACK somehow block, perhaps through a redefinition with no actual code, the unwanted routines from class LIST.

Another problem resulting from STACK being defined as a subclass of LIST is that if the implementation details of LIST are modified, this has a significant effect on the subclass STACK.

We use composition to design our stack. That is, a stack is "composed of" a list. This has the effect of de-coupling the protocol of LIST from STACK. As a consequence, if the implementation details of LIST are modified, while keeping the interface constant, the STACK class must be re-compiled but not modified in any way.

Class STACK is presented in Listing 4.13.

Listing 4.13

```
class STACK[ T ]
-- A generic stack class

 creation
   make

 feature { NONE } -- Protected section
    aList : LIST[ T ];

    make is -- Cannot be used as an ordinary routine
    do
        !!aList;
    ensure
       depth = 0
    end; -- make



 feature -- Public

    push( anItem : T ) is
    do
       aList.insertFront( anItem );
    ensure
       top = anItem;
       depth = old depth + 1;
    end; -- push

    pop is
    require
       depth > 0
    do
       aList.removeFront;
    ensure
       depth = old depth - 1;
       -- top is the last item pushed
    end; -- pop

    top : T is
    require
       depth > 0;
    do
       Result := aList.front;
    end; -- top

    depth : INTEGER is
    do
```

```
        Result := aList.elements;
    end; -- depth

end -- STACK
```

The creation routine, *make*, is in the protected section so that it cannot be invoked as an ordinary routine on an existing instance of STACK. It can be used only to create new instances of STACK.

A test program that exercises class STACK is given in Listing 4.14. Routine *push* is implemented in terms of *insertFront*. Routine *pop* is implemented in terms of *removeFront*.

Listing 4.14   Class STACK_TEST

```
class STACK_TEST

  creation
    start

  feature

    start is
    local
        stack1    : STACK[ INTEGER ];
        value     : INTEGER;
    do
        !!stack1.make;
        stack1.push( 3 );
        stack1.push( 2 );
        stack1.push( 1 );
        io.putstring( "The element on the top of the stack is: "
        );
        io.putint( stack1.top ); io.new_line;
        if stack1.depth > 0 then -- Make sure precondition is
        -- satisfied
           stack1.pop;
        end;
        if stack1.depth > 0 then -- Make sure precondition is
        -- satisfied
           stack1.pop;
        end;
        io.putstring( "The element on the top of the stack is: "
        );
        io.putint( stack1.top ); io.new_line;
    end; -- start

end -- STACK_TEST
```

The program output is:

```
The element on the top of the stack is: 1
The element on the top of the stack is: 3
```

4.2.4   Queue

Class QUEUE is also implemented using composition with a list. That is, a queue is composed of a list.

The implementation details of QUEUE are shown in Listing 4.15.

Listing 4.15   Class QUEUE

```
class QUEUE[ T ]
 creation
    make

feature { NONE }
    aList : LIST[ T ];

    make is
    do
        !!aList;
    ensure
        length = 0
    end; -- make

feature

    insert( anItem : T ) is
    do
        aList.insertBack( anItem );
    ensure
        length = old length + 1;
        length = 1 implies front = anItem
    end; -- insert

    remove is
    require
        length > 0
    do
        aList.removeFront;
    ensure
        length = old length - 1;
        -- front is the oldest item inserted that has not
        -- since been removed.
    end; -- remove

    front : T is
    require
        length > 0;
    do
        Result := aList.front;
    end; -- front

    length : INTEGER is
    do
        Result := aList.elements;
    end; -- length

end -- QUEUE
```

Class QUEUE reuses routines *insertBack* and *removeFront* from its embedded LIST. Like class STACK, class QUEUE has a simple and elegant definition using the powerful design principal of composition.

4.2.5 Search Tree

A binary search tree is an important container class. Such a tree has the property that for any node, all of the elements in the node's left sub-tree are "smaller" than the node element and all of the elements in the node's right sub-tree are "larger" than the node element. If a search tree is relatively balanced (usually a most desirable situation), the number of levels is approximately equal to the logarithm to the base 2 of the number of nodes. This is the characteristic that gives a search tree its attractive search property.

The elements of a binary tree must be "comparable," and if we wish to display the elements they also must be "displayable." Specifically, the operation of "<" and a *display* routine must be defined for the actual type. This allows an "in-order" traversal to be performed that outputs the elements in ascending order.

The basic operations on a search tree are *insert, delete, display* and *ispresent*. The implementation details of *insert* and *display* are presented while leaving the details of *delete* and *ispresent* as an exercise for the reader.

It is desirable that the search tree be generic. But the actual parameter, T, used when an instance of a search tree is created must satisfy the constraints mentioned above. Specifically, it must have the properties of responding to the messages "<" and *display*.

An abstract class COMPARABLE_DISPLAYABLE is constructed to establish this theoretical condition. This deferred class is shown in Listing 4.16.

Listing 4.16 Abstract class COMPARABLE_DISPLAYABLE

```
deferred class COMPARABLE_DISPLAYABLE

  feature

    infix "<" ( other : like Current ) : BOOLEAN is
    deferred
    end; -- "<"

    display is
    deferred
    end; -- display

end -- COMPARABLE_DISPLAYABLE
```

Any effective class that is a descendant of COMPARABLE_DISPLAYABLE must define the operator "<" and the routine *display*.

In Listings 4.17 and 4.18, we show two such classes, COMPARABLE_DISPLAYABLE_INTEGER and COMPARABLE_DISPLAYABLE_STRING

Listing 4.17   Class COMPARABLE_DISPLAYABLE_INTEGER

```
class COMPARABLE_DISPLAYABLE_INTEGER
 inherit
   COMPARABLE_DISPLAYABLE
 creation
   make

 feature -- Public
    value : INTEGER;

    make( aValue : INTEGER ) is
      do
         value := aValue;
      end; -- make

    infix "<" ( other : like Current ) : BOOLEAN is
      do
         Result := value < other.value;
      end; -- "<"

    display is
      do
         io.putint( value );
         io.new_line;
      end; -- display

 end -- COMPARABLE_DISPLAYABLE_INTEGER
```

Listing 4.18   Class COMPARABLE_DISPLAYABLE_STRING

```
class COMPARABLE_DISPLAYABLE_STRING
 inherit
    COMPARABLE_DISPLAYABLE
 creation
    make

 feature -- Public
    value : STRING;

    make( aValue : STRING ) is
      do
         value := clone( aValue );
      end; -- make

    infix "<" ( other : like Current ) : BOOLEAN is
      do
         Result := value < other.value;
      end; -- "<"

    display is
      do
         io.putstring( value );
         io.new_line;
      end; -- display
```

```
end -- COMPARABLE_DISPLAYABLE_STRING
```

Instances of classes COMPARABLE_DISPLAYABLE_INTEGER and COMPARABLE_
DISPLAYABLE_STRING would qualify as actual types for our search tree.

The search tree has an attribute that is an instance of class NODE[T]. This attribute represents the "root" of the tree. The details of class NODE[T] are presented next in Listing 4.19. The export scope is limited to class SEARCH_TREE.

Listing 4.19   Class NODE for the search tree

```
class NODE[ T ]
creation { SEARCH_TREE }
   make, make_leaf

 feature { SEARCH_TREE }
    value       : T;
    left, right : NODE[ T ];

    make( aValue : T; leftChild : NODE[ T ]; rightChild :
      NODE[ T ] ) is
    -- Create an ordinary node in a search tree
    do
       value := aValue;
       left  := leftChild;
       right := rightChild;
    end; -- make

    make_leaf( aValue : T ) is
    -- Create a leaf node in a search tree
    do
       value := aValue;
       left  := Void;
       right := Void;
    end; -- make_leaf

   setLeft( aNode : NODE[ T ] ) is
   do
       left := aNode;
   end; -- setLeft

   setRight( aNode : NODE[ T ] ) is
   do
       right := aNode;
   end; -- setRight

   setValue( aV alue : T ) is
   do
      value := T;
   end; -- setValue

end -- NODE
```

NODE has two creation methods: the first, *make*, allows a value as well as two child nodes to be specified, whereas the second, *make_leaf*, allows only a value to be specified. The two children are automatically set to Void.

The class SEARCH_TREE is presented in Listing 4.20.

Listing 4.20   Class SEARCH_TREE

```
class SEARCH_TREE[ T -> COMPARABLE_DISPLAYABLE ]

  feature { NONE } -- Private
     root : NODE[ T ];

     traverse( aNode : NODE[ T ] ) is
     do
        if aNode /= Void then
           traverse( aNode.left );
           aNode.value.display;
           traverse( aNode.right );
        end;
     end; -- traverse

  feature -- Public
     num_elements : INTEGER;

     insert( element : T ) is
     local
        parent, curr, new_node : NODE[ T ];
     do
        if root = Void then
           !!root.make_leaf( element );
        else
           from curr := root
           until curr = Void or else curr.value.is_equal(
             element )
           loop
              parent := curr;
              if element < curr.value then -- search left
                 curr := curr.left;
                 if curr = Void then
                    !!new_node.make_leaf( element );
                    parent.setLeft( new_node );
                 end;
              else -- search right
                 curr := curr.right;
                 if curr = Void then
                    !!new_node.make_leaf( element );
                    parent.setRight( new_node );
                 end;
              end;
           end;
        end;
     end; -- insert

     display is
     do
        traverse( root );
     end; -- display
  end -- SEARCH_TREE
```

The algorithm for search tree insertion can be reviewed in any basic book on data structures and will not be discussed here.

The routine *traverse*, invoked by routine *display*, is implemented in the protected section of the class (i.e. feature { NONE } section). This routine is for internal use only and should not be accessible by any clients.

As an alternative, the routine *insert* can be implemented recursively. The modified class SEARCH_TREE is shown in Listing 4.21.

Listing 4.21   Modified class SEARCH_TREE that uses recursion for insert

```
class SEARCH_TREE[ T -> COMPARABLE_DISPLAYABLE ]

 feature { NONE } -- Private
    root   : NODE[ T ];

    traverse( aNode : NODE[ T ] ) is
    do
        if aNode /= Void then
            traverse( aNode.left );
            aNode.value.display;
            traverse( aNode.right );
        end;
    end; -- traverse

    insertElement( aNode : NODE[ T ]; element : T ) is
    local
        new_node : NODE[ T ];
    do
        if element < aNode.value then
            if aNode.left = Void then
                !!new_node.make_leaf( element );
                aNode.setLeft( new_node );
            else
                insertElement( aNode.left, element );
            end;
        elseif aNode.value < element then
            if aNode.right = Void then
                !!new_node.make_leaf( element );
                aNode.setRight( new_node );
            else
                insertElement( aNode.right, element );
            end;
        end;
    end; -- insertElement

 feature -- Public
    num_elements : INTEGER;


    insert( element : T ) is
    local
        new_node : NODE[ T ];
    do
```

```
        if root = Void then
            !!root.make_leaf( element );
        else
            insertElement( root, element );
        end;
    end; -- insert

  display is
  do
      traverse( root );
  end; -- display

end -- SEARCH_TREE
```

Finally, a test class, TREE_TEST, is presented in Listing 4.22.

Listing 4.22   Class TREE_TEST

```
class TREE_TEST

 creation
   start

 feature
    str1 : STRING is "Richard";
    str2 : STRING is "Hanne";
    str3 : STRING is "Henrik";
    str4 : STRING is "Erik";
    str5 : STRING is "Marc";

    start is
    local
        tree1 : SEARCH_TREE[ COMPARABLE_DISPLAYABLE_INTEGER
            ];
        tree2 : SEARCH_TREE[ COMPARABLE_DISPLAYABLE_STRING ];

        element1 : COMPARABLE_DISPLAYABLE_INTEGER;
        element2 : COMPARABLE_DISPLAYABLE_INTEGER;
        element3 : COMPARABLE_DISPLAYABLE_INTEGER;
        element4 : COMPARABLE_DISPLAYABLE_STRING;
        element5 : COMPARABLE_DISPLAYABLE_STRING;
        element6 : COMPARABLE_DISPLAYABLE_STRING;
        element7 : COMPARABLE_DISPLAYABLE_STRING;
        element8 : COMPARABLE_DISPLAYABLE_STRING;
    do
        !!element1.make( 10 );
        !!element2.make( 5 );
        !!element3.make( 15 );

        !!element4.make( str1 );
        !!element5.make( str2 );
        !!element6.make( str3 );
        !!element7.make( str4 );
        !!element8.make( str5 );
```

```
                !!tree1;
                tree1.insert( element1 );
                tree1.insert( element2 );
                tree1.insert( element3 );
                tree1.display;
                io.new_line;

                !!tree2;
                tree2.insert( element4 );
                tree2.insert( element5 );
                tree2.insert( element6 );
                tree2.insert( element7 );
                tree2.insert( element8 );
                tree2.display;
                io.new_line;
            end; -- start

      end -- TREE_TEST
```

The program output is:

```
5
10
15

Erik
Hanne
Henrik
Marc
Richard
```

Two trees are created in the test program. The first tree, *tree1*, holds objects of type COMPARABLE_DISPLAYABLE_INTEGER. Three such objects are inserted into the tree. The second tree, *tree2*, holds objects of type COMPARABLE_DISPLAYABLE_STRING. Five such objects are inserted in this tree.

The use of constrained generic parameters has provided the search tree system presented in this section with specifications that ensure that if an illegal type is used as an actual parameter, the compiler will detect and report this error.

4.2.6 "Sortable" Arrays Re-visited

Eiffel provides an array class defined in terms of an unconstrained generic parameter, T. Therefore, an array of any arbitrary base type can be constructed using this array class. Suppose we desire to build an array class that contains "sortable" elements — that is, elements that can be compared. We re-visit the SORTABLE_ARRAY class first introduced in Listing 2.16. We modify this class to provide for greater efficiency and to provide the user with more natural access to its elements.

As indicated in section 2.8, we wish to constrain the actual types that can be used to create instances of a generic array to conform to class COMPARABLE.

One mechanism for achieving this is through composition. We define an array class SORTABLE_ARRAY. This class has an array object as one of its attributes. But the generic parameter specified in the SORTABLE_ARRAY class is constrained to conform to COMPARABLE.

Class SORTABLE_ARRAY is presented in Listing 4.23.

Listing 4.23   Modified Class SORTABLE_ARRAY

```
class SORTABLE_ARRAY[ T -> COMPARABLE ]

creation
    create

feature { NONE }
    data  : SIMPLE_ARRAY[ T ]; -- Efficient array class
    -- supplied by TowerEiffel
    size  : INTEGER;
    lower : INTEGER;
    upper : INTEGER;

feature
    create( first : INTEGER; second : INTEGER ) is
    require
      first <= second;
    do
        size  := second - first + 1;
        lower := first;
        upper := second;
        !!data.make( size );
    ensure
      lower = first;
      upper = second;
      size  = upper - lower + 1
    end; -- create

    sort is
    local
        i, j, maxindex  : INTEGER;
        maximum, temp   : T;
    do
        from i := 0
        until i = size - 1
        loop
            i := i + 1;
            maximum := data.item( 0 );
            maxindex := 0;
            from j := 0
            until j = size - i
            loop
                j := j + 1;
                if data.item( j ) > maximum then
                    maximum  := data.item( j );
                    maxindex := j;
                end;
            end;
```

```
                temp := data.item( size - i );
                data.put( item( maxindex ), size - i );
                data.put( temp, maxindex );
            end;
        end; -- sort

        item( index : INTEGER ) : T is
        require
            valid_index: index >= lower and index <= upper;
        do
            Result := data.item( index - lower );
        end; -- item

        put( value : T; index : INTEGER ) is
        require
            valid_index: index >= lower and index <= upper;
        do
            data.put( value, index - lower );
        ensure
            item( index ) = value;
        end; -- put
end -- SORTABLE_ARRAY
```

The SORTABLE_ARRAY class is composed of an unconstrained generic array, *data*, given by type SIMPLE_ARRAY. This is a special array class supplied by TowerEiffel for efficient array operations. ISE Eiffel supplies a similar kind of special array for efficient computation.

Instances of SIMPLE_ARRAY behave much like ordinary C arrays. That is, they are indexed from zero to one less than the size of the array. In order to make the internal data model transparent to the user, an attribute, *lower*, is defined. This permits users to supply both a lower and upper bound on their SORTABLE_ARRAY. The routines *put* and *item* do the translation from the user's index to the appropriate index of the internal SIMPLE_ARRAY.

The preconditions defined for routines *item* and *put* help the client ensure that the SORTABLE_ARRAY class is used properly.

It is noted that the sorting algorithm used in routine *sort* is inefficient but simple.

A test class is presented in Listing 4.24.

Listing 4.24   Class ARRAY_TEST

```
class ARRAY_TEST

  creation
    start

  feature

    start is
     local
        myArray  : SORTABLE_ARRAY[ DOUBLE ];
        index    : INTEGER;
        r        : RANDOM;
```

```
        time      : TIMER;
    do
        !!r.initialize;
        !!time;
        !!myArray.create( 1, 2000 );
        from index := 0
        until index = 2000
        loop
            index := index + 1;
            myArray.put( r.uniform, index );
        end;
        time.startTiming;
        myArray.sort;
        time.endTiming;
        time.report
    end; -- start

end -- ARRAY_TEST
```

The program output is:

```
Time duration = 2.69989 seconds
```

The timing results shown were run on a SUN IPX workstation using the TowerEiffel compiler with optimization turned on. For purposes of timing, all assertion checking was turned off. This improves the performance of the resulting code. For comparison purposes, the sorting was performed in straight C using the same C compiler that TowerEiffel uses (GNUC). The Eiffel code is about 25 percent faster than the C code.

Two support classes are used in class ARRAY_TEST. The class RANDOM is presented in Chapter 2. The class TIMER is presented in Listing 4.25. The C functions used by TIMER are shown in Listing 4.26.

Listing 4.25   Class TIMER

```
class TIMER

INHERIT
    BASIC; -- for routine double_real

feature { NONE } -- For internal use only
    time1 : DOUBLE;
    time2 : DOUBLE;

    c_start : DOUBLE is
    external "C"
    alias
        "beginTime"
    end; -- c_start

    c_end : DOUBLE is
    external "C"
    alias
        "endTime"
    end; -- c_end;
```

```
feature -- For public use

    startTiming is
    do
        time1 := c_start;
    end; -- start

    endTiming is
    do
        time2 := c_end;
    end; -- end

    report is
    do
        io.putstring( "Time duration = " );
        io.putreal( double_real( ( time2 - time1 ) /
            1000000.0 ) );
        io.putstring( " seconds" );
        io.new_line;
    end; -- report

end -- TIMER
```

Listing 4.26   C functions used for class TIMER

```
#include <time.h>
#include <stdlib.h>

double beginTime()
{
    return ( double ) clock();
}

double endTime()
{
    return ( double ) clock();
}
```

4.3 SUMMARY

Generic parameters allow general purpose reusable software to be constructed without compromising type safety. The Eiffel static type system is able to verify that all of the operations on the formal generic parameters are defined. This type checking is performed without regard to the actual type or types that replace the generic parameter. By contrast, a C++ compiler verifies that the operations specified in a class template are valid for the actual type that is used when creating an instance of the generic class.

Constrained generic parameters in Eiffel allow the supplier to specify precisely the type constraints that must be met by the client in substituting an actual type for the generic type when creating an instance of the generic class.

CHAPTER 5

Inheritance in Eiffel

5.1 THE ROLE OF INHERITANCE IN OBJECT-ORIENTED PROGRAMMING

*I*nheritance is used during object-oriented analysis and design for establishing a hierarchical decomposition of a software system into classes and subclasses. The accepted practice is for classes at the top of an inheritance hierarchy to encapsulate general properties of some domain and for classes lower in the hierarchy to extend and to encapsulate more specialized properties of the domain.

In going from a parent class to its child, *specialization* involves redefining one or more of the parent's routines, *extension* involves adding routines not present in the parent, and *restriction* involves blocking one or more routines of the parent. All three mechanisms may be used simultaneously, but it is most common to use only specialization and extension in going down a class hierarchy.

If only extension is involved in going from a parent class to its child, the child is considered to be a *subtype* of its parent. Its behavior can be characterized by the sum of the parent's behavior and the additional behavior given by the additional routines not present in the parent.

Inheritance is an architectural property of an object-oriented software system. As such, it provides a basis for describing, understanding and later enhancing a software system. As one moves down a class hierarchy, the "is a" or "is kind of" relationship should hold between child class and parent class. That is, the child should be a "kind of" parent class. For example, a car class is a "kind of" vehicle class. A sportscar class is a "kind of" car class.

Inheritance also provides a framework for software reuse. Class libraries and application frameworks are being developed to support object-oriented software development in a variety of object-oriented languages on a variety of operating systems and for a variety of hardware platforms. Interactive Software Engineering provides an application framework called EiffelVision that supports the construction of graphical user interface (GUI) applications running under X-Windows™. A similar tool NeXT Step™, exists for Objective-C, and many such tools are being marketed by C++ vendors to support GUI applications.

Inheritance provides a mechanism for defining new classes that inherit properties from existing classes. Such inheritance is static. The properties of the new classes are defined at compile/link time in terms of the rules that data models (attributes) and operation models (methods) follow in propagating down a class hierarchy. Different object-oriented languages provide the programmer with different constructs and different rules for managing and defining the properties of subclasses in terms of their parents. Eiffel, as we shall see, provides a rich set of constructs that support the construction of class hierarchies.

If a subclass does not redefine any features of its parent but only adds features, it is considered to be a *subtype*. Instances of such a subtype class share the same characteristics as the parent as well as having some additional characteristics not found in the parent. For such a subtype, all of the methods of the parent class are available on instances of the subtype. These methods will produce identical behavior on a subtype instance as on a parent instance.

Let us consider a simple example of a small class hierarchy of subtypes. Such a class hierarchy is shown in Figure 5.1 and uses multiple inheritance.

The attributes and methods of each class follow.

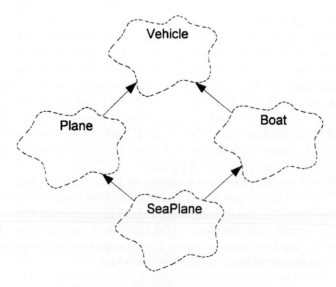

Fig. 5.1 Hierarchy of Vehicle Subtypes

```
Vehicle:
    Attributes: weight, color, price
    Routines: setWeight, setColor, setPrice

Plane:
    Attributes: wingSpan, maxAltitude
    Routines: setWingSpan, setMaxAltitude, setMaxAltitude

Boat:
    Attributes: displacement
    Routines: setDisplacement

SeaPlane:
    Attributes: numberPontoons
    Routines: setNumberPontoons
```

The hierarchy of subtypes given above is quite simple and obviously rather artificial. An instance of class SeaPlane (i.e. a SeaPlane object) is characterized by an internal state with the fields: *weight, color, price, wingSpan, maxAltitude, displacement* and *numberPontoons*. It responds to the messages: *setWeight, setColor, setWingSpan, setWingSpan, setMaxAltitude, setMaxAltitude, setDisplacement, setDisplacement, setNumberPontoons* and *setNumberPontoons*. Moreover, the response of a SeaPlane object to *setWeight* is identical to the response of a Vehicle object to this message. This is required in a subtype relationship.

The purity of the subtype hierarchy is broken if, for example, a method *display* is added to the VEHICLE class. This method should be redefined in each of the subclasses. It is therefore no longer possible to claim that a SeaPlane object will respond to *display* the same way as a Vehicle object. Subtyping has been destroyed.

In this chapter, the rules and mechanisms that Eiffel provides for constructing class hierarchies are carefully examined. Specifically, this chapter focuses on how Eiffel supports the redefinition of features, the renaming of features, exports, joining, expanded classes, deferred classes, repeated inheritance and the propagation of assertions under inheritance.

5.2 OVERALL STRUCTURE OF INHERITANCE CLAUSE

An "inherit" clause may contain one or more sub-sections. If more than one sub-section is specified, the order of specification is important. The following optional sub-sections for a class CHILD inheriting from PARENT are allowed and must be given in the order shown:

```
class CHILD

    inherit
        PARENT
            rename
                --Will discuss in section 5.5
```

```
        export
            -- Will discuss in section 5.6.
        undefine
            -- Will discuss in section 5.7.
        redefine
            -- Will discuss in section 5.3
        select
            -- Will discuss in section 5.5
    end;
    -- Other details of class not shown
end -- CHILD
```

Each of the above bold-faced sub-sections of an "inherit" clause play a potentially important role in defining the inheritance relationship of a subclass to its parent or ancestors. The meaning, purpose and use of each of these sub-sections is explained and illustrated in later sections of this chapter.

5.3   REDEFINITION OF FEATURES

Both attributes and routines may be *redefined* in an Eiffel subclass. Such redefinition destroys the subtype relationship between child and parent.

A simple example of feature redefinition is presented in Listing 5.1. In this example, both the attribute and method of the parent class are redefined in the subclass.

Listing 5.1   Class PARENT

```
class PARENT

  feature { NONE }
     data : A;

  feature
     perform is
     do
         io.putstring(
         "Entering routine perform of class PARENT" );
         io.new_line;
         !!data;
         data.first;
         io.putstring(
         "Leaving routine perform of class PARENT" );
         io.new_line;
     end; -- perform

end -- PARENT
```

Class PARENT contains an attribute *data* of type A. Class A is a simple class with no attributes and only a single routine — *first*. This class is presented in Listing 5.2.

Listing 5.2   Class A

```
class A

feature
   first is
   do
       io.putstring( "In routine first of class A" );
       io.new_line;
     end; -- first

end -- A
```

Class CHILD is inherited from PARENT and redefines both the attribute of its parent, *data*, as well as its method, *perform*. This class is shown in Listing 5.3.

Listing 5.3   Class CHILD

```
class CHILD
inherit
    PARENT
        redefine
          data,
          perform
        end;

 feature { NONE }
     data : B; -- The type B must conform to type A in the
     -- parent class
feature
   perform is -- Redefinition
   do
       io.putstring(
       "Entering routine perform of class CHILD" );
       io.new_line;
       !!data;
       data.first;
       data.second;
       io.putstring(
       "Leaving routine perform of class CHILD" );
       io.new_line;
     end; -- perform
end -- CHILD
```

The *redefine* clause in class CHILD specifies that both *data* and *perform* are redefined in class CHILD.

The redefined attribute *data* in the child class must be of a type that conforms to the type in the parent class. This is an important constraint that affects the redefinition of attributes in Eiffel. For example, it would be illegal to redefine *data* in class CHILD to be of type INTEGER. INTEGER is not a subclass of class A.

Class B is defined as a child of class A. Its implementation is shown in Listing 5.4

Listing 5.4   Class B

```
class B

 inherit
   A -- Share or include all the features of A

 feature
   second is
   do
       io.putstring( "In routine second of class B" );
       io.new_line;
   end; -- second

end -- B
```

Listing 5.5 presents a short test program that exercises classes PARENT and CHILD.

Listing 5.5   Class APPLICATION to test PARENT and CHILD

```
class APPLICATION

 creation
   start

 feature
   start is
   local
       p : PARENT;
       c : CHILD;
   do
       !!p;
       !!c;
       p.perform;
       c.perform;
   end; -- start

end -- APPLICATION
```

The program output is:

```
Entering routine perform of class PARENT
In routine first of class A
Leaving routine perform of class PARENT
Entering routine perform of class CHILD
In routine first of class A
In routine second of class B
Leaving routine perform of class CHILD
```

A more typical example of redefinition is presented next. Suppose that we wish to create classes that model hourly employees and annual employees in a given company. Suppose further that the attributes that define the data model of an hourly employee are: *name, age, gender and hourly wage*. The attributes that

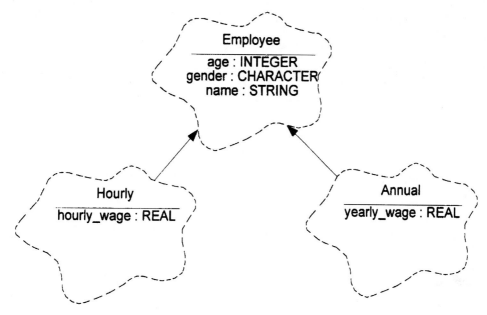

Fig. 5.2 Employee Class Hierarchy

define the data model of an annual employee are: *name, age, gender and annual salary*. We create a parent class, EMPLOYEE, that factors the common attributes of the two more specialized kinds of employee. The class hierarchy, with attributes, is shown in Figure 5.2.

In Listing 5.6, the implementation of the parent class EMPLOYEE is presented.

Listing 5.6   Class EMPLOYEE

```
class EMPLOYEE

creation
    create

feature
    name      : STRING;
    age       : INTEGER;
    gender    : CHARACTER;

    create( aName : STRING; anAge : INTEGER; theGender :
      CHARACTER ) is
    do
        name := clone( aName );
        age := anAge;
        gender := theGender;
    end; -- create
```

```
      display is
      do
         io.putstring( "Name : " ); io.putstring( name );
         io.new_line;
         io.putstring( "Age : " ); io.putint( age );
         io.new_line;
         io.putstring( "Gender: " ); io.putchar( gender );
         io.new_line;
      end; -- display

end -- EMPLOYEE
```

The details of classes HOURLY and ANNUAL are presented in Listings 5.7 and 5.8.

Listing 5.7   Class HOURLY

```
class HOURLY

inherit
    EMPLOYEE
         redefine
              display
          end;

creation
    create_hourly

  feature
     hourly_wage : REAL;

     create_hourly( anEmployee : EMPLOYEE; hourly : REAL ) is
     do
        name          := clone( anEmployee.name );
        age           := anEmployee.age;
        gender        := anEmployee.gender;
        hourly_wage   := hourly;
     end; -- create_hourly

     display is
     do
        io.putstring( "Name : " ); io.putstring( name );
        io.new_line;
        io.putstring( "Age : " ); io.putint( age );
        io.new_line;
        io.putstring( "Gender: " ); io.putchar( gender );
        io.new_line;
        io.putstring( "Wage : " ); io.putreal( hourly_wage );
        io.new_line;
     end; -- display

end -- HOURLY
```

Listing 5.8   Class ANNUAL

```
class ANNUAL

 inherit
     EMPLOYEE
         redefine
             display
         end;

 creation
     create_annual

 feature
     yearly_wage : REAL;

     create_annual( anEmployee : EMPLOYEE; yearly : REAL ) is
     do
         name          := deep_clone( anEmployee.name );
         age           := anEmployee.age;
         gender        := anEmployee.gender;
         yearly_wage   := yearly;
     end; -- create_annual

    display is
    do
        io.putstring( "Name : " ); io.putstring( name );
        io.new_line;
        io.putstring( "Age : " ); io.putint( age );
        io.new_line;
        io.putstring( "Gender: " ); io.putchar( gender );
        io.new_line;
        io.putstring( "Wage : " ); io.putreal( yearly_wage );
        io.new_line;
    end; -- display

 end -- ANNUAL
```

The redefined *display* routines in classes HOURLY and ANNUAL can be criticized because they reproduce the code of routine *display* given in the parent class EMPLOYEE. This could be avoided if the *display* routines of the child classes HOURLY and ANNUAL could call the *display* routine of class EMPLOYEE. If this were done, implementation or code inheritance would be achieved. In section 5.5, where feature renaming is discussed, a simple method for doing this is demonstrated.

5.3.1   Formal Rules for Redefinition

The rules for redefinition are stated below.

- A feature can appear only once in a *redefine* clause;
- A feature that is redefined in a subclass must not be frozen in an ancestor

class (the key word *frozen* used in front of the routine *declaration*— when a feature is "frozen" it cannot be redefined in any descendant class);

- The feature name is the final name of the feature that is inherited (it may have a different name than the feature in the parent class because of renaming (see section 5.5);
- A feature cannot be "redefined" if the inherited feature is deferred (see section 5.4). Such a feature is considered "effected" but not "redefined";
- The signature of the redefined feature must conform to the inherited feature (this implies that the parameters and return value must conform if the inherited feature is a routine, and the attribute must conform if the inherited feature is an attribute);
- A function with no parameters can be redefined as an attribute whose type conforms to the return type of the function (see section 5.3.2); and
- The consequence of a feature redefinition is that all client classes as well as descendant classes will refer to the redefined feature and not the original feature.

5.3.2   Redefining a Function as an Attribute

Can a routine be redefined as an attribute, and can an attribute be redefined as a routine?

Rule: It is possible to redefine a function that has no parameters as an attribute, but it is not possible to redefine an attribute as a function.

The reason why an attribute cannot be redefined as a function can be seen from the following example:

Suppose that some parent class contains an attribute:

```
an_attribute: SOME_TYPE
```

In some routine of this parent class the attribute is assigned the result of some expression that returns SOME_TYPE:

```
an_attribute := some_expression
```

Suppose that in a child class *an_attribute* is redefined as a function that returns SOME_TYPE:

```
an_attribute: SOME_TYPE
```

If the routine of the parent class that contains the assignment of the attribute to the result of an expression were not itself redefined (certainly a reasonable possibility), and if this routine were applied to an instance of the child class in which *an_attribute* is a function that returns SOME_TYPE, the assignment of the function to *some_expression* would make no sense. Therefore, an attribute cannot be allowed to be redefined as a function.

Redefining a function with no parameters that returns a given type with an attribute of a conforming type is consistent with the principle of uniform reference. This principle declares that a client need not know whether a given service is performed through storage or through computation.

Consider the following example that illustrates the redefinition of a function by an attribute. A class COMPLEX that contains the attributes *real_ part* and *imag_part* is defined. Functions *modulus* and *angle* each return REAL and are used to compute the modulus and angle of the complex number from its real and imaginary parts.

Class NEW_COMPLEX is defined as a subclass of COMPLEX. The two functions *modulus* and *angle* are redefined as attributes of type REAL. A private function, *convert*, is introduced in class NEW_COMPLEX in order to provide a mechanism for internally converting *real_part* and *imag_part* to *modulus* and *angle*.

A small segment of class COMPLEX is shown in Listing 5.9, and a small segment of class NEW_COMPLEX is shown in Listing 5.10.

Listing 5.9   A small segment of class COMPLEX with two attributes

```
class COMPLEX

  creation
    make

  feature
    real_part, imag_part : REAL;

    make( re : REAL; im : REAL ) is
    do
        real_part := re;
        imag_part := im;
    end; -- make

    modulus : REAL is
    do
        -- logic for computing modulus from real_part and
        -- imag_part
    end; -- modulus

    angle : REAL is
    do
        -- logic for computing angle from real_part and
        -- imag_part
    end; -- angle

  -- Other routines not shown

end -- COMPLEX
```

Listing 5.10   A small segment of class NEW_COMPLEX with four attributes

```
class NEW_COMPLEX
inherit
```

```
        COMPLEX
          redefine
            modulus, angle
          end;

    creation
       make_complex

    feature { NONE }

       convert is
       do
            -- logic for computing the modulus and angle from
            -- real_part and imag_part
       end; -- convert
 feature -- Public section
       modulus, angle : REAL;

       make_complex( re : REAL; im : REAL ) is
       do
            real_part := re;
            imag_part := im;
            convert;
       end; -- make_complex

   -- Other routines not shown

   end -- NEW_COMPLEX
```

A client could not distinguish whether *modulus* and *angle* is returned through computation or through storage without inspecting the details of the class. The usage would be the same. To get the modulus of complex instance *c*, one would write the expression *c.modulus* regardless of whether *modulus* is an attribute or a function.

5.4 DEFERRED CLASSES AND KEY METHODS

Deferred classes are used in Eiffel to create abstract classes. The definition of such abstract classes and abstract subclasses can be used in object-oriented analysis to establish the highest level structure of the system architecture. If the deferred routines contain pre and postconditions, the definition of the abstract classes also establishes the highest level semantics of the system architecture — a set of contracts that must be met by subclasses.

A deferred class is called abstract because no instances of the class are allowed. Its only purpose is to declare routines and possibly their semantics through assertions that must be made "effective" in one or more descendant classes.

Often, a deferred (abstract) class contains one or more routines that are fully defined (that start with *do*, *once* or *external*). The fully defined routines (methods) are sometimes implemented in terms of the deferred routines. When this is true, the deferred routines may be called key methods (a concept introduced in Smalltalk). Once defined or redefined, the *key methods* give meaning to all the routines of the abstract class. These fully defined methods that are defined in terms of the key methods are generally not redefined in any subclasses.

The notion of key methods is illustrated by considering an abstract class, NUMBER, presented in Listing 5.11. This class is elaborated on in much more detail in Chapter 6.

Listing 5.11   Abstract class NUMBER with key methods

```
deferred class NUMBER

feature { NONE }
   value : ANY

feature

   less_than, infix "<"( anotherNumber : NUMBER ): BOOLEAN
      is
   deferred -- A key method
   end; -- infix "<"

   frozen greater_than, infix ">"( anotherNumber : NUMBER )
     : BOOLEAN is
   do
      Result := Current < anotherNumber;
   end;

   frozen less_than_equal_to( anotherNumber : NUMBER ) :
     BOOLEAN is
   do
      Result := Current < anotherNumber or Current =
        anotherNumber;
   end; -- lessthan_equal_to

   frozen greater_than_equal_to( anotherNumber : NUMBER ) :
     BOOLEAN is
   do
      Result := Current > anotherNumber or Current =
        anotherNumber;
   end; -- greaterthan_equal_to

   infix "+"( anotherNumber : NUMBER ) : NUMBER is
   deferred
   end; -- infix "+"

   infix "-"( anotherNumber : NUMBER ): NUMBER is
   deferred
   end; -- infix "-"
```

```
infix "*"( anotherNumber : NUMBER ) : NUMBER is
deferred
end; -- infix "*"

infix "/"( anotherNumber : NUMBER ) : NUMBER is
deferred
end; -- infix "/"
```

```
end -- NUMBER
```

The methods "<" and "=" are key methods because the fully defined methods ">", *less_than_equal_to*, and *greater_than_equal_to* are dependent on the definitions of the key methods. Furthermore, the fully defined methods are "frozen" in order to assure that they are not redefined in any subclass. Thus, the key methods must be defined, and the dependent methods cannot be redefined. This is a fairly typical design protocol.

Returning briefly to the EMPLOYEE classes of section 5.2, it might be argued that since none of the display code of class EMPLOYEE (see Listings 5.6 through 5.8) is actually inherited but just reproduced, that routine *display* of class EMPLOYEE and, therefore, class EMPLOYEE should be deferred. That is, it should be defined as an abstract class. Since no instances of a deferred class can be created, it is incorrect for such a class to have a creation routine.

Once class EMPLOYEE is declared as deferred, it is no longer correct to consider routine *display* in each of classes HOURLY and ANNUAL to be redefined. This clause must be removed. Routine *display* can surely not be redefined if it was never defined. It is simply made "effective" in classes HOURLY and ANNUAL.

The creation routines in classes HOURLY and ANNUAL must also be modified since they cannot be based on an instance of class EMPLOYEE. The revised code for this application is shown in Listing 5.12. All three revised classes as well as a revised application class are shown.

Listing 5.12   Revised EMPLOYEE classes using a deferred class EMPLOYEE

```
deferred class EMPLOYEE

  feature
    name      : STRING;
    age       : INTEGER;
    gender    : CHARACTER;

    display is
    deferred -- Must be redeclared in subclass
    end; -- display

end -- EMPLOYEE

class HOURLY

  inherit
    EMPLOYEE
```

```
   creation
       create_hourly

    feature
       hourly_wage : REAL;

    feature
       create_hourly( aName : STRING; anAge : INTEGER;
                   aGender : CHARACTER; hourly : REAL ) is
       do
          name := deep_clone( aName );
          age := anAge;
          gender := aGender;
          hourly_wage := hourly;
       end; -- create_hourly

       display is
       do
          -- Same details as Listing 5.7
       end; -- display
end -- HOURLY

class ANNUAL

  inherit
     EMPLOYEE

   creation
       create_annual

    feature
       yearly_wage : REAL;

       create_annual( aName : STRING; anAge : INTEGER;
                   aGender : CHARACTER; annual : REAL ) is
     do
          name := deep_clone( aName );
          age := anAge;
          gender := aGender;
          yearly_wage := annual;
       end; -- create_annual

       display is
       do
          -- Same details as Listing 5.8
       end; -- display

end -- ANNUAL

class APPLICATION

  creation
       start

   feature
```

```
    start is
    local
        employee_1 : HOURLY;
        employee_2 : ANNUAL;
    do
        !!employee_1.create_hourly( "Marc", 17, 'M', 4.25 );
        !!employee_2.create_annual( "Erik", 22, 'M', 36000.0
            );
        io.putstring( "Employee 1" ); io.new_line;
        employee_1.display(); io.new_line;
        io.putstring( "Employee 2" ); io.new_line;
        employee_2.display(); io.new_line;
    end; -- start

end -- APPLICATION
```

Routine *display* is said to be effective in classes HOURLY and ANNUAL. If a subclass does not make a deferred routine effective, the class containing the routine is considered deferred and must be labeled as *deferred*.

5.5   RENAMING AND SELECTION OF FEATURES

As indicated in section 5.2, the various sub-sections of an inheritance clause, if present, must be in the following order:

☞ **rename**
    -- Discussed in this section
export
    -- Will discuss in section 5.6
undefine
    -- Will discuss in section 5.7
redefine ✔
    --Discussed in section 5.3
☞ **select**
    -- Discussed in this section

This section examines the optional "rename" and "select" sub-sections.

Renaming an inherited feature allows a child class, all of its descendants and all of its clients to access a feature of the parent class using a name that the designer of the subclass believes is more suitable for the intended purpose of the subclass than the feature name given by the author of the parent class. This is the intended software engineering purpose of this facility.

Another more technical capability that a "rename" sub-section provides is the capability to correct any name clash that occurs because of multiple inheritance. Such a name clash occurs whenever two or more parents of a subclass use the same feature name.

Renaming a feature inherited from a parent class does not change the semantics of the inherited feature. Only if a feature is renamed and redefined might its semantics be changed.

The structure of a "rename" subclause is the following:

```
rename
    a as b,
    c as d,
    e as f,
    ...
end;
```

where *a*, *c* and *e* are the feature names of parent class features, and *b*, *d* and *f* are the new final names of the inherited features.

A typical situation that might justify renaming is presented in Listings 5.13 and 5.14 that define class FIGURE and subclass CIRCLE. In class FIGURE, the feature *perimeter* is declared. In subclass CIRCLE, this feature is renamed to be *circumference* because this name is more becoming a circle.

Listing 5.13   A segment of class FIGURE

```
class FIGURE

 feature

    -- many features not shown

    perimeter : REAL is
    do
       -- Implementation details not shown
    end; -- perimeter

end -- FIGURE
```

Listing 5.14   A segment of class CIRCLE

```
class CIRCLE

 inherit
    FIGURE
        rename
            perimeter as circumference

        redefine
            circumference
    end;

 feature
    -- other features not shown

    circumference : REAL is
    do
       -- Implementation details not shown
    end; -- circumference
end -- CIRCLE
```

It is again important to note that all clients of class CIRCLE (classes that declare one or more entities to be of type CIRCLE) and all descendants of class CIRCLE will be able to access only the feature *circumference*. The feature *circumference* is also redefined in class CIRCLE because its implementation is different from the implementation of *perimeter* given in class FIGURE.

5.5.1   Accessing a Parent Routine from a Redefined Routine in a Child Class

In Listings 5.6 through 5.8 of section 5.3 classes EMPLOYEE, HOURLY and ANNUAL were defined. It was observed that the routines *display*, in classes HOURLY and ANNUAL, duplicate much of the code of routine *display* in the parent class EMPLOYEE. This raises the question, "Is it possible for the *display* routines in HOURLY and ANNUAL to reuse the code of class EMPLOYEE by invoking the *display* routine of class HOURLY?"

The answer is yes. In order to achieve this code inheritance, the "select" sub-section is introduced and multiple inheritance is used.

Suppose, in class HOURLY, the following inheritance clause is used:

```
class HOURLY

  inherit
    EMPLOYEE
        rename
            display as display_employee
        end;
    EMPLOYEE
        redefine
            display
        select
            display
        end;
```

In the first inheritance of EMPLOYEE, the routine *display* in the parent class is renamed *display_employee*. This implies that any references to the parent routine *display* in class HOURLY, any of its subclasses or any client classes must refer to this parent routine as *display_employee*. The second inheritance subclause implies that a local redefinition of the parent class *display* routine is defined in class HOURLY.

But now a potential ambiguity has been created. Suppose an instance of class HOURLY is defined and assigned to an instance of class EMPLOYEE. Suppose the message *display* is sent to this object. To which version of *display* should the run-time system bind the message *display* — the method *display* defined in the EMPLOYEE class or the redefined method *display* defined in the HOURLY class?

The "select" sub-section indicates that the redefined version of *display* should be selected in this situation resulting from polymorphism and dynamic-binding. If the "select" sub-section were attached to the first inheritance of EMPLOYEE, the parent version of *display* would be selected.

The modified version of class HOURLY is shown in Listing 5.15.

Listing 5.15   Modified class HOURLY

```
class HOURLY

  inherit

      EMPLOYEE
          rename
              display as display_employee
          end;

      EMPLOYEE
          redefine
              display
          select
              display
          end;

  creation
      create_hourly

  feature
      hourly_wage : REAL;

      create_hourly( anEmployee : EMPLOYEE; hourly : REAL ) is
      do
        -- Same details as Listing 5.7
      end; -- create_hourly

      display is
      do
          display_employee; -- This invokes parent class
          -- version of display
              io.putstring( "Wage : " ); io.putreal( hourly_wage );
              io.new_line;
      end; -- display

end -- HOURLY
```

5.5.2   Using Renaming to Resolve Name Clashes

When a child class inherits from two or more parent classes that each use the same feature name, a name clash occurs in the child class. This is one of the basic hazards of multiple inheritance. Eiffel provides a simple and clean resolution of this potential name clash.

Listing 5.16 illustrates the problem. Listing 5.17 presents the solution.

Listing 5.16   Illustration of name clash resulting from multiple inheritance

```
class FIRST


  feature
    common_name : INTEGER;

end -- FIRST

class SECOND

  feature
    common_name : REAL;

end -- SECOND

class THIRD

  inherit

    FIRST;
    SECOND

end -- THIRD
```

The code in Listing 5.16 will not compile because of the clash of the feature
common_name in classes FIRST and SECOND.

Listing 5.17   Using renaming to resolve a name clash

```
class FIRST

  feature
    common_name : INTEGER;

end -- FIRST

class SECOND

  feature
    common_name : REAL;

end -- SECOND

class THIRD
  inherit
    FIRST
        rename
            common_name as first_name
        end;

    SECOND
        rename
            common_name as second_name
```

```
        end

end -- THIRD
```

The attributes of class `THIRD` are *first_name* and *second_name* as a consequence of renaming.

5.6 MODIFYING THE EXPORT STATUS OF INHERITED FEATURES

This section discusses the optional "export" sub-section of an inheritance clause.

> **rename** ✔
> -- Discussed in section 5.5
> ☞ **export**
> -- Discussed in this section
> **undefine**
> -- Will discuss in section 5.7
> **redefine** ✔
> --Discussed in section 5.3
> **select** ✔
> -- Discussed in section 5.5

Recall that the features of a class can be grouped according to their export status. For example:

```
class EXPORT_STATUS

    feature { A, B, C }
        value1 : INTEGER;
    feature { A, D }
        value2 : REAL;
    feature { NONE }
        value3 : DOUBLE;
    -- Other details not shown
```

indicates that the feature *value1* is accessible directly in classes A, B and C, the feature *value2* is directly accessible in classes A and D, and the feature *value3* is inaccessible outside of the class.

When a child class inherits from a parent class, the export status of the features of the parent class remain intact in the child class unless an "export" sub-section appears in an inheritance clause. Suppose, for example, the child class inherits from class `EXPORT_STATUS`, given above. Furthermore, the child class wishes to make the inherited attribute *value1* private. In addition, the child class wants to make *value2* available to all classes. And finally, the child class wishes to restrict *value3* to classes A and B only.

The adaptation of the export status of the inherited features can be accomplished as shown below.

```
    class CHILD
inherit
    EXPORT_STATUS
        export
                { NONE } value1 -- value1 hidden
                { ANY }  value2 -- value2 available anywhere
                { A, B } value3 -- value3 available in classes A
                -- and B
            end;
```

Suppose that the child class wishes to make all of the features of its parent class hidden or protected. It could accomplish this as follows:

```
    class CHILD
        inherit
            EXPORT_STATUS
                export
                    { NONE } all -- all of the parent class
                    -- features are inaccessible
                end;
```

The above inheritance clause implies that all of the features of the parent class are available to class NONE and its descendants. This of course means that all of the features of the parent class are hidden. This might be desirable in cases where only code inheritance is wanted. In such a case, only the routines in the child class and its descendants can access the features of the parent (code inheritance) directly.

5.7 How to "Undefine" a Parent Feature in a Subclass — The Join Mechanism

This section discusses the optional "undefine" sub-section of an inheritance clause.

> **rename** ✔
> -- Discussed in section 5.5
> **export** ✔
> -- Discussed in section 5.6
> ☞ **undefine**
> -- Discussed in this section
> **redefine** ✔
> --Discussed in section 5.3
> **select** ✔
> -- Discussed in section 5.5

The "undefine" sub-section of an inheritance clause allows a child class to declare one or more effective features inherited from its parent as deferred. "Undefining" an inherited feature permits subclasses of the child class to "affect" the feature anew without concern about the history of the feature as specified in the ancestor classes.

The "undefine" sub-section serves another important role. It provides the basis for the joining of features from two or more parent classes into a child class. The join mechanism allows a fusion of abstractions from two or more parent classes. The concept of joining is illustrated with several examples.

In the first example, the routines *display_int* and *display_real* are merged from classes PARTNER1 and PARTNER2. The definition of these classes is given in Listings 5.18 and 5.19

Listing 5.18   Class PARTNER1 to illustrate joining of features

```
class PARTNER1

 feature
    value : INTEGER;

 feature
    setValue( aValue : INTEGER ) is
    do
       value := aValue;
    end; -- setValue

    display_int is
    do
       io.putstring( "value = " );
       io.putint( value );
       io.new_line;
    end; -- display_int

end --PARTNER1
```

Listing 5.19   Class PARTNER2 to illustrate joining of features

```
class PARTNER2

 feature
    value : REAL;

    setValue( aValue : REAL ) is
    do
       value := aValue;
    end; -- setValue

    display_real is
    do
       io.putstring( "value = " );
       io.putreal( value );
       io.new_line;
```

```
        end; -- display_real

    end -- PARTNER2
```

In order to join the routines *display_int* and *display_real* from classes PARTNER1 and PARTNER2, we must *rename* each of these routines and form a common name, say *display*.

Class JOINED, shown in Listing 5.20, performs the necessary renaming, "undefining" and joining.

Listing 5.20   Class JOINED to illustrate joining of features

```
    class JOINED

     inherit
        PARTNER1
            rename
                value as value1,
                setValue as setValue1,
                display_int as display
            undefine
                display
            end;

        PARTNER2
            rename
                value as value2,
                setValue as setValue2,
                display_real as display
            undefine
                display
            end;

     feature

        display is
        do
            io.putstring( "value1 = " );
            io.putint( value1 );
            io.new_line;
            io.putstring( "value2 = " );
            io.putreal( value2 );
            io.new_line;
        end; -- display

    end -- JOINED
```

Class JOINED inherits from PARTNER1 and PARTNER2. From PARTNER1, attribute *value* is renamed to be *value1*, *setValue* to be *setValue1*, and *display_int* as *display*. Then *display* is "undefined." The new definition of *display* in class JOINED serves to "affect" the joined deferred features *display*.

Listing 5.21 shows a short test routine in class APPLICATION.

Listing 5.21   Class APPLICATION to exercise class JOINED

```
class APPLICATION
  creation
      start
  feature
    start is
     local
        myObject : JOINED;
       do
        !!myObject;
        myObject.setValue1( 5 );
        myObject.setValue2( 5.1 );
        myObject.display;
     end; -- start
end -- APPLICATION
```

The program output is:

```
value1 = 5
value2 = 5.1
```

In the next example, two parent classes, PARENT1 and PARENT2, contain the same routine — *common_routine*. In class CHILD, we wish the PARENT1 version of *common_routine* to be the one that prevails. Listing 5.22 shows classes PARENT1, PARENT2 and CHILD.

Listing 5.22   Blocking a common routine in multiple inheritance

```
class PARENT1

  feature

    common_routine( aValue : INTEGER ) : INTEGER is
    do
       Result := aValue * aValue;
    end; -- common_routine

end -- PARENT1

class PARENT2

  feature

    common_routine( aValue : INTEGER ) : INTEGER is
    do
       Result := aValue * aValue * aValue;
    end -- common_routine

end -- PARENT2

class CHILD
```

```
inherit
    PARENT1;

    PARENT2
        undefine
            common_routine
        end;

end -- CHILD

class APPLICATION

creation
    start

feature

    start is
    local
        myObject : CHILD;
    do
        !!myObject;
        io.putstring( "myObject.common_routine( 5 ) = " );
        io.putint( myObject.common_routine( 5 ) );
        io.new_line;
    end; -- start

end -- APPLICATION
```

The program output is:

```
myObject.common_routine( 5 ) = 25
```

This section is concluded by stating some formal rules that govern "undefine" and the joining of deferred routines.

The formal rules for using "undefine" are given below:

- The feature being "undefined" must not be frozen and is not an attribute;
- The feature must be effective in the parent class; and
- The final name must appear only once in the list of undefined features.

The formal rules for joining two deferred routines are:

- The final names of all of the precursors (the inherited features that are being joined) must be the same (renaming may be required to achieve this);
- The final signature of all of the precursors must be the same (redeclaration may be required to achieve this);
- The precondition of the joined routine is the "or" of all the precursors' preconditions; and
- The postcondition of the joined routine is the "and" of all the precursors' postconditions.

5.8 REPEATED INHERITANCE

Repeated inheritance is a special, fairly common and important pattern of multiple inheritance in which two or more ancestors of a class have a common parent. This pattern raises several interesting challenges that are explored in this section. The inheritance sub-sections that have been discussed in previous sections (*rename, undefine, export, redefine* and *select*) are used to control repeated inheritance. Some new language rules associated with repeated inheritance are presented and discussed.

5.8.1 An Example — Vehicle Classes

To begin, let us re-visit the multiple inheritance hierarchy given in section 5.1, the hierarchy of vehicles. The inheritance structure and attributes of each class are repeated below (this is an example of repeated inheritance!)

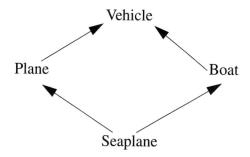

```
Vehicle:
    Attributes: weight, color, price
    Routines: setWeight, setColor, setPrice
Plane:
    Attributes: wingSpan, maxAltitude
    Routines: setWingSpan, setMaxAltitude

Boat:
    Attributes: displacement
    Routines: setDisplacement

SeaPlane:
    Attributes: numberPontoons
    Routines: setNumberPontoons
```

Some partial implementation details of this class hierarchy, which exhibits repeated inheritance, are given in Listings 5.23 through 5.26.

Listing 5.23 Class VEHICLE

```
class VEHICLE
creation
```

```
        make_vehicle

   feature
      weight, speed  : REAL;
      color          : STRING;

      make_vehicle( aWeight : REAL; aSpeed : REAL; aColor :
         STRING ) is
      do
         weight := aWeight;
         speed  := aSpeed;
         color  := clone( aColor );
      end; -- make_vehicle

      -- Details of setWeight, setSpeed, setColor and setPrice
      -- not shown

   end -- VEHICLE
```

Listing 5.24   Class PLANE

```
class PLANE
 inherit
   VEHICLE

 creation
    make_plane

 feature
    wingSpan, maxAltitude: REAL;

    make_plane( aWeight: REAL; aSpeed : REAL; aColor :STRING;
                wSpan: REAL; mAltitude : REAL ) is
    do
        -- Details not shown
    end; -- make_plane

   -- Details of setWingSpan and setMaxAltitude not shown

 end -- PLANE
```

Listing 5.25   Class BOAT

```
class BOAT

 inherit
   VEHICLE

    creation
       make_boat

    feature
       displacement : INTEGER;
```

```
        -- Details of make_boat and setDisplacement not shown

  end -- BOAT
```

Listing 5.26   Class SEAPLANE

```
class SEAPLANE

 inherit
    PLANE;
    BOAT

 creation
    make_seaplane

 feature
    numberPontoons : INTEGER;

    make_seaplane( aWeight : REAL; aSpeed : REAL; aColor :
      STRING; wSpan : REAL; mAltitude : REAL; nPontoons :
      INTEGER ) is
    do
       weight := aWeight;
       speed := aSpeed;
       color := deep_clone( aColor );
       wingSpan := wSpan;
       maxAltitude := mAltitude;
       numberPontoons := nPontoons;

    end; -- make_seaplane

    setNumberPontoons( nPontoons : INTEGER ) is
    do
       numberPontoons := nPontoons;
    end; -- setNumberPontoons

    display is
    do
       io.putstring( "Weight : " ); io.putreal( weight );
       io.new_line;
       io.putstring( "Speed : " ); io.putreal( speed );
       io.new_line;
       io.putstring( "Color : " ); io.putstring( color );
       io.new_line;
       io.putstring( "Span : " ); io.putreal( wingSpan );
       io.new_line;
       io.putstring( "Max Alt : " ); io.putreal( maxAltitude );
       io.new_line;
       io.putstring( "Pontoons: " ); io.putint
       ( numberPontoons ); io.new_line;
    end; -- display

end -- SEAPLANE
```

After reviewing the code of Listings 5.23 through 5.26, you may be wondering how the compiler can distinguish the attributes *weight, speed* and *color* inherited through class PLANE from the same attributes inherited through class BOAT. The answer is that when one or more attributes are inherited through the structure defined as "repeated inheritance," and no grandparent features have been redefined, undefined or renamed, only one copy of the grandparent attribute occurs in the grandchild class.

If classes PLANE and BOAT were each to introduce the same attribute, say *horsepower* : INTEGER, the compiler would emit an error message for class SEA-PLANE. This would occur because the compiler could not distinguish the PLANE version of *horsepower* from the BOAT version of *horsepower*. A name clash would exist. Of course, if the attribute *horsepower* were declared in the grandparent class VEHICLE, there would be no error because only one copy of an attribute inherited through repeated inheritance is defined in the grandchild class. It would not make sense to declare the attribute *horsepower* in class VEHICLE because some vehicles, such as a bicycle, do not have a meaningful *horsepower* attribute. This attribute, therefore, does not belong in class VEHICLE.

Class SEAPLANE in Listing 5.26 has the attributes *weight, speed, color, wing-Span, maxAltitude* and *numberPontoons*. Suppose we wish to allow class SEA-PLANE to have two speed attributes — the maximum speed in the water and the maximum speed in the air (*max_water_speed* and *max_air_speed*). In other words, we do not want only one *speed* attribute to be inherited through the repeated inheritance structure. Furthermore, we wish to add the attribute *horse-power* to classes PLANE and BOAT and have only a single *horsepower* attribute in class SEAPLANE.

In Listing 5.27, we modify the repeated inheritance vehicle hierarchy, specifically classes PLANE, BOAT, and SEAPLANE, in order that: (1) classes PLANE and BOAT each have an attribute *horsepower*, (2) the grandchild class SEAPLANE can access *max_air_speed* and *max_water_speed* independently, and (3) the SEAPLANE class has access to a single attribute *horsepower*. Portions of all three classes are included in Listing 5.27.

Listing 5.27   Modified vehicle classes with horsepower attribute and two speed attributes (Modified code shown in boldface)

```
class PLANE
   inherit
      VEHICLE
         rename
            speed as max_air_speed
         end;

   creation
      make_plane

   feature
      wingSpan, maxAltitude : REAL;
      horsepower            : INTEGER;
```

```
      make_plane( aWeight : REAL; aSpeed : REAL; aColor :
        STRING; wSpan : REAL; mAltitude : REAL; hpower :
        INTEGER ) is
      do
         -- Details not shown
      end; -- make_plane

   -- Other features are the same as in Listing 5.24.

end -- PLANE

class BOAT

inherit
    VEHICLE
        rename
            speed as max_water_speed
        end;

 creation
    make_boat

 feature
    displacement : INTEGER;
    horsepower   : INTEGER;

    make_boat( aWeight : REAL; aSpeed : REAL; aColor :
      STRING; aDisplacement : INTEGER; hpower : INTEGER )
      is
    do
       -- Details not shown
    end; -- make_boat

   -- Other features the same as in Listing 5.25.

end -- BOAT

class SEAPLANE

 inherit
   PLANE
        select
            horsepower, max_air_speed
        end;
    BOAT
        rename
            horsepower as boat_horsepower
        export
            { NONE } boat_horsepower
        end;

 creation
    make_seaplane
```

```
feature
    numberPontoons : INTEGER;

    make_seaplane( aWeight : REAL; airSpeed : REAL;
        waterSpeed : REAL; aColor : STRING; wSpan : REAL;
                mAltitude : REAL; nPontoons : INTEGER;
                hpower : INTEGER ) is
    do
        weight := aWeight;
        max_air_speed := airSpeed;
        max_water_speed := waterSpeed;
        color := deep_clone( aColor );
        wingSpan := wSpan;
        maxAltitude := mAltitude;
        numberPontoons := nPontoons;
        horsepower := hpower;
    end; -- make_seaplane

    setNumberPontoons( nPontoons : INTEGER ) is
    do
        numberPontoons := nPontoons;
    end; -- setNumberPontoons

    display is
    do
        io.putstring( "Weight : " ); io.putreal( weight );
        io.new_line;
        io.putstring( "Max air speed : " ); io.putreal(
            max_air_speed );
        io.new_line;
        io.putstring( "Max water speed : " ); io.putreal(
            max_water_speed );
        io.new_line;
        io.putstring( "Color : " ); io.putstring( color );
        io.new_line;
        io.putstring( "Span : " ); io.putreal( wingSpan );
        io.new_line;
        io.putstring( "Max Alt : " ); io.putreal( maxAltitude
            );
        io.new_line;
        io.putstring( "Pontoons : " ); io.putint( numberPon
            toons );
        io.new_line;
        io.putstring( "Horsepower: " ); io.putint( horsepower
            );
        io.new_line;
    end; -- display

end -- SEAPLANE
```

In Listing 5.27, the "rename" sub-section of the VEHICLE inheritance clause in class PLANE assigns a new name, *max_air_speed*, to class PLANE and all of its descendants and clients. In addition, a new *horsepower* attribute is introduced.

The *make_plane* routine is slightly modified to take these changes into account.

In class BOAT, the "rename" sub-section assigns a new name, *max_water_speed*, to this class and all of its descendants and clients. In addition, the new attribute *horsepower* is introduced. The *make_boat* routine is modified slightly to account for these changes.

The most interesting changes are made in class SEAPLANE. In the inheritance clause for PLANE, a "select" sub-section includes *horsepower* and *max_air_speed*. In the inheritance clause for BOAT, a "rename" sub-section changes *horsepower* to *boat_horsepower* and sets the export status of *boat_horsepower* to NONE.

Since two versions of *horsepower* are now available to SEAPLANE (the *horsepower* attribute from PLANE and the renamed *boat_horsepower* attribute from BOAT), the "select" sub-section in the PLANE inheritance clause tells the system to choose the PLANE version of *horsepower* under dynamic-binding to a seaplane object. The same comment can be made about the two versions of speed in class SEAPLANE.

The "export" sub-section in the BOAT inheritance clause hides the *boat_horsepower* version of the BOAT attribute from any descendants and clients of class SEAPLANE. Therefore, effectively only a single version of *horsepower* is accessible to the clients and descendants of SEAPLANE.

All of the goals stated thus far have been achieved in the vehicle class hierarchy.

Further maintenance is now performed on this vehicle hierarchy. An abstract class called POWERED_VEHICLE is constructed as a subclass of VEHICLE. This class gets the attribute *horsepower*. Another abstract class, NON_POWERED_VEHICLE, is added as a subclass of VEHICLE. This class gets the attribute *power_source*. Class BICYCLE is added as a subclass to this hierarchy, with attribute *frameSize*. Finally, class MOPED is added. This MOPED is a "kind of" POWERED_VEHICLE and is also a "kind of" NON_POWERED_VEHICLE. The use of multiple inheritance handles this situation very nicely. Finally, routine *display* is added to each of the effective subclasses.

Since many of the sub-section features of inheritance clauses presented in earlier sections are used in this example, all of the code for the vehicle classes follows. But before doing this, the revised vehicle class hierarchy with class names and attributes is shown in Figure 5.3.

The code for the revised vehicle classes is given in Listings 5.28 through 5.36.

Listing 5.28   Revised class VEHICLE

```
deferred class VEHICLE

  feature
    weight, speed  : REAL;
    color          : STRING;

    setWeight( aWeight : REAL ) is
    do
```

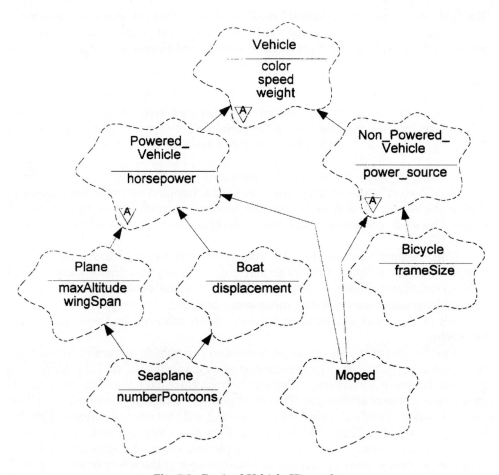

Fig. 5.3 Revised Vehicle Hierarchy

```
    weight := aWeight;
end; -- setWeight

setSpeed( aSpeed : REAL ) is
do
    speed := aSpeed;
end; -- setSpeed

setColor( aColor : STRING ) is
do
    color := deep_clone( aColor );
end; -- setColor

display is
deferred
end;

end -- VEHICLE
```

Listing 5.29   Class POWERED_VEHICLE

```
deferred class POWERED_VEHICLE
 inherit
    VEHICLE -- deferred routine display inherited from VEHICLE
 feature
    horsepower : INTEGER;

    setHorsepower( hpower : INTEGER ) is
     do
         horsepower := hpower;
     end; -- setHorsepower
end -- POWERED_VEHICLE
```

Listing 5.30   Class NON_POWERED_VEHICLE

```
deferred class NON_POWERED_VEHICLE

 inherit
    VEHICLE -- deferred routine display inherited from VEHICLE

 feature
    power_source : STRING;

    setPowersource( source : STRING ) is
    do
       power_source := deep_clone( source );
    end; -- setPowersource

end -- NON_POWERED_VEHICLE
```

Listing 5.31   Revised class PLANE

```
class PLANE

 inherit
    POWERED_VEHICLE
        rename
           speed as max_air_speed
        end;

 creation
    make_plane
 feature
    wingSpan, maxAltitude : REAL;

    make_plane( aWeight : REAL; aSpeed : REAL; aColor :
      STRING; wSpan : REAL; mAltitude : REAL; hpower :
      INTEGER ) is
    do
```

```
                setWeight( aWeight );
                setSpeed( aSpeed );
                setColor( aColor );
                setWingSpan( wSpan );
                setMaxAltitude( mAltitude );
                setHorsepower( hpower );
            end; -- make_plane

            setWingSpan( wSpan : REAL ) is
            do
                wingSpan := wSpan;
            end; -- setWingSpan

            setMaxAltitude( mAltitude : REAL ) is
            do
                maxAltitude := mAltitude;
            end; -- setMaxAltitude

            display is
            do
                io.putstring( "Weight : " );
                io.putreal( weight ); io.new_line;
                io.putstring( "Max air speed : " );
                io.putreal( max_air_speed ); io.new_line;
                io.putstring( "Color : " );
                io.putstring( color ); io.new_line;
                io.putstring( "Wing span : " );
                io.putreal( wingSpan );
                io.new_line;
                io.putstring( "Maximum altitude : " );
                io.putreal( maxAltitude );
                io.new_line;
                io.putstring( "Horsepower : " );
                io.putint( horsepower );
                io.new_line;
            end; -- display

    end -- PLANE
```

Listing 5.32   Revised class BOAT

```
    class BOAT

    inherit
        POWERED_VEHICLE
            rename
                speed as max_water_speed
            end;

    creation
        make_boat

    feature
        displacement : INTEGER;
```

```
    make_boat( aWeight : REAL; aSpeed : REAL; aColor :
      STRING; aDisplacement : INTEGER; hpower : INTEGER )is
do
      setWeight( aWeight );
      setSpeed( aSpeed );
      setColor( aColor );
      setDisplacement( aDisplacement );
      setHorsepower( hpower );
    end; -- make_boat

    setDisplacement( aDisplacement : INTEGER ) is
    do
        displacement := aDisplacement;
    end; -- setDisplacement

    display is
    do
        io.putstring( "Weight : " );
        io.putreal( weight ); io.new_line;
        io.putstring( "Max water speed : " );
        io.putreal( max_water_speed );
        io.new_line;
        io.putstring( "Color : " );
        io.putstring( color );
        io.new_line;
        io.putstring( "Displacement : " );
        io.putint( displacement );
        io.new_line;
        io.putstring( "Horsepower : " );
        io.putint( horsepower );
        io.new_line;
    end; -- display

end -- BOAT
```

Listing 5.33   Revised class SEAPLANE

```
class SEAPLANE

  inherit
    PLANE
        undefine
            display
        select
            horsepower, max_air_speed
        end;

    BOAT
        rename
            horsepower as boat_horsepower
        export
            { NONE } boat_horsepower
        undefine
```

```
            display
        end;

creation
   make_seaplane

feature
    numberPontoons : INTEGER;

    make_seaplane ( aWeight : REAL; airSpeed : REAL;
                    waterSpeed : REAL; aColor : STRING; wSpan :
                    REAL; mAltitude : REAL; nPontoons : INTEGER;
                    displace : INTEGER; hpower : INTEGER ) is
    do
        setWeight( aWeight );
        max_air_speed := airSpeed;
        max_water_speed := waterSpeed;
        setColor( aColor );
        setWingSpan( wSpan );
        setMaxAltitude( mAltitude );
        setNumberPontoons( nPontoons );
        setDisplacement( displace );
        horsepower := hpower;
    end; -- make_seaplane

    setNumberPontoons( nPontoons : INTEGER ) is
    do
        numberPontoons := nPontoons;
    end; -- setNumberPontoons

    display is
    do
        io.putstring( "Weight : " ); io.putreal( weight );
        io.new_line;
        io.putstring( "Max air speed : " ); io.putreal(
          max_air_speed );
        io.new_line;
        io.putstring( "Max water speed : " ); io.putreal(
          max_water_speed );
        io.new_line;
        io.putstring( "Color : " ); io.putstring( color );
        io.new_line;
        io.putstring( "Wing span : " ); io.putreal( wingSpan
          );
        io.new_line;
        io.putstring( "Max altitude : " ); io.putreal(
          maxAltitude );
        io.new_line;
        io.putstring( "Pontoons : " ); io.putint( numberPon
          toons );
        io.new_line;
        io.putstring( "Displacement : " ); io.putint(
          displacement );
        io.new_line;
```

```
            io.putstring( "Horsepower : " ); io.putint(
              horsepower );
            io.new_line;
        end; -- display

    end -- SEAPLANE
```

Listing 5.34   Class BICYCLE

```
class BICYCLE

 inherit
   NON_POWERED_VEHICLE

 creation
   make_bicycle

 feature
    frameSize : INTEGER;

    make_bicycle( aWeight : REAL; aSpeed : REAL; aColor :
      STRING; frame : INTEGER; source : STRING ) is
    do
       setWeight( aWeight );
       setSpeed ( aSpeed );
       setColor( aColor );
       setFrameSize( frame );
       setPowersource( source );
    end; -- make_bicycle

    setFrameSize( frame : INTEGER ) is
    do
       frameSize := frame;
    end; -- setFrameSize

    display is
    do
       io.putstring( "Weight : " );
       io.putreal( weight ); io.new_line;
       io.putstring( "Speed : " );
       io.putreal( speed );
       io.new_line;
       io.putstring( "Color : " );
       io.putstring( color );
       io.new_line;
       io.putstring( "Frame size : " );
       io.putint( frameSize );
       io.new_line;
       io.putstring( "Power source : " );
       io.putstring( power_source );
       io.new_line;
    end; -- display
```

```
    end -- BICYCLE
```

Listing 5.35   Class MOPED

```
class MOPED

  inherit
    POWERED_VEHICLE;
    NON_POWERED_VEHICLE

  creation
    make_moped

  feature

    make_moped( aWeight : REAL; aSpeed : REAL; aColor : STRING;
                hpower : INTEGER; source : STRING ) is
    do
        setWeight( aWeight );
        setSpeed( aSpeed );
        setColor( aColor );
        setHorsepower( hpower );
        setPowersource( source );
    end; -- make_moped

    display is
    do
        io.putstring( "Weight : " );
        io.putreal( weight ); io.new_line;
        io.putstring( "Speed : " );
        io.putreal( speed );
        io.new_line;
        io.putstring( "Color : " );
        io.putstring( color );
        io.new_line;
        io.putstring( "Horsepower : " );
        io.putint( horsepower );
        io.new_line;
        io.putstring( "Power source : " );
        io.putstring( power_source );
        io.new_line;
    end; -- display
  end -- MOPED
```

Listing 5.36   Test class to exercise vehicles

```
class TEST

  creation
    start

  feature

    start is
```

```
          local
              mySeaPlane  : SEAPLANE;
              myBicycle   : BICYCLE;
              myMoped     : MOPED;
          do
              io.putstring( "Seaplane" ); io.new_line;
              !!mySeaPlane.make_seaplane( 42000.0, 250, 25, "Grey",
                  40, 6000, 4, 100000, 4000 );
              mySeaPlane.display;
              io.new_line;
              io.putstring( "Bicycle" );
              io.new_line;
              !!myBicycle.make_bicycle( 25, 30, "Red", 26,
                  "Foot power" );
              myBicycle.display;
              io.new_line;
              !!myMoped.make_moped( 175, 50, "Black", 3,
                  "Foot power" );
              io.putstring( "Moped" ); io.new_line;
              myMoped.display;
              io.new_line;
          end; -- start

      end -- TEST
```

The program output is:

```
Seaplane
Weight : 42000
Max air speed : 250
Max water speed : 25
Color : Grey
Wing span : 40
Max altitude : 6000
Pontoons : 4
Displacement : 100000
Horsepower : 4000

Bicycle
Weight : 25
Speed : 30
Color : Red
Frame size : 26
Power source : Foot power

Moped
Weight : 175
Speed : 50
Color : Black
Horsepower : 3
Power source : Foot power
```

The VEHICLE class is now a deferred class because routine *display* is deferred. Class POWERED_VEHICLE inherits from VEHICLE and introduces the additional attribute *horsepower* and routine *setHorsepower*. It is a deferred class because it does not make the *display* routine "effective." Class NON_POW-ERED_VEHICLE inherits from VEHICLE and introduces the attribute *power_source* and the routine *setPowersource*. It is a deferred class because it also does not make the *display* routine "effective."

Class PLANE inherits from POWERED_VEHICLE. As before, it renames the VEHICLE attribute *speed* as *max_air_speed*. Class PLANE redeclares routine *display* and makes it "effective." Class BOAT, as before, renames *speed* (from VEHICLE) as *max-water_speed*. It also redeclares routine *display* and makes it "effective."

CLASS SEAPLANE inherits from PLANE and BOAT. From PLANE it "undefines" *display* and "selects" *horsepower* and *max_air_apeed*. From BOAT it renames *horsepower* as *boat_horsepower*, as before, exports *boat_horsepower* to NONE and "undefines" display.

The reason for using "undefine" in sub-sections of the PLANE and BOAT inheritance clauses is that this allows a fresh definition of *display* to be defined in class SEAPLANE. The effect of each "undefine" is to make the inherited routine act as if it were deferred in the two parent classes.

Class BICYCLE "single inherits" from class NON_POWERED_VEHICLE and is straightforward.

Class MOPED "multiply inherits" from POWERED_VEHICLE and NON_POW-ERED_VEHICLE. Because no features of class VEHICLE are redeclared above class MOPED, only a single copy of each of the attributes of class VEHICLE are transmitted to class MOPED.

The test routine, *start*, in class TEST declares three objects — *mySeaPlane*, *myBicycle* and *myMoped*, initializes the three objects and displays them. The predictable output is shown below Listing 5.36.

5.8.2   Rules for Repeated Inheritance, Expanded Classes and a Little Language Law

A fundamental rule that governs repeated inheritance is given below.

Suppose that class GRANDCHILD is a subclass of classes PARENT1 and PARENT2. Each of these two classes is a subclass of GRANDPARENT. From this GRANDPARENT class, the features $f_1, ..., f_n$ are inherited.

Any subset of the features $f_1, ..., f_n$ inherited by GRANDCHILD and under the same final name produce a single feature in GRANDCHILD; and

* Any two of the features $f_1, ..., f_n$ inherited under a different name produce two features in GRANDCHILD.

The situation indicated by the first bullet is called "sharing" of features. The situation indicated by the second bullet is called "replication" of features.

Fortunately, Eiffel, unlike some other currently popular object-oriented languages, generally does not require an advanced degree in language law to understand its inheritance facilities. Most of Eiffel's rules and syntax are straightforward. But, a tricky and highly unusual situation can arise if one mixes generic derivation with repeated inheritance. The reader in fact may wish to skip over this rather perverse example upon first reading.

5.8.2.1 Generic Derivation and Repeated Inheritance — A Potential Problem This example is a slightly modified version of an example given in *Eiffel: The Language,* by Bertrand Meyer, page 184. The problem is presented in Listing 5.37.

Listing 5.37   Illustration of conflicting generic derivations — System will not compile

```
class GENERIC_GRANDPARENT[ T ]
 feature

    aRoutine( p : T ) is
    do
       -- Body of routine
    end; -- aRoutine

end -- GENERIC_GRANDPARENT

class PARENT1

 inherit
    GENERIC_GRANDPARENT[ NUMERIC ]

end -- PARENT1

class PARENT2

 inherit
    GENERIC_GRANDPARENT[ STRING ]

end -- PARENT2

class GRANDCHILD

 INHERIT
    PARENT1;
    PARENT2

end -- GRANDCHILD
```

The problem arises in Listing 5.37 because *aRoutine* has a generic parameter of type T. The signature of the inherited *aRoutine* in class PARENT1 is *aRoutine(p : NUMERIC)*, whereas the signature of *aRoutine* in class PARENT2 is *aRoutine(p : STRING)*. Because the signatures are different, a conflict occurs in class GRANDCHILD.

Suppose we try to resolve the conflict by "undefining" *aRoutine* from PARENT1 and PARENT2 and then "redefining" *aRoutine* in class GRANDCHILD. The difficulty results from the fact that the signature of *aRoutine* in class GRANDCHILD must conform to the signatures of *aRoutine* in PARENT1 and PARENT2. Clearly, the only actual parameter that conforms to both NUMERIC and STRING is NONE. This is not very useful!

Therefore, we are truly confounded by this aberration resulting from a repeated inheritance of classes that contain a routine with a generic parameter.

5.8.2.2 Repeated Inheritance Consistency Constraint   We have seen that the sharing of one or more features must not cause any ambiguity. We also have seen that in the case of replication of one or more features, a "select" sub-section must remove any ambiguity arising from attribute replication or conflicting redeclaration. Such ambiguity can arise during dynamic binding.

The repeated inheritance consistency constraint is the following:

A grandchild class in a repeated inheritance structure is valid if and only if the following two conditions hold for *every* feature *f* of the grandparent class:

- If feature *f* is shared in the grandchild class, all the inherited versions of feature *f* are the same feature; and
- If feature *f* is replicated in the grandchild class, and *f* is potentially ambiguous under dynamic-binding, a *select* subclause in exactly one of the inheritance clauses of the grandchild class lists the corresponding version of *f* under its final name in the grandchild class.

5.8.2.3 Inheritance of Expanded Classes   An expanded class may have heirs that are non-expanded or expanded and a non-expanded (normal) class may have heirs that are expanded (and of course non-expanded). In other words, the expansion status of a class has no effect on the rules of inheritance.

5.9   "MIX-INS" OR CODE INHERITANCE AND THE INHERITANCE RELATIONSHIP

In object-oriented software design, it is important that a subclass satisfy the "is a" or "is a kind of" relationship with its parent(s). For example, a *car* is a "kind of" *vehicle*. A *seaplane* is a "kind of" *plane* and a "kind of" *boat*.

As indicated at the beginning of this chapter, if a subclass does not redefine any of its parent's features, it may be considered an extension of its parent. Its behavior is the sum of the behavior of its parent plus the behavior unique to the subclass. It is illogical, from a design perspective, for a subclass to violate this important inheritance relationship. Despite this, it is an accepted practice among some programmers to violate this principle when using the concept of a "mix-in" (a LISP term) or code inheritance.

When a subclass uses a "mix-in," it inherits from one or more parent classes in order to be able to use some features of the inherited classes. As an example, suppose the class SIMULATION requires access to the routines *sine* and *cosine*. The class inherits from class DOUBLE_MATH. By doing this, the body of the routines in class SIMULATION gain direct access to the features of class DOUBLE_MATH. For example, if it is necessary to compute *100 * cosine(x)*, where *x* is an instance of class DOUBLE_MATH, and return the result to *value*, such a routine may include the statement: *value := 100.0 * cosine(x)*. The *cosine* function, because of the "mix-in" and the rules of Eiffel inheritance, is directly accessible in class SIMULATION. Code inheritance has been effectively utilized, but ... at the expense of the "is a" relationship. An instance of class SIMULATION is certainly not a "kind of" DOUBLE_MATH. The proper relationship between SIMULATION and DOUBLE_MATH is a "uses" relationship. That is, class SIMULATION "uses" class DOUBLE_MATH.

Unfortunately, (at least in this author's view) Eiffel 3 does not have a "uses" clause. But such a "uses" relationship can be simulated using the very rich inheritance constructs that have been presented earlier in this chapter. This is illustrated with an example. Listing 5.38 presents the details of class MIXIN. This class simulates a "uses" relationship by using:

```
inherit
    DOUBLE_MATH
        export { NONE } all
```

The inheritance subclause, *export { NONE } all*, assures that none of the features of class DOUBLE_MATH are available to any client of class MIXIN. The code inheritance of class DOUBLE_MATH does extend to the descendants of class MIXIN. That is, routines in descendant classes can access the features of DOUBLE_MATH directly. But clients of these descendant classes cannot access the features of DOUBLE_MATH.

Listing 5.38   Class MIXIN

```
class MIXIN

  -- simulates "uses" DOUBLE_MATH
  inherit
    DOUBLE_MATH
        export
            { NONE } all
        end;
  feature
     compute( argument : DOUBLE ) : DOUBLE is
     do
        Result := 100.0 * cosine( argument );
     end; -- compute
end -- MIXIN
```

Listing 5.39 presents the details of a subclass MY_MIXIN. The routines of this subclass can access the features of DOUBLE_MATH directly. The "uses" relationship, as presently simulated, propagates into all descendant classes.

Listing 5.39   Class MY_MIXIN

```
class MY_MIXIN
  inherit
     MIXIN
  feature
     compute2( argument : DOUBLE ) : DOUBLE is
     do
```

```
        Result := 100.0 * sine( argument );
      end; -- compute2
  end -- MY_MIXIN
```

Finally, Listing 5.40 presents the code of a test program that exercises routines *compute* and *compute2* from classes MIXIN and MY_MIXIN, respectively.

Listing 5.40   Class APPLICATION — Exercises MIXIN and MY_MIXIN

```
class APPLICATION

  creation
    start

  feature

    start is
     local
        myObject : MIXIN;
        object2  : MY_MIXIN;
     do
        !!myObject;
        io.putstring( "myObject.compute = " );
        io.putdouble( myObject.compute( 0.0 ) );
        io.new_line;
        !!object2;
        io.putstring( "object2.compute2 = " );
        io.putdouble( object2.compute2( 0.0 ) );
        io.new_line;
      end; -- start

  end -- APPLICATION
```

Although a "uses" relationship has been simulated using *inherit* DOUBLE_MATH *export { NONE } all*, the "is a" relationship in class MIXIN of Listing 5.38 is violated. One way to avoid the violation of this important principle, and avoid the mix-in, is shown in Listing 5.41.

Listing 5.41   Revised class MIXIN

```
class MIXIN
  creation { NONE }
    make

  feature { NONE }
    math_object : DOUBLE_MATH;

  feature
    make is
    do
        !!math_object;
    end; -- make

    compute( argument : DOUBLE ) : DOUBLE is
```

```
   do
      Result := 100.0 * math_object.cosine( argument );
   end; -- compute

end -- MIXIN
```

Class MIXIN has an attribute *math_object*. This object is used to access the features of class DOUBLE_MATH. In the creation routine of class MIXIN, the *math_object* is brought to life. In routine *compute*, the *cosine* routine is accessed through *math_object*.

Listing 5.42 shows the revised class MY_MIXIN.

Listing 5.42   Revised class MY_MIXIN

```
class MY_MIXIN

  inherit
     MIXIN

  creation
     make -- Inherited from class MIXIN

  feature

     compute2( argument : DOUBLE ) : DOUBLE is
     do
        Result := 100.0 * math_object.sine( argument );
     end; -- compute2

end -- MY_MIXIN
```

The attribute *math_object* and the routine *make* are inherited and accessible in class MY_MIXIN. This attribute is again used to access the features of DOUBLE_MATH.

An even better approach, suggested by Richard Bielak, is to declare *math_object* as follows (in class MIXIN): *math_object : expanded DOUBLE_MATH*. Using this approach, the creation routines of classes MIXIN and MY_MIXIN can be eliminated because a *math_object* will automatically be initialized.

So in summary, if the programmer wishes to be able to access the DOUBLE_MATH routines *sine* and *cosine* directly in class MIX-IN, the "is a" relationship must be violated by using the "mix-in," DOUBLE_MATH. If the programmer desires to preserve the "is a" relationship and avoid a "mixin", an attribute of type DOUBLE_MATH is defined in the class and all access to *sine* and *cosine* is obtained through this attribute. If Eiffel had a "uses" clause, both compromises could be avoided. Class MIXIN would simply "use" class DOUBLE_MATH.

5.10 ITERATORS — AN APPLICATION OF INHERITANCE

Note: The inspiration for this section comes from the paper "Collections and Iterators in Eiffel," scheduled to be published in the *Journal of Object-Oriented*

Programming (JOOP) by Miguel Katrib and Ismael Martinez from the University of Havana, Cuba.

Iteration is a process that allows one to traverse through all of the elements of some collection class such as a list or a tree. Typically, while traversing a collection, some action is taken on each element of the collection.

Many of the collection classes in the Eiffel libraries support iteration. In Listing 5.43, a test class TEST is shown that shows a typical iteration through an instance of library class LINKED_LIST.

Listing 5.43   Class TEST — Iteration through a linked list

```
class TEST

 creation
    start

feature
    myList : LINKED_LIST[ INTEGER ];

    start is
    do
        !!myList.make;
        myList.put_front( 5 );
        myList.put_front( 10 );
        myList.put_front( 15 );
        io.putstring( "The sum of elements in myList = " );
        io.putint( sum );
        io.new_line;
    end; -- start

    sum : INTEGER is
    do
        from myList.start
        until myList.off
        loop
            Result := Result + myList.item;
            myList.forth;
        end;
    end; -- sum

 end -- TEST
```

Routine *sum* in Listing 5.43 directly manipulates *myList*, an instance of class LINKED_LIST with actual parameter INTEGER. Specifically, the events *start*, *off*, *item* and *forth* are sent to the object *myList*. As Katrib and Martinez point out using a similar example, the client is responsible for using the correct ordering of *start*, *off*, *item* and *forth*. Katrib and Martinez suggest that the supplier should take charge of these details and unburden the client from having to know the precise ordering of the iteration functions.

Listing 5.44 presents a deferred class, LINKED_LIST_ITERATOR, that automates the iteration process in a routine named *for_each*. This is the name used by Katrib and Martinez in their JOOP paper.

Listing 5.44   Deferred class **LINKED_LIST_ITERATOR**

```
deferred class LINKED_LIST_ITERATOR[ T ]

 feature
   list : LINKED_LIST[ T ];

   act_on( value : T ) is
   deferred
   end; -- act_on

   for_each is
   do
       from list.start
       until list.off
       loop
           act_on( list.item );
           list.forth;
       end;
   end; -- for_each

end -- LINKED_LIST_ITERATOR
```

The routine *for_each* performs some action on each element of the list.

In order for a client to use the iteration routine *for_each*, the client must create a subclass of LINKED_LIST_ITERATOR. Listing 5.45 presents such an example.

Listing 5.45   Class **MY_LIST_ITERATOR**

```
class MY_LIST_ITERATOR
inherit
    LINKED_LIST_ITERATOR[ INTEGER ]
 creation { APPLICATION }
    make
 feature { APPLICATION }
    sum : INTEGER;

    make( aList : LINKED_LIST[ INTEGER ] ) is
    do
        list := aList;
    end; -- make

   act_on( value : INTEGER ) is
   do
       sum := sum + value;
   end; -- act_on

end -- MY_LIST_ITERATOR
```

Class MY_LIST_ITERATOR defines an attribute *sum* to replace the function that was used in the previous application. The routine *act_on* processes each element of the list by adding the *item* to the previous sum of the items.

Listing 5.46 presents the completed application class, APPLICATION.

Listing 5.46   Class APPLICATION

```
class APPLICATION

creation
  start

feature { NONE }
  myList : LINKED_LIST[ INTEGER ];
  iter   : MY_LIST_ITERATOR;

feature

    start is
    do
        !!myList.make;
        myList.put_front( 5 );
        myList.put_front( 10 );
        myList.put_front( 15 );
        !!iter.make( myList );
        iter.for_each;
        io.putstring( "The sum of elements in myList = " );
        io.putint( iter.sum );
        io.new_line;
    end; -- start
end -- APPLICATION
```

The *start* routine of class APPLICATION in Listing 5.46 creates an object of class MY_LIST_ITERATOR, *iter*. It sends the parameter *myList* into the *make* routine of this class. It then invokes the routine *for_each* through the object *iter*. The client has indeed been unburdened from having to deal with the low-level details of iteration. These low-level details are embedded in the abstract class LINKED_LIST_ITERATOR.

The abstract (deferred) class LINKED_LIST_ITERATOR of Listing 5.44 is too restrictive. It is only applicable when one wishes to perform an iteration on an instance of LINKED_LIST. Listing 5.47 presents a more general abstract iteration class named ITERATION. This class has an attribute *iteration_type* of type SEQUENTIAL[T]. Class SEQUENTIAL defines the protocol for *start, off, item* and *forth*.

In class ITERATION, the *make* routine is not defined as a creation routine because a deferred class cannot have a creation routine. Subclasses of ITERATION inherit routine *make* and declare it to be a creation routine.

Listing 5.47   Class ITERATION

```
deferred class ITERATION[ T ]
```

```
feature
    iteration_type : SEQUENTIAL[ T ];

    make( iterate_on : SEQUENTIAL[ T ] ) is
    do
        iteration_type := iterate_on;
    end; -- make

    act_on( value : T ) is
    deferred
    end; -- act_on

    for_each is
    do
        from iteration_type.start
        until iteration_type.off
        loop
            act_on( iteration_type.item );
            iteration_type.forth;
        end;
    end; -- for_each

end -- ITERATION
```

The required sequence associated with the relatively low-level routines *start*, *off*, *item* and *forth* is hidden in the abstract class ITERATION. The client must define the action to be taken for each element of the collection that is being traversed.

The example presented in this section demonstrates the importance and power of inheritance and composition. Class ITERATION of Listing 5.47 "is composed of" an *iteration_type* attribute of type SEQUENTIAL[T]. The inheritance relationship allows this abstract class to spawn actual iteration subclasses that are customized to perform the actions desired by a client class.

5.11 CONCLUSIONS

- Inheritance is used during object-oriented analysis and design for establishing a hierarchical decomposition of a software system into classes and subclasses;
- The accepted practice is for classes at the top of an inheritance hierarchy to encapsulate general properties of some domain and for classes lower in the hierarchy to extend and encapsulate more specialized properties of the domain;
- *Specialization* involves redefining one or more of the routines of a parent class;
- *Extension* involves adding routines not present in a parent;
- *Restriction* involves blocking one or more routines of a parent;

- In object-oriented software design, it is important that a subclass satisfy the "is a" or "is a kind of" relationship with its parent(s); and
- An "inherit" clause may contain one or more sub-sections. If more than one sub-section is specified, the order of specification is important. The following optional sub-sections for a class are allowed and must be given in the order shown:

```
inherit
    PARENT
        rename
            --Discussed in section 5.5
        export
            -- Discussed in section 5.6.
        undefine
            -- Discussed in section 5.7.
        redefine
            -- Discussed in section 5.3
        select
            -- Discussed in section 5.5
    end;
```

- Both attributes and routines may be *redefined* in an Eiffel subclass;
- Redefined features must be of a type that *conform* to the type in the parent class;
- The signature of a redefined feature must conform to the inherited feature (this implies that the parameters and return value must conform if the inherited feature is a routine and the attribute must conform if the inherited feature is an attribute);
- A function with no parameters can be redefined as an attribute whose type conforms to the return type of the function;
- The consequence of a feature redefinition is that all client classes as well as descendant classes will refer to the redefined feature and not the original feature;
- Renaming an inherited feature allows a child class, all its descendant, and all of its clients to access a feature of the parent class using a name that the designer of the subclass believes is more suitable for the intended purpose of the subclass than the feature name given by the author of the parent class;
- When a child class inherits from a parent class, the export status of the features of the parent class remain intact in the child class unless an "export" sub-section appears in an inheritance clause;
- The "undefine" sub-section of an inheritance clause allows a child class to declare one or more effective features inherited from its parent as deferred;
- *Repeated inheritance* is a special, fairly common and important pattern of

multiple inheritance in which two or more ancestors of a class have a common parent; and

- When one or more attributes are inherited through repeated inheritance, and no grandparent features have been redefined, undefined or renamed, only one copy of the grandparent attribute occurs in the grandchild class.

Polymorphism and Conformance

6.1 POLYMORPHISM AND OBJECT-ORIENTED PROGRAMMING

*P*olymorphism, introduced briefly in section 2.7, is based on the principle that when a routine is invoked through an object, the behavior displayed by the object is based on the actual dynamic type of the object receiving the message, not the static specification of the object type, provided that the actual type conforms to the static specification. A class is said to *conform* to another class if it is the same type as the other class or is a proper descendant of the other class. Thus, it is clear that polymorphism, in the sense just defined, is associated with inheritance. Without inheritance there is no conformance, except in the most trivial sense. Without conformance, there is no polymorphism.

Polymorphism is associated with late-binding (dynamic-binding). When a routine is invoked through an object in an expression such as *anObject.aRoutine*, there may be several possible definitions (methods) for *aRoutine* to bind to. In terms of semantics, it is at run-time that the routine call (message) *aRoutine* is bound to the appropriate method *aRoutine* (the function definition). This soft binding provides a system with great resilience and flexibility.

An Eiffel compiler, during its optimization phase, may occasionally perform early binding of messages to methods if there is no ambiguity regarding the method that is associated with a message (for example there are no subclasses of a given class). This does not affect the semantics of late-binding. An Eiffel programmer should always assume late-binding as a consistent way of thinking about and designing a system.

There is a basic conflict between the requirements of static type checking and dynamic-binding. Static type checking ensures that every object receives legal messages with legal parameters — that is, messages that it can respond to with actual parameters that conform to the formally specified parameters. Dynamic-binding allows a message to be bound to an object after compile/link time — that is, at run-time.

The apparent conflict between static type checking and dynamic-binding when a message is sent to an object is resolved by requiring the compiler to verify that there exists at least one effective routine that can potentially serve as the method that implements the message. This method must be defined in a class that conforms to the static class type of the object receiving the message. If no such effective routine can be found, the compiler flags the offending expression as an error. If several methods can potentially serve as the implementation of the message, the compiler does not attempt to choose a particular method. This is done at run-time when the actual type of the object can be determined.

Listing 6.1 illustrates the concept of late-binding.

**Listing 6.1   Classes that illustrate late-binding and polymorphism
              Note: Each class is defined in a separate file**

```
deferred class FRUIT

  feature
     name : STRING;
     color : STRING;

     set_name( a_name : STRING ) is
     do
         name := a_name.clone( a_name );
     end; -- set_name

     set_color( a_color : STRING ) is
     do
         color := a_color.clone( a_color );
     end; -- set_name

     display is
     deferred
     end; -- display

end -- FRUIT

class APPLE
  inherit
     FRUIT

  feature
     tartness : INTEGER;

     set_tartness( value : INTEGER ) is
     do
```

```
        tartness := value;
    end; -- set_tartness

    display is
    do
        io.putstring( "Name: " );
        io.putstring( name ); io.new_line;
        io.putstring( "Color: " );
        io.putstring( color ); io.new_line;
        io.putstring( "Tartness: " );
        io.putint( tartness ); io.new_line;
    end; -- display

end -- APPLE

-- Code for class PEAR and GRAPE are similiar to APPLE

class APPLICATION
 creation
    start

 feature

    start is
    local
        basket   : ARRAY[ FRUIT ];
        index    : INTEGER;
        anApple  : APPLE;
        aPear    : PEAR;
        aGrape   : GRAPE;
    do
      -- Initialize objects
      !!basket.make( 1, 3 );
      !!anApple;
      anApple.set_name( "Granny Smith Apple" );
      anApple.set_color( "Green" );
      anApple.set_tartness( 7 );
      !!aPear;
      aPear.set_name( "Bartlett Pear" );
      aPear.set_color( "Yellow" );
      aPear.set_ripeness( 3 );
      !!aGrape;
      aGrape.set_name( "Concord Grape" );
      aGrape.set_color( "Purple" );
      aGrape.set_diameter( 2 );
      -- Fill basket with fruit
      basket.put( anApple, 1 );
      basket.put( aPear, 2 );
      basket.put( aGrape, 3 );
      -- Display the fruit
      from index := 0
      until index = 3
      loop
          index := index + 1;
          basket.item( index ).display;
```

```
        end;
      end; -- start

end -- APPLICATION
```

The program output is:

```
Name: Granny Smith Apple
Color: Green
Tartness: 7
Name: Bartlett Pear
Color: Yellow
Ripeness: 3
Name: Concord Grape
Color: Purple
Diameter: 2
```

In Listing 6.1, as fruit objects are accessed from the array, each object responds to the *display* message in its own unique way. The system dynamically determines which of the three *display* routines to use. If a new fruit type were added and a new *display* routine defined, the basic structure of the application program would not have to be modified.

Late-binding and polymorphism leads to a decentralized computational architecture in which each object, at least semantically, becomes its own computing engine. Each object responds to its messages according to the protocol given in its class description. Polymorphism allows the designer to focus on defining the behaviors of each class and not be concerned about selecting the appropriate behaviors when objects receive messages.

Another major application of polymorphism is in the construction of abstract classes. This was done at the end of Chapter 5 in constructing class ITERATION in Listing 5.47. Portions of this class are reproduced in Listing 6.2.

Listing 6.2   Portions of Listing 5.47 — Class ITERATION

```
    deferred class ITERATION[ T ]

    feature
      iteration_type : SEQUENTIAL[ T ];

      -- See Listing 5.47 for missing features

      for_each is
      do
        from iteration_type.start
        until iteration_type.off
        loop
          action( iteration_type.item );
          iteration_type.forth;
        end;
      end; -- for_each

end -- ITERATION
```

In deferred (abstract) class ITERATION, the *iteration_type* is declared to be of type SEQUENTIAL[T]. This allows routine *for_each* to invoke the routines (send the messages) *start*, *off*, *item* and *forth* to attribute *iteration_type* (these methods are available in class SEQUENTIAL). In actuality, *iteration_type* will be an instance of a descendant and, therefore, conforming subclass. You may recall that in Chapter 5, *iteration_type* was initialized to LINKED_LIST.

When the message *for_each* is invoked on an instance of class LIST1_ITERATOR (see section 5.10), the methods *start*, *off*, *item* and *forth*, as available in LINKED_LIST, are invoked on the LINKED_LIST instance. The key idea here is that late-binding and polymorphism guarantee that the correct implementation of these four routines will be bound, at run-time, to the *iteration_type*. The supplier routine, *for_each*, establishes the correct sequence of operations. Each client class is unburdened from having to deal with this low-level issue.

6.2 CONFORMANCE

The rules of conformance in Eiffel determine when a type may be used in place of another type. Since these important rules sit at the heart of the Eiffel type system and are central to the application of polymorphism, this section presents the technical details associated with conformance.

We first consider the problem of the simple assignment of one object to another: $a := b$. This assignment is valid only if the type of b conforms to the type of a. If the type of a is expanded, then the type of b can only be the same as the type of a or its base type.

Conformance plays a central role in determining the validity of many operations in Eiffel. The following operations are valid only if the type of b conforms to the type of a:

- The assignment $a := b$
- Invoking a routine *aRoutine(...., b, ...)*, where a is the formal parameter in the same position as b;
- The creation instruction *!BB!a* that creates an instance of b's type and attaches a to it (*BB* is the assumed name of the type of b);
- The redefinition of a as being of type *BB* in a proper descendant, where a is an attribute, a function or a routine argument;
- The replacement of a *C[..., BB, ..]* when the formal constrained generic parameter is *C[..., T -> AA, ...]* (*AA* is the assumed name of the type of a); and
- The reverse assignment attempt *b ?= a*.

6.2.1 Conformance of Signatures

A signature contains the full type information of a feature. If the feature is a routine, the signature specifies the order and type of its parameters, and its return type. The signature of feature b is said to conform to the signature of a only if:

- The signature of b contains the same number of elements as the signature of a; and
- Every type in the signature of b conforms to the corresponding type in the signature of a (this implies that the result type of b conforms to the result type of a, if any).

6.2.2   Conformance to a Non-generic Type

- If b is of type BB and a is of type AA, then BB conforms directly to AA if and only if the inheritance clause of BB lists AA as one of its parents.

6.2.3   Conformance to a Generic Type

- If a is an instance of class $AA[\ A1,\ A2,\ ...,\ A_n\ ]$, and b is an instance of $BB[\ B1,\ B2,\ ...,\ B_n\ ]$, then b conforms to a if and only if B_i conforms to A_i for values of i from 1 to n;
- A parent of b conforms to a; and
- a and b are of the same type.

6.2.4   Arithmetic Operators and the "Balancing Rule"

The expression 1.5 + 2 may be interpreted as meaning, "Send the message '+' to the REAL object 1.5 with the parameter 2." On the other hand, the expression 2 + 1.5 may be interpreted as meaning, "Send the message '+' to the INTEGER object 2 with the parameter 1.5. This does not make sense since in class INTEGER, the signature of operator "+" is: *infix "+" (other : INTEGER) : INTEGER is* ... Yet our programming experience and mathematical training require us to interpret 2 + 1.5 as adding the integer 2 to the real number 1.5 (converting 2 to a real number) and getting the real number 3.5.

The "balancing rule" may be stated as follows: In evaluating any arithmetic expression with operands of type INTEGER, REAL and DOUBLE, all operands are converted first to the "heaviest" operand in the expression. DOUBLE is heavier than REAL, and REAL is heavier than INTEGER.

6.3   AN APPLICATION OF POLYMORPHISM —THE GENERALITY OF NUMBERS

6.3.1   Background

In Eiffel, as in Smalltalk or any pure object-oriented language, a number such as 27 is an instance of a class such as INTEGER. The statement 27 + 5 can be interpreted as sending the message "+" to the object 27 with the parameter 5.

This formal interpretation is not the way we are normally accustomed to thinking about such a simple addition operation. The operation 27.5 + 5 changes things because now, at least formally, we are applying two operands of different type (objects that are instances of different classes) to the infix "+" operator (we are sending the message "+" to a REAL object with a parameter that is an INTEGER object). In Eiffel, the "balancing rule" given in the previous section causes the system to convert the INTEGER object 5 to a REAL object 5.0 before performing the addition.

What happens when other non-standard numeric types are introduced? How can objects of different numeric types be added or, in general, manipulated arithmetically? How, for example, can we add an INTEGER type to a RATIONAL type or a REAL type to a RATIONAL type, assuming that we have created a RATIONAL type through a class definition?

The original Smalltalk-80 system developed by ParcPlace systems in the 1980s dealt with this issue by developing a conceptual framework called the "generality of numbers." In this scheme, each numeric type is assigned a "generality number." When two distinct numeric types are operated on using an arithmetic operator, the number of lower "generality" is converted to an equivalent number, mathematically speaking, of higher "generality." For example, if an INTEGER type is added to a REAL type, the INTEGER type is first converted to an equivalent number of REAL type and then the operation is carried out.

We develop portions of a system of numeric classes in this section using the principle of the "generality of numbers." Although we hope you will agree that the application is interesting in its own right, it is principally motivated by the opportunity to provide a non-trivial and important illustration of polymorphism. The basic design of the system of numeric classes is dependent on polymorphic behavior. This will be our central focus in discussing the application.

6.3.2 The Application

We first define an abstract class, NUMBER. This class specifies a set of key methods whose implementation is deferred. Class NUMBER also implements the arithmetic operators (we only define the "+" operator in this limited version). The implementation is expressed in terms of the key methods that are made effective in the subclasses. Next, we define the numeric subclasses of NUMBER. These include class INTEGER_TYPE with a "generality" index equal to 10, class RATIONAL_TYPE with a generality index equal to 15, and class REAL_TYPE with generality index equal to 20. The ranking of generality number is based on the observation that any integer can be converted to an equivalent rational (but not the opposite), and any rational number can be converted to an equivalent real (but not the opposite).

Class NUMBER is shown in Listing 6.3.

Listing 6.3   Class NUMBER

```
deferred class NUMBER
-- Parent class for number subclasses
```

```
feature
    generality : INTEGER;

    display is
    deferred
    end; -- display

    coerced( aNumber : NUMBER ) : NUMBER is
    require
         generality: aNumber.generality < generality;
    deferred
    ensure
        Result.generality = generality;
     end; -- coerced

    asFloat : REAL_TYPE is
    deferred
    ensure
        Result.generality = 20;
    end; -- asFloat

    sum_like_type( aNumber : NUMBER ) : NUMBER is
    require
        generality: aNumber.generality = generality;
    deferred
    end; -- sum_like_type

    sum, infix "+" ( aNumber : NUMBER ) : NUMBER is
    do
        if generality < aNumber.generality then
            Result := aNumber + aNumber.coerced( Current );
        elseif generality > aNumber.generality then
            Result := Current + Current.coerced( aNumber );
        else
            Result := Current.sum_like_type( aNumber )
        end
    end; -- sum

end -- class NUMBER
```

We examine the code in deferred class NUMBER of Listing 6.3. The key routines (key methods) are *display*, *coerced* and *asFloat*. Their implementation details are all *deferred*.

The arithmetic operator "+" (and all the other arithmetic operators if they were present) invokes deferred routine *coerced*. In particular, let us analyze the application of "+" in computing *obj1* + *obj2* where first the "generality" number of *obj1* is less than *obj2*, and second when the generality number of *obj1* is greater than *obj2*.

In the first case, the "if" statement, *if generality < aNumber.generality,* is true so that *Result := aNumber + aNumber.coerced(Current).* Routine *coerced* converts *Current* to a mathematically equivalent value whose type matches that of *aNumber*. Then the resulting object (whose class is that of *obj2*) is added to *aNumber*. In the recursive call to "+" in the expression *Result := aNumber + aNumber.coerced(Current),* the two operands are of the same type (that of *obj2*).

The deferred key method *sum_like_type* is invoked. This routine, like all the key routines, is appropriately defined in each subclass.

In the second case (when *obj1* has a higher "generality" number than *obj2*), the expression *Result := Current + Current.coerced(aNumber)* recursively invokes the "+" operator after converting *obj2* to a mathematically equivalent value of the same type as *obj1*. Once again, the deferred routine *sum_like_type* is invoked.

If the "generality" number of both operands is initially the same, the "+" routine immediately invokes the *sum_like_type* routine and produces the appropriate answer.

Polymorphism plays a central role in this design. The design is based on the semantics of routine *coerced*. This routine converts an object of one type to an object of equivalent mathematical value and of a type given by the receiver (the object receiving the message *coerced*). There exist three distinct *coerced* routines in this cluster of classes; one in each of the subclasses INTEGER_TYPE, RATIONAL_TYPE and REAL_TYPE. The "right" choice of *coerced* routine is made at run-time based on the type of the receiver of the message. The use of polymorphism makes the code relatively easy to understand and, therefore, maintain. Without polymorphism, the code would be littered with multi-branch switch-like statements that would add enormous complexity that could only obscure the simplicity of this elegant concept.

Listing 6.4 presents the details of class INTEGER_TYPE.

Listing 6.4   Class INTEGER_TYPE

```
class INTEGER_TYPE

  inherit
    BASIC_ROUTINES -- A mixin
        export { NONE } all;
    end;

    NUMBER

  creation
    make

  feature
    value : INTEGER;

  feature

    make( aValue : INTEGER ) is
    do
       generality := 10;
       value := aValue;
    end; -- Create

    display is
    do
```

```
            io.putstring( "Integer: " );
            io.putint( value ); io.new_line;
        end; -- display

        coerced( aNumber : NUMBER ) : NUMBER is
        do
            -- This routine will never be invoked for INTEGER_TYPE
            Result := Current;
        end; -- coerced

        setValue( aValue : INTEGER ) is
        do
            value := aValue;
        end; -- setValue

        asFloat : REAL_TYPE is
        do
            !!Result.make( integer_to_real( value ) );
        end; -- asFloat

        sum_like_type( aNumber : INTEGER_TYPE ) : INTEGER_TYPE
            is
        do
            !!Result.make( value + aNumber.value );
        end; -- sum_like_type

end -- class INTEGER_TYPE
```

The implementation of all of the routines in Listing 6.4 is straightforward. Routine *coerced* must be made effective even though it will never be applied to an INTEGER_TYPE object (there are no object types with a "generality" lower than INTEGER_TYPE. If this routine were not made effective, class INTEGER_TYPE would be a deferred class. Such a class cannot have instances defined.

Class INTEGER_TYPE simulates a "uses" clause by inheriting from class BASIC_ROUTINES. It needs to use the *integer_to_real* method of this class.

Listing 6.5 presents the details of class RATIONAL_TYPE.

Listing 6.5   Class RATIONAL_TYPE

```
class RATIONAL_TYPE
-- implements rational numbers

  inherit
    BASIC_ROUTINES
        export
            { NONE } all;
        end;

    NUMBER

  creation
    make
```

```
feature { NONE }
    gcd( a, b : INTEGER ) : INTEGER is
    -- Greatest common divisor of a and b using Euclid
    -- algorithm
    require
        positive_arguments: a > 0; b > 0
    local
        x, y : INTEGER;
    do
        from
            x := a;
            y := b
        until x = y
        loop
            if x > y then
                x := x - y
            else
                y := y - x
            end;
        end;
        Result := x;
    end; -- gcd

feature
    numerator     : INTEGER;
    denominator   : INTEGER;

    make( num : INTEGER; den : INTEGER ) is
    require
        den /= 0;
    local
        greatest_common_divisor : INTEGER;
        rescued   : BOOLEAN;
    do
        generality := 15;
        if num = 0 then
            numerator := 0;
            denominator := 1;
        else
            greatest_common_divisor := gcd( abs( num ), abs(
                den ) );
            numerator := num // greatest_common_divisor;
            denominator := den // greatest_common_divisor;
        end;
    end; -- make

    display is
    do
        io.putstring( "Rational: " );
        if denominator = 1 then
            io.putint( numerator );
        else
            io.putint( numerator );
            io.putstring( " / " );
            io.putint( denominator );
        end;
```

```
        io.new_line;
    end; -- display

    coerced( aNumber : INTEGER_TYPE ) : RATIONAL_TYPE is
    do -- convert an INTEGER_TYPE to a RATIONAL_TYPE
        !!Result.make( aNumber.value, 1 );
    end; -- coerced

    asFloat : REAL_TYPE is
    do
        !!Result.make( integer_to_real( numerator ) /
        integer_to_real( denominator ) );
    end; -- asFloat

    sum_like_type( aNumber : RATIONAL_TYPE ) : RATIONAL_TYPE is
    require else
        denominator_not_zero: denominator /= 0;
            aNumber.denominator /= 0
    local
        num : INTEGER;
        den : INTEGER;
    do
        num := numerator * aNumber.denominator +
                aNumber.numerator * denominator;
        den := denominator * aNumber.denominator;
        !!Result.make( num, den );
    end; -- sum_like_type

  invariant
    denominator /= 0;

end -- class RATIONAL_TYPE
```

In Listing 6.5, the routine *gcd*, an abbreviation for greatest common divisor, is put in the protected section of the class (i.e. export to NONE). This routine uses an old algebraic algorithm, the Euclid algorithm, for computing the greatest common divisor. The reader is urged to examine its details closely.

In routine *coerced*, the formal parameter *aNumber* is declared as type INTEGER_TYPE. This is valid because this is the only logical type that has a lower "generality" number than a RATIONAL_TYPE. A new object of type RATIONAL_TYPE is returned by invoking the creation routine on *Result*.

The details of class REAL_TYPE are shown in Listing 6.6.

Listing 6.6   Class REAL_TYPE

```
class REAL_TYPE

  inherit
    NUMBER

creation
    make
```

```
feature
    value : REAL;

    make( aValue : REAL ) is
    do
        generality := 20;
        value := aValue;
    end; -- Create

    display is
    do
        io. putstring( "Float: " );
        io. putreal( value ); io.new_line;
    end; -- display

    coerced( aNumber : NUMBER ) : NUMBER is
    do -- Convert a number of lower generality to a REAL_TYPE
        !REAL_TYPE!Result.make( aNumber.asFloat.value );
    end; -- coerced

    asFloat : REAL_TYPE is
    do
        Result := Current;
    end; -- asFloat

    setValue( aValue : REAL ) is
    do
        value := aValue; -- these are expanded types
    end; -- setValue

    sum_like_type( aNumber : REAL_TYPE ) : REAL_TYPE is
    do
        !!Result.make( value + aNumber.value );
    end; -- sum_like_type

end -- class REAL_TYPE
```

In Listing 6.6, routine *coerced* returns a new object of REAL_TYPE by invoking the creation routine for REAL_TYPE and using *aNumber.asFloat.value* as a parameter. The actual type for *aNumber* might be INTEGER_TYPE or RATIONAL_TYPE. Since both of these types respond to the routine *asFloat*, the role of late-binding and polymorphism is evident again. The "right" version of *asFloat* will be bound at run-time.

Listing 6.7 shows a main driver class that exercises some of the routines of our numeric classes. The output is shown below the details of the class.

Listing 6.7   Class APPLICATION

```
class APPLICATION

creation
```

```
    start

feature
  start is
   local
       anInt      : INTEGER_TYPE;
       aReal      : REAL_TYPE;
       aRational  : RATIONAL_TYPE;
       r1, r2     : RATIONAL_TYPE;
       sum        : NUMBER;
    do
       !!anInt.make( 10 );
       !!aReal.make( 5.1 );
       !!aRational.make( 3, 4 );
       sum := anInt + aReal;
       sum.display;
       sum := aReal + anInt;
       sum.display;
       sum := anInt + aRational;
       sum.display;
       sum := aRational + anInt;
       sum.display;
       sum := aReal + aRational;
       sum.display;
       sum := aRational + aReal;
       sum.display;
       !!r1.make( 3, 2 );
       !!r2.make( 1, 2 );
       sum := r1 + r2;
       sum.display;
       r1.make( 1, 0 );
       r1.display;
       anInt.make( -1 );
       sum := anInt + aRational;
       sum.display;
    end; -- start

end -- class APPLICATION
```

The program output is:

```
Float: 15.1
Float: 15.1
Rational: 43 / 4
Rational: 43 / 4
Float: 5.85
Float: 5.85
Rational: 2
Error in class RATIONAL_TYPE: Zero denominator
The error will be fixed by setting numerator to 10^6 and the
    denominator to 1
Rational: 1000000
Rational: -1 / 4
```

6.3.3 Maintenance

Suppose we wish to add another numeric class, COMPLEX_TYPE, to the cluster of NUMBER classes. We must define only the key methods given in class NUMBER. The code for class COMPLEX_TYPE is presented in Listing 6.8.

Listing 6.8   Class COMPLEX_TYPE

```
class COMPLEX_TYPE

inherit
    NUMBER

creation
    make

feature
    re : REAL;
    im : REAL;

    make( realPart : REAL; imagPart : REAL ) is
    do
        generality := 25;
        re := realPart;
        im := imagPart;
    end; -- Create

    display is
    do
        io.putstring( "Complex: " );
        io.putstring( "< real_part, imag_part > = " );
        io.putstring( "< " ); io.putreal( re );
        io.putstring( ", " ); io.putreal( im );
        io.putstring( " >" ); io.new_line;
    end; -- display

    coerced( aNumber : NUMBER ) : NUMBER is
    do -- Convert a number of lower generality to a
    -- COMPLEX_TYPE
        !COMPLEX_TYPE!Result.make( aNumber.asFloat.value,
            0.0 );
    end; -- coerced

    asFloat : REAL_TYPE is
    -- This routine will never be invoked
    do
        Result := Void;
    end; -- asFloat

    sum_like_type( aNumber : COMPLEX_TYPE ) : COMPLEX_TYPE is
    do
```

```
        !!Result.make( re + aNumber.real, im + aNumber.imag );
    end; -- sum_like_type
```

```
end -- class COMPLEX_TYPE
```

In Listing 6.8, routine *asFloat* returns a *Void* reference. This routine will never be invoked because there is no class with a higher "generality" number.

6.3.4 Summary

Listings 6.3 to 6.8 represent a polymorphic cluster of classes that implement various numeric types. Class NUMBER is an abstract class that defines several key methods. The arithmetic operations are effective (fully defined) in this class and are implemented in terms of one or more of the key methods. The use of polymorphism makes the code simple in structure, flexible in terms of maintenance (as evidenced by the ease with which additional subclasses may be added), and useful because clients can perform mixed mode arithmetic on disparate numeric types. Numeric objects of lower generality number will always be converted to numeric objects of higher generality number before the final arithmetic operation is implemented.

6.4 CONCLUSIONS

In this chapter, the concept of late-binding polymorphism was introduced. Polymorphism was shown to promote a high degree of flexibility in design. The "correct" version of a routine is bound to a message sent to an object at run-time. The actual type of the object receiving a message determines which version of a routine is bound at run-time.

Polymorphism allows a programmer to decentralize the process of software development. Resources may be built in each class that will be bound at run-time to the demands of the application. This transfer of responsibility from the client to the supplier is an important step forward in constructing robust software systems.

C++ && Eiffel
or is it C++ & Eiffel
or is it C++ and Eiffel?
A Clash of Cultures

7.1 THE LANGUAGE WARS?

*L*anguage wars, like real wars, are often caused by ignorance, vested interests, jealousy or personal animosity, but mostly by ignorance. It is easy to attack something when you know little about it. It is not the goal of this chapter to add fuel to any language war fires. By better understanding the differences between Eiffel and C++ — and these differences are profound — a desire to create or perpetuate a war can hopefully be diminished.

This chapter presents a critical and technical comparison of Eiffel and C++. Many opinions will be expressed and backed up, in most cases, by examples and facts.

I do not believe that there need be a war between Eiffel and C++. If there were indeed such a war, I (and many others) would declare C++ the winner and we could all go home! C++ would be declared the winner by observing the number of programmers using this language, by observing the number of compilers and other software tools and products that support C++ development and by observing the number of trade books, professional books and more recently text books that feature C++. This is in addition to the huge number of magazine and journal articles that are devoted to every twist and turn of this complex language. There is no real war between these languages — nor should there be. They were each created to serve a different purpose even though they are often used in the same application areas.

7.1.1   Religion, Politics and, Oh Yes, Programming Languages

There are few subjects for a programmer, save religion or politics, that evoke as much zeal, anger, evangelicalism, and piousness than the choice of programming language. I have seen programmers as well as language designers almost come to blows when arguing in favor of a particular programming language. You would think, after witnessing such "discussions," that the matters being discussed were of life and death. If one steps back a few paces, a discussion of comparative programming languages, while intellectually stimulating, is rather unimportant in the general scheme of things in our troubled world. Nevertheless, some writers continue to wage language wars in the editorial pages of popular magazines, in their columns, at technical conferences, among university faculties and in the halls of many organizations.

7.1.2   The Cultures

C++ and Eiffel were designed to serve different purposes and different cultures. C++ serves as a systems-level and object-oriented programming language; Eiffel serves as a high-level, pure object-oriented software engineering language and as a program design and documentation language. Both, as so typically happens, are being used for a diversity of purposes that may go beyond their original purpose (e.g. doing system-level programming in Eiffel or large-scale, high-level programming in C++). This can lead to trouble or frustration.

C++ has grown out of C and the C culture as a systems level programming language. C++ programming style, program organization and problem solving mindset are greatly influenced by and steeped in the C culture. Cryptic code is often rewarded and considered a badge of honor. In this culture, the execution speed of a program is sometimes the only real figure of merit in evaluating its worthiness. Also, in some subcultures of C, it is considered an asset that there is only a thin safety net to protect the programmer from self (himself or herself, or is it *Current* or *this*?). In some C circles, it is not considered fashionable or even desirable to provide error protection in one's code. It is quite the opposite in the Eiffel culture.

Eiffel, heavily influenced by Ada, was born and bred as a language that features type safety, assertion handling for error protection and requirements specification, and consistency. An Eiffel programmer is expected to be greatly concerned about error protection and error handling. This has always been an important part of the Eiffel culture.

7.1.3   The Readability of C or C++

C++ is an operator-intensive language. Many operators or key words may be used with different meanings in different contexts. An example is the key word *static*. This key word has three distinct uses. Another example is the operator "=." It can be used to mean initialize, assign or establish a "pure virtual" function. This strong reliance on operators can easily lead to unreadable code.

Software maintenance, often acknowledged to be the most expensive part of the software development lifecycle, is affected by the "readability" and "understandability" of the program code. Can one measure the relative "readability" of two different languages, for example C++ and Eiffel? I believe the answer is "yes," although I cannot prove this. Descriptive key words and symbols profoundly affect the ease with which a program can be read. In addition, the principle simply stated as, "what you see is what you get" also affects the ease with which a program can be understood. When this principle holds, "understandability" is greatly enhanced. When the principle fails, the programmer may be in for some surprises and, perhaps, big trouble.

7.1.4   C++ Is a Hybrid Language

C++ includes features to support a mixture of structured programming and object-oriented programming. This is one of the features that makes C++ so appealing to C programmers. One can do C programming in C++ and not utilize any of its object-oriented features. In this sense, C++ is a hybrid language. Although type safety in C++ is supported more than in C, there are usually easy ways to work around the type rules and engage in unsafe programming. Of course, the other side of this coin is that such "unsafe programming" might be, for some, clever or efficient programming. In fact, C++, like C, is dedicated to shaving machine cycles. The language provides the programmer facilities for micro-managing code in order to improve its efficiency.

7.1.5   Complexity of C++

Each class in C++ provides three levels of accessibility: *private*, *protected* and *public*. The semantics of *private* make it possible for a C++ class to be denied direct access to its own features (data members or member functions). This, as we will see later, can become the source of major problems in achieving reusability.

There are also three types of inheritance (derivation is the name used in more parochial C++ circles): *private*, *protected* and *public* derivation. Member functions (routines or methods) in C++ can be specified as being *static, const* or *inline*. Ordinary file-scope functions can be designated as being *friend* functions of a particular class. Moreover, functions in the same scope can be overloaded. This requires the compiler, but perhaps more significantly the programmer, to understand the subtleties associated with determining which overloaded function definition is to be bound to a given function call. When one adds templates and default values for function parameters to this brew, one really has quite a complex programming language.

7.1.6   Complexity of Eiffel

Eiffel is also not a simple programming language. It is a full-feature, commercial, object-oriented, software engineering language designed for industrial strength large-scale applications. As should be evident from Chapters 5 and 6, the inheritance and conformance features of Eiffel are rich but not simple. The assertion handling mechanism, coupled with inheritance, adds additional complexity along with increased power.

Because of the high degree of "readability" inherent in Eiffel, its consistency (most reserved words and symbols have only one purpose), and its purity as an object-oriented language, it is much less complex than C++.

7.1.7   Learning C++ and Eiffel

My experience in teaching both C++ and Eiffel is that one can become proficient in Eiffel in about one quarter the time as in C++ (assuming that the C++ student already has proficiency with the C programming language). Many students have indicated that they were able to use C++ much more effectively after learning Eiffel. I expect that this is because they were forced to do "pure" object-oriented programming in Eiffel, whereas in C++, they could do a mixture of structured and object-oriented programming.

7.2   WHAT YOU GET MAY NOT BE WHAT YOU SEE

After teaching many courses on C++ in industry and at the University of Colorado, it has become evident to me that the single factor that creates the greatest difficulty in mastering C++ is the reality that what you get may not be what you see. C++ has many complex default mechanisms — implications contained in the program code. If a C++ programmer overlooks or does not understand one or more of these default mechanisms, unpredictable results may occur.

7.2.1   Bringing Objects to Life — On the Stack and On the Heap

Objects in C++ are brought to life in the same way as ordinary C language variables — on the stack or on the heap. By declaring a C++ variable to be of a type specified by a class, the declaration itself brings the class instance to life when the block containing the declaration is entered. Constructors (special member functions in the class), if present, provide an opportunity to initialize the fields of a class instance at the moment it is brought to life. Objects may also be brought to life dynamically using the operator *new,* which plays a role similar to the C function *malloc.* Such dynamically created objects can also be initialized at the time of their birth using an explicit call to a constructor in an expression involving the operator *new.* Such dynamic objects are really pointers to objects. In fact, C++ encourages the extensive use of pointers and references in order to control memory management. In some application domains, this control is essential; while in others, it is a nuisance and a potential source for serious errors. The scourge of "memory leakage," as many of these errors are called, is present as a serious hazard in C++ and in any programming language that favors the extensive use of pointers.

Let us consider an example of bringing a single object to life and initializing its attributes at birth in both C++ and Eiffel.

Class A contains an attribute of type String. Class B contains an attribute of class A. Class E contains two String attributes. Class C inherits from B and contains an attribute of type String. And finally, class D inherits from A and contains attributes of types C and E.

Listing 7.1 shows the several files that comprise an implementation in Eiffel. Class D has two creation routines, one with no parameters and one with five parameters.

Listing 7.2 shows the implementation in C++.

Listing 7.1   Eiffel instantiation and initialization

```
class A
 creation
   makeA1, makeA2
 feature { NONE } -- For internal use.
   a1 : STRING;
 feature -- Methods
   makeA1 is
   do
       !!a1.make( 30 );
       a1.fill_blank;
   end; -- makeA1

   makeA2( aString : STRING ) is
   do
       a1 := clone( aString );
   end; -- makeA2

end -- class A


class B
 creation
   makeB1, makeB2
 feature { NONE } -- For internal use.
   b1 : A;
 feature -- Methods
   makeB1 is
   do
       !!b1.makeA1;
   end; -- makeB1

   makeB2( aString : STRING ) is
   do
       !!b1.makeA2( aString );
   end; -- makeB2

end -- B
```

```
class E
 creation
    makeE1, makeE2
 feature { NONE } -- For internal use.
    e1 : STRING;
    e2 : STRING;
 feature -- Methods
    makeE1 is
    do
        !!e1.make( 50 );
        e1.fill_blank;
        !!e2.make( 50 );
        e2.fill_blank;
    end; -- makeE1

    makeE2( str1 : STRING; str2 : STRING ) is
    do
        e1 := clone( str1 );
        e2 := clone( str2 );
    end; -- makeE2

end -- E


class C
inherit
    B
 creation
    makeC1, makeC2
 feature { NONE } -- For internal use
    c1 : STRING;
 feature -- Methods
    makeC1 is
    do
        !!b1.makeA1;
        !!c1.make( 40 );
        c1.fill_blank;
    end; -- makeC1



    makeC2( str1 : STRING; str2 : STRING ) is
    do
        !!b1.makeA2( str2 );
        c1 := clone( str1 );
    end; -- makeC2

end -- C

class D
 inherit
    A
 creation
    makeD1, makeD2
 feature { NONE } -- For internal use.
```

```
      d1 : C;
      d2 : E;
  feature -- Methods
    makeD1 is
    do
        !!a1.make( 30 );
        a1.fill_blank;
        !!d1.makeC1;
        !!d2.makeE1;
    end; -- makeD1

    makeD2( str1 : STRING; str2 : STRING; str3 : STRING; str4
      : STRING;
             str5 : STRING ) is
    do
        !!a1.make( 30 );
        a1.fill_blank;
        !!d1.makeC2( str2, str3 );
        !!d2.makeE2( str4, str5 );
    end; -- makeD2

end -- D



class APPLICATION
 creation
    start
 feature
    start is
    local
        obj : D;
    do
        !!obj.makeD1;
        !!obj.makeD2( "One", "Two", "Three", "Four", "Five"
           );
    end; -- start

end -- APPLICATION
```

Listing 7.2   C++ instantiation and initialization

```cpp
#include <iostream.h>
#include <string.h>
class String
{
    private:
        char *str;
    public:
        String()
        {
          cout << "In null constructor for String\n";
          str = new char[ 30 ];
          str[ 0 ] = '\0';
```

```cpp
        }
        String( char *s )
        {
            cout << "In one parameter constructor for
                String\n";
            strcpy( str = new char[ strlen( s ) + 1 ], s );
        }
        ~String()
        {
            cout << "In destructor for class String\n";
            delete str;
        }
        // Other methods not shown
};
class A
{
    private:
        String a1;
    public:
        A() { cout << "In null constructor for class A\n"; }

        A( char *s ) : a1( s )
        {
            cout << "In one parameter constructor for class
                A\n";
        }
};

class B
{
    private:
        A b1;
    public:
        B() { cout << "In null constructor for class B\n"; }

        B( char *s ) : b1( s )
        {
            cout << "In one parameter constructor for class
                B\n";
        }
};

class E
{
    private:
        String e1;
        String e2;
    public:
        E() { cout << "In null constructor for class E\n"; }

        E( char *str1, char *str2 ) : e1( str1 ), e2( str2 )
        {
            cout << "In two parameter constructor for class
                E\n";
        }
```

```
};


class C : public B
{
    private:
        String c1;
      public:
        C() { cout << "In null constructor for class C\n"; }

        C( char *str1, char *str2 ) : B( str1 ), c1( str2 )
        {
            cout << "In two parameter constructor of class
                C\n";
        }
};

class D : public A
{
    private:
        C d1;
        E d2;
      public:
        D() { cout << "In null constructor for class D\n"; }

        D( char *str1, char *str2, char *str3, char *str4,
          char *str5 ) :
            A( str1 ), d1( str2, str3 ), d2( str4, str5 )
        {
            cout << "In five parameter constructor for class
                D\n";
        }
};

void main()
{
    D obj1;
    D obj2( "One", "Two", "Three", "Four", "Five" );
}
```

The program output is:

```
In null constructor for String
In null constructor for class A
In null constructor for String
In null constructor for class A
In null constructor for class B
In null constructor for String
In null constructor for class C
In null constructor for String
In null constructor for String
In null constructor for class E
In null constructor for class D
In one parameter constructor for String
In one parameter constructor for class A
```

```
In one parameter constructor for String
In one parameter constructor for class A
In one parameter constructor for class B
In one parameter constructor for String
In two parameter constructor of class C
In one parameter constructor for String
In one parameter constructor for String
In two parameter constructor for class E
In five parameter constructor for class D
In destructor for class String
In destructor for class String
In destructor for class String
In destructor for class String
In destructor for class String
In destructor for class String
In destructor for class String
In destructor for class String
In destructor for class String
In destructor for class String
```

7.2.1.1 Discussion of Eiffel Code   In Eiffel, an object is not created by virtue of its declaration as a given type. An ordinary Eiffel variable (of reference type) assumes a default "value" of Void until a creation routine or operator is applied to it. This must be done explicitly. Therefore, in terms of object creation and initalization, what you see is what you get.

In Listing 7.1, the Eiffel implementation, there are two creation routines in each class, one that takes no parameters and one that takes one or more partameters. Consider class B. This class is composed of an attribute *b1* of type A. In creating an instance of class B using *makeB1* with no parameters, the attribute *b1* is created and initialized by explicitly calling the creation routine for *b1*, namely, *!!b1.makeA1*. The attribute *b1* is created in *makeB2* in a similar manner using *!!b1.makeA2(aString)*.

In class D, let us consider the creation routine *makeD2*. The attribute *a1*, inherited from class A, is created explicitly and initialized using *!!a1.make(30)*. Next, the attribute *d1* is created explicitly and initialized using *!!d1.makeC2(str2, str3)*. Finally, the attribute *d2* is created explicitly and initialized using *!!d2.makeE2(str4, str5)*.

The sequence of initialization is under the full control of the programmer. The chain of calls (and therefore output) is a direct consequence of the explicit invocation of the creation routines. This sequence could easily be modified. It is the responsibility of the programmer to ensure that all attributes of a class get properly created and initialized.

7.2.1.2 Discussion of C++ Code   In contrast, let us examine the C++ code of Listing 7.2. Since there is no built-in library class String, such a class is constructed. Two constructors are provided as well as a destructor. Class A provides a null constructor and a one-parameter constructor. The null constructor does not call the constructor of class String. It is activated by default by virtue of the composition relationship. On the other hand, the one-parameter constructor does explicitly call the one-parameter constructor of class String in its initialization list: *A(char *s) : a1(s) { ... }.*

Implicit initialization is more dramatically evident in class D. Here the null constructor does little more than simply announce its presence (the constructors are instrumented with output statements in order that the complex sequence of constructor calls is revealed). The five parameter constructor invokes the parent class one-parameter constructor, the attribute constructor for *d1* and the attribute constructor for *d2*.

In function *main*, *obj1* is born because of the declaration *D obj1*. The null constructor in class D is automatically invoked by virtue of this declaration. The object, *obj2*, is born and then initialized by virtue of the declaration *D obj2(...)*.

An enormous amount of output is generated as a consequence of the two lines of code in function *main* that do no more than declare two variables. A precise set of rules for constructor sequencing governs the initialization sequence and thus the resulting output. The sequence of initialization is a result of the inheritance and composition relationships that are defined by the classes. It is imperative that a C++ programmer understand these constructor sequencing rules, otherwise, the behavior of the C++ code may be surprising and in some cases defective.

7.2.1.3 Constructor Sequence Rules — What You Get is More Than What You See   The rules are: An appropriate constructor in the base class is invoked first. If the constructor requires one or more parameters, it must be invoked explicitly in the initialization list of the derived class constructor. Otherwise, the base class null constructor, if present, is invoked implicitly. Then, if any attributes are present, their constructors are invoked in the order in which the attributes are declared. The attribute constructors follow the same rules as the base class constructor.

In response to the declaration in function main, *D d1*, the inheritance relationship between class D and class A causes the null constructor in class A to be invoked first. This produces the first two lines of output (first the null constructor of the attribute of type *String* is invoked implicitly and then the body of the null constructor of class A). Next, the null constructor for attribute *d1* is invoked implicitly. Since this attribute is of type C, and C inherits from B, and B has an attribute of class A, this inheritance/composition relationship causes the null constructor of A to be invoked again, producing the next two lines of output. Following this, the body of constructor B is invoked, causing the next line of output. Next, the constructor for the attribute *c1* is invoked implicitly, causing the sixth line of output. Finally, the body of constructor C is executed, causing the next line of output. Next, the constructor for the attribute *d2* is invoked. This causes two invocations of the null constructor for class String. Then, the body of constructor E causes the next line of output. And finally, the body of the null constructor of class D causes the eleventh line of output. All eleven of these implicit constructor calls result from just one line of code in function main, namely, *D d1*. The next eleven lines of output are produced by the second line of code in function main. The remaining ten lines of output are produced by the ten implicit calls to the destructor in class String. These deallocate storage from the heap for the ten "C" strings resulting from the five strings produced from d1 and the five strings produced from d2 (see the program output). When the program ends, there is no memory leakage. It is fair to say that in C++, what you get is more than what you see.

7.2.1.4 Some Conclusions

- C++ provides for automatic object initialization through constructors in which constructors of base classes as well as constructors for attributes can be invoked implicitly or explicitly. The initialization order is governed by a precise set of rules. Objects can be allocated statically or dynamically.
- Eiffel provides for only explicit initialization and, therefore, what you see is what you get. It is the responsibility of the Eiffel programmer to actuate directly all creation routines in bringing the attributes of a class to life.
- Eiffel's system of initialization is explicit, whereas C++'s system is partially implicit. Both systems provide the programmer with an opportunity to create safe and completely initialized objects at the time they are created.
- The automatic garbage collection in Eiffel provides additional simplicity and safety by unburdening the programmer from having to deal with memory leakage issues. The price paid may be in performance but always in control. This price may be too high for some applications.
- The destructor mechanism of C++ provides the programmer with a much higher degree of control in determining the mechanism and timing of garbage collection. The price is eternal vigilance in avoiding the scourge of memory leakage.
- Direct control over the garbage collection in Eiffel in cases where performance is critical would be most desirable. No such reliable facilities currently exist.

7.3 What You See May Not Be What You Get

C++ offers the capability to overload functions that exist in the same logical scope. Eiffel does not offer this facility. Many C++ programmers react quite positively when they first learn about this C++ facility. In principle, the goal of function overloading is to simplify the name space in which several functions coexist and to permit the programmer to employ natural naming conventions.

Listing 7.3 presents a simple example that demonstrates the benefit of function name overloading.

**Listing 7.3   Simple example of function name overloading in C++
(Exact Matching)**

```
#include <iostream.h>

int aFunction( int value )
{
    return value * value;
}


float aFunction( float value )
{
    return value * value * value;
}

void main()
{
    int a = 4;
    float b = 5.0;
    cout << aFunction( a ) << " " << aFunction( b ) << endl;
}
```

The program output is:

```
16 125
```

7.3.1   Overloading is a Blessing When Exact Matching to Signatures Occurs

The compiler is able to bind the first call of *aFunction* to the *int* version and the second call to the *float* version based on the perfect signature match of each function call. When exact matches occur, function overloading is a wonderful blessing. It can become a nightmare when an exact match does not occur. Then a set of complex rules must be applied in order to determine whether the call is ambiguous or can be resolved. The problem of course is that the compiler may do the resolution one way and the programmer another. Then, the programmer will fall victim to "what you see (the program text and the perceived binding to a particular overloaded function) may not be what you get."

7.3.2   Exact Matches Occur Only in Heaven!

Listing 7.4 presents several examples where only a trained C++ programmer would be able to predict accurately the actual binding. See whether you can predict the output of the following three programs, or whether any of the function calls in function *main* lead to an error message indicating an ambiguous call.

Listing 7.4   More complex overloading in C++

```
#include <iostream.h>
void f( int a ) { cout << "Version 1\n"; }
void f( long a, int b = 0 ) { cout << "Version 2\n"; }
void main()
{
    f( 5L );
    f( 0 );
}
```

```
#include <iostream.h>
void f( char* a ) { cout << "Version 1\n"; }
void f( void* a ) { cout << "Version 2\n"; }
void f( double ) { cout << "Version 3\n"; }
void main()
{
    int i;
    f( i );
    f( &i );
}
```

```
#include <iostream.h>
    void f( const char* a ) { cout << "Version 1\n"; }
void f( char* a ) { cout << "Version 2\n"; }
void main()
{
    f( "Today is Saturday" );
}
```

7.3.3   Some Conclusions

The overloading of functions in C++, although appealing in purpose, introduces a major source of complexity. When an exact match does not occur, the
actual function binding may be different from what the programmer expects.
Therefore, this facility of C++, if used, should be used with great caution and care.

It is probably the case that Eiffel is much better off not allowing this facility.

7.4   GENERIC FUNCTIONS AND TEMPLATES

C++ and Eiffel both offer a programmer facilities for constructing generic software components — generic classes. C++, in addition, allows ordinary file-scope
functions to be constructed that contain one or more generic parameters. This is
not allowed in Eiffel because the concept of a file-scope function does not exist in
Eiffel. As a pure object-oriented language, the only functions that have meaning
in Eiffel are the routines of a class. Such functions can be invoked only through
an object.

7.4.1   Eiffel Offers Constrained Genericity

As you recall from Chapter 4, Eiffel supports the concept of "constrained
genericity." If a generic parameter is constrained, the actual parameter must

conform to the class specified in the generic parameter constraint. The compiler verifies that the implementation of each routine in the generic class uses operations on the generic parameters that are supported. Furthermore, the constraints, if present, provide formal documentation to the user regarding the requirements that an actual parameter must satisfy in order to use the generic class legally.

7.4.2 C++ is More Permissive

C++ is much more permissive. It is not possible to constrain any generic parameter formally. The C++ compiler *does not verify in advance* that the operations imposed on the generic parameters in the member functions of the generic class are legal. Only when a client creates an instance of a template class (a generic class in C++) does the compiler verify that the actual type supports the operations given in the member functions that are used. In the absence of explicit documentation, the C++ programmer must reverse engineer from the code in the template function the constraints on the actual type(s) that may be used in creating instances of the generic type.

If an Eiffel class were to support a sorting function (arrange its elements from smallest to largest), the class, here called MY_COLLECTION, might be declared as follows:

```
class MY_COLLECTION[ T -> COMPARABLE ]
-- Other details not shown
```

By constraining the parameter T to class COMPARABLE, the client knows that only actual types that may be compared using the comparison operators, "<," ">," "<=," ">=" and "=" would be legal. If this constraint were not present, the compiler would not allow a sorting routine to use any of the above operators. This would impose a serious problem in implementing a sorting algorithm.

7.4.3 A Serious C++ Problem: The Need for Specialized Template Functions

The hybrid nature of C++ introduces a problem for which there is no counterpart in Eiffel, namely the need for specialized template functions. The problem is illustrated in Listing 7.5.

Listing 7.5   The need for specialized template functions in C++

```
#include <iostream.h>
template < class T >
T minimum( T a, T b )
{
    return ( a < b ) ? a : b;
}
```

```
void main() {
    int a = 25, b = 15;
    char *str1 = "BBB",
    *str2 = "AAA";
    cout << minimum( a, b ) << " " << minimum( str1, str2 )
    << endl;
}
```

The program output is:

```
15 BBB
```

This program is defective, although quite legal. The problem occurs when an instance of the generic function is created using an actual parameter of type *char**. The compiler compares the pointers and chooses the one with the smaller memory address rather than choosing the string that is lexically smaller ("AAA"). Pointer comparison is only appropriate when the pointers that are being compared are pointing to the same contiguous storage (an array). This is violated here, but the compiler cannot check this.

The correction of this problem requires that the user specify an exception to the rule in the form of a "specialized template function." This function is normally written directly below the template function, but in general, must appear in the same logical scope as the template function. For this problem, a specialized template function that does the job is the following:

```
char* minimum( char *a, char *b )
{
    return ( strcmp( a, b ) < 0 : a : b ;
}
```

Another final problem that confronts C++ programmers using template classes is one of physical organization. Template functions must be implemented in the header file that contains the definition of the template class. This can impose organizational problems of multiple *includes*. Normally, the implementation of a member function is performed in an executable file, not a header file. C++ requires template functions to be implemented in a header file to allow a client to have direct access to the template code that serves as a pattern.

This potential organizational nightmare does not exist in Eiffel because both the interface as well as the implementation of all class routines must be in the same file.

7.4.4   Some Conclusions

Eiffel provides a programmer with a much richer, rigorous, and in many ways simpler set of constructs for building generic classes. The notation in Eiffel for constructing generic classes is much more readable than in C++. There is never a need for specialized generic routines (exceptions to the rules). The use of constrained generic parameters provides for strong self documentation by formally specifying to a client the precise conditions that must be met by the actual type that is used in place of the generic parameter. The compiler enforces these rules on the template function itself, providing for a more rigorous basis for class construction.

Eiffel supported generic parameters in classes from the very beginning (in the first version of the language), whereas for C++, it was somewhat of an afterthought, coming into the language many years after the first version of the language. As a result, the syntax for C++ template usage is more verbose and cumbersome than the clean and simple syntax used in Eiffel.

7.5 DEFAULT VALUES FOR PARAMETERS

C++ has the capability to provide one or more formal parameters in a function with default values. Once a formal parameter is given a default value, all parameters to its right (lexically speaking) must also be given default values. Eiffel does not offer this facility.

I believe that this C++ facility is extremely useful and lament the fact that it does not exist in Eiffel. Default values can greatly simplify the task of a client module by using the default values suggested by the producer.

My conclusion: Default values for parameters, available in C++, provide an extremely useful facility that is not available in Eiffel.

7.6 ASSERTIONS

The assertion handling facilities of Eiffel distinguish it from most languages, both object-oriented and non-object-oriented. These facilities support the powerful and useful notion of "programming by contract." Fault detection can be built into every Eiffel routine and every Eiffel class using class invariants. Assertion handling is beautifully generalized to support inheritance in which preconditions can be weakened and postconditions strengthened in a descendant class.

C++, at the time of this writing, offers only primitive support for fault detection using function *assert(...)*. If the argument on this function is zero, a run-time failure is induced with a diagnostic message indicating where the failure occurred. There is no distribution of responsibility between the supplier and the client as in Eiffel and no mechanism for propagating fault detection through class derivation. Future releases of C++ promise support for exception handling using the new keywords *try* and *throw*. These features were not available at the time of this writing.

My conclusion: Assertion handling alone might suffice to justify the use of Eiffel. Assertion handling promotes a high level of fault detection and safety. It provides a semi-formal basis for doing "correct" programming and verifying this correctness at run-time. It provides an additional level of self documentation, informing a client about the formal specifications (preconditions) that must be satisfied in order to use a routine or a class.

C++ does not provide any similar facilities.

7.7 VIRTUAL FUNCTIONS AND LATE-BINDING

Late-binding is not just a feature of a programming language but a basic design principle. In Eiffel, as in Smalltalk and Objective-C, late-binding semantics are uniformly applied to all function calls through objects. The actual type of the object receiving a function call determines the version of the routine used rather than the formal type of the object. If an Eiffel compiler is able to optimize out late-binding and replace the call with early-binding, this is done in a manner that is totally transparent to the programmer. This is as it should be. Binding is a low-level issue and a uniform semantic interpretation makes software design more consistent.

In C++, the default mode for binding is early-binding. This promotes efficiency by providing the opportunity for compiler optimization of code. But in C++, late-binding must be enabled by the programmer. In order to accomplish this, some micro-management must be employed by the C++ programmer. Specifically, the member functions that are to be bound at run-time must be specified in a base class as *virtual*. These *virtual* functions must be redefined in a descendant class while preserving the signature of the *virtual* function in the base class. And finally, the *virtual* function must be invoked through a pointer or a reference to an object. Then, the actual type of the object rather than the formal type will be used to determine the version of the function definition to bind to the function call.

There are several fundamental and major problems associated with this process. The first of these problems is illustrated in Listing 7.6.

Listing 7.6   Hazard of virtual functions in C++

```
#include <iostream.h>
class Parent
{
    public:
        virtual int doIt( int value )
        {
            return value * value;
        }
};

class Child : public Parent
{
    public:
        int doIt( int value, int anotherValue = 20 )
        {
            return value * anotherValue;
        }
```

```
};

void main()
{
    Parent *p = new Child();
    cout << p -> doIt( 3 ) << endl;
}
```

The programmer, and perhaps the reader, would expect an output of 60. The reasoning that might be used to justify this expected output is the following: the function *doIt* in the base class Parent is declared to be *virtual*. In function *main*, a pointer to an instance of class Child is substituted for the formally specified pointer to class Parent (this is legal in C++ as well as in Eiffel; class Child conforms to class Parent). The function *doIt(3)* is invoked through the object pointer *p*. One might suspect that the default value of 20 for *anotherValue* would be supplied and the output of 60 produced. Not true!

The redefined function *doIt* in class Child violates one of the requirements for late-binding. The signature of this function does not match the signature of the base class version exactly. Instead of identifying this as an error, as an Eiffel compiler would do under comparable circumstances, it allows this violation to persist without an error. Early-binding is employed and, therefore, the version of *doIt* defined in class Parent is formally bound to the object of type Child. This is a serious problem because the fundamental nature of the design (late-binding) has been compromised. Of course, one should know the rules. In my view, the C++ compiler should protect us from ourselves in this situation. The redefinition of a virtual function should be deemed illegal in C++, but it is not.

Eiffel requires all routine redefinitions to be "conformant" to the version in the ancestor class. This implies that the parameters and the return type must conform to those of the ancestor class. This is strictly enforced by the compiler. Any attempt to change the signature of the ancestor function through redefinition would not be tolerated by the compiler.

Another problem associated with virtual functions in C++ is the need to sometimes supply a downward reference to a member function that really belongs in a descendant class. This problem arises because of the manner in which C++ implements late-binding: the virtual table. A virtual table is constructed in every class in the polymorphic cluster of classes over which the late-binding prevails. Every function that is to enjoy late-binding in the polymorphic cluster must be formally specified in the base class in order that its entry be placed in the virtual table. This problem can cause a major discontinuity in mapping an object-oriented design to C++. A base class should not have to specify member functions that relate to attributes that are defined lower in the hierarchy.

7.7.1 The Clairvoyance Principle

Perhaps the most fundamental and disturbing problem associated with virtual functions in C++ is the very fact that the programmer must choose which functions are to be late-bound and which functions are to be early-bound. This violates the clairvoyance principle (i.e. a class designer should not have to be clairvoyant with respect to predicting the usage of a class). This term was suggested to the author by Randy Dunaieff of Reuters Information Technology in a technical conversation.

Simply stated, how can the designer of a base class in a reusable class library possibly know for which functions some client intends to require late-binding and for which functions the client desires early-binding? In general, there is no way the base class designer can be clairvoyant and have this knowledge, particularly in light of the fact that some users may wish all the functions to be late-bound, whereas other users may require none of the functions to be late-bound. Reusability is, therefore, seriously compromised because of C++'s multiparadigm nature.

Some practitioners have suggested that it might be wise to declare all C++ functions as virtual. The counterargument is that this imposes a fixed overhead on all programmers regardless of whether they wish to use late-binding or not. Under most circumstances, I endorse the suggestion that all C++ functions in a base class be declared as *virtual* in order to support a uniform semantic of design and implementation.

7.7.2   Some Conclusions

Virtual functions in C++ provide support for late-binding. The programmer must decide which functions will enjoy early-binding and which functions will enjoy late-binding. This seriously compromises reusability in designing base classes. The compiler does not enforce the requirement that for late-binding a virtual function redefinition in a descendant class must match the signature of the base class version. This can lead to serious errors. Because of the mechanism of virtual table construction, member functions that have no logical reason for being in the base class may have to be declared there. This forces a compromise in mapping an object-oriented design to a C++ implementation.

None of these problems exist in Eiffel. All functions enjoy late-binding semantics. The compiler verifies that type conformance exists when a routine is redefined in a descendant class. Downward references are never required. Routines can be defined in the subclass in which they belong. The compiler optimizes for early binding automatically without the programmer having to intervene.

7.8   INHERITANCE AND THE CLAIRVOYANCE PRINCIPLE

One of the "buzzwords" that is used when touting the benefits of object-orientation is "reusability." Software reuse may have a scope limited to an individual programmer, a team of programmers, an entire organization or across organizations and individuals. The larger the intended scope for reuse, the more challenging it becomes to satisfy the potentially diverse needs.

7.8.1   Inheritance Provides the Basis for Software Reuse

Inheritance provides the basis for software reuse in object-oriented programming languages. This is most evident when one looks at Smalltalk. Although the language itself is quite small, the standard library includes more than 300 classes and more than 2000 methods. This is just the raw library that is supplied to every Smalltalk programmer; this count does not include the many special purpose classes that are constructed by the programmer, programming team or organization. All of these special purpose classes become first-class members of the Smalltalk programming environment. To learn Smalltalk means to learn the Smalltalk environment. Reuse and its benefit, "incremental problem solving," takes on real meaning when such a highly rationalized hierarchy of classes can be used as-is, or extended through inheritance.

7.8.2   Must a Subclass Designer Have Access to the Source Code of its Ancestors?

A key requirement in extending the Smalltalk hierarchy if one programs in Smalltalk, or extending a hierarchy of classes in C++ or in Eiffel, is the ability for the subclass designer to be able to use language facilities to either block methods from an ancestor class, redefine methods from an ancestor class, combine methods from ancestor classes or even rename methods from an ancestor class without requiring the permission of the ancestor class author or access to the source code of the ancestor class. If one must retrofit features into the ancestor classes because of the needs of the new subclasses, this is a violation of reuse. Reuse does not imply rebuilding; it implies extending an existing hierarchy of classes. This is a most critical issue in object-oriented design and implementation.

C++ and Eiffel are examined with respect to the how their inheritance mechanisms support software reuse. First we look at C++.

7.8.3   How Inheritance in C++ Supports Software Reuse

There are three types of inheritance (derivation) in C++: public derivation, protected derivation and private derivation.

In *public* derivation, achieved by using the key word *public* in front of the base class (e.g. *class B : public A { ... };), the inherited members maintain their access level within the derived class. That is, private members of the base class remain private and inaccessible to the derived class, protected members of the base class remain protected but acessible to the derived class, and public members of the base class, remain public in the derived class.

In *protected* derivation, a capability recently introduced into C++, the key word *protected* is used in front of the base class (e.g. *class B : protected A { ... };). The inherited public and protected members of the protected base class become protected members of the derived class.

In *private* derivation, the key word *private* is used in front of the base class (e.g. *class B : private A { ... };). The inherited public and protected members of a private base class become private members of the derived class.

Private derivation is used in C++ for code reuse only. None of the behavior of the base class is available to instances of the derived class. That is, it is illegal to invoke the public member functions of the base class through an instance of the derived class. The public member functions of the base class are available only within the derived class function definitions and to friends of the derived class.

Behavioral reuse is achieved using public derivation. The public member functions that have not been redefined in the derived class may be invoked, as-is, on instances of the derived class. The behavior of the base class thus propagates to instances of the derived class.

It should be clear from the above discussion that in C++, the semantics of inheritance are controlled by the parent class in a parent-child inheritance relationship. We speak of a public base class, or a protected base class or a private base class. This choice affects what can be done in a descendant class.

7.8.4   An Example that Compares Inheritance in C++ and Eiffel

Before continuing this discussion, two modes of derivation in C++ are compared to Eiffel. We show, side-by-side, in Listings 7.7 and 7.8, public derivation in C++ and Eiffel and private derivation in C++ and Eiffel. This comparison is significant as will be seen shortly.

Listing 7.7   Comparing public derivation in C++ and Eiffel

```
#include <iostream.h>
class A
{
    protected:
        int valueA;
    public:
        void setValueA( int aValue ) { valueA = aValue; }
        void displayA() { cout << valueA; }
};

class B : public A
{
    private:
        int valueB;
    public:
        void setValues( int a_value, int b_value )
        {
            valueA = a_value;
            valueB = b_value;
        }
        void displayB() { displayA(); cout << " " << valueB
            << endl; }
};
void main()
{
```

```
      A objA;
      objA.setValueA( 4 );
      B objB;
      objB.setValues( 5, 6 );
      objA.displayA();
      cout << endl;
      objB.displayB();
    objB.displayA();
    cout << endl;
}
```

The program output is:

```
4
5 6

class A

  feature { NONE } -- Acts like a protected section in C++
    valueA : INTEGER;

  feature
    setValueA( aValue : INTEGER ) is
    do
      valueA := aValue;
    end; -- setValueA

    displayA is
    do
      io.putint( valueA );
    end; -- displayA

end -- A
-----------------------------------------------------------------
class B

inherit
  A

    feature { NONE }
      valueB : INTEGER;

    feature
      setValues( a_value : INTEGER; b_value : INTEGER ) is
      do
        valueA := a_value;
        valueB := b_value;
      end; -- setValues

    displayB is
    do
      displayA;
      io.putstring( " " );
      io.putint( valueB );
      io.new_line;
```

```
        end; -- displayB

end -- B

class APPLICATION
creation
    start

 feature
    start is
    local
        objA : A;
        objB : B;
    do
        !!objA;
        !!objB;
        objA.setValueA( 4 );
        objB.setValues( 5, 6 );
        objA.displayA;
        io.new_line;
        objB.displayB;
        objB.displayA;
        io.new_line;
    end; -- start
end -- APPLICATION
```

The program output is:

```
4
5 6
5
```

The export expression { NONE } in the Eiffel classes creates the same effect as a protected section in C++. It should be mentioned that in Eiffel, there is no way to simulate a private section. It is the Eiffel philosophy that subclass routines must be able to access the attributes in their own class directly . In C++, derived class function definitions cannot access their inherited attributes directly if these attributes are located in the private section of the base class.

Listing 7.8   Comparing private derivation in C++ and Eiffel

```
#include <iostream.h>

class A
{
    // Same details as in Listing 7.7
};

class B : private A
{
    // Same details as in Listing 7.7
};
```

```
void main()
{
 A objA;
 objA.setValueA( 4 );
 B objB;
 objB.setValues( 5, 6 );
 objA.displayA();
 cout << endl;
 objB.displayB();
 // objB.displayA(); This causes an error since displayA was
 // inherited as a private function
    cout << endl;
}
```

The program output is:

```
4
5 6
```

```
-------------------------------------------------------------
class A
    -- Same details as in Listing 7.7
end -- A
-------------------------------------------------------------
class B
inherit
    A
        export
            { NONE } all
          end;
    -- Same remaining details as in Listing 7.7
end -- B
-------------------------------------------------------------
class APPLICATION

 creation
    start

 feature
    start is
    local
        objA : A;
        objB : B;
    do
        !!objA;
        !!objB;
        objA.setValueA( 4 );
        objB.setValues( 5, 6 );
        objA.displayA;
        io.new_line;
        objB.displayB;
        -- objB.displayA; Causes a compiler error message
        -- since displayA is blocked
        io.new_line;
```

```
    end; -- start

  end -- APPLICATION
```

The export clause in class B is responsible for blocking all of class A's public features from being available to instances of class B. It must be noted that Eiffel allows a finer degree of granularity in determining which public features of class A are to be blocked from instances of class B. The export clause can name individual public features of class A as being available to specific classes and their descendants through instances of class B. A similar capability could be achieved in C++ using its friendship facility.

7.8.5   Some Conclusions

So far, it appears that C++ and Eiffel offer a relatively similar capability with respect to public and private derivation. But the really significant difference between C++ and Eiffel is yet to be seen.

Suppose we consider the following typical maintenance problem in both C++ and Eiffel. We assume that the existing hierarchy of classes A and B in which B is privately derived from A is available to us in the form of a class library. Let us assume that we do not have write access to the source code for either class (A or B). The source code for this library is shown in Listing 7.8.

7.8.6   Some Maintenance — Specifications for a New Subclass

We wish to create a subclass C inherited from class B that introduces the attribute *valueC* (of type integer) and the methods *setAllValues* (takes three parameters) and *displayC*, which outputs all three integer attributes. In addition, we wish to enable instances of class C to be able to respond to the message *displayA*.

It must be emphasized that we cannot alter the source code of classes A and B. To do so would violate the principle of software reuse. First, we explore a solution to this problem in Eiffel. Listing 7.9 shows the newly designed subclass C in Eiffel and a new main driver class, APPLICATION. The code for classes A and B is found in Listing 7.8.

Listing 7.9   Software maintenance in Eiffel— New subclass C

```
class C
  inherit
    B
        redefine
          displayA
        select
          displayA
        end;
    B
        rename
```

```
            displayA as display_A
        end;

feature { NONE }
    valueC : INTEGER;

feature
    setAllValues( a_value : INTEGER; b_value : INTEGER;
                  c_value : INTEGER ) is
    do
        setValues( a_value, b_value );
        valueC := c_value;
    end; -- setAllValues

    displayA is
    do
        display_A;
    end; -- displayA

    displayC is
    do
        io.putint( valueA ); io.putstring( " " );
        io.putint( valueB ); io.putstring( " " );
        io.putint( valueC );
        io.new_line;
    end; -- displayC

end -- C

-----------------------------------------------------------

class APPLICATION

creation
    start

feature
    start is
    local
        objA : A;
        objB : B;
        objC : C;
    do
        !!objA;
        !!objB;
        objA.setValueA( 4 );
        objB.setValues( 5, 6 );
        objA.displayA;
        io.new_line;
        objB.displayB;
        -- objB.displayA; Causes an error message
        !!objC;
        objC.setAllValues( 1, 2, 3 );
        objC.displayC;
        objC.displayA;
```

```
        io.new_line;
    end; -- start

end -- APPLICATION
```

Class C in Listing 7.9 is able to access its own attributes directly. This is quite useful in implementing routine *displayC*. It can also access the routine *setValues* defined in class B. This is quite useful in implementing routine *setAllValues*. But what about resurrecting the routine *displayA* from class A that was blocked using private derivation in class B? This is accomplished by multiply inheriting from class B. In the first inheritance clause, *displayA* is redefined and then selected. In the second inheritance clause, *displayA* is renamed *display_A*. The effect of this is to reestablish *displayA* as a legitimate routine to call through instances of class C.

The routine *displayA* could be reestablished in an alternative way, as follows:

```
class C

  inherit
      B
          export
              { ANY } displayA
          end;
-- Remaining details the same as in Listing 7.9
```

The export clause of class C above declares that the inherited routine *displayA* (from an ancestor class) is now available to all clients.

The significant conclusion here is that Eiffel, with its powerful and flexible inheritance mechanism, has permitted true code reuse. There was no need for the designer of classes A and B to be clairvoyant in predicting what the needs of the user might be. The subclass C was designed without having to modify or have access to the source code of the library from which it is derived.

Listing 7.10   Attempted maintenance in C++

```
#include <iostream.h>
class A
{
    protected:
        int valueA;
    public:
        void setValueA( int aValue ) { valueA = aValue; }
        void displayA() { cout << valueA; }
};

class B : private A
{
    private:
        int valueB;
    public:
        void setValues( int a_value, int b_value )
```

```
                {
                    valueA = a_value;
                    valueB = b_value;
                }
            void displayB() { displayA(); cout << " " << valueB <<
                endl; }
        };

        class C : public B
        {
            private:
                int valueC;
            public:
                void setAllValues( int a_value, int b_value, int
                    c_value )
                {
                    valueA = a_value;
                    valueB = b_value;
                    valueC = c_value;
                }
                void displayC()
                {
                    cout << valueA << " " << valueB << " " << valueC
                        << endl;
                }
        };

        void main()
        {
            A objA;
            objA.setValueA( 4 );
            B objB;
            objB.setValues( 5, 6 );
            objA.displayA();
            cout << endl;
            objB.displayB();
            // objB.displayA(); This causes an error since displayA
                is private
            cout << endl;
            C objC;
            objC.setAllValue( 1, 2, 3 );
            objC.displayC();
            objC.displayA();
        }
```

Unfortunately, when the code of Listing 7.10 is compiled, the following error messages are produced:

```
"public.c", line 32: error: C::setAllValues() cannot access
    valueA : A is a private base class
"public.c", line 33: error: C::setAllValues() cannot access
    B::valueB: private member
"public.c", line 38: error: C::displayC() cannot access
    valueA : A is a private base class
```

```
"public.c", line 38: error: C::displayC() cannot access
    B::valueB: private member
"public.c", line 54: error: member setAllValue undefined
"public.c", line 56: error: main() cannot access displayA : A
    is a private base class
```

The private derivation *specified by the library designer, not the user,* has prevented the newly derived class C from directly accessing the attribute *valueA*. As the above error message suggests, A is a private base class (and therefore the attribute *valueA* is not available in class C). The attribute *valueB* cannot be accessed in class C because in C++, as indicated earlier, a function does not have access to all its attributes if they are private attributes in the parent class. Finally, function *main* cannot access *displayA* because A is a private base class and, therefore, appears in class B as a private member function.

True software reuse has not occurred in C++ because of the violation of the clairvoyance principle. The designer of classes A and B would have to be clairvoyant in being able to predict the needs of class designer C. This, of course, is impossible.

7.8.7   More Conclusions

C++ does **not** support general software reuse. Only if the user can modify the classes available in the library that represent the ancestor classes can the user's needs be guaranteed to be satisfied.

Eiffel, with its extremely powerful and flexible inheritance mechanism, does indeed support true software reuse.

It should be pointed out that many outstanding C++ libraries have been developed in problem-specific domains. One popular domain is that of the graphical user interface. Many of the best commercial C++ libraries supply source code to the user so that she or he can modify the ancestor classes. Often, such libraries define all member functions as virtual, use strictly public derivation, use only protected sections for data members, and employ other measures to maximize reuse for client applications within the given domain.

Since the C++ language itself does not provide sufficient facilities to assure a wide scope of reuse, it behooves the C++ developer to establish disciplined protocols for program design.

7.9   MULTIPLE INHERITANCE AND THE CLAIRVOYANCE PRINCIPLE

Eiffel supported multiple inheritance since its first version. C++ introduced support for multiple inheritance in a relatively late version of the language.

One of the thorny problems associated with multiple inheritance regards the issue of whether a single shared copy of an attribute exists in a base class or whether multiple copies of an attribute propagate through various branches of the directed acyclic graph (DAG) that characterizes a multiple inheritance hierarchy.

7.9.1   Virtual Base Classes in C++ and the Clairvoyance Problem

In C++, the keyword *virtual* is used in yet another context to define virtual base classes. A virtual base class ensures that only one copy of an attribute is inherited through a path in the DAG. The clairvoyance problem arises in C++ because the class library designer is forced to make decisions about whether a base class in a DAG is a virtual base class or an ordinary base class. Once such a decision is made, it cannot be undone by a client who wishes to create a class derived from one in the DAG. This problem will be illustrated shortly.

Eiffel's inheritance mechanism avoids the clairvoyance problem by making facilities available in an inheritance clause that allow the designer of a subclass through redefinition, selection and renaming to undo any decision made at a higher level in the hierarchy. This allows true software reuse to be realized.

To illustrate this problem, we create a library consisting of three classes: A, B and C. Classes B and C are derived from virtual base class A. The C++ code for this is shown in Listing 7.11.

Listing 7.11   Another clairvoyance problem in C++

```
#include <iostream.h>
class A
{
   protected:
       int valueA;
   public:
       A( int value ) : valueA( value ) { }
};

class B : virtual public A
{
   protected:
      int valueB;
   public:
       B( int value1, int value2 ) : A( value1 ), valueB(
          value2 ) { }
};

class C : virtual public A
{
   protected:
      int valueC;
   public:
       C( int value1, int value2 ) : A( value1 ), valueC(
          value2 ) { }
};
```

We assume that the user (client) does not have access to the source code given in Listing 7.11. The designer of this library has assured that only one copy of attribute *valueA* will propagate to any descendant class of A. Now, suppose that our user wishes to create a derived class D that multiply inherits from B and C and wishes only one copy of attribute *valueA*. The user is in luck! Because class A has been defined as a virtual base class, only one copy of *valueA* will appear in class D. The code for this class is shown in Listing 7.12 along with a short main driver program.

Listing 7.12   A C++ class multiply inherited from two parent classes

```
class D : public B, public C
{
    protected:
        int valueD;
    public:
        D( int value1, int value2, int value3, int value4 ) :
            A( value1 ), B( value1, value2 ), C( value1,
            value3 ),
            valueD( value4 ) { }
        void display() { cout << valueA << " " << valueB <<
                    " " << valueC << " " << valueD << endl; }
};

void main()
{
 D obj( 1, 2, 3, 4 );
 obj.display();
}
```

The program output is:

```
1 2 3 4
```

7.9.1.1 The Problem   Now suppose that another user (client) wishes to create a class D multiply inherited from B and C and have two separate copies of attribute valueA. Unfortunately, unless the client has access to the source code of the library (classes A, B and C), this cannot be done. The class library designer has already imposed a decision about the sharing of attribute A in any descendant class. Real software reuse has been denied once again in C++.

Listing 7.13   Multiple inheritance system implemented in Eiffel

```
class A

  creation
    makeA

  feature { NONE }
    valueA : INTEGER;

  feature
    makeA( value : INTEGER ) is
    do
        valueA := value;
    end; -- makeA
end -- A
-------------------------------------------------------------
```

```
class B
 inherit
    A
 creation
    makeB

 feature { NONE }
    valueB : INTEGER;

 feature
    makeB( value1 : INTEGER; value2 : INTEGER ) is
    do
       valueA := value1;
       valueB := value2;
    end; -- makeB
end -- B
---------------------------------------------------------
class C
 inherit
    A

 creation
    makeC

 feature { NONE }
    valueC : INTEGER;

 feature
    makeC( value1 : INTEGER; value2 : INTEGER ) is
    do
       valueA := value1;
       valueC := value2;
    end; -- makeC
end -- C
```

Now assume as before that a user (client) wishes to create a class D that multiply inherits from B and C and has only one copy of attribute *valueA*. This class is shown in Listing 7.14.

Listing 7.14 Multiply inherited Eiffel class

```
class D
 inherit
    B;
    C;

 creation
    makeD

 feature { NONE }
    valueD : INTEGER;

 feature
    makeD( value1 : INTEGER; value2 : INTEGER; value3 :
```

```
       INTEGER; value4 : INTEGER ) is
    do
       valueA := value1;
       valueB := value2;
       valueC := value3;
       valueD := value4;
    end; -- makeD

    display is
    do
       io.putint( valueA ); io.putstring( " " );
       io.putint( valueB ); io.putstring( " " );
       io.putint( valueC ); io.putstring( " " );
       io.putint( valueD ); io.putstring( " " );
       io.new_line;
    end; -- display
end -- D

class APPLICATION
 creation
    start


 feature
    start is
    local
       obj : D;
    do
       !!obj.makeD( 1, 2, 3, 4 );
       obj.display;
    end; -- start

end -- APPLICATION
```

The program output is:

```
1 2 3 4
```

The rules of repeated inheritance guarantee that only one copy of attribute *valueA* appears in class D.

7.9.1.2 The Same Maintenance in Eiffel   But, what if now another user wishes to create a class D that preserves two copies of the *valueA* attribute. Can this be done without having access to the source code of classes A, B and C? The answer is yes. The solution is shown in Listing 7.15.

Listing 7.15   Another multiply inherited class in Eiffel

```
class D

 inherit
    B
```

```
        rename
           valueA as valueA_B -- provides valueA through
           -- class B
        select -- Needed to resolve which valueA to choose
        -- under polymorphism
           valueA_B
        end;

    C
        rename
           valueA as valueA_C -- provides valueA through
           -- class C
        end;

creation
    makeD


feature { NONE }
    valueD : INTEGER;

feature
    makeD( value1 : INTEGER; value2 : INTEGER; value3 :
      INTEGER; value4 : INTEGER; value5 : INTEGER ) is
    do
       valueA_B := value1;
       valueA_C := value2;
       valueB := value3;
       valueC := value4;
       valueD := value5;
    end; -- makeD

    display is
    do
       io.putint( valueA_B ); io.putstring( " " );
       io.putint( valueA_C ); io.putstring( " " );
       io.putint( valueB ); io.putstring( " " );
       io.putint( valueC ); io.putstring( " " );
       io.putint( valueD ); io.putstring( " " );
       io.new_line;
    end; -- display

end -- D
```

Through renaming in class D, the desired two separate copies of the *valueA* attribute are available in class D. True software reuse has again been demonstrated in Eiffel.

7.9.2 Conclusions

- Eiffel's powerful and flexible inheritance facilities enable clients to adapt features from a multiple inheritance hierarchy without having to compromise functionality or have access to the source code of the ancestor classes. Reuse is assured.

- C++ requires the class designer to be clairvoyant in determining which base classes are not virtual and which are virtual. Once these decisions are made, they make the library design brittle. Software reuse is shown again to be a fiction in multiple inheritance C++ hierarchies.

7.10 READABILITY OF C++ AND EIFFEL

It is difficult to make qualitative judgements about the relative "readability" of two languages. Yet, we all make such judgments just as we express opinions about restaurants and works of art. Although it is certainly my opinion that Eiffel is much more readable than C++, this opinion being formed after having written and read at least twenty times as much C++ as Eiffel, there is no absolute truth regarding this issue.

In the interest of comparing the "readability" of C++ and Eiffel, segments from two real applications will be presented, one in C++ and the other in Eiffel. Each implementation was written at different times, neither with the intention of being used for such comparison purposes.

Listing 7.16 presents segments from a generic LIST class in Eiffel. Listing 7.17 presents segments of the implementation of the LIST class in C++. The C++ code that I believe may detract from its "readability" is shown in boldface. You be the judge.

Listing 7.18 presents segments of some numeric classes in Eiffel. Listing 7.19 presents segments of the same numeric classes in C++. Some of the C++ code is put in boldface for the same reason as before. You again judge the relative "readability" of each language.

Listing 7.16   Segments of LIST class in Eiffel

```
class LIST[ T ]
  feature
     first    : NODE[ T ];
     last     : NODE[ T ];
     elements : INTEGER; -- The number of elements in the list

     insertFront( anItem : T ) is
     -- Add anItem to the front of the list
     local
        newItem : NODE[ T ];
     do
        if first = Void then
           !!first.make( anItem );
           last := first;
        else
           !!newItem.make( anItem );
```

```
                    newItem.link( first );
                    first := newItem;
                end;
                elements := elements + 1;
            ensure
                elements = old elements + 1;
        end; -- insertFront

        -- Other details not shown
    end -- LIST
    -------------------------------------------------------------
    class NODE[ T ]

     creation
        make
     feature { LIST, ORDERED_LIST }
        value : T;
        next  : NODE[ T ];

        make( initial : T ) is
        do
            value := initial;
        end; -- make

        setValue( aValue : T ) is
        do
            value := aValue;
        end; -- setValue

        link( target : NODE[ T ] ) is
        do
            next := target;
        end; -- link

    end -- NODE
```

Listing 7.17   Segments of List class in C++

```
    #ifndef LIST
    #define LIST
    #include <assert.h>
    #include <iostream.h>
    enum Boolean { FALSE = 0, TRUE };

    template < class T >
    class List
    {
        friend ostream& operator << ( ostream &os, List<T> &aList
            );

        private:
            struct Item
            {
```

```
            Item *next;
            T value;

            Item( T& aValue, Item *ptrNextItem = 0 ) : next(
                ptrNextItem ), value( aValue ) { }
        };

        Item *first;
        Item *last;
        int numElements;
        void destroy();

    public:
        List( void ) { first = last = 0; numElements = 0; }

        // A copy constructor
        List( List<T>& aList );

        // Overloaded assignment operator
        List<T>& operator = ( List<T>& aList );

        ~List( void );

        void insertFront( T& anItem )
        {
            if ( first == 0 )
            {
                first = new Item( anItem );
                last = first;
            }
            else
            {
                Item *pt = new Item( anItem, first );
                first = pt;
            }
            numElements++;
        }

template < class T >
ostream& operator << ( ostream& os, List<T>& aList )
{
    os << "< ";
    List<T>::Item *curr = aList.first;
    do
    {
        if ( curr != aList.first ) cout << ", ";
        cout << curr -> value;
        curr = curr -> next;
    } while ( curr != 0 );
    cout << " >";
    return os;
}

template < class T >
```

```
List<T>::List( List<T>& aList )
{
    first = last = 0;
    Item* curr = aList.first;
    while ( curr != 0 )
    {
        insertBack( curr -> value );
        curr = curr -> next;
    }
}

template < class T >
List<T>& List<T>::operator = ( List<T>& aList )
{
    if ( this != &aList )
    {
        delete first;
        first = last = 0;
        Item* curr = aList.first;
        while ( curr != 0 )
        {
            insertBack( curr -> value );
            curr = curr -> next;
        }
    }
    return *this;
}

// Remaining details not shown
#endif
```

Listing 7.18   Segments of numeric classes in Eiffel

```
deferred class NUMBER
-- Parent class for number subclasses

feature
    generality : INTEGER;

    sum, infix "+" ( aNumber : NUMBER ) : NUMBER is
      do
        if generality < aNumber.generality then
            Result := aNumber + aNumber.coerced( Current );
        elseif generality > aNumber.generality then
            Result := Current + Current.coerced( aNumber );
        else
            Result := Current.sum_like_type( aNumber )
        end
      end; -- add

    -- Remaining details not shown
end -- class NUMBER
```

```
class REAL_TYPE
inherit
    NUMBER

creation
    make

feature { NONE }
    value : REAL;

feature

    coerced( aNumber : NUMBER ) : NUMBER is
    do -- Convert a number of lower generality to a REAL_TYPE
        !REAL_TYPE!Result.make( aNumber.asFloat.value );
    end; -- coerced

    sum_like_type( aNumber : REAL_TYPE ) : REAL_TYPE is
    do
        !!Result.make( value + aNumber.value );
    end; -- sum_like_type
    -- Remaining details not shown

end -- class REAL_TYPE
```

Listing 7.19   Segments of Numeric classes in C++

```
#ifndef NUMBER
#define NUMBER
#include <iostream.h>
class Number
{
    public:
        virtual Number* operator + ( Number& y )
        {
            if ( generality() < y.generality() )
                return ( *( y.coerce( *this ) ) + y );
            else
                return *this + *coerce( y );
        }

        // Remaining details not shown
#endif

// Interface to class Float - Float.h

#ifndef FLOAT
#define FLOAT
#include "Number.h"
#include <iostream.h>

class Float : public Number
{
```

```
      private:
          double value;

          virtual int generality() { return 20; }

      public:
          virtual Number* operator + ( Number& y )
          {
              if ( y.generality() == 20 )
              {
                  Float *f = ( Float* ) &y;
                  return new Float( value + f -> value );
              }
              else
                  return Number::operator + ( y );
          }
          // Remaining details not shown
  };

  #endif
```

It is noted that the extensive use of pointers and references in the C++ code of Listing 7.19 is required in order to enable late-binding, an essential feature of the software design.

7.11 MORE ON THE COMPLEXITY OF C++ AND EIFFEL

Just like it is difficult to compare the relative "readability" of two languages, it is also difficult to compare the relative complexity of two languages. And of course, complexity is related to "readability." One cannot judge the complexity of a language on the basis of the number of reserved words or some other simple measure. C++, for example, uses some of its reserved words in several ways, based on the context. This in fact adds to the complexity of the language. The complexity of a language is related to its consistency — consistency of syntax and semantics. Complexity is also related to the number of special cases and exceptions to rules. Probably the most fundamental question related to the complexity of a language is, "Does the code perform as one would expect?" If this is often a difficult question to answer for a given language then this is an important indicator that the language is complex.

7.11.1 Power, Complexity and Usefulness

Is complexity an undesirable thing? Generally, yes. Although the complexity of a programming language is probably directly related to its power, its complexity may not be directly related to its usefulness. What good is power if it is often misused? Most programmers and software development managers believe that maintaining total intellectual control over the software development process is of paramount importance.

7.11.2 The "++" Part of C++

An increasing number of users are reporting that C++ ranks as one of the most complex commercial programming languages ever created along with PL/1 and Ada. In part, this is due to the hybrid nature of C++. Its constructs and rules must deal with the need to be almost completely upwards compatible with the C programming language. Its support for overloading of functions, overloading of operators, default values for parameters, templates and specialized templates, initialization order of constructors and destructors, virtual functions, virtual base classes, const member functions, static member functions, reference variables, to name a few of C++'s many features, places a heavy burden on programmers attempting to perform the "++" part of going from C to C++. The burden becomes particularly heavy if these same programmers are simultaneously trying to learn about object-oriented software engineering. **I strongly recommend against the practice of using C++ as a vehicle to teach object-oriented programming.**

On the positive side, for at least some people, C++ has spawned an industry of writers, short course presenters and C++ conference promoters who have all capitalized on the opportunity to teach this complex language.

7.11.2.1 What About Eiffel?
As indicated earlier, Eiffel is certainly not a simple programming language. Its complex and powerful rules of inheritance require careful study and practice. But, Eiffel enjoys a benefit that only relatively few programming languages can claim: a high level of consistency. Many of the artifacts that cause great complexity in C++ are notably absent in Eiffel. Eiffel does not support the overloading of functions. It does not distinguish between const member functions, virtual functions, non-virtual functions, virtual base classes, non-virtual classes, etc. Yet, as a pure object-oriented programming language, it is able to achieve a high degree of power, flexibility and most importantly safety.

To provide a simple and typical illustration of the complexity of C++ compared with the relative simplicity of Eiffel, we consider an example. We compare how Eiffel and C++ deal with constant objects. In particular, we consider how one might access the characters of a constant String object. This example presents the "flavor" of how C++ typically does business compared to the way Eiffel typically does business.

In Listing 7.20, a constant string object is constructed in Eiffel and then accessed. In Listing 7.21, portions of a string class in C++ are shown, and a constant string object is constructed and accessed.

Listing 7.20   Constant STRING object in Eiffel

```
class APPLICATION

creation
  start
```

```
feature
    start is
    do
        constant_string.put( 'z', 1 );
        io.putstring( "constant_string = " );
        io.putstring( constant_string );
        io.new_line;
    end; -- start

    constant_string : STRING is
    once
        Result := "abcdefghij";
    end; -- CONSTANT_STRNG

end -- APPLICATION
```

The program output is:

```
constant_string = zbcdefghij
```

The "once" function, *constant_string*, is used to simulate a constant STRING object in Listing 7.20. Unfortunately, it is a poor simulation. By sending the message *constant_string.put('z', 1)*, the so called *constant_string* changes. Eiffel does not provide rigorous support for constant objects.

Listing 7.21   Constant String object in C++

```
#include <iostream.h>

extern "C"
{
    #include <string.h>
}


class String
{
    friend ostream& operator << ( ostream&, const String& );
    private:
        char *str;
    public:
        String() { str = new char[ 1 ]; str[ 0 ] = '\0'; }

        String( char *aString )
        {
            strcpy( str = new char[ strlen( aString ) + 1 ],
                aString );
        }

        char operator [] ( int index ) const
        {
            return str[ index ];
        }
```

```
        /* Another approach
        char& operator [] ( int index ) const { return str[
          index ]; }
        */

        char& operator [] ( int index )
        {
            return str[ index ];
        }

        operator char*() const { return str; }

        // Other details not shown
    };

void main()
{
    const String obj( "abcdefghij" );
    // obj[ 0 ] = 'z'; Error: not lvalue or assignment to
      const type

    // Now we do something nasty!
    char *nasty = obj;
    *nasty = 'z';
    cout << obj << endl;
}
```

7.11.2.2 Unraveling the C++ Code   The C++ code of Listing 7.21 demonstrates two alternative techniques for establishing constant object semantics. The first member function, *operator [ ]*, with the *const* specifier, returns a type *char* and can, therefore, be used only on the right side of an expression. This prevents one from assigning to a constant String object. The second alternative *operator [ ]* with the *const* specifier (commented out in Listing 7.21) returns a reference to a *char* (*char&*). Any attempt to assign a *char* to a constant object will result in an illegal assignment and an error message. It is illegal to assign an ordinary *char* to a reference to a *char*. To the attendee unfamiliar with C++, no attempt will be made to further explain the somewhat bizarre semantics being used here. Even some moderately experienced C++ programmers find this usage somewhat strange.

So, it appears that C++ provides constructs for and, therefore, support for constant objects. Unfortunately, the same language that provides the syntax shown in Listing 7.21 for enforcing constant object semantics also provides a simple and perfectly legal workaround. The last three lines of code in function main (Listing 7.21) shows this workaround. A pointer to *char*, *char *nasty*, is defined and initialized to *obj*. The *char** conversion operator in class String assigns the *str* attribute of *obj* to *nasty*. Then the character "z" sent through this "nasty" pointer to *obj*. The semantics of a constant object have been totally compromised.

7.11.2.3 Conclusion About 'Constant' Objects in C++ and Eiffel It

is, therefore, concluded that neither C++ nor Eiffel provides rigorous support for constant object semantics. This is in light of the fact that C++ promises such semantics but doesn't deliver.

But more to the point of this section, the C++ code of Listing 7.21 relies on fairly complex and subtle language usage — for example, the ability to assign a value to a function because it returns a reference to some type, the overloading of two versions of the *operator [ ]* (one with and one without the const specifier), and the subtlety associated with lvalue or *char&* return values.

None of this complexity is evident in the Eiffel code.

7.12 WHY THE C++ BANDWAGON EFFECT—THE POLITICS OF LANGUAGES

The reasons that large organizations adopt a particular programming language for their projects vary. But among the significant considerations that influence this decision are the following:

- The perception that everyone else is adopting the language and the desire to "keep up with the Joneses;"
- The prestige of the primary vendor and the confidence that the primary vendor will be around in five years to support the language;
- The number of support tools (e.g. CASE tools, language specific-editors, programming frameworks) that are currently available;
- The number of books that explain and illustrate the use of the language;
- The number of vendors that sell and support language compilers and the number of platforms on which the language is available;
- The existence of legacy code; and
- Maybe performance issues and the technical merits of the language itself.

Many conversations over the years with software managers representing large and important organizations suggest that bullets two, three and five above represent the strongest reasons that many companies choose one language over another. The first five bullets are in large measure a consequence of the "bandwagon effect." The rich get richer and more famous. As the reality (or sometimes perception) occurs that a language is being used by many programmers, this in itself stimulates many third-party support products. It also stimulates a tidal wave of books to be published, magazines to be spawned and new technical conferences to come into existence. There is certainly nothing wrong with all of these events. The irony is that the last bullet is the one that often gets overlooked.

C++ has been enjoying a "bandwagon effect" of popularity. This bodes very well for C++'s future. But C++'s high level of complexity, its hybrid nature, its failure to support true software reuse, its inconsistency and its vulnerability to the scourge of memory leakage are causing an increasing number of highly respected writers to report some of C++'s problems and to cause an increasing number of engineers to question their choice of using C++ for high-level, large-scale software development projects. Some of these people have been looking for an alternative.

7.13 CONCLUDING REMARKS

This chapter has compared C++ and Eiffel in terms of their respective complexity, "readability," support for software reuse and support for safe software engineering. It is difficult and perhaps dangerous to keep a score card in each of these areas. Some of what I have expressed is personal opinion and not fact. I have not presented every aspect of each language. To do so would require the space of at least two books. I have attempted, allowing for my own biases, to present cases that capture the spirit and typical usage of each language.

Happy programming in C++, or in Eiffel, or in both!

Case Studies

*P*art 2 presents several moderate-sized examples that show Eiffel in action. The focus in this part of the book is on object modeling at the analysis and design level, and the mapping of the design to an Eiffel implementation.

CHAPTER 8

Object-Oriented Analysis and Design

8.1 OBJECT-ORIENTED MODELING

*T*his chapter introduces and illustrates the Grady Booch approach for performing object-oriented analysis and design. Among the various major and competing methods, this method has been chosen because it is quite straightforward, is nicely supported by the CASE Tool Rational Rose™, supports an iterative approach, provides mechanisms for the validation of the model at each stage and supports object scenarios (use cases). The reader is encouraged to consult[1] for more details. The work products at each stage of modeling will be illustrated in this and subsequent chapters.

The analysis process focuses on the problem domain. Its purpose is to identify and describe the entities that interact in this domain. At every stage of analysis, the analyst looks toward the problem, not the solution.

The design process focuses on the solution, the implementation. Its purpose is to identify additional classes, called design classes, that provide the best utilization of computer memory resources and provide for the greatest run-time optimization. Most of the design classes have little resemblance to the domain classes.

The Booch approach to object modeling provides a seamless transition from analysis to design. Many of the work products and activities are the same at each level. Key Class Abstraction Diagrams and Object Scenario Diagrams are produced during each phase. How would one know whether the class abstraction diagram that is being produced is a work product of analysis or design? The answer is simple. If one is looking in the direction of the problem (trying to understand better the problem and the complex behaviors and data models that describe the problem domain), then one is doing analyis. If one is looking in the direction of the solution and trying, for example, to determine what type of collection class should be used to represent a set of objects, then one is doing design.

Hopefully, the problem clarification that emerges from analysis and the fairly detailed blueprint that emerges from design will map easily into object-oriented programming — implementation in some object-oriented language. We will do all of our implementations in Eiffel.

Booch[1] defines object-oriented analysis as "... *a method of analysis that examines requirements from the perspective of the classes and objects found in the vocabulary of the problem domain.*" He defines object-oriented design as "...*a method of design encompassing the process of object-oriented decomposition and a notation for depicting both logical and physical as well as static and dynamic models of the system under design.*"

The analysis phase of object-modeling centers on formulating key abstractions that correspond to the major elements of the problem space. Classes are used to represent abstractions of the things or entities in the problem domain. For example, a class representing cars and another class representing jet planes would be two key abstractions in a transportation simulation. Actions or the behaviors of the entities in the problem domain are abstracted by the methods or operations that are available to the instances of a class. These instances or objects of a class are characterized by state, some well-defined behavior and unique identity.

At the analysis level, it is important to identify the kinds of relationships that exist among the objects of the problem domain and their respective classes. Additional relationships may be discovered at the design stage. A relationship between two objects includes the knowledge one object has about the other. This knowledge includes what operations can be performed and what behavior results from these operations.

J. Rumbaugh, et al[2] define a *link* relationship as a "physical or conceptual connection between objects." Objects collaborate with other objects through the links they have with these other objects. An object may play several roles in a link relationship:

- It can operate upon other objects but is never operated upon by the other objects;
- It is only operated on by other objects but can never act upon other objects; and
- It can both operate on other objects and be operated upon.

The first type of link is called an actor, the second a server and the third an agent.

Figure 8.1 shows an actor object, an agent object and a server object.

The actor object, aUser, can only send messages to other objects. The agent object, *aButton*, receives a message from the user and sends a message to a display object. The display object *aView*, can only receive messages and is, therefore, a server object.

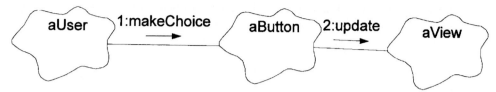

Fig. 8.1 An Actor, Agent and Server

8.2 BASIC STEPS IN OBJECT-ORIENTED ANALYSIS

Analysis is concerned with the classification of the key problem domain entities. Class discovery starts with object discovery. There are standard methods for identifying key classes and their relationships. See, for example, Coad and Yourdon[3].

It is common to examine the similarities and differences among a set of related classes. From this analysis, it may be decided that two classes are best represented as siblings; they have a common parent. Sibling classes should either differ in their number of attributes or have distinct behavior that cannot be accounted for easily by a difference in some value of a parent attribute.

As an example, consider the objects *aDog, aYellowLab, aBlackLab* and *aGoldenRetriever.* What relationship, if any, do these objects have to each other?

It is clear that yellow labs, black labs, and golden retrievers satisfy the "kind of" dog relationship. Each is an instance of a class that is a descendent of *Dog.* But are they instances of three separate sibling classes with *Dog* as a parent class (or some other intervening class such as *FieldDog*)? To answer this, we must determine what the differences are between yellow labs and black labs. If, as I believe is the case, the only significant difference is in the color of the respective dogs, then both yellow labs and black labs should be modeled as instances of a single class, *LabradorRetriever.* This class would have a *color* attribute probably defined in a superclass of *LabradorRetriever.* The value of this *color* attribute would account for the difference between these two closely related varieties of Labrador Retrievers. There are basic behavioral differences between Labrador Retrievers and Golden Retrievers (I can personally attest to this fact). These behavioral differences justify modeling the classes *LabradorRetriever* and *GoldenRetriever* to be two sibling classes with class *FieldDog* as their parent.

In many computer applications, the problem domain objects are themselves fairly abstract. Such objects might include a push button, pull-down menu or a dialog window in a graphical user interface application. These entities must be treated as being as real as chairs, desks, lamps and computer terminals or other physical objects. The graphical user interface objects have a life of their own, albeit an artificial one. Their properties are just as real as the properties of a chair, desk or other physical object. That is because properties themselves are abstractions of reality. For example, how "real" are the blueprints of a house. A real house may be manufactured from a well drawn blueprint, but the blueprint itself consists of just abstract specifications.

The Booch method of analysis and design will be described and illustrated. Domain analysis consists of the following major steps:

1. Define classes in each category.

2. Define aggregation relationships and associations among the classes.

3. Define attributes for classes.

4. Define inheritance relationships for classes.

5. Define operations.

6. Validate and iterate the analysis.

7. The work products at the analysis level include:

- **Class category diagram**. This allows a complex system to be partitioned into groupings or clusters of classes that are logically related.
- **A key abstraction diagram**. This graphically depicts the key classes and the relationships among them. The key classes are those that correspond to the major domain objects. They are easily found from an understanding and representation of the problem domain.
- **The class specifications for all key classes**. Each class specification includes a general description of the class, documentation about each attribute, documentation about each method, a list of superclasses and a description of the relationships to other classes.
- **Object scenario diagrams**. These show all of the key mechanisms associated with the application. The sequence of messages to key objects is depicted graphically on an object-scenario diagram. These may be the most important diagrams in the modeling process because they depict the dynamic aspects of the model. From these diagrams, validation of the class relationships and the class structures can be performed.

Each of these work products will be illustrated in this and later chapters.

- At the design level, attention shifts to the solution domain — the implementation. The Booch method of design involves the following sequence of steps:

1. Define initial architecture supported by implementation prototypes.

2. Determine the logical design. This requires defining data structures, data types, details of many operations and access control for all attributes.

3. Map the logical design to the physical design.

4. Iterate this process and make refinements to both the analysis models and design models.

The work products of design are the same as analysis. Many additional design classes are typically added at the design stage. Additional attributes are usually discovered or required to support the underlying design architecture, and many additional operations are added to each class.

An often asked question is, "when is analysis completed and design begun?" In object-oriented analysis and design there is at best a fuzzy line that separates these two activities. The line is somewhat blurred by the fact that the work products at these distinct stages of modeling are the same. The difference, as indicated earlier, is one of attitude. If the goal of the modeling activity is to explore and better understand and describe the problem domain, the activity is definitely analysis. If the goal is to formulate a solution, the activitiy is design.

The above processes will be illustrated with a detailed example that will go from an informal problem specification to several stages of domain analysis to design and finally to an Eiffel implementation. This in fact was the sequence in which the work was performed. It is reassuring to report that the Eiffel implementation flowed effortlessly from the modeling work products. There were no surprises and not too much creative activitiy at the implementation level.

8.3   A MODELING EXAMPLE — SUPERMARKET CHECKOUT LINES — THE ANALYSIS

Informal specifications: Customers join one of several supermarket lines at a specified average rate and according to a Poisson arrival distribution, which is equivalent to exponential interarrival times. It is also assumed that service times are modeled by an exponential probability density function.

There are three types of checkout lines: express lines for customers with 6 or fewer items, fast lines for customers with 7 to 15 items, and normal lines for all other customers. The average service times for each of these lines are different. As customers arrive in the checkout area, a predetermined fraction of these customers are assumed to qualify for the express line, a fraction for the fast line and the remainder for the normal lines. A customer will always choose the shortest line of the appropriate type and join that line.

The goal of the program is to simulate this behavior and provide a statistical summary. Output will be text. A string of "x's" will be used to dynamically represent each checkout line. Each time a customer completes service, an 'x' is removed from the appropriate string and the shortened string redisplayed on the screen. Likewise, each time a customer joins a line, an 'x' is added to the appropriate string, and the string is redisplayed on the screen. In addition to displaying each line, some cumulative output statistics are also displayed and updated each time a customer completes service. These statistics include: the running average line length for each line, the current clock time in seconds, the total number of customers served to date and the running average wait time in the system (this includes wait time as well as service time).

A typical screen output is shown.

Supermarket Checkout Line Simulation

Express line:	xxxxxxxx	Av line length: 3.45
Fast line 1:	xxxx	Av line length: 2.46
Fast line 2:	xx	Av line length: 1.68
Normal line 1:	xxxxxxxxx	Av line length: 3.06
Normal line 2:	xxxxx	Av line length: 2.97
Normal line 3:	xx	Av line length: 1.96

Clock time: 3597.4
Total customers: 195
Av wait time: 176.2

From the problem description, the following key abstractions from the problem domain are shown in the Class Diagram of Figure 8.2. which identifies some key domain classes: Simulation, Clock, Customer, Display and Checkout. The lines connecting the key domain classes indicate yet-to-be-defined relationships. These relationships will be determined as the analysis progresses.

There are two basic approaches that may be taken in modeling a simulation of this type. The first is a discrete-event model (a term used in simulation theory — nothing to do with object modeling) in which the clock is advanced from one event to another. In this application, events would be customer arrivals and customer departures. Such an approach requires a central control object that coordi-

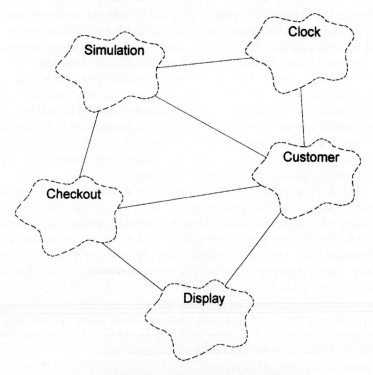

Fig. 8.2 Key Classes for Supermarket

nates and orchestrates the activities of the customers and checkout lines.

The other approach, the one that will be used here, is a discrete-time model. Using this approach, the clock is incremented in uniform segments of time (0.1 seconds in this simulation). At each discrete time unit, the simulation controller determines whether any of the objects are brought into action. That is, the current clock time is compared to the service completion time of each customer being served by a cashier and the next arrival time of a new customer. If the current clock time is equal or greater than the time associated with any of the above-mentioned event times, the simulation controller signals the appropriate customer to perform one of its key mechanisms (i.e. service completion or customer arrival). The key mechanisms themselves involve transactions between the customer object, the cashier object and the display object.

We more closely examine each of the domain classes presented in Figure 8.2 and further explore the nature of the associations and collaborations between them. In the process of doing this, additional key domain classes will be discovered.

The simulation object (instance of class Simulation) is responsible for incrementing the clock and polling each customer being served by a cashier to determine whether their service is completed and polling the next customer that is scheduled to arrive in order to determine whether a key mechanism needs to be triggered. There are two such key mechanisms, as indicated earlier: a customer completing service and a new customer joining the line.

Before the conclusion of each key event (mechanism), the user's screen needs to be updated to show the effect of a checkout line losing a customer or a checkout line gaining a customer. The cumulative output statistics must also be updated after each key event. It seems reasonable that the simulation object should "own" the display. This whole/part relationship or aggregation relationship implies that the display object is brought to life at the same time as the simulation object. If other objects need to update the single display object, they may either contain a reference to the display object as an attribute or use a reference to the display in one or more of their methods.

The simulation object also owns the clock and is solely responsible for communication with it. The clock object is brought to life at the same time as the simulation object.

The simulation object is also responsible for constructing the six cashier objects that are instances of class Checkout. These objects must be brought to life when the simulation object is created.

The simulation object has an association with the next arriving customer. Since it is responsible for creating this next customer, it is appropriate for another aggregation relationship, namely, the simulation object owns a customer object.

Based on the above discussion, the Simulation class has an aggregation relationship with classes Clock, Display, Checkout and Customer. These relationships are shown in Figure 8.3.

The dark circles on the Simulation class indicate that the aggregates belong to it. The dark squares on each of the other classes indicate that the Simulation

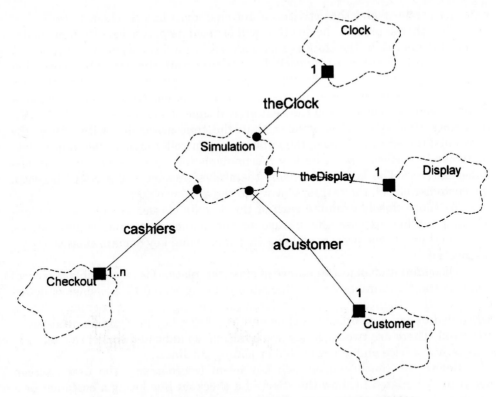

Fig. 8.3 Aggregation Relationships for Class SIMULATION

class owns instances of these other classes. The numeral shown at the end of each line indicates the cardinality of the relationship. For example, the 1..n next to the Checkout class indicates that the Simulation class owns several instances of class Checkout. The hash mark on each relationship indicates that the attribute is hidden from all clients but visible within the protocol of all descendants. That is, from within a routine of a descendant class, the attribute could be accessed directly. In C++ this would imply "protected" visibility. In Eiffel, the export status would be { NONE }.

The labels that are shown on each class relationship indicate the attribute name in class Simulation.

A line of customers is associated with each cashier. It is the responsibility of the cashier to manage this line. It is also the responsibility of each cashier to update the display when a customer joins or departs its line. The Checkout class, therefore, contains a reference to the Display class. This is manifested on the Key Class Diagram by an aggregation relationship that is terminated by a light square. This is shown in Figure 8.4, which includes the additional key class Queue and the aggregation relationship between class Checkout and Display.

In Figure 8.4, there is a "uses" relationship shown between class Checkout

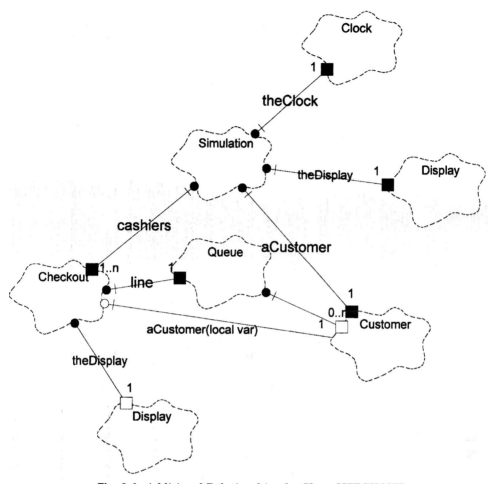

Fig. 8.4 Additional Relationships for Class CHECKOUT

and class Customer. When a customer completes service, this customer must be available to the cashier object.

A cashier object (instance of Checkout) owns a queue. But the queue does not own each customer. As indicated earlier, the simulation object actually owns each customer because it is responsible for creating each customer. Customers are only temporarily stored in the line object (instance of Queue). This is depicted by showing Queue connected to Customer with a light square indicating a reference relationship rather than a value relationship.

The simulation object and each checkout object need access to exponentially distributed random variates. These are used to generate service times and inter-arrival times. Such a TimeInterval class is a specialization of a more general class, Random, that produces uniformly distributed variates from 0 to 1. An inheritance relationship, therefore, exists between class TimeInterval and class

Random. Only one such TimeInterval instance is needed in the simulation even though it must be shared by two classes. The approach used here is to have the simulation object take ownership of the TimeInterval instance and then send a reference to this instance when creating a cashier object. The cashier object can then use the resources of the TimeInterval object through this reference. These additional key classes and relationships are shown in Figure 8.5.

Figure 8.5 indicates that class Checkout has a reference to class TimeInterval, whereas class Simulation owns one instance of TimeInterval and one instance of Random. It is necessary for the simulation object to determine whether a new customer is of type *express fast* or *normal*. This is done by choosing a uniformly distributed random variate using an instance of class Random.

The nine classes in the Class Diagram of Figure 8.5 represent the major or key abstractions of the problem domain. The relationships among these classes are shown. These include aggregation, uses and inheritance relationships.

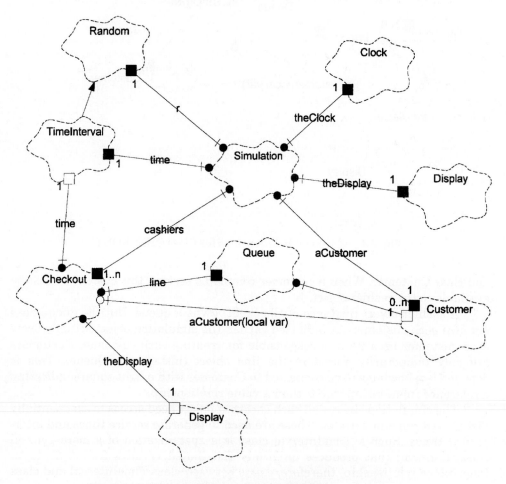

Fig. 8.5 Addition of Classes TIMEINTERVAL and DISPLAY

The semantics that have been described should be documented in each class specification. A typical class specification at this stage of analysis is shown below.

Included in a full class specification is documentation that describes the purpose of a class, a list of its attributes (at this stage of analysis, only a partial list has been discovered), a list of its operations including all parameters and return values (this has not yet been done), and documentation that indicates the semantics of each operation.

The next step in the domain analysis is to identify key operations associated with each class. Many of the key operations are fairly obvious. Each class must contain creation routines. These are responsible for bringing instances of the class to life. They are also responsible for bringing all objects that are owned by the class to life. Access methods are another obvious category of routines for each class. Although it is desirable to keep the interface bandwidth as small as possible, some attributes must be accessible to collaborating classes. Object scenario diagrams assist greatly in identifying key mechanisms and operations for each class.

Class Specifications For Several Key Classes

```
Class name: Simulation
Documentation:
 This is the class that drives the entire simulation. It deter-
 mines the next event after each clock cycle of 0.1 seconds.


Protected Interface:
 Has-A Relationships:
 Clock theClock
 Checkout cashiers
 The simulation contains an array of
 checkout objects. These are initialized
 by the start routine of the simulation.
 Customer aCustomer
 This object represents the next customer
 to arrive at the supermarket. Its
 arrival time is specified when this
 customer object is created.
 TimeInterval time
 Display theDisplay
 Random r
 A uniformly distributed random number
 from 0.0 to 1.0.


Class name: TimeInterval
Documentation:
 A "kind of" random variable that is exponentially
 distributed. Used to generate the interarrival times
```

and the service times in the simulation.
Superclasses: Random

Class name: **Checkout**
Documentation:
This class represents each checkout line. There are
 Three types of lines: express (for customers with 6 or fewer
 items), fast (for customers with 15 or fewer items) and normal
 (for customers with more than 15 items).
Associations:
 Customer aCustomer
Protected Interface:
 Has-A Relationships:
 Display theDisplay
 TimeInterval time
 A reference to the exponential random
 number generator is passed in by
 reference when the instance is created.
 Queue line
 Each checkout station (object) has a line
 (queue) containing one or more customers.
 This queue object is created when the
 instance of checkout is created.

Class name: **Display**
Documentation:
 This class is used to establish the protocol for
 displaying each supermarket line. In addition, the
 following statistics are displayed:
 Av line length (displayed to the right of each line)
 The current clock time
 The number of customers served to date
 The average total waiting time (including service) for
 each customer

   We examine several object scenario diagrams, each representing a key mechanism of the problem domain. The three key mechanisms that are depicted with object scenario diagrams are the following: (1) Choose the next event, (2) Customer completes service, and (3) Customer joins line.
   The first object scenario diagram is shown in Figure 8.6.
   The documentation associated with this diagram follows.

Documentation For Object-Scenario Diagram That Chooses Next Event

Object name:
 aSimulation : Simulation

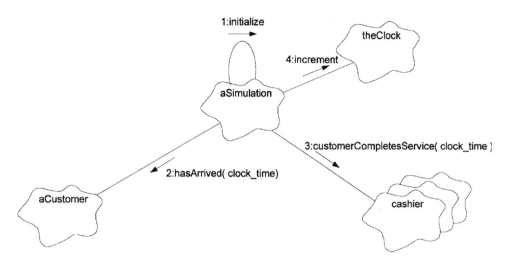

Fig. 8.6 Object-Scenario Diagram — Get Next Event

```
Documentation:
 1:initialize
 Create the following objects:
 r (instance of Random)
 type (contains the attributes express, fast, normal)
time (instance of TimeInterval)
 clock (instance of Clock)
 reuse (instance of Queue)
 theDisplay (instance of Display)
 cashiers (an array of Checkout)
 create each checkout line (the initial service time is
 set to infinity)
 create first customer and assign arrival time

Object name:
 aCustomer : Customer
Documentation:
 2: hasArrived( clock_time )
 In a loop that ends when the clock time is equal or
 greater than some termination time: determine whether
 the next event is a customer arrival.
 if clock.time >= aCustomer.getArrivalTime

Object name:
 cashier : Checkout
Documentation:
 3:customerCompletesService
```

```
Determine whether the next event is the completion of
service for a customer.
if clock.time >= cashiers.item( i ).endService
```

```
Object name:
 theClock : Clock
Documentation:
 4:increment
 Update the clock time by 0.1 seconds.
```

Some elements of the documentation included above bring us close to and perhaps over the fuzzy line that separates domain analysis from design. For example, in the documentation for cashier, the operation *customerCompletesService* (one of the key mechanisms yet to be detailed) specifies a data structure *cashiers.item(i)*.endService. This implies that an array structure will be used to model the collection of cashiers that are contained in the simulation object. This type of decision is a design decision.

Before continuing the modeling, we examine the basic elements of object-oriented design.

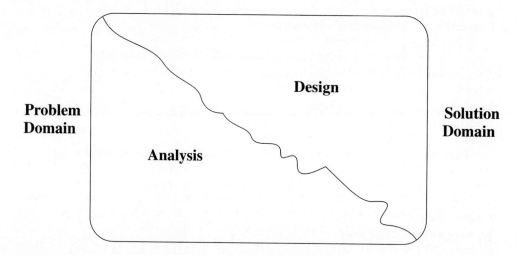

8.4 BASIC STEPS IN OBJECT-ORIENTED DESIGN

Design, in sharp constrast with analysis, focuses on how the domain classes can best be implemented. The concern in design is with the solution, not the problem domain. During the design phase, the work products developed during analysis are further refined. In addition, new design classes are discovered. These classes generally have little or nothing to do with the problem domain. Their primary purpose is to provide a bridge between the problem domain and the physical architecture of the system.

Object-scenario diagrams play a major role in design. They help to identify data structures and other required attributes and routines that provide all of the ingredients required to implement the key mechanisms of the system.

By separating design classes from domain classes, there is a greater likelihood that software reuse can be achieved.

As the progression moves from analysis to design, the work products include the following:

- **Design Class Categories** – New categories of classes that support the implementation.
- **Design Class Diagrams** – These depict the implementation classes.
- **Completed Class Specifications** – These show much more detail than the class specifications at the analysis level. The details of each routine are documented sometimes down to the specification of the appropriate algorithm that is used to implement the routine. Typically, additional attributes are introduced into some domain classes that are for internal use only. Many additional routines, some for internal use, are introduced into existing domain classes and the design classes.
- **Design Object-Scenario Diagrams** – These show the full implementation of the key mechanisms, including those objects that deal with input/output structures and persistent data.

Parts of the design process are illustrated by continuing with the modeling of the supermarket checkout lines.

8.5 SUPERMARKET CHECKOUT LINE SIMULATION CONTINUED — THE DESIGN

The next key mechanism to be modeled is: customer completes service. Instead of deallocating storage for such a customer who is leaving the system (this is done with destructors in C++ and automatically in Eiffel), a design decision is made to recycle the customer object and use it again when a new customer needs to be generated. The old values of attributes are of course replaced with new values. But no new storage needs to be allocated. This should provide for more efficiency in the overall operation of the system. Figure 8.7 presents the object scenario diagram for a customer completing service. Just below this figure is the documentation that explains the actions.

The first event is to remove a customer from the cashier's line. Next, the cashier tells the display to update the number of customers served. The cashier then queries the customer who has completed service for his or her wait time. This information is sent by the cashier to the display. The cashier updates the average line length. This information is sent by the cashier to the display. The eventTime attribute is set to the current clock time. The next service time is computed if there is another customer waiting for service.

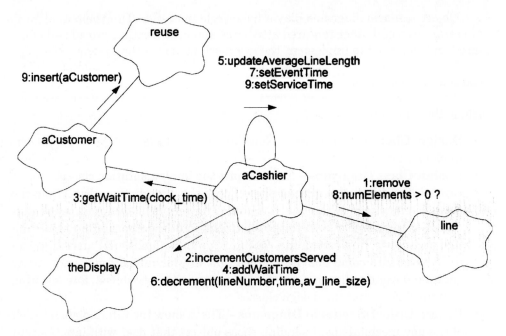

Fig. 8.7 Object-Scenario Diagram of Customer Completing Service

Documentation For Object-Scenario Diagram

```
Object name:
 aCashier : Checkout
Object name:
 line : Queue
Documentation:
1:remove
 Fetch aCustomer from line
 8:numElements > 0?
 Determine whether the line is empty
Object name:
 theDisplay : Display
Documentation:
 2:incrementCustomersServed
 4:addWaitTime
 The display object stores the cumulative wait time
 6:decrement(lineNumber,time,av_line_size)
 Remove an 'x' from the appropriate line, update the
 clock and the average line size.
Object name:
 aCustomer : Customer
Documentation:
```

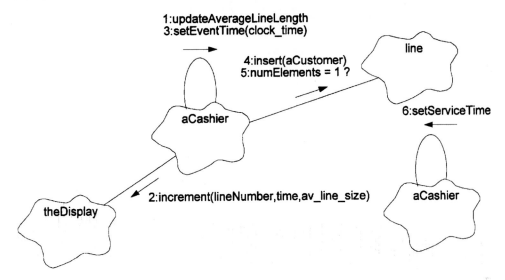

Fig. 8.8 Object-Scenario Diagram — Customer Joins Line

```
3:getWaitTime(clock_time)
```
*Return the difference between arrival_time (an
attribute of Customer) and clock time.*

Object name:
 reuse : Queue
Documentation:
9:insert(aCustomer)
*When a customer leaves the system, it is inserted into this
Queue to enable its reuse the next time a new customer must be
generated.*

From Figure 8.7, several attributes and operations can be identified for existing domain classes. One new class can also be seen (Queue for customer reuse). The key operations shown for class Display are: *incrementCustomers-Served*, *addWaitTime* and *decrement*. The key operations shown for class Checkout are: *updateAverageLineLength*, *setEventTime* and *setServiceTime*. The key operation shown for class Customer is *getWaitTime*.

Figure 8.8 shows the object scenario diagram for the third key mechanism: customer joins line.

The documentation that supports the object scenario diagram of Figure 8.8 is shown below.

Object name:
 aCashier : Checkout
Documentation:
 1:updateAverageLineLength
Every time either an arrival or a departure occurs from

*a given cashier, update the cumulative average line
length.*
*av_line_size := av_line_size + (clock_time -
event_time) * line.numElements*
3:setEventTime(clock_time)
The eventTime must be set to current clock time.
6:setServiceTime (if step 5 is TRUE)
beginService := clock_time
endService := clock_time + service_time

Object name:
 theDisplay : Display
Documentation:
 2:increment(lineNumber,time,av_line_size)
*The parameters sent into the increment message cause an
additional 'x' to be added to the line with given line
number, the current time to be updated and the average
line size to be displayed.*

Object name:
 line : Queue
Documentation:
 4:insert(aCustomer)
Add a customer to the cashier's line.
 5:numElements = 1?
*Test to see whether the customer is the first to join
the line.*

From Figure 8.8, the additional operation *increment* is shown for class Display.

Based on the two key mechanisms of a customer completing service and joining a line shown in Figures 8.7 and 8.8, respectively, a detailed class specification Display is shown below.

Class name: **Display**
Documentation:
 *This class is used to establish the protocol for
 displaying each supermarket line. In addition, the
 following statistics are displayed:*
 Av line length (displayed to the right of each line)
 The current clock time
 The number of customers served to date
 *The average total waiting time (including service) for
 each customer*
Public Interface:
 Operations:

```
addWaitTime
increment
decrement
Protected Interface:
 Has-A Relationships:
 ARRAY[ INTEGER ] line_lengths
 Keeps track of the current line length
 for each line.
INTEGER cust_served
 The total number customers served.
 DOUBLE wait_time
 Contains the total wait time over all
 customers.
Operation name: addWaitTime
Arguments: DOUBLE wt_time
Operation name: increment
Arguments: INTEGER lineNumber, DOUBLE clock_time, DOUBLE
av_line_size
Documentation:
 Displays the effect of adding a customer to a line.
Operation name: decrement
Arguments: INTEGER lineNumber, DOUBLE clock_time, DOUBLE
av_line_size
Documentation:
 Displays the effect of removing a customer from a line.
```

An updated class diagram that shows the design classes integrated with the existing domain classes is presented in Figure 8.9.

In the final class diagram that shows both domain and design classes, shown in Figure 8.9, the new design classes LineType, Array and Queue (for reusing Customers) are shown. The Simulation class attribute *cashiers*, is implemented as an array and is used to house all the checkout lines. An Array is chosen to provide the capability to perform direct indexing to access a particular checkout line. The Array class is shown as owning the checkout lines since the lifetime of the checkout objects is the same as the lifetime of the array (both are created by the simulation object when the simulation is initialized).

The Simulation object is shown as owning single instances of eight classes: Random, Queue, Clock, LineType, Display, Customer, Array and TimeInterval. The classes Array and LineType are typical design classes. LineType encapsulates the three values *express*, *fast* and *normal*. This allows more readable references to these important values. Class Customer is shown as having a *reference type* aggregation relationship to class LineType. This implies that a copy of a LineType instance is sent to a Customer instance when the Customer instance is created. This allows Customer objects to be assigned a type during the execution of their creation routine.

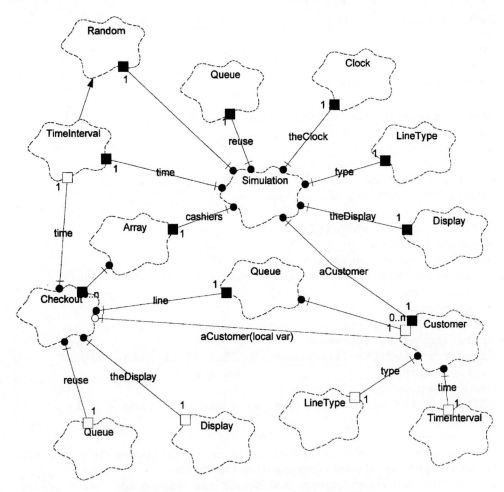

Fig. 8.9 Final Class Diagram with Design Classes

Portions of the final class specifications are shown below. They contain a great deal of detail and should be examined closely.

```
Class name: Clock
Documentation:
 The clock is incremented by 0.1 seconds. After such an
 update, the following possible events are polled to
 determine whether any will occur:
 (1) A new customer arrives
 (2) A customer being served completes service.
Protected Interface:
 Has-A Relationships:
 DOUBLE clock_time
 The instantaneous value of the clock.
```

Class name: **Simulation**
Documentation:
 This is the class that drives the entire simulation.
 It determines the next event after each clock cycle of
 0.1 seconds.
 Operations:
 start
 initialize
 makeCustomer
 selectLine
Protected Interface:
 Has-A Relationships:
 Queue reuse
 Clock theClock
 Customer aCustomer
 This object represents the next customer
 to arrive at the supermarket. Its
 arrival time is specified when this
 customer object is created.
 TimeInterval time
 Display theDisplay
 DOUBLE fraction_express
 The fraction of incoming customers that
 have six or fewer items.
 DOUBLE fraction_fast
 The fraction of incoming customers that
 have between 7 and 15 items.
 DOUBLE reuse_freq
 Keeps track of the number of customers
 that have been recycled through the reuse
 queue.
 LineType type
 Array cashiers
 The cashiers are stored in an Array[CHECKOUT].
 Random r
 A uniformly distributed random number
 from 0.0 to 1.0.
 INTEGER new_allocations
 Keeps track of the number of customers
 that are dynamically allocated.
 The other new customers are recycled
 through the reuse queue.
 Array cashiers
 The cashiers are stored in an Array[CHECKOUT].
Operation name: **start**
Documentation:

Used to trigger the entire simulation.
The main event loop is contained in this routine.
Operation name: **initialize**
Documentation:
 Create the following instance objects:
 (1) r (from Random)
 (2) type (from LineType)
 (3) time (from TimeInterval)
 (4) clock (from Clock)
 (5) reuse (from Queue)
 (6) theDisplay (from Display)
 (7) cashiers (from Array[Checkout]
 (8) aLine (from local variable Checkout)
Operation name: **makeCustomer**
Documentation:
 Get a customer either from the reuse queue, if it is
 not empty, or by dynamic allocation. Assign the
 customer the current clock time, the average interval
 arrival time and the type.
Operation name: **selectLine**
Return Class: INTEGER
Documentation:
 Chooses the smallest line of the appropriate type.

Class name: **LineType**
Documentation:
 Used to encapsulate the three types of lines.
Protected Interface:
 Has-A Relationships:
 unique integer express
 unique integer fast
 unique integer normal

Class name: **Customer**
Documentation:
 Customers line up at cashiers. They are of type {
 express, fast and normal) based on the number of
 items they have. They join the shortest line of the
 appropriate type.
Protected Interface:
 Has-A Relationships:
 DOUBLE arrival_time
 The time that a customer joins a line.
 DOUBLE av_arrival_interval
 A descriptive attribute that describes

the average time between arrivals.
LineType type
A reference to LineType is provided by
the simulation.
TimeInterval time
A reference to this random number object
is provided by the simulation.

Class name: **Checkout**
Documentation:
 This class represents each checkout line. There are
 three types of lines:
 express (for customers with 6 or fewer items), fast
 (for customers with 7 to 15 or fewer items) and normal (for
 customers with more than 15 items).
 Operations:
  make
  serviceCompleted
  customerJoinsLine
Protected Interface:
 Has-A Relationships:
 Queue line
 Each checkout station (object) has a line
 (queue) containing one or more customers.
 This queue object is created when the
 instance of checkout is created.
 Display theDisplay
 Queue reuse
 A reference to the reuse queue is passed
 in from the Simulation object when the
 instance of Checkout is created.
 TimeInterval time
 A reference to the exponential random
 number generator is passed in by
 reference when the instance is created.
 DOUBLE av_ser_time
 This descriptive attribute is set by the
 simulation.
 INTEGER type
 The value is either { express, fast,
 normal }
 DOUBLE beginService
 Records the clock time when a customer in
 the line begins service.
 DOUBLE endService

The computed completion time of the customer being served (infinity if no customer is being served).
DOUBLE eventTime
Records the time of either a customer arrival or departure.
DOUBLE av_line_size
A running sum of products of line size multiplied by the time between events is stored. This value divided by the current clock time forms an estimate of the average line size.
INTEGER lineNumber
The simulation assigns each cashier a line number.
Operation name: **make**
Arguments:
 INTEGER theType
 TIME_INTERVAL t
 DOUBLE service_time
 Display aDisplay
 Queue[Customer] reuse_Q
 INTEGER line_number
Documentation:
 Used to create a new cashier.
Operation name: **serviceCompleted**
Arguments:
 DOUBLE clock_time
Documentation:
 Implements the key mechanism associated with a customer leaving a cashier.
Operation name: **customerJoinsLine**
Arguments:
 DOUBLE clock_time
 Customer aCustomer
Documentation:
 Implements the key mechanism of a customer joining the line of a cashier.

8.6 IMPLEMENTATION OF CHECKOUT LINE SIMULATION

With each of the classes carefully specified and validated through object scenario analysis, it is time to convert the design to a working program. Listing 8.1 shows the details of the SIMULATION class. This class is responsible for bringing to life many class instances.

Listing 8.1   Class SIMULATION

```
creation
    start

feature
  reuse         : QUEUE[ CUSTOMER ];
  cashiers      : ARRAY[ CHECKOUT ];
  aCustomer     : CUSTOMER;
  clock         : CLOCK;
  theDisplay    : DISPLAY;
  type          : LINE_TYPE;
  time          : TIME_INTERVAL;
  fraction_express : DOUBLE is 0.20;
  fraction_fast : DOUBLE is 0.55;
  r             : RANDOM;
  reuse_freq    : INTEGER;
  new_allocations : INTEGER;

  start is -- This routine gets executed first
  local
      lineSelected : INTEGER;
      i : INTEGER;
  do
      initialize;
      from
      until clock.time >= 3600.0 * 4
      loop -- main event loop
         clock.increment;
         -- poll each possible event
         if clock.time >= aCustomer.getArrivalTime then
            -- customer joins a line
            lineSelected := selectLine;
            cashiers.item( lineSelected ).
               customerJoinsLine( clock.time, aCustomer );
          makeCustomer;
         else -- check to see whether a customer completes
         -- service
            from i := 0
            until i = 6
            loop
                i := i + 1;
                if clock.time >= cashiers.item( i ).
                  endService then
                  cashiers.item( i ).serviceCompleted(
                    clock.time );
                end;
            end;
         end;
      end;
      theDisplay.pause;
      theDisplay.close;
      io.putstring(
        "The number of customers taken from the reuse queue = "
        );
```

```
        io.putint( reuse_freq ); io.new_line;
        io.putstring(
          "The number of customers dynamically allocated = " );
        io.putint( new_allocations ); io.new_line;
    end; -- start

    initialize is
    local
        aLine : CHECKOUT;
    do
        !!r.initialize;
        !!type;
        !!time.initialize;
        !!clock.make;
        !!reuse.make;
        !!theDisplay.make;
        !!cashiers.make( 1, 6 );
        !!aLine.make( type.express, time, 50, theDisplay,
          reuse, 1 );
        cashiers.put( aLine, 1 );
        !!aLine.make( type.fast, time, 60, theDisplay, reuse,
          2 );
        cashiers.put( aLine, 2 );
        !!aLine.make( type.fast, time, 80, theDisplay, reuse,
          3 );
        cashiers.put( aLine, 3 );
        !!aLine.make( type.normal, time, 100, theDisplay,
          reuse, 4 );
        cashiers.put( aLine, 4 );
        !!aLine.make( type.normal, time, 120, theDisplay,
          reuse, 5 );
        cashiers.put( aLine, 5 );
        !!aLine.make( type.normal, time, 140, theDisplay,
          reuse, 6 );
        cashiers.put( aLine, 6 );
        makeCustomer;
    end;

    makeCustomer is
    local
        fraction : DOUBLE;
    do
        fraction := r.uniform;
        if fraction <= fraction_express then
            if reuse.numElements > 0 then
                aCustomer := reuse.remove;
                aCustomer.make( clock.time, 10.0, time,
                  type.express );
                reuse_freq := reuse_freq + 1;
            else
                !!aCustomer.make( clock.time, 10.0, time,
                  type.express);
                new_allocations := new_allocations + 1;
            end;
```

```
            elseif fraction <= fraction_fast then
                if reuse.numElements > 0 then
                    aCustomer := reuse.remove;
                    aCustomer.make( clock.time, 20.0, time,
                        type.fast );
                    reuse_freq := reuse_freq + 1;
                else
                    !!aCustomer.make( clock.time, 20.0, time,
                        type.fast );
                    new_allocations := new_allocations + 1;
                end;
            else
                if reuse.numElements > 0 then
                    aCustomer := reuse.remove;
                    aCustomer.make( clock.time, 20.0, time,
                        type.normal );
                    reuse_freq := reuse_freq + 1;
                else
                    !!aCustomer.make( clock.time, 20.0, time,
                        type.normal );
                    new_allocations := new_allocations + 1;
                end;
            end;
        end; -- makeCustomer

    selectLine : INTEGER is
    local
        len4, len5, len6 : INTEGER;
    do
        if aCustomer.type = type.express then
            Result := 1;
        elseif aCustomer.type = type.fast then
            if cashiers.item( 2 ).line.numElements <=
                cashiers.item( 3 ).line.numElements then
                Result := 2;
            else
                Result := 3;
            end;
        else
            len4 := cashiers.item( 4 ).line.numElements;
            len5 := cashiers.item( 5 ).line.numElements;
            len6 := cashiers.item( 6 ).line.numElements;
            if len4 <= len5 and len4 <= len6 then
                Result := 4;
            elseif len5 <= len4 and len5 <= len6 then
                Result := 5;
            else
                Result := 6;
            end;
        end;
    end; -- selectLine

end -- SIMULATION
```

Two key mechanisms are triggered in the *start* routine: *cashiers.item(lineSelected).customerJoinsLine(clock.time, aCustomer)* and *cashiers.item(i).serviceCompleted(clock.time)*.

It is noted that the two fast lines are assigned average service times of 60 and 80 seconds, the express line an average service time of 50 seconds and the three normal lines service times of 100, 120 and 140 seconds. Since customers are always assumed to join the shortest available line, one would expect the average length of the first fast line to be smaller than the second and the average length of the first normal line smaller than the average length of the second normal line, and finally, the average length of the second normal line smaller than the average length of the third normal line. These predictions are indeed born out by the simulation results.

Listing 8.2 presents the details of the next major class in the simulation, class CHECKOUT.

Listing 8.2   Class CHECKOUT

```
class CHECKOUT
-- A checkout line
 creation
    make

 feature
    av_ser_time: DOUBLE;
    type : INTEGER;- express, fast, normal
    line : QUEUE[ CUSTOMER ];
    time : TIME_INTERVAL; - A reference
    theDisplay : DISPLAY; -- A reference
    reuse : QUEUE[ CUSTOMER ];- A reference
    beginService : DOUBLE;
    endService : DOUBLE;
    eventTime : DOUBLE; -- Either arrival or departure
    av_line_size : DOUBLE;
    lineNumber : INTEGER;

 feature
   make( theType : INTEGER; t : TIME_INTERVAL; service_time
      : DOUBLE; aDisplay : DISPLAY; reuse_Q : QUEUE[ CUSTOMER ];
      l_number : INTEGER; ) is
   do
       !!line.make; -- Create an empty queue
       time := t;
       type := theType;
       av_ser_time := service_time;
       theDisplay := aDisplay;
       reuse := reuse_Q;
       lineNumber := l_number;
       eventTime := 0.0;
       endService := 1000000.0;
     end; -- make

   lineLength : INTEGER is
   do
```

```
        Result := line.numElements;
    end; -- lineLength

    setBeginService( clock_time : DOUBLE ) is
    do
        beginService := clock_time;
    end; -- setBeginService

    setEndService( clock_time : DOUBLE ) is
    do
        endService := clock_time + time.interval( av_ser_time
            );
    end; -- setEndService

    serviceCompleted( clock_time : DOUBLE ) is
    local
        aCustomer : CUSTOMER;
    do
        aCustomer := line.remove;
        theDisplay.incrementCustomersServed;
        theDisplay.addWaitTime( aCustomer.getWaitTime(
          clock_time ) );
        -- Update the average line length
        av_line_size := av_line_size +
        ( clock_time - eventTime ) * ( line.numElements + 1
            );
        theDisplay.decrement( lineNumber, clock_time,
                av_line_size / clock_time );
        eventTime := clock_time;
        if line.numElements > 0 then
            beginService := clock_time;
            setEndService( clock_time );
        else
            beginService := 1000000.0;
            endService := 1000000.0;
        end;
        reuse.insert( aCustomer );
    end; -- serviceCompleted

    customerJoinsLine( clock_time : DOUBLE; aCustomer :
      CUSTOMER ) is
    do
        -- Update the average line length
        av_line_size := av_line_size +
                ( clock_time - eventTime ) *
                    line.numElements;
        theDisplay.increment( lineNumber, clock_time,
          av_line_size / clock_time );
        eventTime := clock_time;
        line.insert( aCustomer );
        if line.numElements = 1 then
            beginService := clock_time;
            setEndService( clock_time );
        end;
    end; -- customerJoinsLine

end -- CHECKOUT
```

The routines *serviceCompleted* and *customerJoinsLine* follow the sequence of events given in their respective object scenario diagram. It should be clear that that implementation flows smoothly from the design.

Listing 8.3 presents the details of class CUSTOMER.

Listing 8.3   Class CUSTOMER

```
class CUSTOMER
 creation
   make

   feature
   time                 : TIME_INTERVAL;- This is a reference.
   arrival_time         : DOUBLE;
   type                 : INTEGER;     - express, fast or normal
   av_arrival_interval  : DOUBLE;

   feature
     make( clock_time : DOUBLE; av_arr_time : DOUBLE;
           t : TIME_INTERVAL; cust_type : INTEGER ) is
       do
          time := t;
          type := cust_type;
          av_arrival_interval := av_arr_time;
          arrival_time := clock_time + time.interval(
            av_arrival_interval );
       end; -- create

       getArrivalTime : DOUBLE is
       do
          Result := arrival_time;
       end; -- getArrivalTime

       getWaitTime( clock_time : DOUBLE ) : DOUBLE is
       do
          Result := clock_time - arrival_time;
       end; -- getWaitTime

 end -- CUSTOMER
```

The routines of class CUSTOMER are simple and require no further comments. The details of class DISPLAY are shown in Listing 8.4.

Listing 8.4   Class DISPLAY

```
class DISPLAY
-- Used to display lines
 creation
   make

 feature { NONE }
     line_lengths : ARRAY[ INTEGER ];
```

```
    cust_served  : INTEGER;
    wait_time    : DOUBLE;

    c_init is
    external "C"
    alias
        "init"
    end; -- c_init

    c_display_text is
    external "C"
    alias
        "display_text"
    end; -- c_display_text

    c_display_line( lineNumber : INTEGER; size : INTEGER;
        av_length : DOUBLE ) is
    external "C"
    alias
        "display_line"
    end; -- c_display_line

    c_display_time( clock_time : DOUBLE ) is
    external "C"
    alias
        "display_time"
    end; -- c_display

    c_cust_served( number : INTEGER ) is
    external "C"
    alias
        "cust_served"
    end; -- c_cust_served

    c_av_wait_time( value : DOUBLE ) is
    external "C"
    alias
        "av_wait_time"
    end; -- c_av_wait_time

    c_pause is
    external "C"
    alias
        "pause"
    end; -- c_pause

    c_end_window is
    external "C"
    alias
        "end_window"
    end; -- c_end-window

feature
    make is
    local
        index : INTEGER;
```

```
do
    !!line_lengths.make( 1, 6 );
    from index := 0
    until index = 6
    loop
        index := index + 1;
        line_lengths.put( 0, index );
    end;
    cust_served := 0;
    c_init;
    c_display_text;
end; -- make

addWaitTime( wt_time : DOUBLE ) is
do
    wait_time := wait_time + wt_time;
    avWaitTime( wait_time / cust_served );
end; -- addWaitTime

incrementCustomersServed is
do
    cust_served := cust_served + 1;
    custServed;
end; -- incrementCustomerServed

increment( lineNumber : INTEGER; clock_time : DOUBLE;
av_length : DOUBLE ) is
do
    line_lengths.put( line_lengths.item( lineNumber ) +
        1, lineNumber );
    c_display_line( lineNumber, line_lengths.
        item( lineNumber ), av_length );
    putTime( clock_time );
end; -- increment

decrement( lineNumber : INTEGER; clock_time : DOUBLE;
              av_length : DOUBLE ) is
do
  line_lengths.put( line_lengths.item( lineNumber ) - 1,
      lineNumber );
    c_display_line( lineNumber, line_lengths.
      item( lineNumber ), av_length );
    putTime( clock_time );
end; -- decrement

putTime( clock_time : DOUBLE ) is
do
    c_display_time( clock_time );
end; -- putTime

custServed is
do
    c_cust_served( cust_served );
end; -- custServed

avWaitTime( value : DOUBLE ) is
do
```

```
        c_av_wait_time( value );
    end; -- avWaitTime

  pause is
   do
      c_pause;
   end; -- pause;

   close is
   do
      c_end_window;
   end; -- close

end -- DISPLAY
```

Many of the routines of class DISPLAY are implemented using the C programming language. These C routines use the curses library that is available on many UNIX platforms. The C code that is associated with class DISPLAY is presented in Listing 8.5.

Listing 8.5   C routines associated with class DISPLAY

```c
#include <curses.h>

void init()
{
    initscr();
    clear();
}

void display_text()
{
    move( 8, 27 );
    addstr( "Supermarket Simulation by Richard Wiener" );
    move( 10, 1 );
    addstr( "Express line : " );
    move( 11, 1 );
    addstr( "Fast line 1 : " );
    move( 12, 1 );
    addstr( "Fast line 2 : " );
    move( 13, 1 );
    addstr( "Normal line 1: " );
    move( 14, 1 );
    addstr( "Normal line 2: " );
    move( 15, 1 );
    addstr( "Normal line 3: " );
    move( 17, 1 );
    addstr( "Clock time: " );
    move( 18, 1 );
    addstr( "Total customers: " );
    move( 19, 1 );
    addstr( "Av wait time: " );
    move( 10, 60 );
    addstr( "Av line length: " );
    move( 11, 60 );
```

```
        addstr( "Av line length: " );
        move( 12, 60 );
        addstr( "Av line length: " );
        move( 13, 60 );
        addstr( "Av line length: " );
        move( 14, 60 );
        addstr( "Av line length: " );
        move( 15, 60 );
        addstr( "Av line length: " );
        refresh();
    }


    void display_line( int lineNumber, int size, double av_size )
    {
        char str[ 100 ];
        int i;
        move( 9 + lineNumber, 15 );
        clrtoeol();
        refresh();
        for ( i = 0; i < size; i++ )
            str[ i ] = 'x';
        str[ i ] = '\0';
        move( 9 + lineNumber, 15 );
        addstr( str );
        move( 9 + lineNumber, 60 );
        addstr( "Av line length: " );
        move( 9 +lineNumber, 77 );
        sprintf( str, "%0.2f", av_size );
        addstr( str );
        refresh();
    }


    void display_time( double clock_time )
    {
        char str[ 100 ];
        move( 17, 15 );
        sprintf( str, "%0.1f", clock_time );
        addstr( str );
        refresh();
    }


    void cust_served( int number )
    {
        char str[ 100 ];
        move( 18, 20 );
        sprintf( str, "%d", number );
        addstr( str );
        refresh();
    }


    void av_wait_time( double value )
    {
        char str[ 100 ];
        move( 19, 20 );
        sprintf( str, "%0.1f", value );
        addstr( str );
```

```
        refresh();
    }

    void pause()
    {
        getch();
    }

    void end_window()
    {
        endwin();
    }
```

The details of class CLOCK are shown in Listing 8.6.

Listing 8.6   Class CLOCK

```
class CLOCK
 creation
    make

 feature { NONE }
    clock_time : DOUBLE;

 feature
    make is
    do
       clock_time := 0.0;
    end;

    increment is
    do
       clock_time := clock_time + 0.1;
    end; -- increment

    time : DOUBLE is
    do
       Result := clock_time;
    end; -- time

end -- CLOCK
```

Listing 8.7 shows the details of class LINE_TYPE.

Listing 8.7   Class LINE_TYPE

```
class LINE_TYPE
-- for classifying checkout line types and customer types

 feature
    express  : INTEGER is unique;
    fast     : INTEGER is unique;
    normal   : INTEGER is unique;

end -- LINE_TYPE
```

And finally, the details of class TIME_INTERVAL are presented in Listing 8.8.

Listing 8.8   Class TIME_INTERVAL

```
class TIME_INTERVAL -- Generates exponential arrival and
                    -- service times

  inherit
    RANDOM;

    C_MATH -- uses relationship
       export { NONE } all
    end;

  creation
    initialize

  feature
    interval( av_interval : DOUBLE ) : DOUBLE is
    -- Computes either an exponentially distributed arrival
    -- or service time
    do
       Result := -av_interval * log( uniform );
    end; -- interval

end -- TIME_INTERVAL
```

The details for class RANDOM and class QUEUE were presented in Part 1 of the book.

8.7 SIMULATION OUTPUT

Supermarket Simulation by Richard Wiener

Express line:		Av line length: 1.77
Fast line 1:		Av line length: 1.07
Fast line 2:		Av line length: 0.95
Normal line 1:	xxxxx	Av line length: 5.13
Normal line 2:	xxxxxx	Av line length: 4.96
Normal line 3:	xxxxx	Av line length: 4.93

Clock time: 14395.0
Total customers: 767
Av wait time: 343.9

Only 39 customers were dynamically allocated. The remaining customers were obtained from the reuse queue.

REFERENCES

1. Booch G., *Object-Oriented Analysis and Design: With Applications (Second Edition)*, Benjamin-Cummings, 1994.

2. Rumbaugh J., M. Blaha, W. Premerlani, F. Eddy and W. Lorensen, *Object-Oriented Modeling and Design,* Prentice-Hall, Inc., 1991.

3. Coad P. and E. Yourdon, *Object-Oriented Analysis, Second Edition*, Prentice-Hall, Inc., 1991.

An Ecological Simulation

9.1 INTRODUCTION

*T*he Supermarket Checkout Line Simulation example used in the previous section to illustrate some of the steps associated with object-oriented analysis and design was relatively simple in structure. Inheritance relationships played a minor role. There were no examples of polymorphism or abstract classes.

The goal of the example in this section is to define a specification for an artificial system of moderate complexity with its own complete and unambiguous set of rules that will provide a further opportunity to explore the process of object-oriented domain analysis and design. Because of the additional complexity of this example compared with the previous one, the implementation will showcase more of Eiffel's powerful capabilities and allow us to see Eiffel in action.

9.2 INFORMAL REQUIREMENTS

The system to be modeled and implemented is an ecological simulation. The "ocean" is represented by a two-dimensional grid of cells of specified dimensions. Some of the cells are empty, while others contain species of fish, including plankton, tuna, shark and crab. In addition, dead tuna and dead sharks represent debris that occupy cell space until a crab is able to scavenge the carcass and clean up the garbage. Without crabs serving as garbage collectors, all of the cells would eventually become occupied with dead tuna or dead sharks. Some cells are designated as "obstacle" cells. Their only purpose is to block the movement of active cells that tend to migrate around the two-dimensional ocean space.

We wish to simulate the effect of active cells moving at random from one cell position to another. Using a single thread of control, only one active cell can move at a given time. Included among the active cells are tuna, shark and plankton. Crabs can become active only when they are in the vicinity of either dead tuna or dead sharks. Otherwise they remain passive.

A food chain is created in which sharks can attack, kill and eat other sharks, sharks can kill and eat tuna, and tuna can eat plankton. Tuna and sharks must eat within a certain period of time, otherwise they die of starvation (and become potential food for the crabs). Plankton can never starve. Plankton, tuna and sharks can also reproduce after they have moved a specified number of times. A complex ecology is created in which each of the species goes through periods of population expansion and decay. Under some circumstances, a specie may become extinct. The goal of the simulation is to observe and record the population dynamics of each specie.

The behavior of each of the sea creatures is specified below:

9.2.1   Characteristics Shared By All Sea Creatures

Reproduction: Plankton, tuna and sharks are assigned a reproduction interval, a random integer taken from a specified uniform probability density function, when they are born. When the sea creature has moved a number of times equal to or greater than this reproduction interval (since its last reproduction has occurred) it is qualified to reproduce, providing that it can move according to its rules of movement. When the sea creature moves to an adjacent cell, it leaves its offspring in the cell that was just vacated. Normally, a sea creature will reproduce when it has reached a move number (since the last reproduction) exactly equal to its assigned reproduction interval. Only when it cannot move at this epoch will it continue to attempt to move and reproduce during subsequent moves.

Starvation: Tuna and sharks are assigned a starvation interval, a random integer taken from a specified uniform probability density function, when it is born. When such a creature reaches a move number (since last eating) that is equal to this starvation interval, it will die if it is unable to kill another appropriate sea creature in the food chain and eat it during this move. When a tuna or shark starves, its carcass remains passive in the cell in which it starved. This carcass can be cleaned-up only by a crab.

Area of Movement: Each specie has the potential to move to one of eight surrounding cells. This set of cells includes the cell directly north, directly northeast, directly east, directly south-east, directly south, directly south-west, directly west and directly north-west. Each specie's specific rules of movement are discussed next.

9.2.2   Specific Rules of Movement For Each Sea Creature

Plankton: When a plankton is "told" to move, its biological reproduction clock is incremented by one. It searches for an empty cell in the set of eight cells surrounding it. If the plankton finds more than one empty cell among this set, it chooses one at random, with an equal likelihood assigned to each empty cell. If all of the surrounding cells are occupied, the plankton does not move. If the plankton's reproduction clock is equal to or greater than its reproduction interval, it leaves an offspring in the cell that it has vacated during its move. Its reproduction clock is reset to zero.

It is noted that the population of plankton increases through reproduction and decreases by being eaten by tuna.

Tuna: When a tuna is "told" to move, its biological reproduction clock and starvation clock are incremented by one. It searches the set of eight adjoining cells (see "Area of Movement" above) to determine whether one or more of these cells contain a plankton. If one or more plankton are in this set, it chooses one randomly. If the tuna can eat, it moves to occupy the cell of the plankton that it has killed. Its starvation clock is reset to zero. It will die if it cannot eat when the current starvation clock equals the starvation interval assigned to that tuna. Otherwise, the tuna attempts to move to an empty cell using the same move logic as that defined above for the plankton. If the tuna qualifies for reproduction using the same logic as given for the plankton, it leaves an offspring in the cell that it has vacated and resets its reproduction clock.

It is noted that the population of tuna increases through reproduction and decreases through starvation and being eaten by sharks.

Shark: When a shark is "told" to move, its biological reproduction clock and starvation clock are incremented by one. It searches the set of eight adjoining cells (see "Area of Movement" above) to determine whether one or more of these cells contain a tuna. If tuna are present, it chooses a tuna at random, moves to its location, eats and resets its starvation clock to zero. If the shark cannot eat (no tuna around it) and its starvation clock equals the starvation interval, it searches for another shark in the set of eight cells surrounding it. If one or more are found, it chooses one randomly. It "attacks" this other shark. If another shark cannot be found, it dies.

Each shark is assigned a size value equal to one when it is born. Each time the shark eats, its size value is increased by one unit. If a shark "attacks" another shark (this can only happen if the shark has been unable to find a tuna and its starvation clock equals the starvation interval), it kills it and eats it if its own size is greater than the size of the attacked shark. In that case, it moves to the location of the killed shark and resets its starvation clock to zero. Otherwise, the shark that it attacked moves to the location of the attacking shark, kills it, eats it and sets its own starvation clock to zero.

If none of the above events occurs, the shark follows the same behavior as a tuna (it attempts to move to an empty cell and reproduces if it qualifies for such reproduction).

It is noted that the population of sharks increases through reproduction and decreases through starvation and being eaten by other sharks.

Crabs: When a crab is "told" to move, it can only move if it finds either a dead tuna or dead shark among the set of eight surrounding cells (see "Area of Movement" above). If the crab finds one or more such dead creatures, it chooses one at random, eats it and moves to its location. It then attempts to move again immediately by searching the new set of eight surrounding cells. It continues in this manner until it can no longer find a dead tuna or shark among its eight surrounding cells. A crab cannot be eaten, does not reproduce, and cannot die of starvation. Only a fixed number of crabs are assigned to the ocean when the simulation initializes the ocean.

Obstacle: An obstacle is completely passive. It cannot move and it blocks the movement of all other creatures.

9.2.3   Overall Flow of Simulation

The simulation creates and initializes the two-dimensional ocean, populating it with a predetermined number of plankton, tuna, sharks, crabs and obstacles. These creatures are initially deposited in randomly chosen cell positions. A simulation cycle is then begun. Such a cycle involves telling *number_rows* * *number_columns* creatures to "move," where *number_rows* and *number_columns* represent the dimensions of the ocean grid. If such a "move" command is received by either an empty cell or obstacle cell, it ignores the request. If a tuna, shark, plankton or crab cell is told to "move," it follows the rules of movement appropriate for its type.

During each simulation cycle, the "move" command is sent sequentially to a random sequence of cells. For each "move" in the simulation cycle, a random row and random column is chosen, and that cell is told to "move." It is, therefore, possible for some creatures to be told to "move" several times during a given cycle and other creatures to be ignored (not told to move). Over many simulation cycles, each cell has the same probability of receiving the "move" command.

The user is prompted for the number of simulation cycles to be executed. The ocean is initialized with the specified number of cells deposited at random positions. The simulation continues to run until either the number of sharks is zero, the number of tuna is zero or the requisite number of simulation cycles have been executed.

9.2.4   Simulation Output

After each simulation cycle (number of rows multiplied by number of columns "moves"), the number of tuna, sharks, plankton, dead fish, dead sharks and empty cells are displayed on the screen. A running graph is plotted containing the character 'T' for tuna, 'S' for sharks and 'P' for plankton. The vertical position of each of these three characters with respect to a horizontal axis is proportional to the current population of the particular specie. At each successive cycle, the horizontal position of the three characters is moved to the right by one unit.

9.3   ANALYSIS

An inspection of the problem domain suggests that there are several distinct types of sea creatures. We "discover" a hierarchy of cell classes by carefully

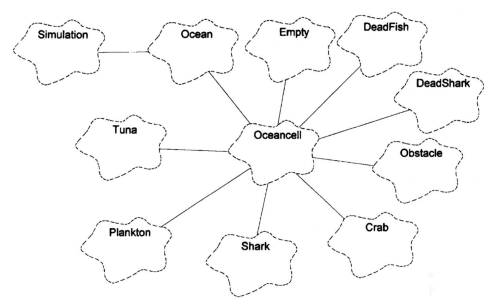

Fig. 9.1 Major Classes in Ecological Simulation

examining the similarities and differences in the attributes and behaviors of the various sea creatures.

Each of the sea creature types mentioned in the problem description are serious candidates for the major abstraction classes. These include Simulation, Ocean, Oceancell, Plankton, Tuna, Shark, Crab, Obstacle, Empty, DeadTuna and DeadShark.

These eleven classes are shown in the first Key Abstraction Class Diagram of Figure 9.1. In this figure, class Simulation is shown as having an association with class Ocean, class Ocean as having an association with class Oceancell, and class Oceancell as having an association with classes Tuna, Plankton, Shark, Crab, Obstacle, Empty, DeadFish and DeadShark.

The description of the problem domain suggests the following rough initial decomposition of classes: A simulation contains an ocean (owns the ocean object as an aggregation relationship). The ocean contains references to cells. These cells include obstacle cells, empty cells, plankton cells, tuna cells shark cells, crab cells, dead fish cells and dead shark cells.

This initial decomposition is shown in the next Class Abstraction Diagram given in Figure 9.2 which suggests that all of the protocol common to Oceancell's decendants is factored into class Oceancell. The triangular annotation with an A indicates that class Oceanell is an abstract class (i.e. deferred class). In order to determine whether it is reasonable for this class to be the only abstract class that contains all of the common attributes and behavior of the species mentioned above, we examine and list the similarities and differences in behavior among the various kinds of cells.

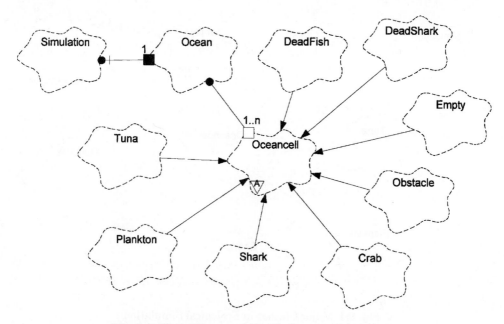

Fig. 9.2 Class Diagram 2 For Ecological Simulation

9.3.1   Similarities and Differences Among The Various Kinds of Cells

- Plankton, tuna and shark move to an adjoining cell according to their specific rules of movement peculiar to their species. Part of their behavior is shared, namely the way they seek to choose a random empty position if this becomes appropriate. All three species have an assigned reproduction interval and use the same rules for reproduction.
- Tuna and shark will starve if they do not eat but have specific ways of dealing with starvation (i.e. a tuna just dies whereas a shark attempts to "attack" another shark in order to survive). Their basic protocol for movement is the same (except for different prey).
- Plankton cannot starve but share the same reproduction rules as tuna and shark.
- Crabs cannot starve and cannot reproduce and can only move when in the vicinity of dead tuna or dead sharks. A crab never moves to an empty cell.
- Empty cells, obstacle cells, dead tuna, and dead sharks share the same behavior: they ignore a command to move and remain passive.

Each of the cell classes must have a reference to the ocean that they are part of in order to be able to determine their eight surrounding neighbors. This implies that class Oceancell has an aggregation relationship to class Ocean (by reference). Each subclass of Oceancell acquires this reference to an ocean through inheritance. Each cell must know its coordinate in the ocean. Each cell

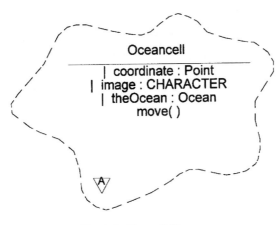

Fig. 9.3 Class Cell

type must have a unique image character. Each cell type must be able to respond to the "move" message (even if it does nothing). Each cell must be able to return its image. This suggests that Oceancell have the attributes shown in Figure 9.3. The message *move* is deferred.

The list of similarities and differences given above suggests that the Oceancell subclasses be partitioned based on the following considerations: (1) Can a cell reproduce and move to an empty location (this behavior unifies subclasses Plankton, Tuna and Shark), (2) Is a cell passive (this behavior unifies subclasses Empty, Obstacle, DeadFish and DeadShark), (3) Can a cell collect garbage and move multiple times (this characteristic is unique to class Crab), and (4) Can a cell kill another cell but also die of starvation (this characteristic unifies subclasses Tuna and Shark)?

From this analysis, the effective class Scavenger is created as a subclass of Oceancell. The instances of this subclass are crabs. These creatures cannot reproduce, cannot die of starvation and cannot move to an empty cell. Their characteristics are quite unique and, therefore, justify a separate branch on the inheritance tree.

A close examination of the passive cells (empty, obstacle, dead tuna and dead shark) reveal that their behavior and attributes are identical. Their only difference is in the value of their image attribute. Therefore, it is incorrect to consider them separate subclasses as done earlier. Instead, an effective class Passive is created as a subclass of Oceancell.

The common characteristics of the cells that can reproduce are defined in another abstract class, Reproducible. This abstract class is defined as a subclass of Oceancell. The key mechanism, *reproduce*, is defined in this class. The attributes *reproduction_clock* and *reproduction_interval* in this abstract class support the mechanism of determining when a reproducible ocean cell qualifies for reproduction.

The list of similarities and differences given above suggests one final discrimination among the subclasses of Reproducible. Two of the three types of cells

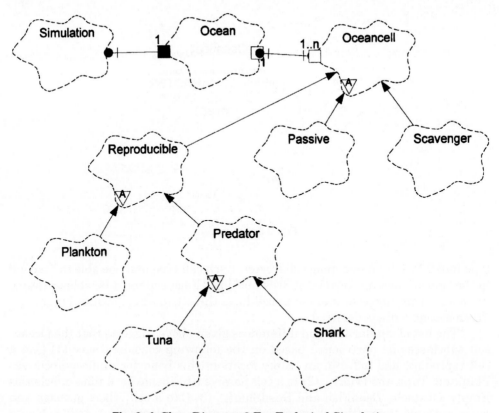

Fig. 9. 4 Class Diagram 3 For Ecological Simulation

that can reproduce can kill prey and can starve (tuna and sharks). Another abstract class, Predator, is defined to capture and factor the common characteristics of such predator ocean cells. These cells need the attributes *starvation_interval* and *starvation_clock* to support the mechanism of determining when a predator ocean cell qualifies for starvation.

The classes Tuna and Shark are subclasses of Predator, whereas the subclass Plankton is a subclass of Reproducible.

The above classification completes our initial domain analysis. The results of this analysis appear in Figure 9.4.

Several of the domain classes with their key attributes and abstractions are shown in Figure 9.5.

The class specifications for some of the key domain classes are given below.

```
Class name: Oceancell
Public Interface:
 Operations:
 move
```

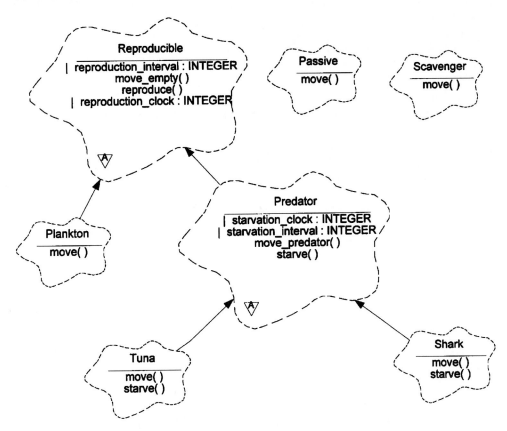

Fig. 9.5 Class Diagram With Attributes For Ecological Simulation

```
Protected Interface:
 Has-A Relationships:
 Ocean theOcean
 The reference to the ocean that allows
 each cell type to determine its
 neighboring cells.
 CHARACTER image
 The character representation of the cell
 Point coordinate
 The location of the cell in the ocean.
Operation name: move
 A deferred routine that is implemented in the
 subclasses.


Class name: Shark
 Superclasses: Predator, Reproducible, Oceancell
Public Interface:
```

 Operations:
 starve
Operation name: **starve**
 This method supports the mechanism for this specie to
 starve.
Operation name: **move**
 This method supports the mechanism for this specie to move.

Class name: **Tuna**
 Superclasses: Predator, Reproducible, Oceancell
Public Interface:
 Operations:
 starve
Operation name: **starve**
 This method supports the mechanism for this specie to
 starve.
Operation name: **move**
 This method supports the mechanism for this specie to move.

Class name: **Plankton**
 Superclasses: Reproducible, Oceancell
Public Interface:
 Operations:
move
Operation name: **move**
 This method is defined to support the particular move
 mechanism for this specie.

Class name: **Reproducible**
Documentation:
 Accounts for the common characteristics of classes
 Plankton, Tuna and Shark.
Hierarchy:
 Superclasses: Oceancell
Public Interface:
 Operations:
 move_empty
 reproduce
Protected Interface:
 Has-A Relationships:
 INTEGER reproduction_interval
 The number of required moves since the
 last reproduction before reproduction can
 occur again.
 INTEGER reproduction_clock
 The number of moves since the last

reproduction event.

Operation name: **move_empty**
 This method supports the mechanism of searching for and
 moving to an empty cell.
Operation name: **reproduce**
 This supports the common mechanism of leaving an
 offspring in the cell just vacated after a move.

Class name: **Passive**
 Superclasses: Oceancell
Public Interface:
 Operations:
 move
Operation name: **move**
 Nothing happens in response to this message.

Class name: **Scavenger**
 Superclasses: Cell
Public Interface:
 Operations:
move
Operation name: **move**
 A crab searches for a dead tuna or dead shark among its
 eight neighbors. If it finds one or more, it chooses
 one randomly and moves to that location. It continues
 to move along as it can.

Class name: **Predator**
 Superclasses: Reproduce, Oceancell
 Operations:
 predator_move
 starve
Protected Interface:
 Has-A Relationships:
 INTEGER starvation_interval
 A shark must kill a prey within this
 number of moves since its last kill. If
 it does not, it will starve.
 INTEGER starvation_clock
 The number of moves since the last kill.
Operation name: **move_predator**
The move method is redefined to include the possibility
of starvation and supports the common mechanism of tuna and
shark moves.

Operation name: **starve**
This is a deferred method that is implemented in each
of the subclasses. It represents the mechanism
associated with starvation.

9.4 THE DESIGN

The domain analysis has involved a careful process of classification and has produced 10 domain classes (see Figure 9.4). Now we change the direction of our
concern from the problem domain to the solution. We consider the key behavioral
mechanisms identified during the domain analysis. This will allow us to validate
the domain classes, perhaps discover the need for new classes and new relationships among the existing classes, introduce specific design classes, and discover
new attributes and methods throughout the class hierarchy.

When we are done with the design, the implementation should follow
smoothly and somewhat seamlessly.

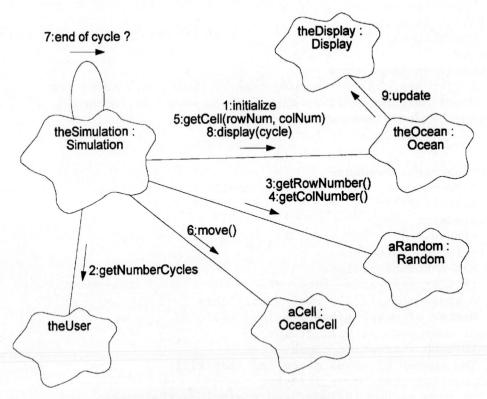

Fig. 9.6 Object Scenario Diagram for Main Event Loop

The specific key mechanisms that are examined closely are the following:

- The simulation event loop;
- *move_empty* as defined in class Reproducible;
- *reproduce* as defined in class Reproducible;
- *move_predator* as defined in class Predator;
- *move* as defined in class Scavenger;
- *starve* as defined in class Tuna, and
- *starve* as defined in class Shark

Figure 9.6 shows the object-scenario diagram for the main event loop.

9.4.1   Explanation of Main Event Loop Object-Scenario Diagram

The simulation object sends the message *initialize* to the ocean object. The user is prompted for the number of cycles to run the simulation. A random row and column are chosen. The cell with given row and column is sent the message *move*. When an iteration of the event loop is completed, the display is updated. If the number of tuna or sharks is zero at this moment, the simulation is terminated.

Figure 9.7 shows the second object-scenario diagram for the move-empty mechanism in class Reproducible.

9.4.2   Explanation of *move_empty* Mechanism in Class Reproducible

Object *aReproducible* sends itself the message *neighboringCoords(empty_ image)*. A collection of points is returned (possibly empty). The object sends itself the message *moveTo* after choosing a random coordinate in the collection returned

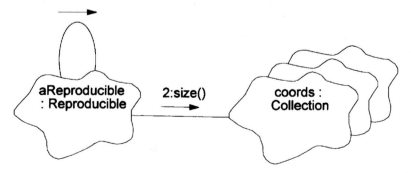

Fig. 9.7 Mechanism move_empty in Class Reproducible

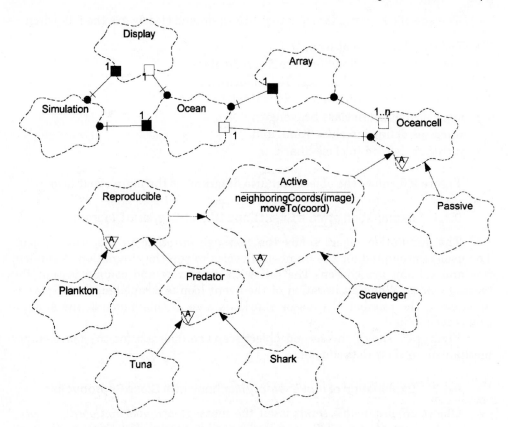

Fig. 9.8 Updated Class Diagram For Ecological Simulation

This raises a basic architectural issue. In what class are these behaviors contained? If the answer is class Reproducible as indicated in Figure 9.7, then how will a Scavenger object access these methods? If the answer is class Ocean-cell, then why should all the passive objects (dead tuna, dead shark, obstacle and empty cell) inherit protocol for moving?

We have discovered the need for another class: class Active. This new class Active is an abstract class. As a direct descendant of class Oceancell, it does not redefine the *move* method and, therefore, no instances of this class are legal. Abstract class Active defines the two behaviors *neighboringCoords* and *moveTo*. All ocean cell classes that inherit from Active need this behavior and inherit this behavior

The revised class diagram is shown in Figure 9.8.

In addition to showing the new abstract class Active in Figure 9.8, the class Display is shown as being owned by Simulation and referenced in class Ocean. Class Ocean is also shown as containing an instance of Array, which contains from 1..n references to Oceancell. Oceancell, as before, contains a single refer-ence to Ocean.

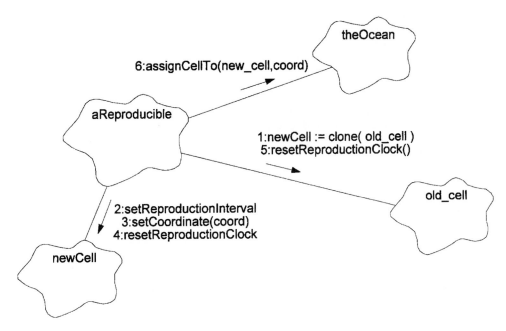

Fig. 9.9 Object-Scenario Diagram for Reproduce in Class Reproducible

As typically occurs during the process of analysis and design, additions and modifications are made based on the insight obtained by studying each key mechanism in detail.

Figure 9.9 depicts the third key mechanism, using an object-scenario diagram that describes the operation of *reproduce* in class Reproducible.

9.4.3 Explanation of *reproduce* Mechanism in Class Reproducible

The method *reproduce* in class Reproducible takes *old_cell* and *coord* as parameters. It makes a clone of this cell. This clone allocates separate storage for *newCell* and copies the fields of *old_cell* (these fields include *coordinate, image, reproduction_interval, reproduce_clock* and a reference to ocean, *theOcean*). A *reproduction_interval* is set for *newCell,* using the deferred method *setReproductionInterval* (implemented in each Reproducible subclass) and its *reproduction_clock* is set to zero. The *reproduction_clock* is set to zero for the *old_cell*. Finally, the *newCell* is assigned to *theOcean.* at position *coord*.

The method *setReproductionInterval* involves the second use of polymorphism in this design. The first use is method *move* in class Oceancell.

The ability to make a clone of the the input cell (*old_cell*) and obtain a *newCell* of the same type and with the same values for its attributes allows us to avoid a branch statement that determines the type of *old_cell* before creating a *newCell*. The clone mechanism, which is part of the protocol of all Eiffel objects, is an important and powerful facility.

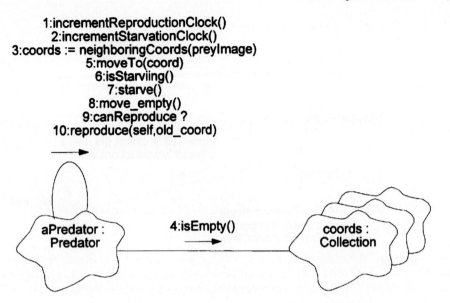

1:incrementReproductionClock()
2:incrementStarvationClock()
3:coords := neighboringCoords(preyImage)
5:moveTo(coord)
6:isStarviing()
7:starve()
8:move_empty()
9:canReproduce ?
10:reproduce(self,old_coord)

aPredator :
Predator

4:isEmpty()

coords :
Collection

Fig. 9.10 Mechanism for move_predator in Class Predator

Figure 9.10 depicts the fourth key mechanism for *move_predator* in abstract class Predator.

9.4.4   Explanation of Key Mechanism *move* in Class Predator

When a predator object (either instance of Tuna of Shark) is told to move, it first increments its reproduction clock and starvation clock. It then searches for a prey (based on the parameter *prey_image*) in its surrounding neighborhood. If the collection of coordinates is not empty, it chooses one at random and moves to

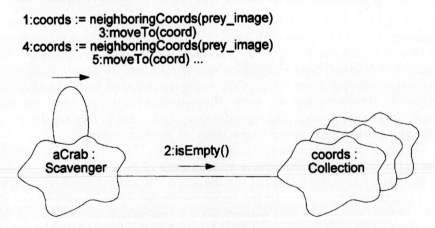

1:coords := neighboringCoords(prey_image)
3:moveTo(coord)
4:coords := neighboringCoords(prey_image)
5:moveTo(coord) ...

aCrab :
Scavenger

2:isEmpty()

coords :
Collection

Fig. 9.11 Object-Scenario Diagram for Move in Class Scavenger

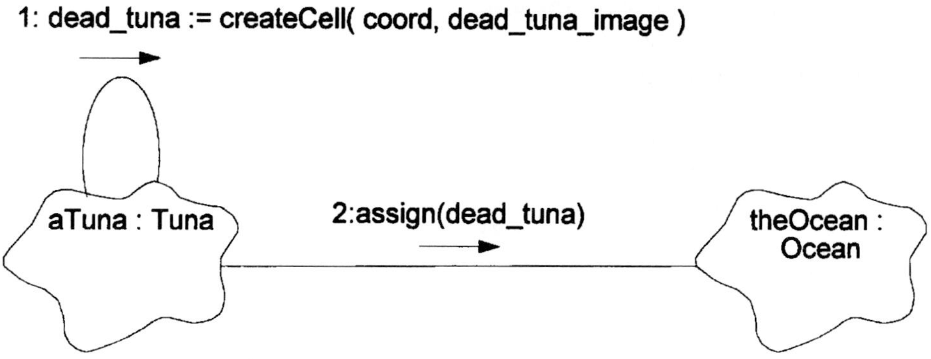

1: dead_tuna := createCell(coord, dead_tuna_image)

Fig. 9.12 Object-Scenario Diagram — starve Mechanism for Class Tuna

that location, feeding on the prey. If the array of coordinates is empty, the object determines whether it is starving, and if so, receives the polymorphic message *starve* (deferred in class Predator). It then attempts to move using the *move_ empty* mechanism defined in class Reproducible (see Figure 9.7). Finally, if a move has occurred (either because of killing a prey or moving to an empty location), it determines whether it can reproduce, and if so, does this.

The third polymorphic method, *starve*, is identified in this key mechanism.

The fifth key mechanism, *move*, in class Scavenger is depicted in Figure 9.11.

9.4.5 Explanation of Key Mechanism *move* in Class Scavenger

When a crab is told to move it searches for dead tuna or dead sharks in its immediate vicinity. If it finds such a prey, it kills it and moves to that position. It repeatedly tries to move until it can no longer find any prey. This mechanism allows a single crab to "clean-up" a large area of dead fish.

Figure 9.12 depicts the sixth key mechanism, *starve*, as defined in class Tuna.

9.4.6 Explanation of *starve* Mechanism for Class Tuna

When a tuna starves, it immediately creates a new instance of class Passive with a *dead_tuna* image. It then assigns this cell to the ocean.

Figure 9.13 shows the final key mechanism, *starve,* for class Shark.

9.4.7 Explanation of Key Mechanism *starve* for Class Shark

A starving shark first determines whether there exists one or more sharks in its vicinity. If so, it chooses one at random. It obtains its size and compares it to its own size. If its own size is equal or larger, it attacks, kills and moves to this position. Otherwise, the intended victim is assigned to the atacking shark's position in the ocean.

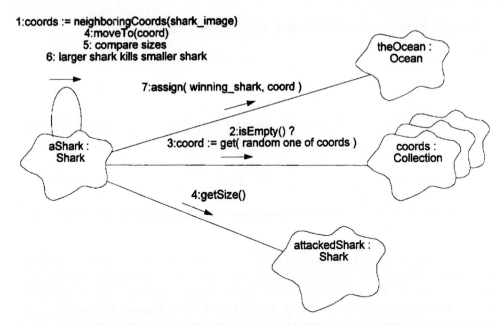

1:coords := neighboringCoords(shark_image)
4:moveTo(coord)
5: compare sizes
6: larger shark kills smaller shark

7:assign(winning_shark, coord)

2:isEmpty() ?
3:coord := get(random one of coords)

4:getSize()

Fig. 9.13 Object-Scenario Diagram for Starve in Class Shark

We have completed our examination of the key mechanisms in the ecological simulation. There are some details that have been left out. For example, when an active object moves to another position, either empty or one that contains a prey, if it does not reproduce, it must replace the cell that it vacated with an empty cell (instance of class Passive with *empty_cell* image).

Based on an inspection of all the object-scenario diagrams, a modified class diagram is shown in Figure 9.14. This shows all of the required associations implied by the object-scenario diagrams.

The refined Class Diagram of Figure 9.14 shows the addition of classes Random and Collection. Classes Active, Scavenger, Reproducible and Predator have an association with class Collection because they need to examine their eight adjoining neighbors.

A set of class specifications is the final work product in preparation for the Eiffel implementation. The level of detail in these class specifications is commensurate with the details provided by the domain analysis and design. Some room for modification or addition must be made at the implementation level.

It may be necessary to perform one final pass on the Class Diagram or some of the object-scenario diagrams if the implementation reveals errors in the model(s) of the key mechanisms.

The class specifications of some key classes are given below.

Class name: **Oceancell**
This is an abstract class that is the root of a
hierarachy of cell classes.

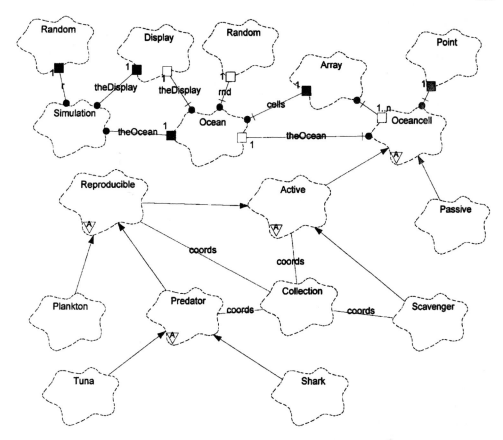

Fig. 9.14 Refined Class Diagram For Ecological Simulation

```
Protected Interface:
 Has-A Relationships:
 Ocean theOcean
 This is a reference relationship.
 Display theDisplay
 This is a reference relationship.
 CHARACTER image
 Point coordinate
Operation name: move
 This is a deferred method.
Operation name: setCoordinate


Class name: Shark
 A sea creature that can reproduce and must eat to live.
 Its prey are tuna.
Operation name: move
```

Class name: **Tuna**
 *A sea creature that can reproduce and must eat to live.
 Plankton are its prey.*
Operation name: **move**

Class name: **Plankton**
 *This class can reproduce, are prey to tuna but do not
 have to eat.*
Operation name: **move**

Class name: **Ocean**
 *This class contains a two-dimensional array of ocean
 cells. It also contains descriptive attributes
 concerning the number of each type of ocean cell. This
 class is responsible for initializing the ocean and
 transmitting the message move to each ocean cell.*
Protected Interface:
 Has-A Relationships:
 Display theDisplay
 Random rnd
 Array cells
 INTEGER numPlankton
 INTEGER numTuna
 INTEGER numSharks
 INTEGER numCrabs
 INTEGER numDeadTuna
 INTEGER numDeadSharks
 INTEGER av_tuna_r
 INTEGER av_shark_r
 INTEGER av_plankton_r
 INTEGER av_tuna_s
 INTEGER av_shark_s
 CHARACTER empty_image
 CHARACTER obstacle_image
 CHARACTER tuna_image
 CHARACTER shark_image
 CHARACTER crab_image
 CHARACTER plankton_image
 CHARACTER dead_tuna_image
 CHARACTER dead_shark_image
Operation name: **initialize(r : Random)**
Operation name: **display(cycles : INTEGER)**

Class name: **Simulation**
 *This is the root class for the simulation. It prompts
 the user for the number of simulation cycles, starts*

the simulation and controls when it ends.
Public Interface:
 Has-A Relationships:
 Ocean theOcean
 Display theDisplay
 Random r
Operation name: **run**
 This is the method that controls the length of the
 simulation. It is the first method to be called in
 this root class.

Class name: **Reproducible**
 Accounts for the common characteristics of classes
 Plankton, Tuna and Shark. These creatures can all
 reproduce.
Protected Interface:
 Has-A Relationships:
 INTEGER reproduction_interval
 The number of required moves since the
 last reproduction before reproduction can
 occur again.
 INTEGER reproduce_clock
 The number of moves since the last
 reproduction event.
Operation name: **reproduce(old_cell : Reproducible; coord :**
Point)
 This supports the common mechanism of leaving an
 offspring in the cell just vacated after a move.
Operation name: **move_to_empty**
Operation name: **resetReproductionClock**

Class name: **Passive**
 Contains the common protocol for obstacles, empty
 cells, dead fish and dead sharks. All of these
 creatures do nothing in response to the move method.
Operations: **move**
 Nothing happens in response to this message.

Class name: **Scavenger**
Operation name: **move**
 A crab searches for a dead tuna or dead shark among its
 eight neighbors. If it finds one or more, it chooses
 one randomly and moves to that location. It continues
 to move along as it can.

Class name: **Predator**

*This abstract class factors the protocol common to
those sea creatures that must eat to live.*
Protected Interface:
 Has-A Relationships:
 INTEGER starvation_interval
 *A shark must kill a prey within this
 number of moves since its last kill. If
 it does not, it will starve.*
 INTEGER starvation_clock
 The number of moves since the last kill.

Operation name: **predator_move**
 *The move method is defined to include the possibility
 of starvation and the common mechanisms of tuna and
 shark movement.*
Operation name: **starve**
 *This is a deferred method that is implemented in each
 of the subclasses. It represents the mechanism
 associated with starvation.*
Operation name: **resetReproductionInterval**
 A deferred method that is defined in the subclasses.

Class name: **Active**
 *This class factors all protocol common to ocean cells
 that can move to an empty cell.*
Protected Interface:
 Has-A Relationships:
 Collection[Point] offset
 *This is a once method that defines a
 collection of 8 offsets representing the
 north, north-east, east, south-east,
 south, south-west, west and north-west
 neighbors of any point in the ocean.*
Operation name: **moveTo (coord : Point)**

When should design end and implementation begin? I am a strong believer in developing implementation prototypes for the various key abstraction classes as the design progresses. This, like object scenario diagrams, provides important validation information regarding the sufficiency of each class's attributes, its associations with other classes and whether there are missing classes.

Programming is a legitimate and important phase of the development process. If the modeling has been done well, there should be few significant surprises at the implementation level. The real payoff for having established a sound architecture is the high likelihood of program correctness and the strong probability that maintenance will be an easy process.

Using the work products produced thus far (Figures 9.1 through 9.14 and the class specifications), we proceed to examine the Eiffel implementation of the Ecological Simulation.

9.5 EIFFEL IMPLEMENTATION

The major key abstraction classes, SIMULATION and OCEAN, are presented and discussed first. Then, the abstract classes, OCEANCELL, ACTIVE, REPRODUCIBLE and PREDATOR, which factor protocol common to their respective subclasses, are presented and discussed. Next, the effective classes, TUNA, SHARK, PLANKTON, PASSIVE and SCAVENGER, are presented and discussed. Following this, class DISPLAY is presented.

The root class of the Ecological Simulation is class SIMULATION. This class is presented in Listing 9.1.

Listing 9.1   Class SIMULATION

```
class SIMULATION -- root class
 creation
    run

 feature
    theOcean    : OCEAN;
    theDisplay  : DISPLAY;
    r           : RAND;

  run is
  local
      cycles   : INTEGER;
      i        : INTEGER;
      nrows, ncols : INTEGER;
      row, col : INTEGER;
      iterations : INTEGER;
  do
      io.new_line; io.new_line;
      io.
        putstring( "Ecological Simulation by Richard Wiener" );
      io.new_line; io.new_line;
      io.
        putstring( "Enter the number of simulation cycles:" );
      io.readint;
      iterations := io.lastint;
      !!r.initialize;
      !!theDisplay.initialize;
      !!theOcean.initialize( r, theDisplay );
      nrows := theOcean.NUM_ROWS;
      ncols := theOcean.NUM_COLS;
      theOcean.display( 0 );
      from cycles := 0
      until cycles = iterations or theOcean.numTuna = 0 or
              theOcean.numSharks = 0
```

```
        loop
            cycles := cycles + 1;
            from i := 0
            until i = nrows * ncols
            loop
                i := i + 1;
                row := r.valueBetween( 1, nrows );
                col := r.valueBetween( 1, ncols );
                if theOcean.cells.item( row, col ) /= Void
                    then
                        theOcean.cells.item( row, col ).move;
                    end;
                end;
                theOcean.display( cycles );
            end;
            theDisplay.pause;
            theDisplay.close;
        end; -- run

    end -- SIMULATION
```

The *run* routine communicates with its attribute *theOcean* and tells each of its attributes to *move*. Instead of implementing empty ocean cells as an instance of Passive, as suggested in the design, it is more efficient to assign empty cell locations to the value Void. This removes the need for having to allocate (and automatically deallocate) storage for empty cells as they are produced and removed during the execution of the simulation. This is why it is necessary to verify that *theOcean.cells.item(row, col) /= Void* before sending this ocean cell the message *move*.

Text graphics, using the standard UNIX package curses, are employed. More about this when class DISPLAY is discussed. The *run* routine finishes its work by causing the user's screen to pause and then closes this screen and returns control to the ordinary X-window under which the program is run.

Class OCEAN is shown in Listing 9.2.

Listing 9.2   Class OCEAN

```
class OCEAN
    creation
        initialize

    feature
        numPlankton   : INTEGER;
        numTuna       : INTEGER;
        numSharks     : INTEGER;
        numCrabs      : INTEGER;
        numDeadTuna   : INTEGER;
        numDeadSharks : INTEGER;
        cells         : ARRAY2[ ACTIVECELL ];
        rnd           : RAND;
        NUM_ROWS      : INTEGER is 50;
        NUM_COLS      : INTEGER is 20;
```

```
      NUMBER_TUNA  : INTEGER is 50;
      NUMBER_SHARKS : INTEGER is 10;
      NUMBER_PLANKTON : INTEGER is 250;
      NUMBER_CRABS : INTEGER is 40;
      NUMBER_OBSTACLES : INTEGER is 30;
      AV_TUNA_R     : INTEGER is 6;
      AV_SHARK_R    : INTEGER is 10;
      AV_PLANKTON_R : INTEGER is 1;
      AV_TUNA_S     : INTEGER is 4;
      AV_SHARK_S    : INTEGER is 9;
      EMPTY_IMAGE  : CHARACTER is '-';
      OBSTACLE_IMAGE : CHARACTER is '#'
      TUNA_IMAGE    : CHARACTER is 'T';
      SHARK_IMAGE   : CHARACTER is 'S';
      CRAB_IMAGE    : CHARACTER is 'C';
      PLANKTON_IMAGE : CHARACTER is 'P';
      DEADTUNA_IMAGE : CHARACTER is 't';
      DEADSHARK_IMAGE : CHARACTER is 's';
      theDisplay   : DISPLAY;

      initialize( r : RAND; the_display : DISPLAY ) is
      do
         rnd := r;
          theDisplay := the_display;
          !!cells.make( NUM_ROWS, NUM_COLS );
          -- Initialize cells
          addObstacles;
          addSharks;
          addTuna;
          addPlankton;
          addCrabs;
      end; -- initialize

      TUNA_R : INTEGER is
      do
          Result := AV_TUNA_R + rnd.valueBetween( -2, 2 );
      end -- TUNA_R

      SHARK_R : INTEGER is
      do
          Result := AV_SHARK_R + rnd.valueBetween( -3, 3 );
      end -- SHARK_R

      PLANKTON_R : INTEGER is
      do
          Result := AV_PLANKTON_R + rnd.valueBetween( -1, 1 );
      end -- PLANKTON_R

      SHARK : INTEGER is
      do
          Result := AV_SHARK_R + rnd.valueBetween( -2, 2 );
      end -- SHARK_R

      TUNA_S : INTEGER is
      do
          Result := AV_TUNA_S + rnd.valueBetween( -2, 2 );
```

```
end; -- TUNA_S

SHARK_S : INTEGER is
do
    Result := AV_SHARK_S + rnd.valueBetween( -3, 3 );
end; -- SHARK_S


voidCellCoord : POINT is
 local
    row, col : INTEGER;
 do
    from
    row := rnd.valueBetween( 1, NUM_ROWS );
    col := rnd.valueBetween( 1, NUM_COLS )
    until cells.item( row, col ) = Void
    loop
        row := rnd.valueBetween( 1, NUM_ROWS );
        col := rnd.valueBetween( 1, NUM_COLS );
    end;
    !!Result.make( col, row );
end; -- voidCellCoord

resetTotals is
do
    numTuna := 0;
    numSharks := 0;
    numPlankton := 0;
    numDeadTuna := 0;
    numDeadSharks := 0;
end; -- resetTotals

display( cycles : INTEGER ) is
local
    row, col : INTEGER;
do
    resetTotals;
    -- Scan the cells and tabulate the number of
    -- creatures
    from row := 0
    until row = NUM_ROWS
    loop
        row := row + 1;
        from col := 0
        until col = NUM_COLS
        loop
            col := col + 1;
            if cells.item( row, col ) /= Void then
                cells.item( row, col ).count; -- each cell
            -- type counts itself
            end;
        end;
    end;
    if cycles > 0 then
        theDisplay.update( cycles, numTuna, numSharks,
```

```
                    numPlankton,
                    numDeadTuna, numDeadSharks,
                    NUM_ROWS * NUM_COLS - numTuna - numSharks
                    - numPlankton - NUMBER_OBSTACLES -
                    NUMBER_CRABS - numDeadTuna -
                    numDeadSharks );
        end;
    end; -- display

incrementNumTuna is
 do
    numTuna:= numTuna + 1;
 end; -- incrementNumTuna

incrementNumPlankton is
 do
    numPlankton := numPlankton + 1;
 end; -- incrementNumPlankton

incrementNumSharks is
 do
    numSharks := numSharks + 1;
 end; -- incrementNumSharks

incrementNumDeadTuna is
 do
    numDeadTuna := numDeadTuna + 1;
 end; -- incrementNumDeadTuna

incrementNumDeadSharks is
 do
    numDeadSharks := numDeadSharks + 1;
 end; -- incrementNumDeadSharks

assignCellTo( aCell : ACTIVECELL; pt : POINT ) is
 do
    cells.put( aCell, pt.y, pt.x );
 end; -- assignCellTo

cellAt( pt : POINT ) : ACTIVECELL is
 require
    pt_x_not_too_small : pt.x > 0;
    pt_y_not_too_small : pt.y > 0;
    pt_x_not_too_large : pt.x <= NUM_COLS;
    pt_y_not_too_large : pt.y <= NUM_ROWS;
 do
    Result := cells.item( pt.y, pt.x );
 end; -- cellAt

addSharks is
 local
    aCoord   : POINT;
    count    : INTEGER;
    aCell    : SHARK;
 do
```

```
          from count := 0
          until count = NUMBER_SHARKS
          loop
              count := count + 1;
              aCoord := voidCellCoord;
              !!aCell.create( aCoord, SHARK_IMAGE, SHARK_R,
                 SHARK_S, Current );
              cells.put( aCell, aCoord.y, aCoord.x );
          end;
      end; -- addSharks

  addObstacles is
   local
      aCoord    : POINT;
      count     : INTEGER;
      aCell     : PASSIVE;
   do
      from count := 0
      until count = NUMBER_OBSTACLES
      loop
          count := count + 1;
          aCoord := voidCellCoord;
          !!aCell.create( aCoord, OBSTACLE_IMAGE, Current
             );
          cells.put( aCell, aCoord.y, aCoord.x );
      end;
   end; -- addObstacles

  addTuna is
   local
      aCoord    : POINT;
      count     : INTEGER;
      aCell     : TUNA;
   do
      from count := 0
      until count = NUMBER_TUNA
      loop
          count := count + 1;
          aCoord := voidCellCoord;
          !!aCell.create( aCoord, TUNA_IMAGE, TUNA_R,
             TUNA_S, Current );
          cells.put( aCell, aCoord.y, aCoord.x );
      end;
   end; -- addTuna

  addPlankton is
   local
      aCoord    : POINT;
      count     : INTEGER;
      aCell     : PLANKTON;
   do
      from count := 0
      until count = NUMBER_PLANKTON
      loop
```

```
            count := count + 1;
            aCoord := voidCellCoord;
            !!aCell.create( aCoord, PLANKTON_IMAGE,
                PLANKTON_R, Current );
            cells.put( aCell, aCoord.y, aCoord.x );
        end;
    end; -- addPlankton

    addCrabs is
    local
        aCoord    : POINT;
        count     : INTEGER;
        aCell     : SCAVENGER;
    do
        from count := 0
        until count = NUMBER_CRABS
        loop
            count := count + 1;
            aCoord := voidCellCoord;
            !!aCell.create( aCoord, CRAB_IMAGE, Current );
            cells.put( aCell, aCoord.y, aCoord.x );
        end;
    end; -- addCrabs


end -- class OCEAN
```

Class OCEAN contains many descriptive attributes. All of these attributes were identified in the class specifications given as one of the design work products. The actual reproduction interval assigned for a new tuna, new shark or new plankton is given by the appropriate function, such as TUNA_R. These functions assign a uniformly distributed random variate with specified mean value.

The creation routine, *initialize*, for class OCEAN stores references to class OCEAN (attribute *theOcean*), class DISPLAY (attribute *theDisplay*), and class RANDOM (attribute *rnd*). The routines *addObstacles*, ..., *addCrabs*, called in this creation routine, assign various types of sea creatures to random coordinates in the ocean.

The most interesting routine in class OCEAN is *display*. The first task of this routine is to take inventory of each type of sea creature. Using a structured approach, a multibranch *if* statement might be written as follows:

```
if cells.item( row, col ).image = 'T' then
    incrementTunaCount;
elseif cells.item( row, col ).image = 'S' then
    incrmentSharkCount;
...
end;
```

A better approach is to define another polymorphic method, *count*, in class OCEANCELL and send this message to each non-void cell. In other words, let each subclass of OCEANCELL count itself. After this is done, the current population of each sub-species is sent to the update routine of class DISPLAY.

Listing 9.3 presents the details of the abstract root class of the cell hierarchy, class OCEANCELL.

Listing 9.3   Class OCEANCELL

```
deferred class OCEANCELL
  -- Abstract super class for a hierarchy of cell types

  feature
    theOcean      : OCEAN;
      image       : CHARACTER;
      coordinate  : POINT;

      count is
         deferred
      end; -- count

      move is
         deferred
      end; -- move

      setCoordinate( pt : POINT ) is
      do
         coordinate := pt;
      end; -- setCoordinate

  end -- OCEANCELL
```

There is no creation routine for class OCEANCELL because it is an abstract (deferred) class. The polymorphic routine move must be defined in all effective subclasses of OCEANCELL.

Listing 9.4 presents the details of the abstract class ACTIVE. This class contains the common protocol for all sea creatures that can move in some way. The name of this class is changed to ACTIVECELL to avoid a name clash with another class ACTIVE defined in the standard ISE base library.

Listing 9.4   Class ACTIVECELL

```
deferred class ACTIVECELL
  inherit
    OCEANCELL

  feature
    offset : COLLECT[ POINT ] is
    local
        west, nwest,
        north, neast,
        east, seast,
        south, swest : POINT;
        clt : COLLECT[ POINT ];
    once
        !!clt.make( 8 );
```

```
            !!west.make( -1, 0 );
            !!nwest.make( -1, 1 );
            !!north.make( 0, 1 );
            !!neast.make( 1, 1 );
            !!east.make( 1, 0 );
            !!seast.make( 1, -1 );
            !!south.make( 0, -1 );
            !!swest.make( -1, -1 );
        clt.insert( west );
        clt.insert( nwest )
        clt.insert( north );
        clt.insert( neast );
        clt.insert( east );
        clt.insert( seast );
        clt.insert( south );
        clt.insert( swest );
        Result := clt;
    end; -- initialize

moveFromTo( fromPt : POINT; toPt : POINT ) is
 require
        fromPt_not_Void : fromPt /= Void;
        toPt_not_Void : toPt /= Void;
 do
        Current.setCoordinate( toPt );
        theOcean.assignCellTo( Current, toPt );
        theOcean.assignCellTo( Void, fromPt );
 end; -- moveFromTo

neighboringCoords( withImage : CHARACTER ) : COLLECT
    [ POINT ] is
 local
        index      : INTEGER;
        aPoint     : POINT;
        validCoords : COLLECT[ POINT ];
 do
        !!validCoords.make( 8 );
        from index := 0
        until index = 8
        loop
            index := index + 1;
            aPoint := coordinate + offset.get( index );
            if aPoint.x < 1 then aPoint.setX(
                theOcean.NUM_COLS ); end;
            if aPoint.y < 1 then aPoint.setY(
                theOcean.NUM_ROWS ); end;
            if aPoint.x > theOcean.NUM_COLS then aPoint.setX
                ( 1 ); end;
            if aPoint.y > theOcean.NUM_ROWS then aPoint.setY
                ( 1 ); end;
            if cellImageMatches( aPoint, withImage ) then
                validCoords.insert( aPoint );
            end;
        end;
        Result := validCoords;
```

```
        end; -- neighboringCoords

        cellImageMatches( aPoint : POINT; anImage : CHARACTER )
          : BOOLEAN is
        do
            if theOcean.cellAt( aPoint ) = Void then
                Result := anImage = theOcean.EMPTY_IMAGE
            else
                Result := theOcean.cellAt( aPoint ).image =
                    anImage;
            end;
        end; -- cellImageMatches

    end -- class ACTIVECELL
```

The design documentation specified a method *moveTo(pt : POINT)*. The actual implementation adds a second parameter and is renamed *moveFromTo(fromPt : POINT; toPt : POINT)*. This permits this routine to assign a value Void to the *fromPt*.

The routine *neighboringCoords* returns a collection, possibly empty, of points that contain the specified image. This routine is needed by all of the effective sea creature classes except instances of PASSIVE. The approach used is to add the current coordinate of the ocean cell to each of the eight offset values (stored as a fixed collection of points). Then, for each of these eight neighboring points, the routine *cellImageMatches* is invoked. This routine returns "True" if the neighboring cell contains the appropriate image, otherwise it returns "False."

Listing 9.5 presents the abstract class REPRODUCIBLE. This class factors all of the protocol common to the three classes that can reproduce.

Listing 9.5   Class REPRODUCIBLE

```
    deferred class REPRODUCIBLE
     inherit
        ACTIVECELL

    feature
        reproduction_interval : INTEGER;
        reproduction_clock : INTEGER;

      move_to_empty : BOOLEAN is
      local
            coords : COLLECT[ POINT ];
            old_coord : POINT;
      do
            coords := neighboringCoords( theOcean.EMPTY_IMAGE );
            if coords.size > 0 then
              old_coord := coordinate;
              coordinate := coords.get( theOcean.rnd
                .valueBetween( 1, oords.size ) );
            moveFromTo( old_coord, coordinate );
```

```
            Result := TRUE;
        else
            Result := FALSE;
        end;
    end; -- move_to_empty

 resetReproductionClock is
  do
      reproduction_clock := 0;
  end; -- resetReproductionClock

 setReproductionInterval is
      deferred
  end; -- setReproductionInterval

 reproduce( old_cell : REPRODUCIBLE; coord : POINT ) is
 local
      new_cell : REPRODUCIBLE;
 do
      new_cell := clone( old_cell );
      new_cell.setReproductionInterval;
      new_cell.setCoordinate( coord );
      new_cell.resetReproductionClock;
      old_cell.resetReproductionClock;
      theOcean.assignCellTo( new_cell, coord );
  end; -- reproduce

end -- class REPRODUCIBLE
```

The routine *setReproductionInterval* is deferred. Each of the effective sub-classes of REPRODUCIBLE must implement this routine according to their own statistical characteristics.

The routine *reproduce* is very important and quite interesting. At this level of the class hierarchy, this routine has no knowledge of any of its subclasses. Yet, is is being called upon to produce a new instance of one of its subclasses. This is accomplished quite elegantly using the *clone* function derived from class ANY. Storage for a *new_cell* is dynamically allocated, and the fields of this ocean cell are initially a copy of the fields of the *old_cell*. As long as the type of the *old_cell* conforms to type REPRODUCIBLE, this strategy works. Some of the attributes of the *new_cell* are changed appropriately for a newborn cell. Specifically, the newborn's reproduction interval is set, its coordinate is set and its reproduction clock is reset to zero. Finally, the reproduction clock of the *old_cell* is also set to zero. All of these events were modeled in one of the object-scenario diagrams at the design level.

Listing 9.6 presents the details of abstract class PREDATOR.

Listing 9.6   Class PREDATOR

```
deferred class PREDATOR
 inherit
    REPRODUCIBLE
```

```
feature
    starvation_interval : INTEGER;
    starvation_clock : INTEGER;

    predator_move( prey : CHARACTER ) is
    local
        old_coord : POINT;
        coords    : COLLECT[ POINT ];
        moved     : BOOLEAN;
        old_starvation_clock : INTEGER;
        old_starvation_interval : INTEGER;
        old_size : INTEGER;
        theShark : SHARK;
        isAShark : BOOLEAN;
    do
      theShark ?= theOcean.cellAt( coordinate );
      isAShark := theShark /= Void; -- is receiver a shark?
      old_coord := coordinate;
      reproduction_clock := reproduction_clock + 1;
      starvation_clock := starvation_clock + 1;
      coords := neighboringCoords( prey );
      if coords.size > 0 then -- kill prey
          starvation_clock := 0;
          coordinate := coords.get( theOcean.
            rnd.valueBetween( 1,
                coords.size ) );
          moveFromTo( old_coord, coordinate );
          if reproduction_clock >= reproduction_interval
            then
             old_starvation_interval :=
               starvation_interval;
            setStarvationInterval;
            if isAShark = TRUE then
               old_size := theShark.size + 1;
               theShark.setSize( 1 );
            end;
            reproduce( Current, old_coord );
            if isAShark then
               theShark.SetSize( old_size );
            end;
            starvation_interval :=
               old_starvation_interval;
          end;
        else -- could not kill prey
          if starvation_clock = starvation_interval then
             starve;
          else
              moved := move_to_empty;
              if moved and reproduction_clock >=
                  reproduction_interval then
              old_starvation_clock := starvation_clock;
              old_starvation_interval :=
              starvation_interval;
              setStarvationInterval;
              starvation_clock := 0;
```

```
                    if isAShark = TRUE then
                        old_size := theShark.size;
                        theShark.setSize( 1 );
                    end;
                    reproduce( Current, old_coord );
                    if isAShark then
                        theShark.setSize( old_size );
                    end;
                    starvation_clock := old_starvation_clock;
                    starvation_interval :=
                    old_starvation_interval;
                    end;
                end;
            end;
        end; -- predator_move

    resetStarvationClock is
    do
        starvation_clock := 0;
    end; -- resetStarvationClock

    setStarvationInterval is
        deferred
    end; -- setStarvationInterval

    starve is
        deferred
    end; -- starve
end -- PREDATOR
```

The routine *predator_move* in this abstract class is the most complex routine among all the classes. This routine must account for all of the protocol of sea creatures that must eat to live and have a particular kind of prey (tuna and shark). The complexity occurs because of the need to determine whether the particular predator type is a shark. It is necessary to make this determination because newborn sharks must have a *size* attribute of one. This value must be temporarily set in the *old_cell* that is sent to routine *reproduce* (from class REPRODUCIBLE). The *reproduce* routine blindly copies all of the attribute values of *old_cell* into the *new_cell*.

How can a routine of class PREDATOR know whether it is a SHARK type predator or a TUNA type predator? The mechanism used in routine *predator_move* is to use reverse assignment (*theShark ?= theOcean.cellAt(coordinate)). Normally, it would be illegal to have the target of an assignment not conform to its source. The reverse assignment operator allows this violation of the conformance principle. If the target of the assignment, *theShark*, is not *Void*, then the predator type (*Current*) is indeed a shark.

In the branches of the *predator_move* logic that allow reproduction, the *size* of the current shark is set to zero before invoking the reproduce routine. Then following this routine, the *size* is set back to its old value.

Two deferred methods, *starve* and *setStarvationInterval*, are declared. They are both defined in the two effective subclasses SHARK and TUNA.

Listing 9.7 presents the code for the PREDATOR subclass TUNA.

Listing 9.7   Class TUNA

```
class TUNA
 inherit
    PREDATOR

 creation
    create

 feature
    create( pt : POINT; anImage : CHARACTER; reprod :
      INTEGER; starvation : INTEGER; anOcean : OCEAN ) is
    do
       theOcean := anOcean;
       coordinate := pt;
       image := anImage;
       reproduction_interval := reprod;
       starvation_interval := starvation;
       reproduction_clock := 0;
       starvation_clock := 0;
    end; -- create

    count is
    do
        theOcean.incrementNumTuna;
    end; -- count

    setReproductionInterval is
    do
        reproduction_interval := theOcean.TUNA_R;
    end; -- setReproductionInterval

    setStarvationInterval is
    do
        starvation_interval := theOcean.TUNA_S;
    end; -- setStarvationInterval

   move is
    do
        predator_move( 'P' );
    end; -- move

    starve is
    local
        deadtuna : PASSIVE;
    do
       !!deadtuna.create( coordinate,
          theOcean.DEADTUNA_IMAGE,
                theOcean );
```

```
              theOcean.assignCellTo( deadtuna, coordinate );
         end; -- starve

   end -- TUNA
```

The payoff for factoring the protocol common to all predators occurs here. The method *move* is implemented in one line. The method *starve* creates an instance of a dead tuna at the present coordinate.

Listing 9.8 presents the details of class SHARK.

Listing 9.8   Class SHARK

```
class SHARK
 inherit
    PREDATOR

 creation
    create

 feature
    size : INTEGER;

    create( pt : POINT; anImage : CHARACTER; reprod : INTEGER;
      starvation : INTEGER; anOcean : OCEAN ) is
    do
       theOcean := anOcean;
       coordinate := pt;
       image := anImage;
       reproduction_interval := reprod;
       starvation_interval := starvation;
       reproduction_clock := 0;
       starvation_clock := 0;
    end; -- create

    count is
    do
       theOcean.incrementNumSharks;
    end; -- count

    setReproductionInterval is
    do
       reproduction_interval := theOcean.SHARK_R;
    end; -- setReproductionInterval

  setStarvationInterval is
    do
       starvation_interval := theOcean.SHARK_S;
    end; -- setStarvationInterval

    setSize( value : INTEGER ) is
    do
       size := value;
```

```
        end; -- setSize

        move is
        do
            predator_move( 'T' );
        end; -- move

        starve is
        local
            deadshark : PASSIVE;
            coords    : COLLECT[ POINT ];
            shark_coord : POINT;
            otherShark : SHARK;
        do
          coords := neighboringCoords( theOcean.SHARK_IMAGE );
          if coords.size > 0 then -- there is a neighboring
          -- shark
              shark_coord := coords.get( theOcean.rnd.
                  valueBetween( 1, coords.size ) );
              otherShark ?= theOcean.cellAt( shark_coord );
              if size > otherShark.size then
                  moveFromTo( coordinate, shark_coord );
                  resetStarvationClock;
              else
                  moveFromTo( shark_coord, coordinate );
                  otherShark.setCoordinate( coordinate );
                  otherShark.resetStarvationClock;
              end;
          else -- no neighboring shark
              !!deadshark.create( coordinate,
                  theOcean.DEADSHARK_IMAGE, theOcean );
              theOcean.assignCellTo( deadshark, coordinate );
          end;
        end; -- starve

    end -- SHARK
```

The method *starve* involves a little complexity. Reverse assignment must again be used in order to allow a shark object as the target of assignment where the source is an OCEANCELL object. In this case, there is no need to test for a non-void value since it is known that a shark object resides at the given cell position .

Listing 9.9 presents the details of class PLANKTON.

Listing 9.9   Class PLANKTON

```
class PLANKTON
 inherit
    REPRODUCIBLE

 creation
    create
```

```
feature

    create( aPoint : POINT; anImage : CHARACTER;
            reprod : INTEGER; anOcean : OCEAN ) is
    do
        theOcean := anOcean;
        coordinate := aPoint;
        image := anImage;
        reproduction_interval := reprod;
        reproduction_clock := 0;
    end; -- create

    count is
    do
        theOcean.incrementNumPlankton;
    end; -- count

    setReproductionInterval is
    do
        reproduction_interval := theOcean.PLANKTON_R;
    end; -- setReproductionInterval

    move is
    local
        old_coord : POINT;
        moved : BOOLEAN;
    do
        old_coord := coordinate;
        reproduction_clock := reproduction_clock + 1;
        moved := move_to_empty;
        if moved and reproduction_clock >=
          reproduction_interval then
            reproduce( Current, old_coord );
        end;
    end; -- move

end -- class PLANKTON
```

The protocol for *move_empty*, defined in the parent class REPRODUCIBLE, and the protocol for *reproduce*, also defined in REPRODUCIBLE, make it quite easy to implement the "move" logic for a plankton.

Listing 9.10 presents the details of class PASSIVE.

Listing 9.10   Class PASSIVE

```
class PASSIVE
 inherit
    ACTIVECELL

creation
    create
```

```
feature
   create( aCoord : POINT; anImage : CHARACTER; anOcean :
      OCEAN ) is
   do
      theOcean := anOcean;
      image := anImage;
      coordinate := aCoord;
   end;

   count is
   do
      if image = theOcean.DEADTUNA_IMAGE then
         theOcean.incrementNumDeadTuna;
      elseif image = theOcean.DEADSHARK_IMAGE then
         theOcean.incrementNumDeadSharks;
      end;
   end; -- count

   move is
   do -- intentionally blank
   end; -- move

end -- class PASSIVE
```

You will agree that the "move" logic for a passive cell is the simplest of all the "move" implementations shown thus far. The count routine must employ a multibranch statement because there are no subclasses of PASSIVE that could be used for a polymorphic implementation. Although such multibranch statements are to be discouraged, their occasional use is justified.

Listing 9.11 presents the details of class SCAVENGER.

Listing 9.11   Class SCAVENGER

```
class SCAVENGER
 inherit
   ACTIVECELL

 creation
   create

 feature
   create( pt : POINT; anImage : CHARACTER; anOcean : OCEAN
      ) is
   do
      theOcean := anOcean;
      coordinate := pt;
      image := anImage;
   end; -- create

   count is
   do -- We do not wish to count crabs
```

```
        end; -- count

    move is
    local
        coords    : COLLECT[ POINT ];
        moved     : BOOLEAN;
        old_coord : POINT;
    do
        coords := neighboringCoords( theOcean.DEADTUNA_IMAGE
          );
        if coords.size > 0 then
            moved := TRUE;
            old_coord := coordinate;
            coordinate := coords.get( theOcean.rnd.
              valueBetween( 1, coords.size ) );
          moveFromTo( old_coord, coordinate );
        else
            coords := neighboringCoords(
              theOcean.DEADSHARK_IMAGE );
            if coords.size > 0 then
                moved := TRUE;
                old_coord := coordinate;
                coordinate := coords.get( theOcean.rnd.
                  valueBetween( 1, coords.size ) );
                moveFromTo( old_coord, coordinate );
            end;
        end;
        if moved then
            move;
        end;
    end; -- move

end -- SCAVENGER
```

In routine *move*, a crab first attempts to eat a dead tuna. If it cannot, it attempts to eat a dead shark. If either of these attempts is successful, it recursively invokes *move* and tries to move again. If both attempts fail, the crab just stays where it is.

Listing 9.12 presents the details of class DISPLAY.

Listing 9.12   Class DISPLAY

```
class DISPLAY
 creation
    initialize

 feature { NONE }
    c_init is
    external "C"
    alias
        "init"
```

```
            end; -- c_init

        c_display_text is
        external "C"
        alias
            "display_text"
        end; -- c_display_text

        c_update( cycle : INTEGER; num_tuna : INTEGER; num_sharks :
            INTEGER; num_plankton : INTEGER; num_dead_fish : INTEGER;
            num_dead_sharks : INTEGER; num_empty : INTEGER ) is
        external "C"
        alias
            "graph"
        end; -- c_update

        c_pause is
        external "C"
        alias
            "pause"
        end; -- c_pause

        c_end_window is
        external "C"
        alias
            "end_window"
        end; -- c_end-window

feature
        initialize is
        do
            c_init;
            c_display_text;
        end; -- make

        update( cycle : INTEGER; num_tuna : INTEGER; num_sharks
            : INTEGER; num_plankton : INTEGER; num_dead_fish :
            INTEGER; num_dead_sharks : INTEGER; num_empty :
            INTEGER is
        do
            c_update( cycle, num_tuna, num_sharks, num_plankton,
            num_dead_fish, num_dead_sharks, num_empty );
        end; -- update

        pause is
        do
            c_pause;
        end; -- pause;

        close is
        do
            c_end_window;
        end; -- close
```

```
end -- DISPLAY
```

Each of the public routines of class DISPLAY is implemented by a private routine that invokes a "C" function. These "C" functions are defined in a file that is presented in Listing 9.13.

Listing 9.13   "C" functions for class DISPLAY

```c
#include <curses.h>

void init()
{
    initscr();
    clear();
}

void display_text()
{
    move( 60, 50 );
    addstr( "Ecological Simulation by Richard Wiener" );
    refresh();
}

void graph( cycle, tuna, sharks, plankton, dead_f, dead_s,
    empty )
int cycle;
int tuna;
int sharks;
int plankton;
int dead_f;
int dead_s;
int empty;
{
    int ht_tuna = tuna / 10;
    int ht_sharks = sharks / 10;
    int ht_plankton = plankton / 10;
    char str[ 10 ];
    if ( ht_tuna > 49 )
        ht_tuna = 49;
    if ( ht_sharks > 49 )
        ht_sharks = 49;
    if ( ht_plankton > 49 )
        ht_plankton = 49;
    move( 50 - ht_tuna, cycle );
    addch( 'T' );
    move( 50 - ht_sharks, cycle );
    addch( 'S' );
    move( 50 - ht_plankton, cycle );
    if ( ht_plankton > 0 )
        addch( 'P' );
    move( 54, 1 );
    addstr( "Cycle: " );
    move( 54, 8 );
```

```
sprintf( str, "%d", cycle );
addstr( str );
move( 55, 1 );
addstr( "Tuna: " );
move( 55, 7 );
sprintf( str, "%d", tuna );
if ( tuna < 10 )
{
    str[ 1 ] = ' ';
    str[ 2 ] = ' ';
    str[ 3 ] = '\0';
}
else if ( tuna < 100 )
{
    str[ 2 ] = ' ';
    str[ 3 ] = '\0';
}
addstr( str );
move( 55, 20 );
addstr( "Shark: " );
move( 55, 27 );
sprintf( str, "%d", sharks );
if ( sharks < 10 )
{
    str[ 1 ] = ' ';
    str[ 2 ] = ' ';
    str[ 3 ] = '\0';
}
else if ( sharks < 100 )
{
    str[ 2 ] = ' ';
    str[ 3 ] = '\0';
}
addstr( str );
move( 55, 40 );
addstr( "Plankton: " );
move( 55, 50 );
sprintf( str, "%d", plankton );
if ( plankton < 10 )
{
    str[ 1 ] = ' ';
    str[ 2 ] = ' ';
    str[ 3 ] = '\0';
}
else if ( plankton < 100 )
{
    str[ 2 ] = ' ';
    str[ 3 ] = '\0';
}
addstr( str );
move( 56, 1 );
addstr( "Dead fish: " );
move( 56, 12 );
sprintf( str, "%d", dead_f );
if ( dead_f < 10 )
```

```
    {
        str[ 1 ] = ` `;
        str[ 2 ] = ` `;
        str[ 3 ] = `\0`;
    }
    else if ( dead_f < 100 )
    {
        str[ 2 ] = ` `;
        str[ 3 ] = `\0`;
    }
    addstr( str );
    move( 56, 20 );
    addstr( "Dead sharks: " );
    move( 56, 33 );
    sprintf( str, "%d", dead_s );
    if ( dead_s < 10 )
    {
        str[ 1 ] = ` `;
        str[ 2 ] = ` `;
        str[ 3 ] = `\0`;
    }
    else if ( dead_s < 100 )
    {
        str[ 2 ] = ` `;
        str[ 3 ] = `\0`;
    }
    addstr( str );
    move( 56, 40 );
    addstr( "Empty cells: " );
    move( 56, 53 );
    sprintf( str, "%d", empty );
    if ( empty < 10 )
    {
        str[ 1 ] = ` `;
        str[ 2 ] = ` `;
        str[ 3 ] = `\0`;
    }
    else if ( empty < 100 )
    {
        str[ 2 ] = ` `;
        str[ 3 ] = `\0`;
    }
    addstr( str );
    refresh();
}

void pause()
{
    getch();
}

void end_window()
{
    endwin();
}
```

9.6 INITIAL CONCLUSIONS

An analysis, design and Eiffel implementation of an Ecological Simulation have been presented in this chapter. The analysis and design models and Eiffel implementation demonstrate the use of abstract classes (there are four of them) and the use of late-binding in connection with five methods (*move, count, starve, setReproductionInterval* and *setStarvationInterval*). The interplay among the classes is quite interesting and provides for alternative design architectures.

The reader is encouraged to perform a different design than the one presented here. There is no absolute right and wrong in doing a design. All classes should satisfy the consistency principle, which states that: (1) a class is a "kind of" all its ancestors, (2) all attributes make sense (including those inherited from ancestors), and (3) all methods make sense (including those inherited from ancestors). In doing such a redesign, different abstract classes should be identified based on a different partitioning of the common and separate features of the sea creatures.

It was stated earlier that the ultimate payoff for a well-designed system is ease of maintenance. In order to test this concept, a new requirement will be added to the original specifications and some maintenance performed to see how well the current design supports changes in the problem domain.

9.7 MAINTENANCE ON THE ECOLOGICAL SIMULATION

9.7.1 New Requirement

Suppose a new Scavenger type, *Super_Crab*, is added to the sea of ocean cells. This super crab can reproduce, moves and eats exactly like an ordinary crab (it cleans up dead fish and dead sharks) but only stays alive for a predefined length of time. This time interval is fixed and set at 38 time units. When a super crab's time is up, it disappears from the ocean. The only way the population of super crabs can sustain themselves is to reproduce before their time is up. While they are alive, super crabs help ordinary crabs clean up the debris of dead tuna and dead shark that litter the ocean.

We wish to add this new *Super_Crab* type to our ecological mix and display the number of such creatures after each simulation cycle along with the population values of the existing sea creatures. The image for this super crab is 'X.'

9.7.2 More Analysis

The new Super_Crab class is a "kind of" Scavenger and a "kind of" Reproducible type. It needs protocol from each of these classes. A Super_Crab instance needs an attribute *age* that determines whether it is time to die. Its move method is a modification of the move method of class Scavenger because of the requirement that it die when it reaches a certain age.

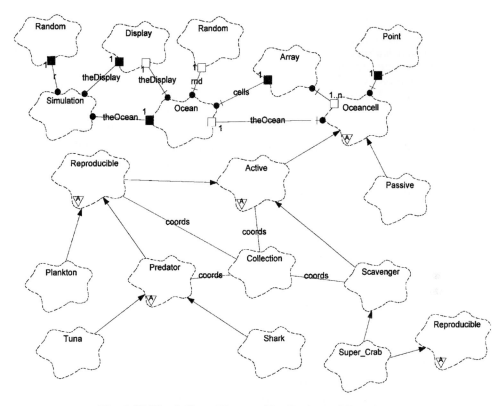

Fig. 9.15 Final Class Diagram For Ecological Simulation

Since protocol from classes Reproducible and Scavenger are both needed for Super_Crab, multiple inheritance is used to capture this protocol. It is important to apply the consistency rule to determine whether too much is inherited. If this is the case, a more drastic reconfiguration of the class architecture is required.

From class Reproducible, the attributes *reproduction_interval* and *reproduction_clock* are inherited. Both of these logically belong to the new class Super_Crab. The methods *resetReproductionClock*, *setReproductionInterval* and *reproduce* also belong in class Super_Crab to support the mechanism of reproduction.

From class Scavenger, the method *move* is inherited. This behavior is needed in class Super_Crab. The consistency principle is satisfied.

Figure 9.15 shows the modified class diagram including the new class Super_Crab.

9.7.3 More Design

An object-scenario diagram that describes the mechanism for a super crab to move is shown in Figure 9.16.

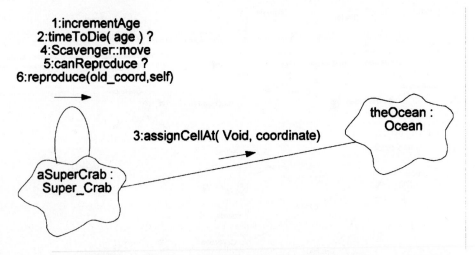

1:incrementAge
2:timeToDie(age) ?
4:Scavenger::move
5:canReproduce ?
6:reproduce(old_coord,self)

3:assignCellAt(Void, coordinate)

theOcean :
Ocean

aSuperCrab :
Super_Crab

Fig. 9.16 Mechanism for Move in Class Super_Crab

When a super_crab instance receives the *move* message, it increments its age. If it is time to die, it assigns its current coordinate position to a void cell in the ocean. If not, it invokes the protocol for moving that is defined in class Scavenger. It then determines whether it has moved and whether it qualifies for reproduction. If so, it calls *reproduce*. It will have to set its *age* parameter to zero temporarily (so the *new_cell* object produced in routine *reproduce* gets the right value for the *age* of the newborn *super_crab*) and then reset its age to the old value after completing reproduction.

9.7.4   Implementation Changes

The classes that are affected by this maintenance are OCEANCELL and DIS-PLAY. The modifications that must be made in these two classes are relatively minor and will not be presented.

The new class SUPER_CRAB is shown in Listing 9.14

Listing 9.14   Class SUPER_CRAB

```
class SUPER_CRAB
 inherit
   REPRODUCIBLE;

     SCAVENGER
         rename
            move as scavenger_move
         redefine
```

```
                count, create
            end;

        SCAVENGER
            redefine
                move, count, create
            select
                move
            end;

creation
    create

feature
    age       : INTEGER;
    lifespan  : INTEGER;

    create( pt : POINT; anImage : CHARACTER; anOcean : OCEAN
        ) is
    do
        theOcean := anOcean;
        coordinate := pt;
        image := anImage;
        lifespan := 38;
        reproduction_interval := 35;
      age := 0;
    end; -- create

    count is
    do
        theOcean.incrementNumSuperCrabs;
    end; -- count

    setReproductionInterval is
    do
        reproduction_interval := theOcean.SUPER_CRAB_R;
    end; -- setReproductionInterval

    move is
    local
        old_coord : POINT;
        old_age   : INTEGER;
        moved     : BOOLEAN;
    do
        old_coord := coordinate;
        age := age + 1;
        reproduction_clock := reproduction_clock + 1;
        if age >= lifespan then
            theOcean.assignCellTo( Void, coordinate );
        else
            scavenger_move;
            moved := old_coord /= coordinate;
            if reproduction_clock >= reproduction_interval
```

```
                    and moved then
                      old_age := age;
                      age := 0;
                      reproduce( Current, old_coord );
                      age := old_age;
                   end;
                end;
           end; -- move

      end -- SUPER_CRAB
```

The class SUPER_CRAB inherits once from REPRODUCIBLE and twice from SCAVENGER. This enables the routine *move* from class SCAVENGER (renamed *scavenger_move)* to be accessible within routine *move* of class SUPER_CRAB. The methods *create*, *move* and *count* are redefined in class SUPER_CRAB.

9.8 FINAL CONCLUSIONS

Although it could rightly be argued that the maintenance just performed was artificially set up and, therefore, not at all representative of the typical type of maintenance encountered in real software systems, the partitioning of the system provided an excellent framework to add an additional ocean cell subclass that was multiply inherited from two existing subclasses. In more typical maintenance situations, additional intermediate abstract classes might have to be constructed that provide the appropriate mix of protocol needed in the new subclass.

The Ecological Simulation, like the examples before it, provides furthur evidence that Eiffel makes the transition from design to implementation straightforward and painless.

One final suggestion. Lest you take for granted the ease with which the design just performed mapped to Eiffel, try, as an exercise, implementing the same design in C++. You may be in for a painful surprise. This type of "reality therapy" will remind you not to take a well-crafted language like Eiffel for granted. Eiffel does not get in the way!

A Game of Strategies and Investment

10.1 INTRODUCTION

An analysis, design and Eiffel implementation of a game of strategies and investment is presented in this chapter. This game, inspired by the popular game of Monopoly®, was invented and used by the author as a semester project in a graduate course on Object-Oriented Analysis and Design given at the University of Colorado at Colorado Springs. This game leads to a richer and more complex set of modeling relationships than the Ecological Simulation presented in Chapter 9 and provides the basis for another look at the process of object-oriented analysis, design and Eiffel implementation. Like the example presented in Chapter 9, the major goal of this example is to showcase Eiffel's powerful capabilities and once again see Eiffel in action.

10.2 INFORMAL REQUIREMENTS

The game consists of four players, named A, B, C and D, and a board with 20 positions on it. There is no required human intervention in this game. Your computer program, through its various objects and mechanisms, will be responsible for playing out a complete game, presenting the user with simple output to be described below and announcing the winner at the end.

There is no entity, such as a centralized game controller, that has any knowledge of the 20 board positions. The four players, A, B, C and D, are all initialized to start at position 1. Each board position knows of the next board position and the 20th board position knows of the 1st position.

Each of the players is randomly assigned one of three investment strategies, 1, 2 or 3, at the beginning of the game. Each player starts with an account balance of $50,000. As the game progresses, the original investment strategy may be replaced with another (one of the remaining two). Such swaps may occur from time-to-time for each player as the game progresses. Each player has no control over these investment strategy swaps.

The referee tells each of the players in turn (first player A, then B, then C, then D) to move. In response to this, the player rolls a die with an equal probability of outcomes from 1 to 6 and moves that number of board positions forward.

The game ends in one of two ways: (1) The referee has told each player to move 5000 times (each sequence of four "move" commands is defined as a move cycle), or (2) One of the players is out of money. If a player is out of money, it must inform the referee who then ends the game and causes the winner to be announced. When the game ends, the player with the most money is declared the winner. Property is not valued in computing the player with the most money. The referee has no other function than telling each of the players to move in turn and counting the number of move cycles so the game can be terminated (if in fact the game hasn't already been terminated because of bankruptcy).

There are two kinds of board positions: chance and property.

If a player lands on a chance position, the following possible actions may occur: (1) The player may acquire additional money immediately, (2) The player may lose some money immediately, (3) The player may get a replacement investment strategy, (4) The player may be asked to make another move determined again by a random roll of a die, or (5) The player may be given the option to purchase unowned property.

If a player lands on a property position, the following possible actions may occur: If the property is not owned, the player will be offered the opportunity to purchase the property at a preset price associated with the board position. The player's decision to purchase or not purchase will be based on the investment strategy it's currently using. If the property is owned by another player, the player will pay a fixed rental penalty directly to a banker who will convey this rent to the owner. The rent is based on the number of investment units (the Monopoly® equivalent of houses) built on the property by the owner. If the property is owned by the player who has landed on the property, the player will be offered the opportunity to purchase from 0 to 5 additional investment units. These investment units on an owned property offer the advantage of increasing the rental fee obtained if another player lands on the property. There is no limit to the number of investment units that can be "built" on an owned property. The decision regarding the number of investment units to purchase (from 0 to 5) will be based on the player's current investment strategy.

The output must be updated at the conclusion of every player's move or when rent is paid to another player. The format for the output is shown below (without the three dots, of course) for a typical output (here, two players happen to be on the same board position).

Cash A	Cash B	Cash C	Cash D
20799	52114	78043	15398

Move cycle: 12		Owned By	Number Units
1:			
2: A		B	12
3:			
4: C, D			
5:		D	
6:		B	2
7:			
8:			
9:			
10:			
...			
19: B			
20:		A	5

The referee must transmit the updated move cycle number at the beginning of each new move cycle to the display. After each move, each player must transmit its current cash and board position to the display. The display must also be updated each time rent is paid to another player (in order to keep the display of the current cash values current). These data, as indicated in the sample output display given above, are shown on the user's screen.

The specifications for each board position are given below:

Position 1: If a player lands on or passes this board position, the player "earns" $200 (like passing "GO" in Monopoly®). That is the only function of position 1.

Position 2: This is a property position. It's cost is $2000. It's rent is $200. Investment units cost $1000 each. For each investment unit, the rent goes up by $100. In general, the following algorithm holds for all property units: Rent is 1/10 the cost of the property. Rent is increased by 1/10 the cost of each additional investment unit. Investment units always cost 1/2 as much as the property. All arithmetic is integer arithmetic with normal truncation. This algorithm allows a property position to be characterized uniquely by its cost. As an example, if the property on position 2 has three investment units on it, it will cost another player $500 if it lands on this property (1/10 the worth of the $2000 property and the three investment units).

Position 3: This is a chance position. If a player lands on this position, it receives a new investment strategy randomly chosen from 1 to 3 with equal likelihood. It is possible that it will receive the same investment strategy that it already has (1/3 probability).

Position 4: This is another chance position. A player landing on this position has its cash amount changed by a random integer uniformly distributed from –$300 to $300.

Position 5: This is a property position. The cost to purchase the property is $500. Using the algorithm given above, it would cost the owning player $250 to purchase one additional investment unit and cost a non-owning player landing on this position $50 rent plus an extra $25 for each investment sitting on the property. The owning player would be offered the opportunity to purchase between 0 and 5 additional investment units each time it lands on this board position.

Position 6: This is a property position. The cost is $800.

Position 7: This is a chance position. A player landing on this position has its cash amount changed by a random integer uniformly distributed from –$500 to $500.

Position 8: This is a chance position. A player landing on this position must "throw" the die and move again.

Position 9: This is a property position. The cost is $1200.

Position 10: This is a chance position. If a player lands on this position, it receives a new investment strategy randomly chosen from 1 to 3 with equal likelihood. It is possible that it will receive the same investment strategy that it already has (1/3 probability).

Position 11: This is a property position. The cost is $900.

Position 12: This is a chance position. The player immediately receives a bonus of 5 percent of its current cash amount.

Position 13: This is a property position. The cost is $500.

Position 14: This is a chance position. The player immediately receives a penalty of 5 percent of its current cash amount.

Position 15: This is a property position. The cost is $1500.

Position 16: This is a chance position. If a player lands on this position, it receives a new investment strategy randomly chosen from 1 to 3 with equal likelihood. It is possible that it will receive the same investment strategy that it already has (1/3 probability). In addition, a player landing on this position has its cash amount changed by a random integer uniformly distributed from –$200 to $200.

Position 17: This is a property position. The cost is $3000.

Position 18: This is a chance position. A player landing on this position has its cash amount changed by a random integer uniformly distributed from $50 to $250.

Position 19: This is a chance position. A player landing on this position is given the option of purchasing the first unowned property (in position 20 or 1 or 2, etc.).

Position 20: This is a property position. The cost is $700.

All monetary transactions (one player paying another rent, player receiving or losing money on a chance board position, player receiving $200 every time it completes a circuit, players paying for a property or additional investment units) are handled by a banker. Players do not communicate directly with other players. The banker cannot ever run out of money.

It was stated earlier that when a player is offered the option of purchasing a property (when landing on an unowned property) or offered the option of purchasing from 0 to 5 additional investment units (when later landing on its own property), it makes its decision by "using" its current investment strategy. The algorithms for each of the three investment strategies are given below.

If a player has investment strategy 1: This is a random strategy. When offered the opportunity to purchase an unowned property, it will decide by a "flip of a fair coin" (i.e. equal chance of accepting or rejecting), provided that it has more cash than the cost of the property. Its decision to purchase between 0 and 5 investment units when later landing on its own property is made by choosing a uniformly distributed random integer from 0 to 5 (providing it has enough cash to make the purchase). For example, if the random integer chosen is 3, and the player lacks the cash to buy 3 units, it then elects to buy no units.

If a player has investment strategy 2: This is an aggressive strategy. When offered an unowned property, it will always purchase it if it has the cash to cover the purchase price (a player must always have at least one dollar remaining after a purchase — bankruptcy cannot occur as a result of a purchase). When given an opportunity to buy between 0 and 5 additional investment units, it will always purchase the largest number that it has the cash on hand to cover. That is, it will try to purchase 5 units if it has the cash. If not, it will try to purchase 4 units, and so on.

If a player has investment strategy 3: This is a conservative strategy that is based on the player's current cash and rent receipts. When offered the opportunity to purchase an unowned property, it will purchase this property provided that it has at least five times the cost of the property in current cash. When offered the opportunity to purchase between 0 and 5 investment units on its own property, it will purchase as many investment units as it can subject to the following constraints: (1) It has greater than five times as much cash as the total outlay for the additional investment unit(s), and (2) The rent already earned from the property exceeds 1/4 the cost of the additional investment units.

When a player runs out of money because it lands on another player's property and must pay rent, or a chance board position imposes a monetary penalty, it cannot sell its property or investment units to acquire additional cash. Property and investment units are not deemed to have any monetary value for avoiding bankruptcy. Their only value is in acquiring wealth during the game. When a player runs out of cash it must inform the referee. The referee then asks the banker which of the remaining players has the most cash, ends the game and asks the banker to tell the display to name the winning player.

Each class should limit access to its attributes as much as possible (have the smallest interface bandwidth). That is, each player should know as little about the board position it's on as is feasible, each board position should know as little about the player that has landed on it as is feasible, and the referee knows nothing about any of the players or board positions. In fact, only the banker has direct access to information about the current cash amount of all players and can reveal this information only to the display at the end of the game. Of course each player knows its own cash amount that it must transmit to the display after each move.

10.3 ANALYSIS

Analysis as seen in Chapters 8 and 9 involves the "discovery" of problem domain classes, an identification of the responsibilities and collaborations of the classes, an identification of their attributes and finally their methods. The game, specified in section 10.2, provides an opportunity to investigate a rich set of modeling relationships involving roughly two dozen classes.

Based on the informal problem specification given in section 10.1, Figure 10.1 identifies the major problem domain classes.

The key domain classes include Referee, Player, Banker, Random, Investment_Strategy, Position and Display. The lines connecting the classes indicate an association between the classes. At the earliest stage of analysis, the nature of the associations are not yet known.

From the problem description, it is evident that each player "contains" a particular type of investment strategy from among three choices. It is also clear that there are two distinctly different types of board positions: those that involve property investments and rent and those that involve chance. This suggests that classes Investment_Strategy and Position be defined as abstract classes. Class Investment_Strategy has subclasses Strategy1, Strategy2 and Strategy3. Class Position has subclasses Property and Chance.

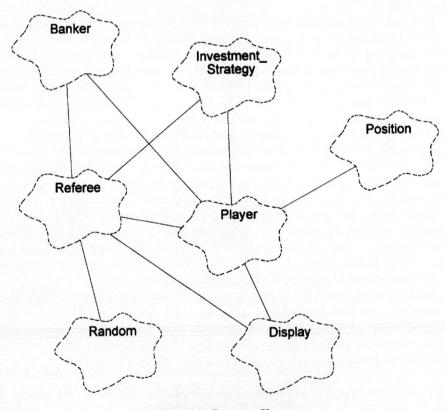

Fig. 10.1 Domain Classes

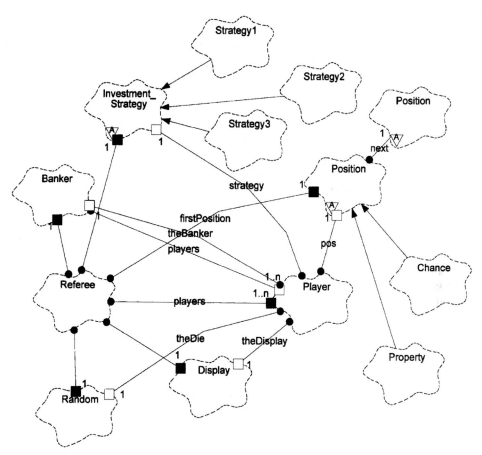

Fig. 10.2 Domain Class Diagram

Figure 10.2 shows these additional classes and also indicates much more precise relationships among the classes defined in Figure 10.1.

Class Referee "owns" a Banker object, an Investment_Strategy object (either Strategy1, Strategy2 or Strategy3), a Position object (either a Property or Chance object), a set of Player objects, a Display object and a Random object. This class is responsible for bringing these objects to life and providing appropriate initialization. It is important to emphasize that ownership does not imply free access to the attributes of these classes. The features that may be accessed in each of the classes Referee owns are specified in the respective class descriptions.

Class Player has references to a Position object, an Investment_Strategy object, a Banker object, a Random object and a Display object. These references are provided to a Position object when it is initialized. The Position object that each Player object references changes as the player moves across the board. The Investment_Strategy object may also change in response to a particular chance position.

Abstract class Position is shown as having ownership of another Position object. This implies a linked-list relationship among the Position objects.

From the problem description, it is possible to identify some key attributes and aggregation relationships associated with the domain classes. These are listed below.

Class Referee
theBanker – aggregation relationship with class Banker
theDisplay – aggregation relationship with class Display
firstPosition – aggregation relationship with class Position
theDie – aggregation relationship with class Random
cycle – attribute of type integer

Class Player
id – attribute of type character
pos – reference to class Position
balance – attribute of type integer
strategy – reference to class Investment_Strategy
theBanker – reference to class Banker
theReferee – reference to class Referee

Class Position (Abstract Class)
next – aggregation relationship with class Position
cost – attribute of type integer
boardPosition – attribute of type integer

10.4 DESIGN

In order to model the methods of each of the domain classes, the key mechanisms associated with the problem must be identified and then modeled. There are 15 such key mechanisms that are modeled using object-scenario diagrams. From these object-scenario diagrams, additional design classes are added, additional

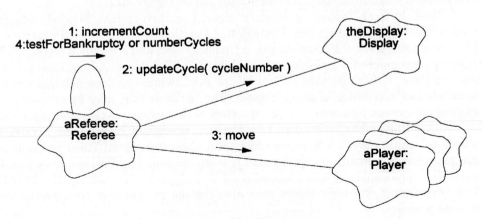

Fig. 10.3 Referee Control

attributes, aggregation relationships and associations are discovered among the existing domain classes, and the methods of each class are identified.

The first key mechanism involves the game control by the referee. The object-scenario diagram of Figure 10.3 shows this mechanism.

The referee first increments the counter. The new cycle number is sent to the display object. The four players are instructed to move. The referee tests for bankruptcy or the required number of cycles being completed in order to determine whether the game has ended. From this diagram, it is evident that class Referee must have an added attribute, *bankruptcy*, of type *Boolean*. It must test this attribute after each move and move cycle.

The next key mechanism, Figure 10.4, shows the movement of a player. It shows aPlayer object throwing a die and getting its number of board positions to traverse. It then obtains the next board position and determines from this position whether it is entitled to collect two hundred dollars. When the player arrives on its destination board position, it interacts with the position. This interaction is shown in subsequent object-scenario diagrams. Upon completing the interaction with the board position, the player updates its position and current cash balance with the display. The key player method, *interact*, is identified in this object-scenario diagram. The method *collectTwoHundred* is identified for class

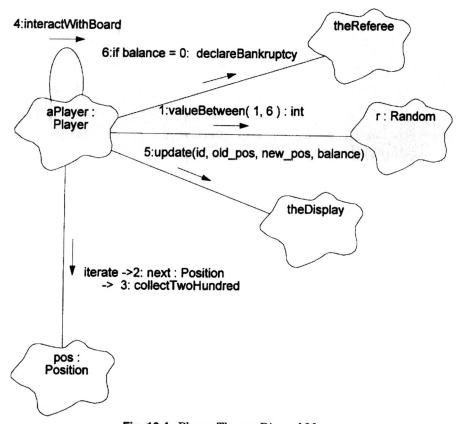

Fig. 10.4 Player Throws Die and Moves

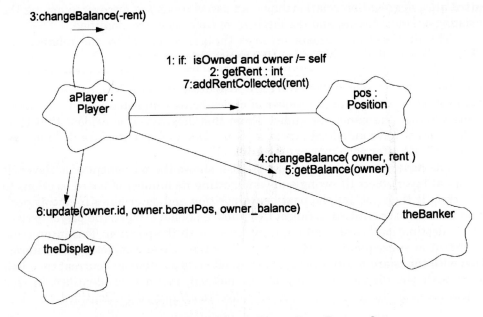

Fig. 10.5 Interact with Board: Player Pays Rent to Owner

Position and the method *update* for class Display.

The next four object-scenario diagrams show the details of the various mechanisms associated with the method *interact*. The first of these "interact" mechanisms involves a player landing on a board position owned by another player and having to pay rent. This diagram is shown in Figure 10.5

The first step for the player is to determine whether the position it is on is owned, and if so, whether it is owned by itself. If the answers to these two questions are yes and no, respectively, it computes the rent owed from the position object that it is on (has a reference to). It decrements its cash balance by this rent. The player then requests that the banker increment the owner's (another Player object) cash balance by the rent. The player then requests that the banker obtain the current cash amount of this owner. Finally, the player updates the display with the new cash amount of the property owner who has collected rent.

Figure 10.6 shows the next "interact" key mechanism — a player landing on its own property and considering whether to add investment units.

The player first determines whether the position it is on is owned and, if so, whether it is owned by itself. If the answers to these two questions are both yes, the player obtains the rent collected to date from its position as well as the cost of purchasing additional investment units. It sends the message *purchaseUnits* to its attribute *strategy* with its cash balance, the cost of the property and the rent collected to date as parameters. The function returns the number of units purchased. If the number of units purchased is positive, the player decrements its cash balance by the cost of the units. Next, the player updates the number of investment units contained on its property by sending the message *addInvestmentUnits* to its position. Finally, it sends the message *units* to the display with

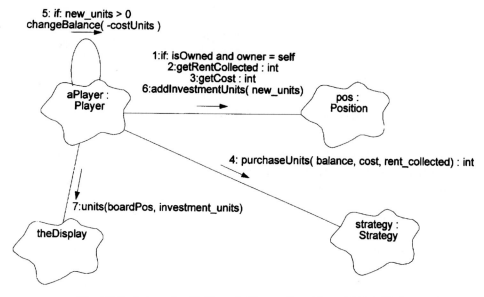

Fig. 10.6 Interact with Board: Player Considers Adding Units

its board position and the current number of investment units as parameters. From this scenario diagram, the methods *units* in class Display, *purchaseUnits* in class Investment_Strategy and *addInvestmentUnits* in class Position are identified.

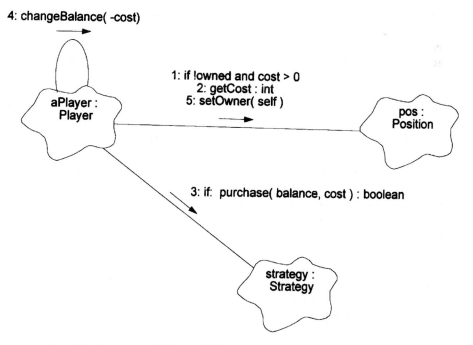

Fig. 10.7 Interact with Board: Player Considers the Purchase of Property

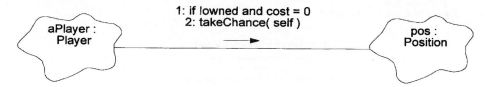

Fig. 10.8 Interact with Board: Chance Position

Figure 10.7 shows the third "interact" mechanism — landing on an unowned property and considering its purchase.

After the player verifies that the position is not owned and has a positive cost (chance positions are unowned and have a zero cost), it gets the cost of the property and sends this value and its current cash balance as parameters to the *purchase* method of class Investment_Strategy. If the purchase function returns a value True, the player decrements its balance by the cost of the property and sends the message *setOwner* to the position.

From this scenario, the methods *purchase* from class Strategy and *setOwner* from class Position are identified.

Figure 10.8 provides the final "interact" mechanism for class Player. In this scenario, a player lands on a chance position. Once the player determines that the property is not owned and has a cost of zero, it sends the message *takeChance(self)* to its Position reference.

The mechanism associated with a player's declaration of bankruptcy (having zero balance after a move) is shown in Figure 10.9.

When the referee detects a state of bankruptcy as a consequence of a player's move, it sends the message *announceWinner* to the banker with parameters *thePlayers* and *theDisplay*. These references are used by the banker object to compute the cash balance of each player and to send the display the winner of the game.

The three investment strategies, modeled as Investment_Strategy subclasses Strategy1, Strategy2 and Strategy3 are shown in Figures 10.10 through 10.12.

There are five distinct types of chance mechanisms. Each is modeled with an object-scenario diagram. These are shown in Figures 10.13 through 10.17.

Figure 10.13 shows the mechanism of a player landing on a change strategy chance position.

The chance mechanism of changing balance by a random amount between lower and upper is shown in Figure 10.14.

The chance mechanism of landing on a position that requires a player to move again is shown in Figure 10.15.

The chance mechanism of adding or subtracting 5 percent of a player's current cash balance is shown in Figure 10.16.

The more complex chance mechanism of a player being directed to purchase the first available property is shown in Figure 10.17.

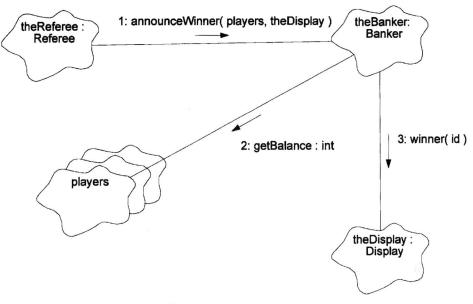

Fig. 10.9 Bankruptcy

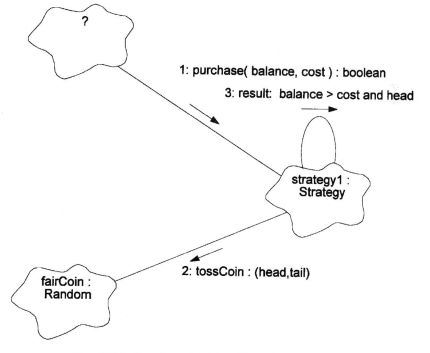

Fig. 10.10 Purchase Decision Using Strategy 1

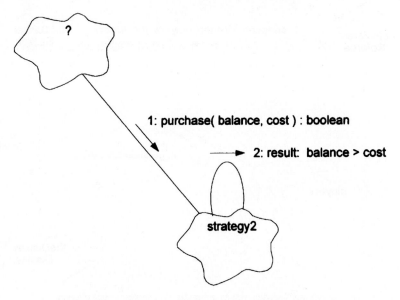

Fig. 10.11 Purchase Decision Using Strategy 2

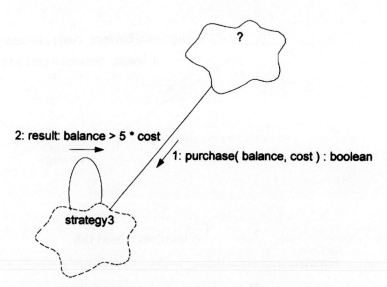

Fig. 10.12 Purchase Decision Using Strategy 3

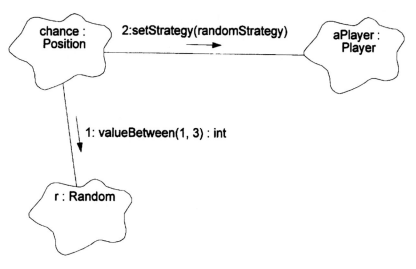

Fig. 10.13   Take Chance: Change Strategy

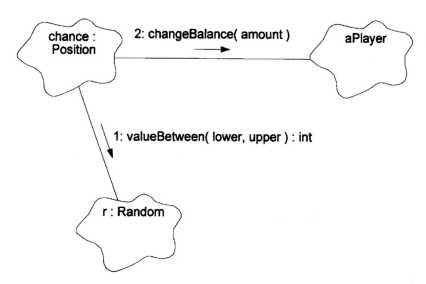

Fig. 10.14   Take Chance: Change Balance

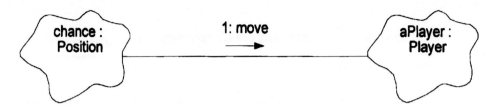

Fig. 10.15   Take Chance: Move Again

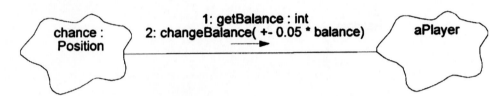

Fig. 10.16   Take Chance: Add (subtract) Five Percent

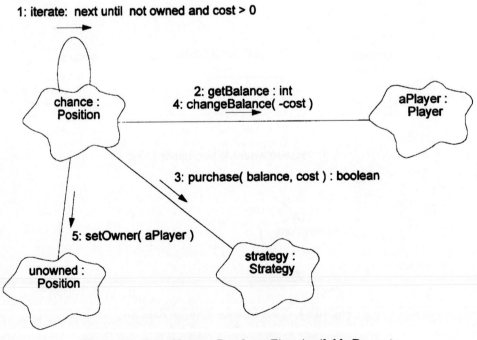

Fig. 10.17   Take Chance: Purchase First Available Property

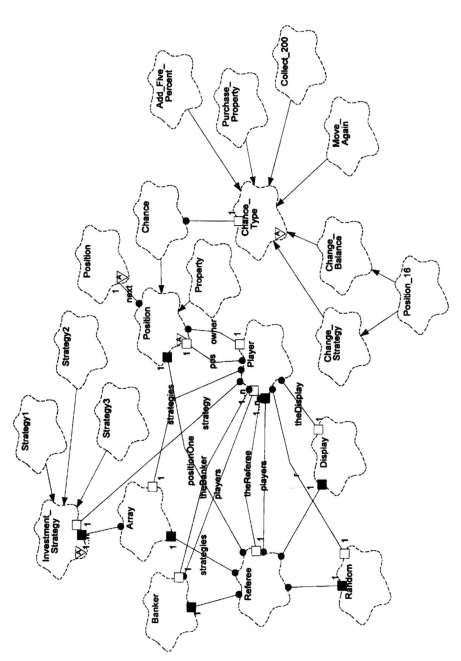

Fig. 10.18 Design Class Diagram

The object-scenario diagrams presented in Figures 10.3 through 10.17 form the basis for the final class diagram given in Figure 10.18. In addition to the domain classes shown in the class diagram of Figure 10.2, many additional design classes have been added.

A key design decision concerns the relationship between class Chance, a subclass of Position, and the various specialized chance types. An obvious choice might be to make the various chance types subclasses of class Chance. An alternative approach is used here. An abstract class Chance_Type is introduced. It contains six subclasses shown in Figure 10.18. Every instance of class Chance contains an instance of class Chance_Type or in actuality an instance of one of Chance_Type's subclasses. The common behavior of all of the subclass chance types is factored into class Chance_Type.

10.5 EIFFEL IMPLEMENTATION

The class diagram of Figure 10.18 plus the numerous object-scenario diagrams form the basis for the Eiffel implementation. Although most of the key mechanisms have been identified at the design level, there is still some room for some low-level design decisions to be made at the implementation level.

The first class to be implemented is class REFEREE. This class has the responsibility to build the game board, initialize the four players, construct the Display object, build the Banker object, initialize the Random object and control the overall simulation. The details of this class are shown in Listing 10.1

Listing 10.1   Class REFEREE

```
class REFEREE
-- Main driver class for game simulation
 creation
    initialize

 feature
    theBanker    : BANKER;
    strategies   : ARRAY[ INVESTMENT_STRATEGY ];
    players      : ARRAY[ PLAYER ];
    theDisplay   : DISPLAY;
    positionOne  : CHANCE;
    r            : RANDOM;
    bankrupt     : BOOLEAN;
    cycle        : INTEGER;

    initialize is
    local
        player1, player2, player3, player4 : PLAYER;
        s1, s2, s3 : INVESTMENT_STRATEGY;
        strategy_number : INTEGER;
        aCollectTwoHundred : COLLECT_TWO_HUNDRED;
    do
```

```
      !!r.initialize;
      !!strategies.make( 1, 3 );
      !STRATEGY1!s1.make( r );
      strategies.put( s1, 1 );
      !STRATEGY2!s2.make( r );
      strategies.put( s2, 2 );
      !STRATEGY3!s3.make( r );
      strategies.put( s3, 3 );
      !!theDisplay.initialize;
      !!positionOne.make( 1 )
      !!aCollectTwoHundred;
       positionOne.setType( aCollectTwoHundred );
      createBoard;
      !!theBanker;
      !!players.make( 1, 4 );
      strategy_number := r.valueBetween( 1, 3 );
      !!player1.make( 'A', 50000, positionOne,
               strategies.item( strategy_number ),
      theDisplay, theBanker, r, strategies, Current );
      strategy_number := r.valueBetween( 1, 3 )
      !!player2.make( 'B', 50000, positionOne,
               strategies.item( strategy_number ),
      theDisplay, theBanker, r, strategies, Current );
      strategy_number := r.valueBetween( 1, 3 );
      !!player3.make( 'C', 50000, positionOne,
               strategies.item( strategy_number ),
      theDisplay, theBanker, r, strategies, Current );
      strategy_number := r.valueBetween( 1, 3 );
      !!player4.make( 'D', 50000, positionOne,
               strategies.item( strategy_number ),
      theDisplay, theBanker, r, strategies, Current );
      players.put( player1, 1 );
      players.put( player2, 2 );
      players.put( player3, 3 )
      players.put( player4, 4 );
      play_game;
      theDisplay.pause;
      theDisplay.close;
   end; -- initialize

createBoard is
 local
    aProperty : PROPERTY;
    nextProperty : POSITION;
    aChance  : CHANCE;
    aChance_Type : CHANCE_TYPE;
 do
   -- Set up board position 2
   !!aProperty.make( 2, 2000 );
   positionOne.setNext( aProperty );
   nextProperty := aProperty;

   -- Set up board position 3
   !!aChance.make( 3 );
   !NEW_STRATEGY!aChance_Type;
```

```
aChance.setType( aChance_Type );
nextProperty.setNext( aChance );
nextProperty := aChance;

-- Set up board position 4
!!aChance.make( 4 );
!CHANGE_BALANCE!aChance_Type.make( -300, 300 );
aChance.setType( aChance_Type );
nextProperty.setNext( aChance );
nextProperty := aChance;

-- Set up board position 5
!!aProperty.make( 5, 500 );
nextProperty.setNext( aProperty );
nextProperty := aProperty;

-- Set up board position 6
!!aProperty.make( 6, 800 );
nextProperty.setNext( aProperty );
nextProperty := aProperty;

-- Set up board position 7
!!aChance.make( 7 );
!CHANGE_BALANCE!aChance_Type.make( -500, 500 );
aChance.setType( aChance_Type );
nextProperty.setNext( aChance );

nextProperty := aChance;

-- Set up board position 8
!!aChance.make( 8 );
!MOVES_AGAIN!aChance_Type;
aChance.setType( aChance_Type );
nextProperty.setNext( aChance );
nextProperty := aChance;

-- Set up board position 9
!!aProperty.make( 9, 1200 );
nextProperty.setNext( aProperty );
nextProperty := aProperty;

-- Set up board position 10
!!aChance.make( 10 );
!NEW_STRATEGY!aChance_Type;
aChance.setType( aChance_Type );
nextProperty.setNext( aChance );
nextProperty := aChance;

-- Set up board position 11
!!aProperty.make( 11, 900 );
nextProperty.setNext( aProperty );
nextProperty := aProperty;

-- Set up board position 12
!!aChance.make( 12 );
```

```
            !ADD_FIVE_PERCENT!aChance_Type;
            aChance.setType( aChance_Type );
            nextProperty.setNext( aChance );
            nextProperty := aChance;

            -- Set up board position 13
            !!aProperty.make( 13, 500 );
            nextProperty.setNext( aProperty );
            nextProperty := aProperty;

            -- Set up board position 14
            !!aChance.make( 14 );
            !SUBTRACT_FIVE_PERCENT!aChance_Type;
            aChance.setType( aChance_Type );
            nextProperty.setNext( aChance );
            nextProperty := aChance;

            -- Set up board position 15
            !!aProperty.make( 15, 1500 );
        nextProperty.setNext( aProperty );
            nextProperty := aProperty;

            -- Set up board position 16
            !!aChance.make( 16 );
            !NUMBER16!aChance_Type.make( -200, 200 );
            aChance.setType( aChance_Type );
            nextProperty.setNext( aChance );
            nextProperty := aChance;

            -- Set up board position 17
            !!aProperty.make( 17, 3000 );
            nextProperty.setNext( aProperty );
            nextProperty := aProperty;

            -- Set up board position 18
            !!aChance.make( 18 );
            !CHANGE_BALANCE!aChance_Type.make( 50, 250 );
            aChance.setType( aChance_Type );
            nextProperty.setNext( aChance );
            nextProperty := aChance;

            -- Set up board position 19
            !!aChance.make( 19 );
            !PURCHASE_NEW_PROPERTY!aChance_Type;
            aChance.setType( aChance_Type );
            nextProperty.setNext( aChance );
            nextProperty := aChance;

          -- Set up board position 20
            !!aProperty.make( 20, 700 );
            nextProperty.setNext( aProperty );
            nextProperty := aProperty;

            -- Link back to board position 1
            nextProperty.setNext( positionOne );
```

```
end; -- createBoard

play_game is
local
    index       : INTEGER;
     decade     : INTEGER;
do
    from cycle := 0
    until bankrupt = TRUE or cycle = 5000
    loop
        cycle := cycle + 1;
        theDisplay.updateCycle( cycle );
        from index := 0
        until bankrupt = TRUE or index = 4
        loop
            index := index + 1;
            players.item( index ).move;
        end;
    end;
    if bankrupt = TRUE then
        theBanker.announceWinner( players, theDisplay );
    end;
end; -- play_game

declareBankruptcy is
do
    bankrupt := True;
end; -- setBankrupt


end -- REFEREE
```

Class REFEREE is responsible for creating and initializing many of the objects that are used in the software system. Routine *initialize* triggers the application. First, the random number object, r, is initialized. Next, the array of three strategies is initialized. Then, the creation routines of each Strategy subclass are called with a reference to *r* passed in as a parameter. The three Strategy subclasses are installed in the *strategies* array. Next, the Display object, *theDisplay*, is initialized. Chance object *positionOne* is initialized. Then, the Chance_Type object *aCollectTwoHundred* is initialized. The attribute *aCollectTwoHundred* is next installed in the Chance object.

The *createBoard* routine sets up a long sequence of events. Each board position is initialized individually using either a Property object or a Chance object and its associated Chance_Type subclass. We examine one such Property position and one such Chance position in detail.

The code for performing the initialization of board position 9 is given below:

```
-- Set up board position 9
!!aProperty.make( 9, 1200 );
nextProperty.setNext( aProperty );
nextProperty := aProperty;
```

The first parameter, 9, specifies the board position, whereas the second parameter, 1200, specifies the cost of the property.

Next, the initialization of position number 18 is shown.

```
-- Set up board position 18
!!aChance.make( 18 );
!CHANGE_BALANCE!aChance_Type.make( 50, 250 );
aChance.setType( aChance_Type );
nextProperty.setNext( aChance );
nextProperty := aChance;
```

Board position 18 is one of several that is an instance of the CHANCE subclass CHANGE_BALANCE. This position requires two initialization parameters, lower limit and upper limit, that specify the range from which a random amount is either paid to or taken from the player landing on this position. First a CHANCE instance *aChance* is created with board position parameter, 18. Then, an instance of CHANCE_TYPE, aChance_Type, is created with the two parameters 50 and 250. Then, the object aChance_Type is installed as an attribute in the object *aChance*. The remaining two statements perform the required linking of the previous board position to the new board position.

The routine *play_game* called near the end of routine *initialize* implements the referee's key mechanism for starting and controlling the duration of the game. Each of the two nested loops test first for bankruptcy. This causes the game to end abruptly as soon as one of the players has a cash balance of zero. The inner loop sends the message *move* to each player in turn. This key mechanism is implemented in class PLAYER, shown in Listing 10.2.

Listing 10.2 Class PLAYER

```
class PLAYER
 creation { REFEREE }
   make

 feature { POSITION, BANKER }
    theDisplay : DISPLAY;

 feature { PLAYER, BANKER, POSITION }
    id : CHARACTER;

 feature { PLAYER, PURCHASE_NEW_PROPERTY }
    pos : POSITION;

 feature { BANKER, CHANCE_TYPE }
    balance : INTEGER;

 feature { CHANCE_TYPE }
    strategy : INVESTMENT_STRATEGY;
    strategies : ARRAY[ INVESTMENT_STRATEGY ];

 feature { NONE }
    theBanker : BANKER;
    theReferee : REFEREE;

    make( theId : CHARACTER; theBalance : INTEGER; p :
```

```
        POSITION; aStrategy : INVESTMENT_STRATEGY; aDisplay :
        DISPLAY; aBanker : BANKER; rnd : RANDOM;
        s : ARRAY[ INVESTMENT_STRATEGY ]; aReferee :
        REFEREE ) is
do
     id := theId;
     balance := theBalance;
     pos := p;
     strategy := aStrategy;
     theDisplay := aDisplay;
     theBanker := aBanker;
     r := rnd;
     strategies := s;
     theReferee := aReferee;
end; -- make

interactWithBoard is
local
     chancePosition : CHANCE;
do
     if pos.isOwned and then pos.owner /= Current then
         -- player lands on property owned by another
         -- player
         payOwner;
   elseif pos.isOwned and then pos.owner = Current then
         -- player lands on his/her own property and
         -- considers purchasing units
         considerPurchasingUnits;
   elseif not pos.isOwned and then pos.cost > 0 then
         -- player lands on unowned property and considers
         -- purchase
         considerPurchase;
   elseif not pos.isOwned and then pos.cost = 0 then
         -- player has landed on a chance position
         chancePosition ?= pos; -- this must be satisfied
         chancePosition.takeChance( Current );
     end;
end; -- interact

payOwner is
local
     aProperty       : PROPERTY;
     rent            : INTEGER;
     owner_balance   : INTEGER;
do
     aProperty ?= pos; -- This must be satisfied
     rent := aProperty.cost // 10 +
     aProperty.investment_units * aProperty.cost // 20;
     if rent < balance then
         theBanker.changeBalance( pos.owner, rent );
     else
         theBanker.changeBalance( pos.owner, balance );
     end;
     owner_balance := theBanker.getBalance( pos.owner );
     theDisplay.update( pos.owner.id,
```

```
              pos.owner.pos.boardPosition,
              pos.owner.pos.boardPosition, owner_balance );
          aProperty.addRentCollected( rent );
          changeBalance( -rent );
       end; -- payOwner

    considerPurchase is
    do
        if strategy.purchase( balance, pos.cost ) then
            changeBalance( -pos.cost );
            pos.setOwner( Current );
        end;
    end; -- considerPurchase

    considerPurchasingUnits is
    local
        aProperty      : PROPERTY;
        rent_collected : INTEGER;
        new_units      : INTEGER;
    do
        aProperty ?= pos; -- This must be satisfied
        rent_collected := aProperty.rent_collected;
        new_units := strategy.purchaseUnits( balance,
            aProperty.cost, rent_collected );
        if new_units > 0 then
            changeBalance( -new_units * pos.cost // 2 );
            aProperty.addInvestmentUnits( new_units );
            theDisplay.units( pos.boardPosition,
                aProperty.investment_units );
        end;
    end; -- considerPurchasingUnits

    delay is
    local
        index : INTEGER;
        z     : REAL;
    do
        z := 1.00;
        from index := 0
        until index = 150000
        loop
            index := index + 1;
            z := z * 1.0001
        end;
    end; -- delay

feature { CHANCE_TYPE }
    r : RANDOM;

  feature { REFEREE, CHANCE_TYPE }

    move is
    local
        dice      : INTEGER;
```

```
            count     : INTEGER;
            old_pos   : INTEGER;
        do
          old_pos := pos.boardPosition;
          dice := r.valueBetween( 1, 6 );
          from count := 0
          until count = dice
          loop
              count := count + 1;
              pos := pos.next;
              if pos.collectTwoHundred then
                  changeBalance( 200 );
              end;
          end;
          interactWithBoard;
          theDisplay.update( id, old_pos, pos.boardPosition,
            balance );
          if balance = 0 then
              theReferee.declareBankruptcy;
          end;
          delay;
        end; -- move

    setStrategy( aStrategy : INVESTMENT_STRATEGY ) is
    do
        strategy := aStrategy;
    end; -- setStrategy

feature { CHANCE_TYPE, BANKER }

    changeBalance( amount : INTEGER ) is
    do
        balance := balance + amount;
        if balance < 0 then
            balance := 0;
        end;
    end; -- changeBalance

invariant
    balance >= 0;

end -- PLAYER
```

The reader will notice that the attributes of class PLAYER are distributed
into feature sections, each having a different export scope. This is a very nice
capability of Eiffel. It allows the Eiffel programmer precise control over the
accessibility of each attribute. In short, it allows the software system to satisfy
the specification that each class provide the tightest possible interface bandwidth. Attributes are visible only where they are required. This is in sharp contrast to the typical C++ practice of putting all attributes in the private section of
a class (sometimes protected section) and all member functions in the public section of the class. The same selective export control can be achieved in C++ by
making all members private and then controlling export scope using friendship.

In my view, this is a much less elegant approach than the one offered by Eiffel.

The *move* routine implements the object-scenario diagram given in section 10.4. Since there is no central and all-knowing game controller that has a global knowledge of the entire board, each player must query each board position that it lands on to see whether it is entitled to receive the bonus of 200 dollars that occurs once per cycle.

The routine *interactWithBoard* encapsulates the four mechanisms for a player to interact with the board position that it is on.

The first mechanism, a player landing on a property owned by another player and paying rent to the other player, is tested for by the *if* statement:

```
if pos.isOwned and then pos.owner /= Current then
    payOwner;
```

The second mechanism, a player landing on his or her own property and possibly adding investment units, is tested for by the *if* statement:

```
elseif pos.isOwned and then pos.owner = Current then
    considerPurchasingtUnits;
```

The third mechanism, a player landing on an unowned property and being offered the opportunity to purchase this property, is tested for by the *if* statement:

```
elseif not pos.isOwned and then pos.cost > 0 then
    considerPurchase;
```

The final mechanism, a player landing on a chance position, is tested for by the *if* statement:

```
elseif not pos.isOwned and the pos.cost = 0 then
    chancePos ?= pos;
    chancePosition.takeChance( Current );
```

The present design assigns all position objects to have the attributes *owner* and *cost*. A position is detected as a chance position if its owner has a value *Void* and its cost is zero. It might properly be argued that the attributes *owner* and *cost* belong one level down in the Position hierarchy, namely in class PROPERTY. After all, does a chance position really have an owner and really have a cost? If such a modification were made to the architecture of the system, a different mechanism for determining the interplay between player and board position would have to be used. This will be explored further in Section 10.6 when the present design is critically examined and some modifications suggested.

Continuing the discussion of the present approach, if a chance position is detected, another inelegant segment of code resulting from the present design is used, namely, the downward reference through reverse assignment of local variable *chancePos* to *pos*. If this were attempted as an ordinary assignment, it would violate the principle of conformance that requires the source of the assignment to be of a type that conforms to the target of the assignment. Exactly the opposite is true here. The controlling *elseif* clause guarantees that the actual type of *pos* serving as the source of the reverse assignment must be of type Chance.

The reader should verify that each of the four routines called in the *interactWithBoard* routine correspond exactly to the object scenario diagrams presented in Section 10.4.

One of these four routines, *considerPurchasingUnits*, must also use a downward reference through reverse assignment to assign *aProperty* to *pos*. This is because class PROPERTY has the two attributes *rent_collected* and *investment_units* not present in the parent class POSITION. Because of the controlling *elseif* clause, this reverse assignment is guaranteed to always be valid. The routine *purchaseUnits*, defined in class INVESTMENT_STRATEGY as a deferred routine and made effective in classes Strategy1, Strategy2 and Strategy3, takes the three parameters *balance*, *cost* and *rent_collected*. The third of these parameters is actually only needed by class Strategy3 and is discarded in the *purchaseUnits* routines of classes Strategy1 and Strategy2. It might properly be argued that this is a flaw in the design. Why should three parameters be "hard-wired" into a polymorphic routine in order to take care of the worst case, Strategy3, that actually needs these three parameters. What if future maintenance would add a fourth strategy that needs four or five parameters? This issue will also be discussed in the design criticism of Section 10.6.

The *delay* routine serves only to slow the execution of the program down to a speed where the output is more easily understandable to the user. The need for this routine would be dependent on the desires of the user and the speed of his or her computer.

Listing 10.3 presents the code for the abstract class POSITION.

Listing 10.3   Class POSITION

```
deferred class POSITION
  feature { PLAYER, CHANCE_TYPE }
    next : POSITION;

  feature { PLAYER, CHANCE_TYPE }
    cost          : INTEGER;
    owner         : PLAYER;
    boardPosition : INTEGER;

    setOwner( theOwner : PLAYER ) is
    do
        owner := theOwner;
        theOwner.theDisplay.owner( theOwner.id,
          boardPosition );
    end; -- setOwner

  feature { REFEREE }

    setNext( nextPosition : POSITION ) is
    do
        next := nextPosition;
    end; -- setNext
```

```
feature { PLAYER }

    isOwned : BOOLEAN is
    do
        Result := owner /= Void;
    end; -- isOwned

    collectTwoHundred : BOOLEAN is
    deferred
    end; -- collectTwoHundred

end -- POSITION
```

This abstract class serves as the parent of subclasses Property and Chance. As indicated before, the decision to put the attributes *cost* and *owner* in this abstract class is questionable and will be examined critically in Section 10.6.

The routine *collectTwoHundred* is deferred. This is the reason that class POSITION is an abstract class.

Listing 10.4 shows the details of class PROPERTY.

Listing 10.4   Class PROPERTY

```
class PROPERTY
 inherit
    POSITION

 creation { REFEREE }
    make

 feature { NONE }

    make( number : INTEGER; price : INTEGER ) is
    do
        boardPosition := number;
        cost := price;
    end; -- make

 feature { PLAYER }

    rent_collected    : INTEGER;
    investment_units  : INTEGER;

    addRentCollected( rent : INTEGER ) is
    require
        positive : rent > 0;
    do
        rent_collected := rent_collected + rent;
    end; -- addRentCollected


    addInvestmentUnits( amount : INTEGER ) is
    require
        too_many : amount <= 5;
    do
```

```
        investment_units := investment_units + amount;
    end; -- addInvestmentUnits

    collectTwoHundred : BOOLEAN is
    do
        Result := FALSE;
    end; -- collectTwoHundred

end -- PROPERTY
```

All of the routines of this class are simple and require no explanation. The creation routine, *make*, is shown as having an export scope that is limited to class REFEREE. This assures that Property instances can only be created in class REFEREE. This is in the spirit of keeping the interface bandwidth of class PROPERTY to a minimum.

Listing 10.5 shows the code for class CHANCE.

Listing 10.5   Class CHANCE

```
class CHANCE

  inherit
    POSITION

  creation { REFEREE }
    make

  feature { NONE }
    type : CHANCE_TYPE;

  feature { NONE }
    make( number : INTEGER ) is
    do
        boardPosition := number;
    end; -- make

  feature { REFEREE }
    setType( chanceType : CHANCE_TYPE ) is
    do
        type := chanceType;
    end; -- setType

  feature { PLAYER }

    takeChance( aPlayer : PLAYER ) is
    do
        type.takeChance( aPlayer );
    end; -- takeChance

    collectTwoHundred : BOOLEAN is
    do
        Result := type.collectTwoHundred;
    end; -- collectTwoHundred
```

```
end -- CHANCE
```

This is an effective class. Instances will be created. Each Chance instance contains a reference to one of the subclasses of abstract class CHANCE_TYPE. When the message *takeChance* is sent to a Chance instance, this message is passed to the Chance_Type subclass. This is the mechanism used here to allow for various chance behaviors. The alternative would be to make class CHANCE an abstract class with routine *takeChance* deferred. There would then be a collection of Chance subclasses. Both methods appear to be about equal for modeling this problem.

Listing 10.6 shows the abstract class CHANCE_TYPE.

Listing 10.6 Class CHANCE_TYPE

```
deferred class CHANCE_TYPE
-- Encapsulates behavior of CHANCE position

 feature { CHANCE }

    takeChance( aPlayer : PLAYER ) is
    deferred
    end; -- takeChance

    collectTwoHundred : BOOLEAN is
    do
        Result := FALSE;
    end; -- collectTwoHundred
end -- CHANCE_TYPE
```

The routine *collectTwoHundred* is defined as returning False as a default mode since only one of the 20 board positions has this board position return True. In Listing 10.12, in class COLLECT_TWO_HUNDRED, this routine is redefined and returns True.

The various specialized subclasses of CHANCE_TYPE are presented in Listings 10.7 through 10.14. Each of these subclasses exactly follows an object-scenario diagram of Section 10.4.

Listing 10.7 Class CHANGE_BALANCE

```
class CHANGE_BALANCE
-- Changes the balance of a player
 inherit
    CHANCE_TYPE


 creation { REFEREE }
    make

 feature { NONE }
    lower_limit : INTEGER; -- of interval of chance
```

```
    upper_limit : INTEGER; -- of interval of chance

    make( lower : INTEGER; upper : INTEGER ) is
    do
        lower_limit := lower;
        upper_limit := upper;
    end; -- make

feature { CHANCE }

    takeChance( aPlayer : PLAYER ) is
    local
        change_by : INTEGER;
    do
        change_by := aPlayer.r.valueBetween( lower_limit,
            upper_Limit );
        aPlayer.changeBalance( change_by );
    end; -- takeChance

end -- CHANGE_BALANCE
```

Listing 10.8   Class NEW_STRATEGY

```
class NEW_STRATEGY
-- Gives player a new investment strategy
 inherit
    CHANCE_TYPE

 feature { CHANCE }
    takeChance( aPlayer : PLAYER ) is
    local
        strategy_number : INTEGER;
    do
        strategy_number := aPlayer.r.valueBetween( 1, 3 );
        aPlayer.setStrategy( aPlayer.strategies.item(
            strategy_number ) );
    end; -- takeChance

end -- NEW_STRATEGY
```

Listing 10.9   Class PURCHASE_NEW_PROPERTY

```
class PURCHASE_NEW_PROPERTY
-- Player allowed to purchase first available property
 inherit
    CHANCE_TYPE

 feature { CHANCE }

    takeChance( aPlayer : PLAYER ) is
    local
        nextProperty : POSITION;
        count     : INTEGER;
    do
        from nextProperty := aPlayer.pos;
```

```
                until count = 20 or
                   ( nextProperty.owner = Void and then
                       nextProperty.cost > 0 )
            loop
                 count := count + 1;
                 nextProperty := nextProperty.next;
            end;
            if count < 20 then
                if aPlayer.strategy.purchase( aPlayer.balance,
                   nextProperty.cost ) then
                      aPlayer.changeBalance( -nextProperty.cost );
                      nextProperty.setOwner( aPlayer );
                end;
            end;
        end; -- takeChance

end -- PURCHASE_NEW_PROPERTY
```

Listing 10.10   Class ADD_FIVE_PERCENT

```
class ADD_FIVE_PERCENT
-- Add five percent to the player's balance
 inherit
    CHANCE_TYPE

 feature { CHANCE }

    takeChance( aPlayer : PLAYER ) is
    do
       aPlayer.changeBalance( aPlayer.balance // 20 );
    end; -- takeChance

end -- ADD_FIVE_PERCENT
```

Listing 10.11   Class SUBTRACT_FIVE_PERCENT

```
class SUBTRACT_FIVE_PERCENT
-- Subtract five percent to the player's balance
 inherit
    CHANCE_TYPE

 feature { CHANCE }

    takeChance( aPlayer : PLAYER ) is
    do
       aPlayer.changeBalance( -aPlayer.balance // 20 );
    end; -- takeChance

end -- SUBTRACT_FIVE_PERCENT
```

Listing 10.12   Class COLLECT_TWO_HUNDRED

```
class COLLECT_TWO_HUNDRED
-- Give player 200 dollars every time it lands on this
-- position
```

```
    inherit
      CHANCE_TYPE
          redefine
              collectTwoHundred
          end;


   feature { CHANCE }

      takeChance( aPlayer : PLAYER ) is
      do
      end; -- takeChance


      collectTwoHundred : BOOLEAN is
      do
          Result := TRUE;
      end; -- collectTwoHundred

   end -- COLLECT_TWO_HUNDRED
```

Listing 10.13   Class MOVES_AGAIN

```
class MOVES_AGAIN
-- Allows player to move again
 inherit
    CHANCE_TYPE

 feature { CHANCE }

    takeChance( aPlayer : PLAYER ) is
    do
        aPlayer.move;
    end; -- takeChance

end-- MOVES_AGAIN
```

Listing 10.14   Class NUMBER16

```
class NUMBER16
-- For board position 16
 inherit
    NEW_STRATEGY
        rename
            takeChance as new_strategy_takeChance
        end;

    CHANGE_BALANCE
        rename
            takeChance as change_balance_takeChance
        end;

    CHANGE_BALANCE
        redefine
            takeChance
        select
```

```
            takeChance
        end;

  creation
    make

  feature { CHANCE }

    takeChance( aPlayer : PLAYER ) is
    do
        new_strategy_takeChance( aPlayer );
        change_balance_takeChance( aPlayer );
    end; -- takeChance

end -- NUMBER16
```

A loop is constructed that ends when 20 positions have been visited or when a board position has been obtained that satisfies the two conditions for an unowned property: *nextProperty.owner = Void and nextProperty.cost > 0*. The player is then given the option of purchasing the property.

Multiple inheritance is implemented according to the design specification of Figure 10.18 in Listing 10.14. This is an example of behavioral or code inheritance. The routines *takeChance* from class CHANGE_BALANCE and *takeChance* from class CHANGE_STRATEGY are both used in implementing the *takeChance* routine of class NUMBER16.

Listings 10.15 through 10.18 show the implementation details of INVEST-MENT_STRATEGY and its three subclasses Strategy1, Strategy2 and Strategy3.

Listing 10.15   Class INVESTMENT_STRATEGY

```
    deferred class INVESTMENT_STRATEGY

  feature { NONE }
    r : RANDOM;

  feature { PLAYER, CHANCE_TYPE }

    make( rnd : RANDOM ) is
    do
        r := rnd;
    end; -- make

    purchase( balance : INTEGER; cost : INTEGER ) : BOOLEAN
        is
    deferred
    end; -- purchase

    purchaseUnits( balance : INTEGER; cost : INTEGER;
                rent_collected : INTEGER ) : INTEGER is
    deferred
    end; -- purchaseUnits

end -- INVESTMENT_STRATEGY
```

Listing 10.16   Class Strategy1

```
class STRATEGY1
 inherit
    INVESTMENT_STRATEGY

 creation { REFEREE }
    make

 feature

    purchase( balance : INTEGER; cost : INTEGER ) : BOOLEAN
      is
    do
       Result := r.uniform <= 0.5 and balance > cost;
    end; -- purchase

    purchaseUnits( balance : INTEGER; cost : INTEGER;
                 rent_collected : INTEGER ) : INTEGER is
    local
       get : INTEGER;
    do
       get := r.valueBetween( 0, 5 );
       if get > 0 and then balance > get * cost // 2 then
          Result := get;
       else
          Result := 0;
       end;
    end; -- purchaseUnits

end -- STRATEGY1
```

Listing 10.17   Class STRATEGY2

```
class STRATEGY2
 inherit
    INVESTMENT_STRATEGY

 creation { REFEREE }
    make

 feature

    purchase( balance : INTEGER; cost : INTEGER ) : BOOLEAN
      is
    do
       Result := balance > cost;
    end; -- purchase

    purchaseUnits( balance : INTEGER; cost : INTEGER;
                 rent_collected : INTEGER ) : INTEGER is
    do
       if balance > 5 * cost // 2 then
          Result := 5;
```

```
         elseif balance > 4 * cost // 2 then
            Result := 4;
         elseif balance > 3 * cost // 2 then
            Result := 3;
         elseif balance > 2 * cost // 2 then
            Result := 2;
      elseif balance > cost // 2 then
            Result := 1;
         else
            Result := 0;
         end;
      end; -- purchaseUnits

end -- STRATEGY2
```

Listing 10.18   Class STRATEGY3

```
class STRATEGY3
 inherit
     INVESTMENT_STRATEGY

 creation { REFEREE }
     make

 feature

     purchase( balance : INTEGER; cost : INTEGER ) : BOOLEAN
       is
     do
        Result := balance > 5 * cost;
     end; -- purchase

     purchaseUnits( balance : INTEGER; cost : INTEGER;
                 rent_collected : INTEGER ) : INTEGER is
     do
        if balance > 25 * cost // 2 and rent_collected > 5 *
          cost // 8 then
            Result := 5;
        elseif balance > 20 * cost // 2 and rent_collected >
          4 * cost // 8 then
            Result := 4;
        elseif balance > 15 * cost // 2 and rent_collected >
          3 * cost // 8 then
            Result := 3;
        elseif balance > 10 * cost // 2 and rent_collected >
          2 * cost // 8 then
            Result := 2;
        elseif balance > 5 * cost // 2 and rent_collected >
          cost // 8 then
            Result := 1;
        else
            Result := 0;
        end;
     end; -- purchaseUnits
```

```
      end -- STRATEGY3
```

Listing 10.19 presents the details of class BANKER.

Listing 10.19   Class Banker

```
class BANKER

  feature { PLAYER }

    changeBalance( theOwner : PLAYER; amount : INTEGER ) is
      do
         theOwner.changeBalance( amount );
      end; -- changeBalance

    getBalance( theOwner : PLAYER ) : INTEGER is
    do
         Result := theOwner.balance;
      end; -- getBalance

  feature { REFEREE }

    announceWinner( players : ARRAY[ PLAYER ]; theDisplay :
       DISPLAY ) is
    local
         balances : ARRAY[ INTEGER ];
         index    : INTEGER;
         max, max_index : INTEGER;
    do
         !!balances.make( 1, 4 );
         from index := 0
         until index = 4
         loop
            index := index + 1;
            balances.put( players.item( index ).balance,
               index );
         end;
         max := balances.item( 1 );
         max_index := 1;
         from index := 1
         until index = 4
         loop
            index := index + 1;
            if balances.item( index ) > max then
               max := balances.item( index );
               max_index := index;
            end;
         end;
         theDisplay.winner( players.item( max_index ).id );
      end; -- announceWinner

end -- BANKER
```

Finally, the details of class DISPLAY are shown in Listing 10.20. The associated file of "C" functions that the DISPLAY class uses is given in Listing 10.21.

The curses package is once again used to provide the capability of writing to a particular coordinate on the screen.

Listing 10.20   Class DISPLAY

```
class DISPLAY
 creation { REFEREE }
    initialize

 feature { NONE }

    c_init is
    external "C"
    alias
       "init"
    end; -- c_init

    c_display_text is
    external "C"
    alias
       "display_text"
    end; -- c_display_text

    c_update_cycle( cycle : INTEGER ) is
    external "C"
    alias
       "update_cycle"
    end; -- c_update_cycle

    c_update( id : CHARACTER; old_pos : INTEGER; new_pos :
       INTEGER;
                balance : INTEGER ) is
    external "C"
    alias
       "update"
    end; -- c_update

   c_owner( id : CHARACTER; pos : INTEGER ) is
    external "C"
    alias
       "owner"
    end; -- c_owner

    c_winner( id : CHARACTER ) is
    external "C"
    alias
       "winner"
    end; -- c_winner

    c_units( pos : INTEGER; number : INTEGER ) is
    external "C"
    alias
       "units"
    end; -- c_units

    c_pause is
```

```
        external "C"
        alias
            "pause"
        end; -- c_pause

        c_end_window is

        external "C"
        alias
            "end_window"
        end; -- c_end-window

feature { BANKER }
        winner( id : CHARACTER ) is
        do
            c_winner( id );
        end; -- winner

feature { POSITION }
        owner( id : CHARACTER; pos : INTEGER ) is
        do
            c_owner( id, pos );
        end; -- owner

feature { REFEREE, PLAYER }
        initialize is
        do
            c_init;
            c_display_text;
        end; -- make

    updateCycle( cycle : INTEGER ) is
        do
            c_update_cycle( cycle );
        end; -- updateCycle

        update( id : CHARACTER; old_pos : INTEGER; new_pos :
            INTEGER;
                balance : INTEGER ) is
        do
            c_update( id, old_pos, new_pos, balance );
        end; -- update

        units( pos : INTEGER; number : INTEGER ) is
        do
            c_units( pos, number );
        end; -- units

        pause is
        do
            c_pause;
        end; -- pause;

        close is
        do
            c_end_window;
        end; -- close

end -- DISPLAY
```

Listing 10.21   C Functions Used in Class DISPLAY

```
#include <curses.h>

void init()
{
    initscr();
    clear();
}

void display_text()
{
    move( 1, 45 );
    addstr( "Game Simulation by Richard Wiener" );
    move( 5, 1 );
    addstr( "Current Cash of A" );
    move( 5, 25 );
    addstr( "Current Cash of B" );
    move( 5, 50 );
    addstr( "Current Cash of C" );
    move( 5, 75 );
    addstr( "Current Cash of D" );
    move( 8, 1 );
    addstr( "Move Cycles: " );
    move( 10, 1 );
    addstr( "1:" );
    move( 11, 1 );
    addstr( "2:" );
    move( 12, 1 );
    addstr( "3:" );
    move( 13, 1 );
    addstr( "4:" );
    move( 14, 1 );
    addstr( "5:" );
    move( 15, 1 );
    addstr( "6:" );
    move( 16, 1 );
    addstr( "7:" );
    move( 17, 1 );
    addstr( "8:" );
    move( 18, 1 );
    addstr( "9:" );
    move( 19, 1 );
    addstr( "10:" );
    move( 20, 1 );
    addstr( "11:" );
    move( 21, 1 );
    addstr( "12:" );
    move( 22, 1 );
    addstr( "13:" );
    move( 23, 1 );
    addstr( "14:" );
    move( 24, 1 );
    addstr( "15:" );
    move( 25, 1 );
```

```
        addstr( "16:" );
        move( 26, 1 );
        addstr( "17:" );
        move( 27, 1 );
        addstr( "18:" );
        move( 28, 1 );
        addstr( "19:" );
        move( 29, 1 );
        addstr( "20:" );
        move( 9, 30 );
        addstr( "Owner" );
        move( 9, 40 );
        addstr( "Investment Units" );
        refresh();
}

void update_cycle( int cycle )
{
        char str[ 20 ];
        move( 8, 14 );
        sprintf( str, "%d", cycle );
        addstr( str );
        refresh();
}

void update( char id, int old_pos, int new_pos, int cash )
{
        char str[ 20 ];
        sprintf( str, "%d", cash );
        if ( id == 'A' )
        {
           move( 6, 5 );
           addstr( "  " );
           move( 6, 5 );
           addstr( str );
           move( 9 + old_pos, 5 );
           addch( ' ' );
          move( 9 + new_pos, 5 );
           addch( 'A' );
        }
        else if ( id == 'B' )
        {
           move( 6, 30 );
           addstr( "  " );
           move( 6, 30 );
           addstr( str );
           move( 9 + old_pos, 10 );
           addch( ' ' );
           move( 9 + new_pos, 10 );
           addch( 'B' );
        }
        else if ( id == 'C' )
        {
           move( 6, 55 );
```

```
            addstr( " " );
            move( 6, 55 );
            addstr( str );
            move( 9 + old_pos, 15 );
            addch( ' ' );
            move( 9 + new_pos, 15 );
            addch( 'C' );
        }
        else
        {
            move( 6, 80 );
            addstr( " " );
            move( 6, 80 );
            addstr( str );
            move( 9 + old_pos, 20 );
            addch( ' ' );
            move( 9 + new_pos, 20 );
            addch( 'D' );
        }
        refresh();
}


void owner( char id, int pos )
{
    move( 9 + pos, 30 );
    addch( id );
    refresh();
}


void units( int pos, int amount )
{
    char str[ 20 ];
    move( 9 + pos, 40 );
    sprintf( str, "%d", amount );
    addstr( str );
    refresh();
}


void winner( char id )
{
    move( 35, 40 );
    addstr( "The winner of the game is: " );
    move( 35, 67 );
    addch( id );
    move( 1, 1 );
    refresh();
}


void pause()
{
    getch();
}
```

```
void end_window()
{
    endwin();
}
```

All of the code for Version 1 of the Game of Investments and Strategy has been presented. The implementation has followed the class diagram and object-scenario diagrams closely and has led to a relatively effortless Eiffel implementation with few surprises.

The next section critically examines some of the design decisions made for Version 1. This will lead to Version 2.

10.6 CRITICAL EXAMINATION OF THE DESIGN OF VERSION 1 — THE MOTIVATION FOR VERSION 2

There are no absolute "rights" and "wrongs" in the craft of design. This, despite the long lists of admonitions offered by many methodologists suggesting, "Thou shall or shall not do this," or "that," or "something else." Such rule-based design defies the essential creative process that is involved in producing a sound software architecture. Unless one can predict with certainty the future maintenance requirements of the software system, it is impossible to evaluate how "robust" or "resilient" a particular architecture is.

The general guidelines put forth in Chapter 8 for producing a consistent class hierarchy are reasonable guidelines. If every class in a hierarchy satisfies the "is a" or "is kind of" relationship with all its ancestors, this makes the decomposition of the system easier to understand. Perhaps it could be argued that this contributes to ease of maintenance. This contention cannot be proven. The same holds for the other two consistency principles: all of the attributes of a given class (i.e. those inherited from ancestors and those defined in the class) should logically apply for every class in the system, all methods available to instances of a class (i.e. inherited methods as well as those defined in the class) should logically apply for every class in the system.

As indicated in Section 10.5, small aspects of the Version 1 design could be criticized on reasonable grounds as violating the consistency principle that deals with attributes logically applying.

In class POSITION, one of the key abstract classes of the software system, the attributes *cost* and *owner* are defined. The values that these two attributes have are used to discriminate four important cases in the *interactWithBoard* routine of class PLAYER. Since a Player instance has a reference to the Position that it has landed on, it is able to determine what type of action is appropriate by using the values of the attributes *owner* and *cost* directly.

Specifically, if *owner* is Void and *cost* is zero, then a *takeChance* message is sent to the Position object. If *owner* is Void and *cost* is non-zero, then a *considerPurchase* message is invoked. If *owner* is not Void and not equal to the Player object, then the *payOwner* routine is invoked. Finally, if *owner* is not Void and equal to the Player object, then the *considerPurchasingUnits* routine is invoked.

So, from a pragmatic software engineering viewpoint, one can argue that the above design choice is justified because it makes the selection of key mechanism (the type of transaction between player and board position) relatively easy to determine. But, ... the attributes *cost* and *owner* do not really belong to a Position object. They really belong to a Property object. A Chance object should not inherit a *cost* attribute or an *owner* attribute. They are not logically related to the concept of a chance position. Saying that a chance position has zero cost is not logically the same as saying that cost is not relevant to a chance position. Similarly, saying that a chance position has a Void owner is not logically the same as saying that an owner is not relevant to a chance position.

The difficulty or conflict is only present because the Version 1 design designates the Player object as responsible for selecting the appropriate key mechanism of the Player/Position transaction. What if the Position object were made responsible for this selection?

What if the Player object sent its Position object the message *pos.hereIAm(Current)*. This method would be deferred in abstract class POSITION.

In class PROPERTY, which would now have the two attributes *cost* and *owner* (where it could again be argued they have always belonged), the method *hereIAm(Current)* might be handled as follows:

```
hereIAm( aPlayer : PLAYER ) is
local
    rent : INTEGER;
do
    if owner /= Void and then owner /= aPlayer then
        rent := cost // 10 + cost * investment_units // 20;
        aPlayer.payOwner( owner, rent );
        rent_collected := rent_collected + rent;
    elseif owner = aPlayer then
        aPlayer.considerAddingUnits( Current );
    elseif owner = Void then
        aPlayer.considerAddingUnits( Current );
    elseif owner = Void then
        aPlayer.considerPurchase( Current );
    end;
end; -- hereIAm
```

Now, the dispatching of key mechanism is being done local to a Property instance, where the attributes *owner* and *cost* really fit.

In class CHANCE, the *hereIAm(Current)* method might be handled as follows:

```
hereIAm( aPlayer : PLAYER ) is
do
    type.hereIAm( aPlayer );
end; -- hereIAm
```

Polymorphism, through late-binding, determines how a Position instance responds to hereIAm in the Version 2 design. If the actual type of the Position subclass is Property, one of the three property transactions occurs, otherwise the chance transaction occurs. All of the details of the Version 2 changes are presented in Section 10.7. In Version 2, there is no need to determine the type of transaction at the Player level through the use of the artificial attributes *cost* and *owner*.

A crucial question that must be answered as a result of modifying the architecture of the Version 1 design is how will the chance mechanism associated with board position 19, namely, allowing the player to advance to the first unowned position and have the option of purchasing it, now work? The original mechanism, presented in Listing 10.9, heavily relies on the availability of *cost* and *owner* in class POSITION. This is because the mechanism depends on advancing from position 19 one position at a time and determining whether the new position is a property position. This can effectively be done by testing the values of the attributes *owner* and *cost*.

In the modified architecture of Version 2, the new mechanism for advancing to the first property position is the following:

```
hereIAm( aPlayer : PLAYER ) is
local
    nextProperty : PROPERTY;
    count        : INTEGER;
    nextPosition : POSITION;
do
    from nextPosition := aPlayer.pos;
        nextProperty ?= nextPosition;
    until count = 20 or
            ( nextProperty /= Void and then nextProperty.owner
                = Void )
    loop
        count := count + 1;
        nextPosition := nextPosition.next;
        nextProperty ?= nextPosition;
    end;
    if count < 20 then
        -- See Section 10.7 for the remaining details
end; -- hereIAm
```

The local variable *nextPosition* is used to advance from one board position to the next one, whereas the local variable *nextProperty* is used to test whether the next board position is a property position. The access *nextProperty.owner* is done only when the test *nextProperty /= Void* has been passed.

The last criticism of the Version 1 design involves the choice of parameters to pass to the Investment_Strategy routines *purchase* and *purchaseUnits*. In Version 1, the three parameters *balance*, *cost* and *rent_collected* are used. In the Version 2 design, the two parameters *aPlayer* and *aPosition* are used instead. This provides for more generality and a better potential to respond to future maintenance changes.

The revised classes PLAYER, POSITION, PROPERTY, CHANCE, CHANCE_TYPE, IN-

VESTMENT_STRATEGY, STRATEGY1, STRATEGY2, STRATEGY3 and PURCHASE_NEW_PROP-
ERTY are presented in Section 10.7

10.7 Version 2 of the Game of Strategies and Investment

Listing 10.22 presents the revised classes from Version 1 that correct the defi-
ciencies of Version 1 that were discussed in the previous section.

Listing 10.22 Modified Classes of Version 2

```
class PLAYER
 creation { REFEREE }
    make

 feature { POSITION, BANKER }
    theDisplay : DISPLAY;

 feature { PLAYER, BANKER, POSITION }
    id : CHARACTER;

 feature { PLAYER, PURCHASE_NEW_PROPERTY }
    pos : POSITION;

 feature { BANKER, CHANCE_TYPE, INVESTMENT_STRATEGY }
    balance : INTEGER;

 feature { CHANCE_TYPE }
    strategy    : INVESTMENT_STRATEGY;
    strategies  : ARRAY[ INVESTMENT_STRATEGY ];

 feature { PROPERTY }
    payOwner( owner : PLAYER; amount : INTEGER ) is
    local
       owner_balance : INTEGER;
    do
       if amount < balance then
         theBanker.changeBalance( owner, amount );
       else
         theBanker.changeBalance( owner, balance );
       end;
       owner_balance := theBanker.getBalance( owner );
       theDisplay.update( owner.id, owner.pos.boardPosition,
         owner.pos.boardPosition, owner_balance );
     changeBalance( -amount );
    end; -- payOwner
    considerAddingUnits( aProperty : PROPERTY ) is
    local
       new_units : INTEGER;
    do
```

```
      new_units := strategy.purchaseUnits( Current,
        aProperty );
      if new_units > 0 then
        changeBalance( - new_units * aProperty.cost // 2
          );
        aProperty.addInvestmentUnits( new_units );
        theDisplay.units( aProperty.boardPosition,
            aProperty.investment_units );
      end;
    end; -- considerAddingUnits

    considerPurchase( aProperty : PROPERTY ) is
    do
      if strategy.purchase( Current, aProperty ) then
        changeBalance( -aProperty.cost );
        aProperty.setOwner( Current );
      end;
    end; -- considerPurchase


feature { NONE }
    theBanker : BANKER;
    theReferee : REFEREE;

    make( theId : CHARACTER; theBalance : INTEGER; p :
        POSITION; aStrategy : INVESTMENT_STRATEGY; aDisplay :
          DISPLAY; aBanker : BANKER; rnd : RANDOM; s :
          ARRAY[ INVESTMENT_STRATEGY ]; aReferee :
          REFEREE ) is
    do
      -- same as Version 1
    end; -- make

  delay is
    do
      -- same as Version 1
    end; -- delay


featuPπre { CHANCE_TYPE }
    r : RANDOM;

  feature { REFEREE, CHANCE_TYPE }

    move is
    local
      dice     : INTEGER;
      count    : INTEGER;
      old_pos  : INTEGER;
    do
      old_pos := pos.boardPosition;
      dice := r.valueBetween( 1, 6 );
      from count := 0
      until count = dice
      loop
        count := count + 1;
        pos := pos.next;
```

```
                if pos.collectTwoHundred then
                    changeBalance( 200 );
                end;
            end;
            pos.hereIAm( Current );
            theDisplay.update( id, old_pos, pos.boardPosition,
                balance );
            if balance = 0 then
                theReferee.declareBankruptcy;
            end;
            delay;
        end; -- move

        setStrategy( aStrategy : INVESTMENT_STRATEGY ) is
        do
            -- same as Version 1
        end; -- setStrategy
feature { CHANCE_TYPE, BANKER }
    changeBalance( amount : INTEGER ) is
    do
        -- same as Version 1
    end; -- changeBalance
invariant
    balance >= 0;

end -- PLAYER
deferred class POSITION

 feature { PLAYER, CHANCE_TYPE }
    next          : POSITION;
    boardPosition : INTEGER;

 feature { REFEREE }

    setNext( nextPosition : POSITION ) is
    do
        next := nextPosition;
    end; -- setNext

feature { PLAYER }

    hereIAm( aPlayer : PLAYER ) is
    deferred
    end; -- hereIAm

    collectTwoHundred : BOOLEAN is
    deferred
    end; -- collectTwoHundred

end -- POSITION

class PROPERTY
 inherit
    POSITION
        rename
```

```
                    hereIam as propertyTransaction
            end;

    creation { REFEREE }
        make

     feature { PLAYER, CHANCE_TYPE, INVESTMENT_STRATEGY }
        cost  : INTEGER;
        owner : PLAYER;

        setOwner( theOwner : PLAYER ) is
        do
            owner := theOwner;
            theOwner.theDisplay.owner( theOwner.id,
              boardPosition );
        end; -- setOwner

    feature { PLAYER }

        propertyTransaction( aPlayer : PLAYER ) is
        local
            rent : INTEGER;
        do
            if owner /= Void and then owner /= aPlayer then
                rent := cost // 10 + cost * investment_units //
                  20;
                aPlayer.payOwner( owner, rent );
                rent_collected := rent_collected + rent;
            elseif owner = aPlayer then
                aPlayer.considerAddingUnits( Current );
            elseif owner = Void then
                aPlayer.considerPurchase( Current );
            end;
        end; -- propertyTransaction

    feature { NONE }

        make( number : INTEGER; price : INTEGER ) is
        do
            boardPosition := number;
            cost := price;
        end; -- make

    feature { PLAYER, INVESTMENT_STRATEGY }
        rent_collected : INTEGER;
        investment_units : INTEGER;

        addInvestmentUnits( amount : INTEGER ) is
        require
            too_many : amount <= 5;
        do
            investment_units := investment_units + amount;
        end; -- addInvestmentUnits

      collectTwoHundred : BOOLEAN is
      do
```

```
            Result := FALSE;
        end; -- collectTwoHundred

end -- PROPERTY

class CHANCE
 inherit
     POSITION
         rename
             hereIAm as takeChance
         end;

creation { REFEREE }
     make

 feature { NONE }
     type : CHANCE_TYPE;

 feature { NONE }
     make( number : INTEGER ) is
     do
         boardPosition := number;
     end; -- make

feature { REFEREE }
     setType( chanceType : CHANCE_TYPE ) is
     do
         type := chanceType;
     end; -- setType

feature { PLAYER }

     takeChance( aPlayer : PLAYER ) is
     do
         type.takeChance( aPlayer );
     end; -- takeChance

     collectTwoHundred : BOOLEAN is
     do
         Result := type.collectTwoHundred;
     end; -- collectTwoHundred

 end -- CHANCE

class PURCHASE_NEW_PROPERTY
-- Player given opportunity to purchase first available
        property
 inherit
     CHANCE_TYPE

 feature { CHANCE }

     takeChance( aPlayer : PLAYER ) is
     local
         nextProperty : PROPERTY;
         count : INTEGER;
```

```
           nextPosition : POSITION;
      do
           from  nextPosition := aPlayer.pos;
                  nextProperty ?= nextPosition
           until count = 20 or
                  ( nextProperty /= Void and then
                     nextProperty.owner = Void )
           loop
              count := count + 1;
              nextPosition := nextPosition.next;
              nextProperty ?= nextPosition;
           end;
           if count < 20 then
             if aPlayer.strategy.purchase( aPlayer,
                nextProperty ) then
                  aPlayer.changeBalance( -nextProperty.cost );
                  nextProperty.setOwner( aPlayer );
             end;
           end;
      end; -- takeChance

end -- PURCHASE_NEW_PROPERTY

deferred class INVESTMENT_STRATEGY

  feature { NONE }
     r : RANDOM;

  feature { PLAYER, CHANCE_TYPE }

     make( rnd : RANDOM ) is
     do
        r := rnd;
     end; -- make

     purchase( aPlayer : PLAYER; aProperty : PROPERTY ) :
        BOOLEAN is
     deferred
     end; -- purchase

     purchaseUnits( aPlayer : PLAYER; aProperty : PROPERTY) :
        INTEGER is
     deferred
     end; -- purchaseUnits

end -- INVESTMENT_STRATEGY

class STRATEGY1
  inherit
     INVESTMENT_STRATEGY

  creation { REFEREE }
     make

  feature
```

```
    purchase( aPlayer : PLAYER; aProperty : PROPERTY ) :
      BOOLEAN is
    do
        Result := r.uniform <= 0.5 and aPlayer.balance >
          aProperty.cost;
    end; -- purchase

    purchaseUnits( aPlayer : PLAYER; aProperty : PROPERTY) :
          INTEGER is
    local
        get : INTEGER;
    do
        get := r.valueBetween( 0, 5 );
        if get > 0 and then aPlayer.balance > get *
          aProperty.cost // 2 then
          Result := get;
        else
          Result := 0;
        end;
    end; -- purchaseUnits

end -- STRATEGY1

class STRATEGY2
  inherit
      INVESTMENT_STRATEGY

  creation { REFEREE }
    make

  feature

    purchase( aPlayer : PLAYER; aProperty : PROPERTY ) :
      BOOLEAN is
    do
        Result := aPlayer.balance > aProperty.cost;
    end; -- purchase

    purchaseUnits( aPlayer : PLAYER; aProperty : PROPERTY) :
      INTEGER is
    do
        if aPlayer.balance > 5 * aProperty.cost / 2 then
          Result := 5;
        elseif aPlayer.balance > 4 * aProperty.cost // 2 then
          Result := 4;
        elseif aPlayer.balance > 3 * aProperty.cost // 2 then
          Result := 3;
        elseif aPlayer.balance > 2 * aProperty.cost // 2 then
          Result := 2;
        elseif aPlayer.balance > aProperty.cost // 2 then
          Result := 1;
        else
          Result := 0;
        end;
    end; -- purchaseUnits
```

```
    end -- STRATEGY2

    class STRATEGY3
     inherit
        INVESTMENT_STRATEGY

     creation { REFEREE }
        make

     feature

        purchase( aPlayer : PLAYER; aProperty : PROPERTY ) :
          BOOLEAN is
        do
           Result := aPlayer.balance > 5 * aProperty.cost;
        end; -- purchase

        purchaseUnits( aPlayer : PLAYER; aProperty : PROPERTY) :
          INTEGER is
        do
           if aPlayer.balance > 25 * aProperty.cost // 2 and
              aProperty.rent_collected > 5 * aProperty.cost //
                 8 then
                   Result := 5;
           elseif aPlayer.balance > 20 * aProperty.cost // 2 and
              aProperty.rent_collected > 4 * aProperty.cost //
                 8 then
                   Result := 4;
           elseif aPlayer.balance > 15 * aProperty.cost // 2 and
              aProperty.rent_collected > 3 * aProperty.cost //
                 8 then
              Result := 3;
           elseif aPlayer.balance > 10 * aProperty.cost // 2 and
              aProperty.rent_collected > 2 * aProperty.cost //
                 8 then
              Result := 2;
           elseif aPlayer.balance > 5 * aProperty.cost // 2 and
              aProperty.rent_collected > aProperty.cost // 8
                 then
              Result := 1;
           else
              Result := 0;
           end;
        end; -- purchaseUnits

    end -- STRATEGY3
```

10.8 CONCLUDING REMARKS

After you, the reader, carefully compare the Version 2 implementation with Version 1, I believe you will agree that Version 2 is an improvement. Are further improvements in the design still possible? The answer to such a question is generally yes. But the engineering process requires that an adequate level of development be performed within a fixed time period. Therefore, once a stable and comfortable design has been achieved, practical considerations usually suggest that one quit.

If a clearly written and up-to-date set of analysis and design models (e.g. various types of Booch diagrams and class specifications) is maintained throughout the modification process, this makes the task of future maintenance changes much easier and safer.

You may wish to start from scratch and consider a totally different software model for this game of strategies and investments. Another useful exercise might be to add additional specifications to make the game more interesting and see how the present model stands up to such changes. If the modifications are highly localized, this would indicate that the present model (Version 2) is stable and fairly robust. If many of the existing classes have to be gutted and completely rewritten, this would indicate that the present model is highly unstable.

Simulated Annealing

11.1 MOTIVATION

*T*he goal of this chapter is to demonstrate the application of the object model and Eiffel to an interesting and important heuristic algorithm that may be used to approximate the solution to a wide variety of difficult combinatorial optimization problems. The algorithm is simulated annealing. In actuality, simulated annealing represents a family of algorithms, each specialized to a particular problem but all unified by a common approach and set of behaviors that can be encapsulated in an abstract class. Each particular application of simulated annealing is then implemented as a subclass. The important structure and much of the protocol of the simulated annealing algorithm is captured for reuse in the abstract root class.

There has been much less published about the application of object-oriented design to the area of algorithm design than the more popular application areas of graphical user interfaces, databases and system simulations. There is certainly no basis for believing that the object paradigm is less effective in this application area. This fact serves as additional motivation for ending this book with a chapter that features the application of objects to the design of algorithms.

There is a common belief in the software community that object-oriented languages, although elegant and perhaps useful for large-scale software development, are inherently too inefficient to be useful for general algorithm design. Maybe C++ is viewed as an exception to this belief because of its low-level almost object-oriented assembly language character. But, certainly other object-oriented languages, including Eiffel, are generally assumed to impose an inordinate level of overhead that makes the computational efficiency of an object-oriented implementation prohibitively expensive. Since it is well known, and will be seen in later sections of this chapter, that simulated annealing is a computationally intensive family of algorithms, an important secondary goal of doing an Eiffel implementation of simulated annealing is to explore the performance of the finished Eiffel code with that of an algorithmically equivalent C implementation. C is only one small step above an assembly language and generally recognized to be extremely efficient. So the run-time performance of the pure and elegant Eiffel language will be compared with the run-time performance of the less pure but fast C language. The comparisons will be included in the last section of this chapter.

So, what is simulated annealing?

11.2 COMBINATORIAL OPTIMIZATION AND SIMULATED ANNEALING

Many important systems that form the basis for algorithm design may assume a very large number of states, each with an associated cost, given by a cost function. The goal in such problems is to find a state that maximizes or minimizes the cost function. Such problems are called combinatorial optimization problems. A worst-case approach is to enumerate all possible states, compute the cost associated with each and choose the largest or smallest. Thus, the word combinatorial is used to describe such problems.

Two classic combinatorial optimizations problems that have served as a source of major challenge in the algorithm design community are the Travelling Salesperson Problem and the Discrete Knapsack Problem. Many interesting scheduling problems and many graph theoretic problems may be categorized as combinatorial optimization problems. Because of the irregular shape of the mathematical surface of the cost function in n-dimensional space for many combinatorial optimization problems, traditional optimization techniques such as gradient search, usually based on calculus, perform poorly or not at all. Figure 11.1 shows a segment of a typical irregular surface shown in two dimensions for such a combinatorial problem

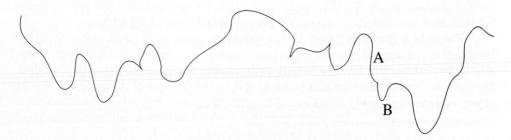

Fig. 11.1 Typical Irregular Mathematical Surface of Combinatorial Problem

If the initial position on the surface is A, and the goal is to compute the global minimum, a typical gradient search technique will force a solution down into the first local valley, point B in this case, where the solution will remain trapped. This local valley in all likelihood will be much higher on the surface than the global minimum.

11.2.1 Stochastic Search

A common technique for finding the approximate maximum or minimum for a combinatorial optimization problem is called stochastic search. This technique involves the evaluation of the cost function at many states, randomly (stochastically) chosen. The best (minimum or maximum) state is saved and updated as many randomly generated points flood the mathematical surface. The process is generally repeated several times, and the best of the best states is chosen. For a typical combinatorial problem, only a very small fraction of the total number of states is visited.

An informal description of a stochastic search algorithm is the following:

1. Choose a random starting state and compute its cost.

2. Randomly reconfigure the ordering of the elements (choose another state) and compute a new cost.

3. If the cost of the new configuration is better than the previous configura-tion, store this new configuration and update, if appropriate, the best configuration to-date. If the new configuration has a worse cost than the previous one, discard it and restore the previous configuration.

4. Continue steps 2 and 3 many times until a "reasonable" effort has been expended in finding a solution.

5. Repeat the entire process several times.

11.2.2 Annealing of Metals

Annealing is a process employed in the fabrication of metal objects. When metal is shaped, small regions of stress often develop because of deformations at the atomic level. These stress regions make the material more prone to fatigue and failure. Annealing attempts to correct this defect.

If you are now wondering whether this section of the book was transplanted accidently from a chemical engineering book in production at the same time (such things have happened!) be reassured that our compass is still pointing at software development using Eiffel.

In 1953, N. Metropolis, A. Rosenbluth, M. Rosenbluth, A. Teller, and E. Teller published a seminal paper in the *Journal of Chemical Physics,* Vol 21, pp 1087–1091, in which they drew an analogy between the annealing of metals and the solution of combinatorial optimization problems. They, like other brilliant scientists have done before, were able to bridge a gap between two seemingly unrelated disciplines: the molecular vibration of molecules through many states and the simulated vibration of a stochastic system through its more artificial states. Before pursuing this analogy further, let us continue to explore the annealing process for metals.

When regions of stress develop in a metal, these regions have relatively high energy. The stress could be removed if the molecules of the metal could be rearranged. Unfortunately, at room temperature most metals do not have enough thermal energy to rearrange their molecules. The process of annealing involves first raising the temperature of the metal, typically by immersing the metal in a hot bath. The bath temperature is very carefully controlled and the metal is slowly cooled. During this slow cooling process, the molecules are gradually "frozen" into place. If the annealing process is not rushed, the metal will end up with lower energy than before and no regions of stress. If the cooling process is performed too quickly, there will be insufficient time for the atomic structure to relax completely and the metal will end up with excess energy and might fracture too easily.

The average energy, E, of the constituent atoms is a function of the absolute temperature. As the temperature decreases, the average energy decreases. In a typical annealing process, in the temperature regions where the slope of the energy versus temperature curve is the most negative (i.e. sharpest decrease in energy per unit change in temperature), the temperature should be lowered the most slowly. The "cooling curve," which models the temperature of the bath as a function of time, must, therefore, be adjusted to allow for the most gradual cooling when the energy of the metal versus temperature has the most negative slope. This is often known in advance from previous experience or must be determined empirically.

For metals, the ratio of the average number of molecules with high energy to low energy, N_{hi}/N_{lo}, as a function of temperature is given by:

$$\frac{N_{hi}}{N_{lo}} = e^{\frac{(E_{lo} - E_{hi})}{kT}}$$, where k is Boltzmann's constant and T is measured in

degrees Kelvin.

11.2.3 Annealing Applied to Combinatorial Optimization — Simulated Annealing

Simulated annealing is a heuristic stochastic algorithm technique that follows the following sequence of steps:

1. Choose a starting temperature. The temperature parameter is controlled artificially by the user by constructing a "cooling curve." This must be supplied before the algorithm begins.

2. Randomize the starting configuration and compute its cost.

3. Reconfigure the ordering of the elements randomly and compute a new cost.

4. If the new configuration has a better cost than the previous, store this new configuration and compare it to the best configuration to-date, updating the best to-date if necessary. If the new configuration has a worse cost than the previous, determine the probability of accepting this new lower cost configuration from the "metropolis" probability density function. Such an "uphill" move allows the search to climb out of a local valley. At high temperatures the probability of accepting an "uphill" move is much greater than at low temperatures.

5. Continue the previous two steps and test for thermal equilibrium. This occurs when it is detected that no further reconfigurations produce statistically significant new results.

6. Continue steps 3 to 5 until the solution is "frozen."

7. Store the results and start over again.

The "metropolis" probability density function is the following:

$$\text{ProbAcceptingScore}(\text{score}_{new}) = e^{\frac{(\text{score}_{new} - \text{score}_{previous})}{\text{temperature}}}, \text{ where temperature is a param-}$$

eter that is controlled by the simulated annealing program.

It is noted that the worse $score_{new}$ is with respect to $score_{previous}$, the lower the probability is of accepting this new score. The higher the value of the temperature parameter, the higher the probability of accepting the new score. As the temperature approaches infinity, all new scores would be accepted. As the temperature approaches zero, no new scores that are worse than the previous (i.e. no "uphill" moves) would be accepted.

Simulated annealing is an art as well as a science. Like programming itself, it is a craft. Determining when thermal equilibrium has been reached requires fine-tuning of a set of parameters. Determining a suitable "cooling curve" is an iterative process that, like the parameters that determine thermal equilibrium, requires iteration and fine-tuning. If the cooling is done too slowly, the algorithm will work fine but take excessively long to complete its work. If the cooling is done too rapidly, the execution time of the algorithm will be shortened, but at the expense of the answer that it provides. The same comments apply to the parameters that determine when thermal equilibrium has been achieved.

The fundamental issues that all simulated annealing implementations must deal with are the following:

- What should be the initial value of the parameter temperature?
- When should the temperature be lowered (determined by the parameters for thermal equilibrium)?
- By what factor should the temperature be lowered (determined by the "cooling curve")?
- When should the simulated annealing process be terminated (this is usually set by a required minimum temperature that must be reached)?
- How should the system be reconfigured (this is the most challenging issue in applying simulated annealing to a particular problem)?

There are no absolute right and wrong answers to any of the questions raised above. A successful simulated annealing balances efficiency and accuracy. The experience of many researchers suggests that simulated annealing offers a high level of accuracy in solving otherwise intractable problems with a reasonable level of efficiency. This contention will be examined later in this chapter in solving the Travelling Salesperson Problem (TSP) using simulated annealing.

11.3 THE COMPONENTS OF THE ALGORITHM

Two key components of simulated annealing are examined in this section. These include: (1) the overall flow of the algorithm and (2) the determination of thermal equilibrium.

11.3.1 The Overall Flow of the Algorithm

After appropriate parameters have been initialized, a loop is run that terminates when the attribute is frozen of class STATUS is True.

In the loop, the following actions are taken:

- tryNewTemperature
- getNewTemperature

The first function, *tryNewTemperature*, contains a loop. This loop contains the following actions and is terminated when thermal equilibrium is detected:

- reconfigure
- decide
- checkEquilibrium

The first action, *reconfigure*, is problem specific. The system is put into a new state by a random move from the current state.

The second action, *decide*, determines whether to accept the new configuration or reject it. If the score associated with the new configuration is "better" than the previous score, the new configuration is always accepted. If the new score is "worse" than the old score, the "metropolis" density function is invoked to determine the acceptance or rejection of the new configuration. At low temperatures or for large uphill moves, the probability is small that acceptance will take place.

The third action, *checkEquilibrium*, uses a number of statistical criteria to determine whether statistical stability among the scores is detected at the particular value of the parameter temperature. The factors that enter into this determination include: (1) the number of successes (accepted scores), (2) the number of failures (rejected scores), and (3) the number of scores that are within the 1/2 standard deviation limits from the mean score for the score data at the particular temperature. The details are shown in the next sub-section. In order to protect the system from getting bogged down at a particular temperature, an upper bound concerning the number of reconfigurations that are allowed to occur at any temperature is set in advance. Hopefully, this upper bound will be exercised only rarely.

The action *getNewTemperature*, the second action of the first loop, lowers the parameter temperature using the "cooling curve" that is supplied in advance.

11.3.2 Determining Thermal Equilibrium

The structure of the algorithm for determining whether thermal equilibrium has been achieved is given in pseudo-code as follows:

```
if numberSuccesses + numberFailures > ULTIMATE_LIMIT then
    setEquilibrium( True );
elseif numberSuccesses >= SUCCESS_MIN then
    if inHalfSigma > -IN_HALF_SIGMA_LIMIT then
        setEquilibrium( True );
    end;
else
    if outHalfSigma > OUT_HALF_SIGMA_LIMIT then
        if numberSuccesses > FIRST_LIMIT then
            setEquilibrium( True );
        else
            setInHalfSigma( 0 );
            setOutHalfSigma( 0 );
        end;
    end;
end;
```

In words, the first test protects the system from remaining at a given temperature forever.

The second test ensures that a certain minimum number of successful reconfigurations have occurred. Then, if the number of scores within 1/2 standard deviation limits from the mean exceeds a threshold, thermal equilibrium is achieved.

If the number of successes is less than the certain minimum and the number of scores lying outside the 1/2 standard deviation limits from the mean exceeds a given threshold, then if the number of successes is greater than FIRST_LIMIT, thermal equilibrium is achieved. This allows progress to be made even in the presence of many outlier scores, providing that a minimum number of successful score has been achieved. In the presence of many outlier scores, if a minimum number of successful scores has not been achieved, the parameters *inHalfSigma* and *outHalfSigma* are reset to zero.

11.4 ABSTRACT CLASS ANNEALING AND SUPPORTING CLASS STATE

The deferred class ANNEALING factors the protocol that is common to all applications that use simulated annealing for later reuse. This includes attributes and routines. Listing 11.1 presents the details of this abstract class. In order to develop a simulated annealing application, a subclass of ANNEALING must be created that defines all of the deferred routines and redefines some of the attributes.

Listing 11.1   Class ANNEALING

```
deferred class ANNEALING
--Abstract class for simulated annealing

 feature { NONE } -- For internal use
     cost          : ANY; -- Will be redefined in subclass
     oldSolution   : ANY; -- Will be redefined in subclass
     currentSolution: ANY; -- Will be redefined in subclass
     bestSolution  : ANY; -- Will be redefined in subclass
     coolingCurve  : SIMPLE_ARRAY_2D[ DOUBLE ];
     status        : STATE; -- Contains annealing state
     -- variables
     consts        : CONSTANTS; -- Must be defined by user
     r             : RANDOM; -- Random number object
     math          : C_MATH; -- For sqrt, fabs

 feature

     initialize is
     do
         !!r.initialize;
         !!consts;
         !!status.initialize;
         initializeCost;
         initializeOldSolution;
         initializeCurrentSolution;
         initializeBestSolution;
         initializeCoolingCurve;
         status.setNextIndex( 1 );
         status.setTemperatureRatio( 0.75 );
         run;
     end; -- initialize

     initializeOldSolution is
     deferred
     end; -- initializeOldSolution

     initializeCurrentSolution is
     do
         copySolution( currentSolution, oldSolution );
     end; -- initializeCurrentSolution

     initializeBestSolution is
     do
         copySolution( bestSolution, oldSolution );
     end; -- initializeBestSolution

     initializeCoolingCurve is
     deferred
     end; -- initializeCoolingCurve
```

```
initializeCost is
deferred
end; -- initializeCost

betterThan( newScoreValue : INTEGER; scoreValue :
   INTEGER ) :
             BOOLEAN is
-- True if either ( newScore > score ) or ( newScore <
-- score )
-- depending on application
deferred
end; -- betterThan

computeScoreLimit( avCost : DOUBLE; halfSigma : DOUBLE )
   : DOUBLE is
-- Either avCost + halfSigma or avCost - halfSigma
deferred
end; -- computeScoreLimit

compareScoreLimit( newScore : INTEGER; scoreLimit :
   DOUBLE ) :
             BOOLEAN is
-- True if either ( newScore > scoreLimit ) or ( newScore
-- < scoreLimit )
-- depending on application
deferred
end; -- compareScoreLimit

getCostCurrentSolution : INTEGER is
deferred
end; -- getCostCurrentSolution

getCostBestSolution : INTEGER is
deferred
end; -- getCostBestSolution


displaySolution is
deferred
end; -- displaySolution

reconfigure( forward : BOOLEAN ) is
deferred
end; -- reconfigure

displayBestSolution is
deferred
end; -- displayBestSolution

copySolution( target : ANY; source : ANY ) is
deferred
end; -- copySolution

initNewTemperature is
do
```

```
        status.setNumberSuccesses( 0 );
        status.setNumberFailures( 0 );
        status.setEquilibrium( False );
        status.setInHalfSigma( 0 );
        status.setOutHalfSigma( 0 );
        status.setTotalScore( 0.0 );
        status.setTotalScore2( 0.0 );
        if status.temperature < consts.tempMin then
           status.setIsFrozen( True );
        end;
   end; -- initNewTemperature

 getNewTemperature is
  do
        if status.temperature < coolingCurve.item( 1,
          status.nextIndex ) then
           status.setTemperatureRatio( coolingCurve.item( 2,
             status.nextIndex ) );
           status.setNextIndex( status.nextIndex + 1 );
        end;
        status.setTemperature( status.temperatureRatio *
          status.temperature );
   end; -- getNewTemperature


  checkEquilibrium is
  -- Set equlibrium to True if appropriate conditions are
  -- satisfied
 do
        if status.numberSuccesses + status.numberFailures >
             consts.ULTIMATE_LIMIT then
           status.setEquilibrium( True );
        elseif status.numberSuccesses >= consts.successMin
          then
           if status.inHalfSigma > consts.inHalfSigmaLimit
             then
              status.setEquilibrium( True );
           end;
        else
           if status.outHalfSigma > consts.outHalfSigmaLimit
             then
              if status.numberSuccesses > consts.firstLimit
                then
                 status.setEquilibrium( True );
              else
                 status.setInHalfSigma( 0 );
                 status.setOutHalfSigma( 0 );
              end;
           end;
        end;
   end; -- checkEquilibrium

  update is
  -- Statistics are updated
  local
```

```
        s          : DOUBLE;
        averageC : DOUBLE;
        lastTotalSuccess : INTEGER;
    do
        if status.numberSuccesses > 0 then
            averageC := status.totalScore / status.
                numberSuccesses;
            status.setAvScore( averageC + consts.scale );
            s := status.totalScore2 /
                    status.numberSuccesses - averageC *
                    averageC;
            if s >= 0.0 then
                status.setSigma( math.sqrt( s ) );
            else
                status.setSigma( 0.0 );
            end;
            status.setHalfSigma( 0.5 * status.sigma );

            status.setScoreLimit( computeScoreLimit(
                status.avScore,
                    status.halfSigma ) );
        else
            status.setAvScore( status.score );
            status.setSigma( 0.0 );
        end;
        if status.temperature < consts.tempMin then
            status.setIsFrozen( True );
        end;
    end; -- update

decide is
-- Either accept new configuration or restore old one
local
    sCost : DOUBLE;
    acceptable : BOOLEAN;
    difference : DOUBLE;
do
    acceptable := False;
    status.setNewScore( getCostCurrentSolution );
    if betterThan( status.newScore, status.score ) then
        if betterThan( status.newScore, status.bestScore
            ) then
            status.setBestScore( status.newScore );
            copySolution( bestSolution, currentSolution );
            status.setBestTemperature( status.temperature
                );
        end;
        acceptable := True;
    elseif status.temperature > 0.0 then -- uphill move
        if r.uniform < math.exp( -math.fabs( status.score
            - status.newScore ) /
                status.temperature ) then
            acceptable := True;
            status.setUphill( status.uphill + 1 );
        end;
```

```
        end;
    if acceptable then
        status.setScore( status.newScore );
        sCost := status.newScore - consts.scale;
        status.setTotalScore( status.totalScore + sCost
            );
        status.setTotalScore2( status.totalScore2 + sCost
            * sCost );
        status.setNumberSuccesses( status.
            numberSuccesses + 1 );
        status.setTotalSuccesses( status.totalSuccesses +
            1 );
        difference := status.avScore - status.score;
        if difference < 0.0 then
            difference := -difference;
        end;
        if difference < status.halfSigma then
            status.setInHalfSigma( status.inHalfSigma + 1
                );
        else
            status.setOutHalfSigma( status.outHalfSigma +
                1 );
        end;
    else
        reconfigure( False );
        status.setNumberFailures( status.numberFailures +
            1 );
        status.setTotalFailures( status.totalFailures + 1
            );
    end;
  end; -- decide

tryNewTemperature is
 do
    from initNewTemperature
    until status.equilibrium = True
    loop
        reconfigure( True );
        decide;
        checkEquilibrium;
    end;
    update;
    if status.quench = False then
        from
        until compareScoreLimit( status.newScore,
            status.scoreLimit ) or
        ( status.numberSuccesses + status.numberFailures
            ) >=
            consts.ULTIMATELIMIT
        loop
            reconfigure( True );
            decide;
        end;
    end;
 end; -- tryNewTemperature
```

```
            report is
            do
                io.putstring( "Total number of steps: " );
                io.putint( status.steps ); io.new_line;
                io.putstring( "Temperature: " );
                io.putreal( status.temperature.to_real );
                io.new_line;
                io.putstring( "Total successes: " );
                io.putint( status.totalSuccesses ); io.new_line;
                io.putstring( "Total failures: " );
                io.putint( status.totalFailures ); io.new_line;
                io.putstring( "Up hill moves: " );
                io.putint( status.uphill ); io.new_line;
                io.putstring( "Current score: " );
                io.putint( status.score ); io.new_line;
                io.putstring( "The best score: " );
                io.putint( status.bestScore ); io.new_line;
                io.putstring( "The best temperature: " );
                io.putreal( status.bestTemperature.to_real );
                io.new_line;
                io.putstring( "The average score: " );
                io.putreal( status.avScore.to_real );
                io.new_line;
                io.putstring( "The standard dev: " );
                io.putreal( status.sigma.to_real );
                io.new_line;
                io.new_line; io.new_line;
            end; -- report

            run is
            local
                time    : TIMER;
                index   : INTEGER;
                seconds : REAL;
            do
                !!time.make
                initNewTemperature;
                from index := 0
                until index = 1000
                loop
                    index := index + 1;
                    reconfigure( True );
                end;
                -- Reset number of steps to 0
                status.setSteps( 0 );
                status.setScore( getCostCurrentSolution );
                io.putstring( "Initial score = " ); io.putint(
                getCostCurrentSolution );
                io.new_line;
                status.setBestScore( status.score );
                from status.setIsFrozen( False )
                until status.isfrozen = True
                loop
                    tryNewTemperature;
                    -- report;
```

```
            if status.temperature > 0.0 then
                getNewTemperature;
            end;
        end;
        -- Quench isfrozen configuration
        status.setQuench( True );
        tryNewTemperature;
        update;
        seconds := time.get_elapsed_seconds;
        report;
        io.new_line;
        displayBestSolution;
        io.new_line;
        io.putstring( "The time for the simulated annealing =
            " );
        io.putreal( seconds );
        io.putstring( " seconds.%N" );
    end; -- run

end -- ANNEALING
```

The attributes *cost*, *oldSolution*, *currentSolution* and *bestSolution* are problem-specific and must be redefined in a subclass. Since these attributes are specified to be of type ANY, they can be redefined to be any supplied type or type provided in an Eiffel library in a subclass.

The attribute *status* of type STATE contains many variables that characterize the instantaneous state of the simulated annealing system. These variables have to be accessed through the attribute *status*.

The attribute *consts* contains many parameters that have to be set by the user for a particular problem. These parameters have to be accessed through this attribute.

The attribute *r* is of the same type RANDOM that is used in the case studies of Chapters 8, 9 and 10.

Finally, the attribute, *math*, allows the routines *sqrt* and *fabs* to be accessed through this attribute. Rather than inherit from the TowerEiffel class C_MATH, as is so often done in the existing Eiffel literature, math routines are handled as attributes.

Most of the deferred routines require no explanation. The routine *betterThan* requires some comment. In some applications, a new score is better than an old score if it is larger. In other applications, a new score is better if it is smaller (e.g. TSP). Each application defines the sense of "better" by providing an effective routine for *betterThan*.

The statistical details given in routines *update* and *decide* compute running statistics for the mean score and standard deviation score at a given temperature. The parameter *scale*, accessed through the attribute *consts,* is used to reduce floating point round-off error in computing a running standard deviation.

Some of the algorithm structure given in Listing 11.1 was inspired by conversations and correspondence with Michael P. McLaughlin. His September 1989 *Dr. Dobbs Journal* article on simulated annealing provided my first contact and introduction to this family of algorithms.

The routine *tryNewTemperature* first invokes *initNewTemperature*. This routine initializes several statistics that are reset at every new temperature. An action loop then invokes routines *reconfigure*, *decide* and *checkEquilibrium* until temperature equilibrium is True. Upon completing this loop, routine *update* is invoked. This routine updates aggregate statistics such as the average score to-date and the standard-deviation to-date. After doing this update of statistics, further reconfigurations are performed if the latest score is an outlier (a score that is not within a *scoreLimit* value given in class STATE). This is to ensure that the final configuration at a given temperature is statistically representative of the population of scores obtained at that given temperature.

Listing 11.2 contains the details of class STATE. This class contains a large set of parameters that have export scope ANNEALING. The attributes are directly assessable to class ANNEALING and any of its descendants. These attributes capture the state and provide general support for the methods of class ANNEALING.

Listing 11.2   Class STATE

```
class STATE
-- Describes the mathematical state of an ANNEALING object

 creation
     initialize

 feature { ANNEALING } -- Available only to class ANNEALING

     nextIndex    : INTEGER; -- index in coolingCurve
     numberSuccesses: INTEGER; -- successful moves at given
     -- temperature
     numberFailures: INTEGER; -- failed moves at given
     -- temperature
     equilibrium : BOOLEAN; -- stability at the given
     -- temperature
     sigma        : DOUBLE; -- a measure of the dispersion of
     -- scores
     inHalfSigma  : INTEGER; -- number of moves within half
     -- sigma
     outHalfSigma : INTEGER; -- number of moves outside of
     -- half sigma
     halfSigma    : DOUBLE; -- value above or below avCost
     -- that is 1/2 sd
     temperature  : DOUBLE; -- controls the annealing process
     bestTemperature: DOUBLE; -- the temperature associated
     -- with bestScore
     isfrozen     : BOOLEAN; -- true when no further moves are
     -- possible
     temperatureRatio: DOUBLE; -- factor by which to change
     -- temperature
     totalScore   : DOUBLE; -- total score at a given
     -- temperature
     avScore      : DOUBLE; -- the running average at a given
     -- temperature
     scoreLimit   : DOUBLE; -- the avScore plus or minus the
```

```
-- halfSigma
totalScore2  : DOUBLE; -- a normalized cost used for
-- computing sigma
score        : INTEGER; -- the cost of the last move
newScore     : INTEGER; -- the cost of the current move
bestScore    : INTEGER; -- the best score to date
totalFailures: INTEGER; -- the total number of failures
totalSuccesses: INTEGER; -- the total number of
-- successes
quench       : BOOLEAN; -- freeze the system
uphill       : INTEGER; -- the total number of uphill
-- moves to date
steps        : INTEGER; -- the total number of moves to
-- date

initialize is
 do
     temperature := 100000.0;
     bestTemperature := temperature;
 end; -- initialize

 -- Set methods

 setnextIndex( value : INTEGER ) is
 do
     nextIndex := value;
 end;

 setnumberSuccesses( value : INTEGER ) is
 do
     numberSuccesses := value;
 end;

 setnumberFailures( value : INTEGER ) is
 do
     numberFailures := value;
 end;

 setinHalfSigma( value : INTEGER ) is
 do
     inHalfSigma := value;
 end;

 setoutHalfSigma( value : INTEGER ) is
 do
     outHalfSigma := value;
 end;

 setScore( value : INTEGER ) is
 do
     score := value;
 end;

 setNewScore( value : INTEGER ) is
 do
```

```
         newScore := value;
      end;

      setBestScore( value : INTEGER ) is
      do
         bestScore := value;
      end;

   setTotalSuccesses( value : INTEGER ) is
      do
         totalSuccesses := value;
      end;

      setTotalFailures( value : INTEGER ) is
      do
         totalFailures := value;
      end;

      setUphill( value : INTEGER ) is
      do
         uphill := value;
      end;

      setSteps( value : INTEGER ) is
      do
         steps := value;
      end;

      setEquilibrium( value : BOOLEAN ) is
      do
         equilibrium := value;
      end;

      setQuench( value : BOOLEAN ) is
      do
         quench := value;
      end;

   setIsFrozen( value : BOOLEAN ) is
      do
         isFrozen := value;
      end;

      setSigma( value : DOUBLE ) is
      do
         sigma := value;
      end;

      setHalfSigma( value : DOUBLE ) is
      do
         halfSigma := value;
      end;

      setTemperature( value : DOUBLE ) is
      do
```

```
        temperature := value;
   end;

   setBestTemperature( value : DOUBLE ) is
   do
        bestTemperature := value;
   end;

  setTemperatureRatio( value : DOUBLE ) is
   do
        temperatureRatio := value;
   end;

   setTotalScore( value : DOUBLE ) is
   do
        totalScore := value;
   end;

   setAvScore( value : DOUBLE ) is
   do
        avScore := value;
   end;

   setScoreLimit( value : DOUBLE ) is
   do
        scoreLimit := value;
   end;

   setTotalScore2( value : DOUBLE ) is
   do
        totalScore2 := value;
   end;

 end -- STATE
```

11.5 SOLUTION OF TRAVELLING SALESPERSON PROBLEM

To illustrate how a particular simulated annealing problem can be solved by
constructing a subclass of ANNEALING, the challenging and well known Travelling Salesperson Problem (TSP) is solved in this section. A 20-city problem is
chosen because a known solution exists. The raw data represent actual dis-
tances between 20 American cities.

Every means is taken in the implementation to optimize the run-time performance of the result because of the computational intensity of the algorithm.
The details of subclass TSP are given in Listing 11.3.

Listing 11.3   Class TSP

```
class TSP
-- 20 city travelling salesperson problem
```

```
inherit
    ANNEALING
    redefine
        cost, oldSolution, currentSolution, bestSolution
    end;

creation
    initialize -- inherited from parent class ANNEALING

feature { NONE } -- For internal use

    NUMBER_CITIES : INTEGER is 20;
    cost          : SIMPLE_ARRAY_2D[ INTEGER ]; -- Redefined
    oldSolution   : SIMPLE_ARRAY[ INTEGER ]; -- Redefined
    bestSolution  : SIMPLE_ARRAY[ INTEGER ]; -- Redefined
    currentSolution: SIMPLE_ARRAY[ INTEGER ]; -- Redefined
    -- currentSolution[ 1 ] is the city visited just after
    -- city 1,
    -- currentSolution[ 19 ] is the final city visited
    -- before returning to city 1
    segment       : SIMPLE_ARRAY[ INTEGER ];

    displayOrder( order : SIMPLE_ARRAY[ INTEGER ] ) is
    local
        index : INTEGER;
    do
        io.putstring( "1 -> " );
        from index := 0
        until index = NUMBER_CITIES - 1
        loop
            index := index + 1;
            io.putint( order.item( index ) );
                io.putstring( "-> " );
        end;
        io.putstring( "1" ); io.new_line;
    end; -- displayOrder

    getCost( order : SIMPLE_ARRAY[ INTEGER ] ) : INTEGER is
    local
        cst   : INTEGER;
        index : INTEGER;
    do
        cst := cost.item( 1, order.item( 1 ) );
        from index := 0
        until index = NUMBER_CITIES - 2
        loop
            index := index + 1;
            cst := cst + cost.item( order.item( index ),
                order.item( index + 1 ) );
        end;
        Result := cst + cost.item( order.item( NUMBER_CITIES
            - 1 ), 1 );
    end; -- getCost
```

```
feature
    initializeOldSolution is
    local
        index : INTEGER;
    do
        !!oldSolution.make( NUMBER_CITIES );
        !!currentSolution.make( NUMBER_CITIES );
        !!bestSolution.make( NUMBER_CITIES );
        from index := 0
        until index = NUMBER_CITIES - 1
        loop
            index := index + 1;
            oldSolution.put( index + 1, index );
        end;
    end; -- initializeOldSolution


    initializeCost is
    local
        index : INTEGER;
    do
        !!cost.make( NUMBER_CITIES + 1, NUMBER_CITIES + 1 );
        -- Initialize cost matrix with zeros
        from index := 0
        until index = NUMBER_CITIES
        loop
            index := index + 1;
            cost.put( 0, index, index );
        end;
        cost.put( 184, 1, 2 ); cost.put( 184, 2, 1 );
        cost.put( 292, 1, 3 ); cost.put( 292, 3, 1 );
        cost.put( 195, 2, 3 ); cost.put( 195, 3, 2 );
        cost.put( 449, 1, 4 ); cost.put( 449, 4, 1 );
        cost.put( 310, 2, 4 ); cost.put( 310, 4, 2 );
        cost.put( 215, 3, 4 ); cost.put( 215, 4, 3 );
        cost.put( 670, 1, 5 ); cost.put( 670, 5, 1 );
        cost.put( 540, 2, 5 ); cost.put( 540, 5, 2 );
        cost.put( 380, 3, 5 ); cost.put( 380, 5, 3 );
        cost.put( 288, 4, 5 ); cost.put( 288, 5, 4 );
        cost.put( 516, 1, 6 ); cost.put( 516, 6, 1 );
        cost.put( 357, 2, 6 ); cost.put( 357, 6, 2 );
        cost.put( 232, 3, 6 ); cost.put( 232, 6, 3 );
        cost.put( 200, 4, 6 ); cost.put( 200, 6, 4 );
        cost.put( 211, 5, 6 ); cost.put( 211, 6, 5 );
        cost.put( 598, 1, 7 ); cost.put( 598, 7, 1 );
        cost.put( 514, 2, 7 ); cost.put( 514, 7, 2 );
        cost.put( 434, 3, 7 ); cost.put( 434, 7, 3 );
        cost.put( 566, 4, 7 ); cost.put( 566, 7, 4 );
        cost.put( 436, 5, 7 ); cost.put( 436, 7, 5 );
        cost.put( 381, 6, 7 ); cost.put( 381, 7, 6 );
        cost.put( 618, 1, 8 ); cost.put( 618, 8, 1 );
        cost.put( 434, 2, 8 ); cost.put( 434, 8, 2 );
        cost.put( 493, 3, 8 ); cost.put( 493, 8, 3 );
        cost.put( 787, 4, 8 ); cost.put( 787, 8, 4 );
        cost.put( 814, 5, 8 ); cost.put( 814, 8, 5 );
```

```
cost.put( 642, 6, 8 ); cost.put( 642, 8, 6 );
cost.put( 295, 7, 8 ); cost.put( 295, 8, 7 );
cost.put( 881, 1, 9 ); cost.put( 881, 9, 1 );
cost.put( 697, 2, 9 ); cost.put( 697, 9, 2 );
cost.put( 719, 3, 9 ); cost.put( 719, 9, 3 );
cost.put( 790, 4, 9 ); cost.put( 790, 9, 4 );
cost.put( 632, 5, 9 ); cost.put( 632, 9, 5 );
cost.put( 697, 6, 9 ); cost.put( 697, 9, 6 );
cost.put( 224, 7, 9 ); cost.put( 224, 9, 7 );
cost.put( 320, 8, 9 ); cost.put( 320, 9, 8 );
cost.put( 909, 1, 10 ); cost.put( 909, 10, 1 );
cost.put( 964, 2, 10 ); cost.put( 964, 10, 2 );
cost.put( 955, 3, 10 ); cost.put( 955, 10, 3 );
cost.put( 1020, 4, 10 ); cost.put( 1020, 10, 4 );
cost.put( 974, 5, 10 ); cost.put( 974, 10, 5 );
cost.put( 952, 6, 10 ); cost.put( 952, 10, 6 );
cost.put( 541, 7, 10 ); cost.put( 541, 10, 7 );
cost.put( 341, 8, 10 ); cost.put( 341, 10, 8 );
cost.put( 318, 9, 10 ); cost.put( 318, 10, 9 );
cost.put( 978, 1, 11 ); cost.put( 978, 11, 1 );
cost.put( 892, 2, 11 ); cost.put( 892, 11, 2 );
cost.put( 1031, 3, 11 ); cost.put( 1031, 11, 3 );
cost.put( 1246, 4, 11 ); cost.put( 1246, 11, 4 );
cost.put( 1352, 5, 11 ); cost.put( 1352, 11, 5 );
cost.put( 1180, 6, 11 ); cost.put( 1180, 11, 6 );
cost.put( 843, 7, 11 ); cost.put( 843, 11, 7 );
cost.put( 538, 8, 11 ); cost.put( 538, 11, 8 );
cost.put( 747, 9, 11 ); cost.put( 747, 11, 9 );
cost.put( 441, 10, 11 ); cost.put( 441, 11, 10 );
cost.put( 654, 1, 12 ); cost.put( 654, 12, 1 );
cost.put( 597, 2, 12 ); cost.put( 597, 12, 2 );
cost.put( 803, 3, 12 ); cost.put( 803, 12, 3 );
cost.put( 1018, 4, 12 ); cost.put( 1018, 12, 4 );
cost.put( 1154, 5, 12 ); cost.put( 1154, 12, 5 );
cost.put( 1104, 6, 12 ); cost.put( 1104, 12, 6 );
cost.put( 766, 7, 12 ); cost.put( 766, 12, 7 );
cost.put( 461, 8, 12 ); cost.put( 461, 12, 8 );
cost.put( 749, 9, 12 ); cost.put( 749, 12, 9 );
cost.put( 634, 10, 12 ); cost.put( 634, 12, 10 );
cost.put( 380, 11, 12 ); cost.put( 380, 12, 11 );
cost.put( 504, 1, 13 ); cost.put( 504, 13, 1 );
cost.put( 503, 2, 13 ); cost.put( 503, 13, 2 );
cost.put( 722, 3, 13 ); cost.put( 722, 13, 3 );
cost.put( 937, 4, 13 ); cost.put( 937, 13, 4 );
cost.put( 1043, 5, 13 ); cost.put( 1043, 13, 5 );
cost.put( 806, 6, 13 ); cost.put( 806, 13, 6 );
cost.put( 986, 7, 13 ); cost.put( 986, 13, 7 );
cost.put( 722, 8, 13 ); cost.put( 722, 13, 8 );
cost.put( 1042, 9, 13 ); cost.put( 1042, 13, 9 );
cost.put( 954, 10, 13 ); cost.put( 954, 13, 10 );
cost.put( 784, 11, 13 ); cost.put( 784, 13, 11 );
cost.put( 404, 12, 13 ); cost.put( 404, 13, 12 );
cost.put( 276, 1, 14 ); cost.put( 276, 14, 1 );
cost.put( 460, 2, 14 ); cost.put( 460, 14, 2 );
cost.put( 568, 3, 14 ); cost.put( 568, 14, 3 );
```

```
cost.put( 725, 4, 14 ); cost.put( 725, 14, 4 );
cost.put( 946, 5, 14 ); cost.put( 946, 14, 5 );
cost.put( 817, 6, 14 ); cost.put( 817, 14, 6 );
cost.put( 874, 7, 14 ); cost.put( 874, 14, 7 );
cost.put( 894, 8, 14 ); cost.put( 894, 14, 8 );
cost.put( 1214, 9, 14 ); cost.put( 1214, 14, 9 );
cost.put( 1185, 10, 14 ); cost.put( 1185, 14, 10 );
cost.put( 1218, 11, 14 ); cost.put( 1218, 14, 11 );
cost.put( 660, 12, 14 ); cost.put( 660, 14, 12 );
cost.put( 452, 13, 14 ); cost.put( 452, 14, 13 );
cost.put( 780, 1, 15 ); cost.put( 780, 15, 1 );
cost.put( 964, 2, 15 ); cost.put( 964, 15, 2 );
cost.put( 1072, 3, 15 ); cost.put( 1072, 15, 3 );
cost.put( 1229, 4, 15 ); cost.put( 1229, 15, 4 );
cost.put( 1450, 5, 15 ); cost.put( 1450, 15, 5 );
cost.put( 1321, 6, 15 ); cost.put( 1321, 15, 6 );
cost.put( 1378, 7, 15 ); cost.put( 1378, 15, 7 );
cost.put( 1326, 8, 15 ); cost.put( 1326, 15, 8 );
cost.put( 1646, 9, 15 ); cost.put( 1646, 15, 9 );
cost.put( 1672, 10, 15 ); cost.put( 1672, 15, 10 );
cost.put( 1410, 11, 15 ); cost.put( 1410, 15, 11 );
cost.put( 1030, 12, 15 ); cost.put( 1030, 15, 12 );
cost.put( 626, 13, 15 ); cost.put( 626, 15, 13 );
cost.put( 476, 14, 15 ); cost.put( 476, 15, 14 );
cost.put( 529, 1, 16 ); cost.put( 529, 16, 1 );
cost.put( 644, 2, 16 ); cost.put( 644, 16, 2 );
cost.put( 789, 3, 16 ); cost.put( 789, 16, 3 );
cost.put( 1004, 4, 16 ); cost.put( 1004, 16, 4 );
cost.put( 1184, 5, 16 ); cost.put( 1184, 16, 5 );
cost.put( 1001, 6, 16 ); cost.put( 1001, 16, 6 );
cost.put( 1214, 7, 16 ); cost.put( 1214, 16, 7 );
cost.put( 950, 8, 16 ); cost.put( 950, 16, 8 );
cost.put( 1270, 9, 16 ); cost.put( 1270, 16, 9 );
cost.put( 1213, 10, 16 ); cost.put( 1213, 16, 10 );
cost.put( 1043, 11, 16 ); cost.put( 1043, 16, 11 );
cost.put( 632, 12, 16 ); cost.put( 632, 16, 12 );
cost.put( 219, 13, 16 ); cost.put( 219, 16, 13 );
cost.put( 436, 14, 16 ); cost.put( 436, 16, 14 );
cost.put( 419, 15, 16 ); cost.put( 419, 16, 15 );
cost.put( 805, 1, 17 ); cost.put( 805, 17, 1 );
cost.put( 698, 2, 17 ); cost.put( 698, 17, 2 );
cost.put( 917, 3, 17 ); cost.put( 917, 17, 3 );
cost.put( 1132, 4, 17 ); cost.put( 1132, 17, 4 );
cost.put( 1238, 5, 17 ); cost.put( 1238, 17, 5 );
cost.put( 1055, 6, 17 ); cost.put( 1055, 17, 6 );
cost.put( 1113, 7, 17 ); cost.put( 1113, 17, 7 );
cost.put( 842, 8, 17 ); cost.put( 842, 17, 8 );
cost.put( 1162, 9, 17 ); cost.put( 1162, 17, 9 );
cost.put( 1027, 10, 17 ); cost.put( 1027, 17, 10 );
cost.put( 779, 11, 17 ); cost.put( 779, 17, 11 );
cost.put( 473, 12, 17 ); cost.put( 473, 17, 12 );
cost.put( 195, 13, 17 ); cost.put( 195, 17, 13 );
cost.put( 637, 14, 17 ); cost.put( 637, 17, 14 );
cost.put( 634, 15, 17 ); cost.put( 634, 17, 15 );
cost.put( 256, 16, 17 ); cost.put( 256, 17, 16 );
```

```
            cost.put( 1181,  1, 18 ); cost.put( 1181, 18,  1 );
            cost.put( 1007,  2, 18 ); cost.put( 1007, 18,  2 );
            cost.put( 1226,  3, 18 ); cost.put( 1226, 18,  3 );
            cost.put( 1441,  4, 18 ); cost.put( 1441, 18,  4 );
            cost.put( 1547,  5, 18 ); cost.put( 1547, 18,  5 );
            cost.put( 1364,  6, 18 ); cost.put( 1364, 18,  6 );
            cost.put( 1375,  7, 18 ); cost.put( 1375, 18,  7 );
            cost.put( 1080,  8, 18 ); cost.put( 1080, 18,  8 );
            cost.put( 1134,  9, 18 ); cost.put( 1134, 18,  9 );
            cost.put( 1138, 10, 18 ); cost.put( 1138, 18, 10 );
            cost.put( 783, 11, 18 ); cost.put( 783, 18, 11 );
            cost.put( 611, 12, 18 ); cost.put( 611, 18, 12 );
            cost.put( 563, 13, 18 ); cost.put( 563, 18, 13 );
            cost.put( 1046, 14, 18 ); cost.put( 1046, 18, 14 );
            cost.put( 759, 15, 18 ); cost.put( 759, 18, 15 );
            cost.put( 624, 16, 18 ); cost.put( 624, 18, 16 );
            cost.put( 368, 17, 18 ); cost.put( 368, 18, 17 );
            cost.put( 1548,  1, 19 ); cost.put( 1548, 19,  1 );
            cost.put( 1444,  2, 19 ); cost.put( 1444, 19,  2 );
            cost.put( 1630,  3, 19 ); cost.put( 1630, 19,  3 );
            cost.put( 1845,  4, 19 ); cost.put( 1845, 19,  4 );
            cost.put( 1984,  5, 19 ); cost.put( 1984, 19,  5 );
            cost.put( 1801,  6, 19 ); cost.put( 1801, 19,  6 );
            cost.put( 1726,  7, 19 ); cost.put( 1726, 19,  7 );
            cost.put( 1431,  8, 19 ); cost.put( 1431, 19,  8 );
            cost.put( 1685,  9, 19 ); cost.put( 1685, 19,  9 );
            cost.put( 1477, 10, 19 ); cost.put( 1477, 19, 10 );
            cost.put( 1134, 11, 19 ); cost.put( 1134, 19, 11 );
            cost.put( 1033, 12, 19 ); cost.put( 1033, 19, 12 );
            cost.put( 906, 13, 19 ); cost.put( 906, 19, 13 );
            cost.put( 1389, 14, 19 ); cost.put( 1389, 19, 14 );
            cost.put( 1094, 15, 19 ); cost.put( 1094, 19, 15 );
            cost.put( 967, 16, 19 ); cost.put( 967, 19, 16 );
            cost.put( 711, 17, 19 ); cost.put( 711, 19, 17 );
            cost.put( 404, 18, 19 ); cost.put( 404, 19, 18 );
            cost.put( 1547,  1, 20 ); cost.put( 1547, 20,  1 );
            cost.put( 1454,  2, 20 ); cost.put( 1454, 20,  2 );
            cost.put( 1668,  3, 20 ); cost.put( 1668, 20,  3 );
            cost.put( 1883,  4, 20 ); cost.put( 1883, 20,  4 );
            cost.put( 1994,  5, 20 ); cost.put( 1994, 20,  5 );
            cost.put( 1811,  6, 20 ); cost.put( 1811, 20,  6 );
            cost.put( 1879,  7, 20 ); cost.put( 1879, 20,  7 );
            cost.put( 1584,  8, 20 ); cost.put( 1584, 20,  8 );
            cost.put( 1776,  9, 20 ); cost.put( 1776, 20,  9 );
            cost.put( 1632, 10, 20 ); cost.put( 1632, 20, 10 );
            cost.put( 1267, 11, 20 ); cost.put( 1267, 20, 11 );
            cost.put( 1053, 12, 20 ); cost.put( 1053, 20, 12 );
            cost.put( 944, 13, 20 ); cost.put( 944, 20, 13 );
            cost.put( 1427, 14, 20 ); cost.put( 1427, 20, 14 );
            cost.put( 1196, 15, 20 ); cost.put( 1196, 20, 15 );
            cost.put( 1005, 16, 20 ); cost.put( 1005, 20, 16 );
            cost.put( 749, 17, 20 ); cost.put( 749, 20, 17 );
            cost.put( 442, 18, 20 ); cost.put( 442, 20, 18 );
            cost.put( 251, 19, 20 ); cost.put( 251, 20, 19 );
      end; -- initializeCost
```

```
displaySolution is
do
    displayOrder( currentSolution );
end; -- displaySolution


displayBestSolution is
do
    displayOrder( bestSolution );
end; -- displayBestSolution

initializeCoolingCurve is
do
    !!coolingCurve.make( 10, 10 );
    coolingCurve.put( 3000.0, 1, 1 ); coolingCurve.put(
        0.85, 2, 1 );
    coolingCurve.put( 2000.0, 1, 2 ); coolingCurve.put(
        0.87, 2, 2 );
    coolingCurve.put( 1500.0, 1, 3 ); coolingCurve.put(
        0.89, 2, 3 );
    coolingCurve.put( 1000.0, 1, 4 ); coolingCurve.put(
        0.90, 2, 4 );
    coolingCurve.put( 500.0, 1, 5 ); coolingCurve.put(
        0.95, 2, 5 );
    coolingCurve.put( 300.0, 1, 6 ); coolingCurve.put(
        0.97, 2, 6 );
    coolingCurve.put( 200.0, 1, 7 ); coolingCurve.put(
        0.95, 2, 7 );
    coolingCurve.put( 100.0, 1, 8 ); coolingCurve.put(
        0.90, 2, 8 );
    coolingCurve.put( 0.0, 1, 9 ); coolingCurve.put( 0.0,
        2, 9 );
end; -- initializeCoolingCurve

betterThan( newScore : INTEGER; score : INTEGER ) :
    BOOLEAN is
do
    Result := newScore < score;
end; -- betterThan

computeScoreLimit( avgCost : DOUBLE; halfSigma : DOUBLE
    ) : DOUBLE is
do
    Result := avgCost + halfSigma;
end; -- computeScoreLimit

compareScoreLimit( newScore : INTEGER; scoreLimit :
    DOUBLE ) : BOOLEAN is
do
    Result := newScore <= scoreLimit;
end; -- compareScoreLimit

getCostCurrentSolution : INTEGER is
do
```

```
    Result := getCost( currentSolution );
end; -- getCostCurrentSolution

getCostBestSolution : INTEGER is
do
    Result := getCost( bestSolution );
end; -- getCostCurrentSolution

reconfigure( forward : BOOLEAN ) is
local
    i, j, k, temp, index1, index2, len, distance:
      INTEGER; d : DOUBLE;
do
    if forward = True then
        status.setSteps( status.steps + 1 );
        copySolution( oldSolution, currentSolution );
        -- A section of path is removed and then replaced
        -- with the same cities
        -- running in opposite order
        index1 := r.valueBetween( 1, NUMBER_CITIES - 1 );
        d := r.uniform;
        if d < 0.333333 then
            distance := 1;
        elseif d < 0.60348 then
            distance := 2;
        elseif d < 0.82247 then
            distance := 3;
        else
            distance := 4;
        end;
        index2 := index1 + distance;
        if index2 > NUMBER_CITIES - 1 then
            index2 := index2 - NUMBER_CITIES + 1;
        end;
        i := index1;
        j := index2;
        if i < j then
            from
            until i >= j
            loop
                temp := currentSolution.item( i );
                currentSolution.put( currentSolution.
                item( j ), i );
                currentSolution.put( temp, j );
                i := i + 1;
                j := j - 1;
            end;
        else -- i > j
            from k := 0
            until k >= distance // 2
            loop
                k := k + 1;
                temp := currentSolution.item( i );
                currentSolution.put( currentSolution.
```

```
            item( j ), i );
            currentSolution.put( temp, j );
            i := i + 1;
            if i = NUMBER_CITIES then
              i := 1;
            end;
            j := j - 1;
            if j = 0 then
              j := NUMBER_CITIES - 1;
            end;
          end;
        end;
      else -- Forward is False
        copySolution( currentSolution, oldSolution );
      end;
    end; -- reconfigure

    copySolution( target : SIMPLE_ARRAY[ INTEGER ] ; source
                  :SIMPLE_ARRAY[ INTEGER ] ) is
    do
      target.copy( source );
    end; -- copySolution

end -- TSP
```

The attributes *cost*, *oldSolution*, *currentSolution* and *bestSolution* are redefined. The TowerEiffel classes `SIMPLE_ARRAY` and `SIMPLE_ARRAY_2D` are used instead of the usual `ARRAY` and `ARRAY2`. ISE Eiffel provides similar classes in its library. These array classes mimic simple C language arrays. Their index range is from 0 to the upper bound specified in their creation routines and is not dynamically changeable. These "simple" arrays provide for much faster access time and, therefore, speed up the overall execution time of the algorithm. In order to simplify the use array indices, the lowest index used in each array is 1. This is compensated for by over-dimensioning each array by one. This allows a "natural" indexing scheme to be used rather than a C-like indexing scheme.

The routine *displayOrder* iterates through the *order* array and outputs the sequence of cities in a tour. The routine *getCost* also iterates through the *order* array and computes the cost of a given tour.

The routine *initializeOldSolution* initializes the simple arrays *oldSolution*, *currentSolution* and *bestSolution*. It then loads the array *oldSolution* with a tour consisting of the consecutive sequence of integers.

The routine *betterThan* returns True if *newScore* is less than *oldScore*.

Routine *reconfigure* is perhaps the most interesting and most important. It provides the basis for moving the solution from one state to another. A section of path is selected by choosing a random starting point, *index1*, and random ending point, *index2*. The separation between the starting and ending point is chosen from a discrete exponential probability density function. Once a section of path is chosen, it is removed and replaced with the same cities running in opposite order.

The values of the "cooling curve" loaded in routine *initializeCoolingCurve* are determined iteratively and experimentally. For values of the temperature parameter above 3000, a new temperature is computed as the fraction 0.85 of the previous temperature. Between temperature values of 2000 and 3000, the multiplicative factor increases to 0.87. The highest value of the multiplicative factor occurs when the temperature parameter is between 200 and 300 degrees. This is based on several runs and the observation that it is in this temperature range that the greatest changes occur in score as a function of temperature. In such an interval it is desirable to reduce the temperature parameter more gradually than in regions where the score does not change significantly.

The values for various constants, given in class CONSTANTS, must also be experimentally determined over a series of runs.

The values chosen for the 20-city TPS are shown in Listing 11.4

Listing 11.4   Class CONSTANTS

```
class CONSTANTS
-- Must be supplied by the user

  feature { ANNEALING } -- Available only to class ANNEALING

    ULTIMATE_LIMIT: INTEGER is 15000;
    successMin    : INTEGER is 600;
    firstLimit    : INTEGER is 8000;
    ultimateLimit: INTEGER is 12000;
    inHalfSigmaLimit: INTEGER is 600;
    outHalfSigmaLimit: INTEGER is 1200;
    scale         : DOUBLE is 6000.0;
    tempMin       : INTEGER is 70;

end -- CONSTANTS
```

The larger the values of the constants, the greater the execution time for the simulated annealing and perhaps the greater the accuracy of the result within some limits. All of the constants affect the determination of when thermal equilibrium has occurred. It is essential that the simulation makes progress by reducing the temperature and eventually "freezing" some solution. If the value ULTIMATE_LIMIT is set too high, the number of computations at a given temperature might become excessive without any commensurate benefit in accuracy. Only experimentation and careful observation can determine reasonable, not optimum, values for these constants.

11.6 PERFORMANCE COMPARISONS

Listing 11.5 shows the details of class SIMULATED_ANNEALING and typical output. To achieve maximum run-time efficiency, the routine *collection_off* is invoked from class MEMORY. The creation routine, *make*, invokes the creation routine of the simulation. That is all.

Listing 11.5   Class SIMULATED_ANNEALING

```
class SIMULATED_ANNEALING

  inherit
    MEMORY -- for collection_off

  creation
    make

  feature

    make is
      local
          simulation : TSP; -- User's ANNEALING subclass
      do
          collection_off; -- Turns off garbage collection
          !!simulation.initialize;
      end; -- make

end -- SIMULATED_ANNEALING
```

11.6.1 Eiffel Solution

A typical output run of the Eiffel system is shown below. The best score of 6747 is the known optimum solution and occurs in 8 out of 10 runs.

```
Total number of steps: 392375
Temperature: 58.9968
Total successes: 129626
Total failures: 262749
Up hill moves: 71573
Current score: 7423
The best score: 6747
The best temperature: 200.649
The average score: 7563.94
The standard dev: 129.358

1 -> 14 -> 15 -> 16 -> 13 -> 17 -> 19 -> 20 -> 18 -> 12 -> 11
-> 10 -> 8 -> 9 -> 7 -> 5 -> 6 -> 4 -> 3 -> 2 -> 1
The time for the simulated annealing = 37.5485 seconds.
```

11.6.2 C Solution

The output produced by a C program that is based on the same algorithm is given below.

```
Number steps = 468657
Total successes = 151137
Total failures = 316520
uphill = 71872
score = 6747
```

```
average score = 6749.43
 sigma = 30.38
The best cost = 6747
The best configuration:
 1 -> 2 -> 3 -> 4 -> 6 -> 5 -> 7 -> 9 -> 8 -> 10 -> 11 -> 12
    -> 18 -> 19 -> 20
    -> 17 -> 13 -> 16 -> 15 -> 14 -> 1

The time for the 33-city problem = 33.75 seconds.
```

11.6.3 Conclusions From This Example

The Eiffel and C output tours are almost the reverse of each other. Both produce the optimum tour cost of 6747. The Eiffel program runs roughly between 10 and 15 percent slower (based on other comparison runs not shown) than the C solution.

Even though the Eiffel program execution time is slightly slower than the C program execution time, it would be unfair to characterize the Eiffel performance as unreasonably slow.

The structure provided by the Eiffel solution through abstract class ANNEALING, which factors all of the code that is required in all simulated annealing applications, offers a great benefit to the designer of a new simulated annealing. The user of this abstract class must provide meaningful definitions for several attributes, several simple routines, and routine *reconfigure*, and the values for several constants that affect the determination of thermal equilibrium.

Although the C code is not shown here, it lacks the elegance, readability, reusability and ease of use present in the Eiffel solution. But it runs slightly faster!

11.7 FINAL WORDS

It is my hope that the presentation of the Eiffel language in Part 1 of the book and the case studies in Part 2 inspire you to experience the joy of Eiffel software development.

Appendix

SAMPLE OF "STANDARD" EIFFEL STYLE

The following Eiffel code incorporates the basic elements of Eiffel style recommended in the book *Eiffel: The Language* (ETH), by Bertrand Meyer. Many programmers in the Eiffel community have adopted this as a "standard" Eiffel style. The details of this style are presented in the 15 page Appendix A of ETH and are illustrated here by example.

The first sample of code selected is from Chapter 1, section 1.2.4. The reader may wish to compare the author's personal non-standard Eiffel style used in that section with the "standard" style illustrated here.

```
class FOUNTAIN_PEN inherit
    PEN

creation
    make

feature
    ink_volume : INTEGER;

    make (aColor : STRING; aPrice : INTEGER; anInkColor :STRING;
      aPointThickness : INTEGER; anInkVolume : INTEGER) is
        do
            set_color (a_color);
            set_price (a_price);
            set_ink_color (an_ink_color);
            set_point_thickness (a_point_thickness);
```

```
            set_ink_volume (an_ink_volume);
        end; -- make

    set_ink_volume (volume : INTEGER) is
        do
            ink_volume := volume;
        end; -- setInkVolume

    stats is
        do
            -- Details not shown
        end; -- stats


end -- FOUNTAIN_PEN
```

The second example is taken from Listing 5.27. The reader may again wish to compare the original with the "standard" formatting shown here.

```
class PLANE inherit
    VEHICLE
            rename
                speed as max_air_speed
            end;

    creation
        make_plane

    feature

        wingSpan, maxAltitude : REAL;
        horsepower                : INTEGER;

        make_plane (aWeight : REAL; aSpeed : REAL; aColor : STRING;
            wSpan : REAL; mAltitude : REAL; hpower :INTEGER) is
          do
           -- Details not shown
          end; -- make_plane
```

-- Other features are the same as in Listing 5.24.

```
end -- PLANE
```

The final example is taken from Listing 5.44, repeated here so that the reader can directly compare the original to the "standard" version.

Original Listing 5.44

```
deferred class LINKED_LIST_ITERATOR[ T ]
 feature
    list : LINKED_LIST[ T ];

    act_on( value : T ) is
    deferred
    end; -- act_on
```

```
        for_each is
        do
            from list.start
            until list.off
            loop
                act_on( list.item );
                list.forth;
            end;
        end; -- for_each


    end -- LINKED_LIST_ITERATOR.
```

Listing 5.44 Using "Standard" Formatting

```
    deferred class LINKED_LIST_ITERATOR[ T ] feature
        list : LINKED_LIST[ T ];

        act_on (value : T) is
            deferred
            end; -- act_on

        for_each is
            do
                from list.start
                until list.off
                loop
                    act_on (list.item);
                    list.forth;
                end;
            end; -- for_each
    end -- LINKED_LIST_ITERATOR
```

Index

A